Built in Detroit

A Story of the UAW,
a Company, and a Gangster

Bob Morris

iUniverse LLC
Bloomington

BUILT IN DETROIT
A STORY OF THE UAW, A COMPANY, AND A GANGSTER

iUniverse books may be ordered through booksellers or by contacting:

iUniverse LLC
1663 Liberty Drive
Bloomington, IN 47403
www.iuniverse.com
1-800-Authors (1-800-288-4677)

Because of the dynamic nature of the Internet, any web addresses or links contained in this book may have changed since publication and may no longer be valid. The views expressed in this work are solely those of the author and do not necessarily reflect the views of the publisher, and the publisher hereby disclaims any responsibility for them.

Any people depicted in stock imagery provided by Thinkstock are models, and such images are being used for illustrative purposes only.

Certain stock imagery © Thinkstock.

ISBN: 978-1-4759-9435-3 (sc)
ISBN: 978-1-4759-9436-0 (hc)
ISBN: 978-1-4759-9437-7 (e)

Library of Congress Control Number: 2013910808

Printed in the United States of America.

iUniverse rev. date: 11/25/2013

To Elise and Leo:

May these pages help you to know your great-grandfather

CONTENTS

FOREWORD

This is a book about the labor movement, the city of Detroit, and my friend Ken Morris. *Built in Detroit* is a story primarily about the United Automobile Workers (UAW) union from 1935 through the 1950s. It is a period of which I know little; yet, I am pleased that many years ago I was able to provide important information regarding the development of several chapters of this book.

I came to know Ken Morris in the early 1970s. I decided to run for the United States Congress in 1973, in the newly created Eighteenth Congressional District in the southern part of Oakland and Macomb counties in southeast Michigan. The district was ripe for a Democrat in the upcoming 1974 election. Although I had never run for elective office, I wanted to be the Democratic Party's candidate. First, however, I had to win a four-way primary election. The influential UAW and others were hesitant to support a person who had never run for political office. Ken Morris was one of the UAW regional directors in my district and was incredibly influential in ensuring UAW neutrality in the race. By being neutral, I had a chance to develop a campaign that reached the residents of the Eighteenth Congressional District. Ken's help was crucial. It did not hurt that I was already great friends with his son Greg and that Bob, the author of this book, worked on my campaign! I won the primary election and had to face the Republican incumbent in November.

After a strong general election campaign, aided by the Richard Nixon–Watergate scandal, I was off to Washington, where I spent eight years in Congress. I saw and worked with Ken on a regular basis. In 1979, the Chrysler Corporation was near collapse, the potential of which meant the unemployment of tens of thousands of people. I sat on the key congressional committee that would address any potential legislation on this issue, so I called Ken to see if there was something I could do. Ken connected me with the UAW president, Doug Fraser; and working with the UAW, Chrysler CEO Lee Iacocca, and the Carter administration, I led the fight for and sponsored the Chrysler Loan Guarantee Act, legislation signed into law by President Jimmy Carter in January 1980.

During my time in Congress, Ken never sought political favors—that was not his style. Only once did he ask for some help. While I was vaguely aware that Ken had been a victim of severe violence decades earlier, I was not aware of the specifics of the incident. Like many Detroiters, I knew that labor leaders were subject to physical attacks by unsavory people. I knew about the assassination attempts on the lives of Walter and Victor Reuther, but I did not know much more beyond that. One day Ken contacted me and asked if I could get the transcripts of the 1951 Detroit hearings held by the US Senate Special Committee to Investigate Organized Crime in Interstate Commerce, chaired by Senator Estes Kefauver.

After some digging, we found the thousand-page volume of the Detroit hearings. What few people knew was that besides the testimony at the hearings, the volume's appendix included the secret testimony of the 1946 Wayne County one-man grand jury that had been created to investigate labor violence at the Briggs Manufacturing Company and included numerous references to the Ken Morris beating. I only recently learned that Ken spent hours reviewing and marking up these transcripts to learn what was behind the violence perpetrated upon him and his UAW colleagues.

Bob Morris brings the pages of these transcripts and much of the UAW's history to life. In *Built in Detroit*, we learn about the development of the UAW, the battles with companies, the early internal struggles within the union, the challenges union members had to ensure a strong and honest union, and so much more. Author Bob Morris deftly portrays many of the leaders of labor's cause, including the Reuther brothers, Emil Mazey, Gus Scholle, George Edwards, and many others. He also tells a story that is unique to Detroit. It is the story of a thriving city and the factories that gave the city life. And in the case of the

Briggs Manufacturing Company, it shows how a company that played loose with the law ultimately floundered, its Detroit heritage largely forgotten.

These pages tell a history about Detroit and the labor movement that most of us simply do not know. It is an important history, one that more people should understand. I hope you will enjoy these pages, for they tell an excellent story.

One final note: I was elected Michigan's governor in 1982. As in my first election, Ken continued to be one of my most valuable supporters. As governor, I had the pleasure of reappointing Ken to the Michigan Unemployment Commission and as a member of the Oakland University Board of Trustees. I sought Ken's counsel throughout my career, and he was my friend until the day he died.

—Governor James J. Blanchard
1983-1991

Introduction

OUR FATHER NEVER TALKED ABOUT it, but from our earliest days, my brother Greg and I were aware of "the beating." Occasionally, our dad mentioned it in a speech, but more often someone, a family acquaintance (as opposed to a family friend), made references to the beating. Then, at some point, we saw a photograph of our battered and beaten father in a hospital bed, and any doubts we might have had were dispelled. We always knew that violence was part of the early days of the United Automobile Workers (UAW), and now it was personal.

From 1955 to 1983, our dad, Ken Morris, worked sixteen hours, seven days a week, as an elected UAW International Executive Board member. In this role, he served as a UAW regional director and represented UAW membership primarily on the east side of Detroit and the expanding suburbs to the north. His passion was the UAW and the labor movement. Our mother, Doris, had to share her husband with the union and the union's members on a 24-7 basis.

During the week, Dad was usually out of the house by six or seven o'clock and did not get home before nine o'clock at night. On weekend evenings, Dad and Mom usually had functions to attend, and Greg and I were left with babysitters. Our mother insisted that on weekends, Dad spend time with "the boys," which meant going to UAW meetings, conferences, or political events with Dad. Greg and I were usually the only kids in the crowd, but we thought nothing of it. Riding to and from those meetings in our 1955 Plymouth, or later in our 1958 white Dodge, Greg and I often asked Dad about the history of the UAW—and what wonderful stories we heard.

**Ken Morris, as president of UAW Local 212
with the author, about 1954**

My brother and I probably romanticized many of the stories, but we learned so much. We learned that Walter Reuther was not the first elected UAW president. Instead, it was a man named Homer Martin, a poor leader who almost destroyed the fledgling UAW. We learned how companies, led by Henry Ford's right-hand man, a thug named Harry Bennett, hired unsavory characters to break the UAW and the working men and women the union represented. We learned that the UAW was a different type of union—more socially active than many other unions. The UAW fought for the rights of working people so they could have good and decent lives, regardless of their ethnic background or gender, but the union also sought social and economic justice for all.

At the meetings, we had the opportunity to hear some of the great leaders of a generation. We heard, and in some instances met, Adlai Stevenson, John F. Kennedy, Hubert Humphrey, Martin Luther King Jr., Michigan Governor G. Mennen Williams, and many others. We met and knew great local labor leaders, including Emil Mazey, Gus Scholle, Doug Fraser, Leonard Woodcock, Roy Reuther, Victor Reuther, and so many others.

And then there was Walter. Walter Reuther was unlike anyone we'd ever know. His speeches were long, full of visionary views of what could be, and they covered so many issues and provided great information. I most remember his comments about why the UAW was active in politics. He said that what you win at the bargaining table for the bread box can be taken away at the ballot box. He talked about the old days of UAW organizing, but he always brought his speeches into the current problems of the 1950s or 1960s. He was a special man and a great leader, who died way too early in life.

What Greg and I did not appreciate at the time was how young these leaders were when they began achieving success. In their twenties or early thirties, these labor activists were negotiating wage and benefit contracts with major corporations, fighting political battles inside their unions, and occasionally making decisions to call a strike. They were smart and ambitious people. These people would have been successful at whatever careers they chose.

During these Saturday or Sundays with Dad, we talked about everything. Or we so we thought; not once did our father ever talk about the Briggs beating—the violent attack that nearly took his life.

In her book, *A Daughter Strikes*, Elizabeth Reuther described the shooting of her father as "the accident." Like our family, she wrote that her family never talked about Walter's shooting—it was just there, like a shadow. What we never understood as children was that our families were linked by a single thread: the underworld gang that beat our father nearly to death in 1946 were in all likelihood the same thugs that tried to kill Walter Reuther with a shotgun blast through his kitchen window in 1948.

. . . .

It is hard to explain to most people, but the UAW and CIO activists were a different breed of people. These people were consumed by the passion of involvement in building a union, and to a small degree, I was able to hear some of the stories and know some of the key players upon which the UAW was built. Yet it is also important that people understand that the vast majority of UAW members were not social ideologues or people of great visionary attributes. Rather, the UAW was (and is) composed of everyday working people who believed their organization made a difference in America's quality of life.

Ken Morris, my dad, played a significant but not pivotal role in the development of the UAW. By this, I mean that the UAW would have grown into a great union with or without Ken's participation. Ken did not make the difference, but he certainly helped provide the human fabric that made this union so unique. While many UAW leaders and labor pioneers could have told similar stories or more detailed stories of the union's early days, this book is my attempt to tell a story of the UAW. I have tried to make an honest presentation of the times but make no mistake: I've tried to tell the story through Ken's eyes and his perspective. I only wish that he had lived long enough to read and critique these pages.

. . . .

There are many people who believe that unions, the UAW in particular, are the reason the United States is experiencing an economic decline. They argue that the unions are the reason that manufacturing jobs left our country and the reason for our economic doldrums. I could not disagree more with such assumptions. The UAW has, in most cases, argued and fought for benefits and good working conditions for its members. Can one blame the UAW for fighting for health care and good wages for them? It was also the companies who negotiated with the union and agreed to these benefits, and it was the companies who negotiated away so many of their own management rights. Is this the UAW's fault? Finally, can the UAW be blamed for the auto industry's inability to design and build cars that attract US customers, while at the same time, Japan and European companies designed better and more fuel-efficient vehicles for the US marketplace?

Perhaps if companies had been more progressive in dealing with workers seventy-five years ago, the relationship between workers and the companies they worked for might have been different. But in fact, history shows that the auto industry of the 1920s and 1930s simply treated the worker as a commodity, nothing more.

When the UAW organized the auto industry seventy-five years ago, the automobile industry was an American monopoly. It had no competition from other countries. To be sure, the UAW fought for benefits and job security. It did not foresee the decline of the US auto industry coupled with the rise of Japanese and other worldwide auto companies. No one did. The assumption in the early and middle twentieth century was that the auto industry would always be in the United States.

When there was trouble and the automobile industry needed help, the auto executives came to the UAW. In the 1979–80 recession, the Chrysler Corporation was facing bankruptcy and sought help from the federal government in what became known as the Chrysler Loan Guarantee Act, or otherwise known as the Chrysler bailout. It appeared to many that the US government and Chrysler CEO Lee Iacocca saved Chrysler, and that could not be further from the truth. While the US loan guarantee was a huge and necessary component, the difference was the Chrysler workers. Former UAW president Doug Fraser negotiated with Chrysler over worker concessions. These concessions provided more in savings for Chrysler than new revenue from the government's loan program. Both were critical, but without the effort of the UAW and its members, Chrysler would have failed.

More recently, as General Motors and Chrysler went through bankruptcy, the UAW negotiated company-wide policies to save the companies, including Ford. Wages, benefits, and job security programs were slashed or restructured. Without the cooperative assistance of the UAW, the American auto industry probably would have died.

I wish the American auto industry had designed cooler, more fuel-efficient, and better cars, but they didn't. I wish Americans would buy more American-made products, but they won't. This is a discussion that is not part of this book and best saved for another time. The point is, simply blaming trade unions for our problems in the auto industry or the American economy is wrong, and it is the easy way out of a far more complex economic and political problem.

· · · · · · · · · · · · · ·

This story has evolved from the rides taken by two sons and a father in vintage American cars. My research proved those stories to be viable and accurate. This book could not have been written without the resources of the Walter P. Reuther Labor Archives at Wayne State University—particularly through the assistance of William Lefevre and Elizabeth Clemens. Ken Morris left several published and unpublished oral histories—either at the labor archives or in his personal files—and they have been used extensively in this project. Oral histories and other documents at the archives have been invaluable. Other significant source work was found at the Library of Michigan and the Detroit Public Library. Interviews with Jane Briggs Hart, the late Doug Fraser, and the late Larry Mazey were extremely important in placing events into appropriate context. Also, several people took time to read the manuscript, and they provided outstanding critique and suggestions. Of course, my fabulous wife, Terry Ahwal, looked at these pages in their original form and provided many suggestions. My brother, Greg Morris, and his wife, Audrey, offered invaluable thoughts and suggestions. Dr. Jeremy Hughes and Dr. Paul Connors read the initial manuscript and offered thousands of suggestions and challenges. Other readers and advisors included Marc Stepp, Bob Lent, Craig Bryson, and Dave Dempsey. The support of Paul Massaron was invaluable. Governor James J. Blanchard has been a friend and mentor to me. I so appreciate his foreword to the book, and I know it would have pleased Ken immensely.

I believe that what is in these pages is accurate and true. However, as indicated, much of this story comes from oral histories, memorandums, newspapers, and other documents that were written from specific points of view. For those looking for more detailed accounts of the UAW early years, great resources can be found in the materials cited in the bibliography. I have generally based the quotations on specific statements from newspapers, oral histories, and other documented sources. Many of the quotes are from letters and other documents which have been reproduced verbatim, errors included. In one chapter, I incorporated a signed statement into a conversation that may well have taken place. The quotes of this conversation are accurate and noted in the chapter notes.

· · · · · · · · · · · · · ·

The stories my brother and I heard were riveting. We assumed that most people knew of the labor struggles of the 1930s and the rise of the labor movement. As we grew older, we learned that only a few people understood the context of labor's rise and its history. This story will hopefully help people understand the life of early UAW activists and why they took the actions that they did. Enjoy!

PROLOGUE

THE BEATING:
MAY 31, 1946

Prologue

"Well, little lady, why don't you ...
go straight back to Nebraska."

IT WAS LATE ON FRIDAY. Everyone had already left Local 212's headquarters except for Ken Morris and the local's custodian. Ken had been doing paperwork for over an hour, as he stood up, lit a Chesterfield cigarette, took a drag, and walked over to the window overlooking Mack Avenue from his second-story office. He looked down at the working-class street located on the east side of Detroit. It had been raining hard, a weather front having moved through the city, bringing terrific thunderstorms and dropping the temperature dramatically.

Mack Avenue was still wet, with few people walking on the sidewalks. Some cars were moving up and down the street, with the tires making a swishing sound on the wet pavement. He faintly heard the electric motor of a streetcar a few blocks away. To his left, Ken saw the various storefronts across the street. His eyes landed on Sammy's barbershop. He made a note to himself to see Sam the next week. It was a holiday weekend, Memorial weekend 1946. Memorial Day had been on Thursday, today had been a workday, and the weekend promised to be relaxing. Perhaps he would play nine holes of golf with Emil or Bill Mazey at the Chandler Park Golf Course.

He thought briefly about Detroit's big event: the huge Detroit Golden Jubilee, celebrating the fiftieth anniversary of the automobile. A massive parade was planned tomorrow for Woodward Avenue, Detroit's main street. A number of UAW leadership participated, but Ken was not interested in that sort of celebration.

The last few months had been pretty damn good, he thought. He'd returned to Detroit from the Army Air Corps with his wife, whom he met during the war three years earlier. Upon his return, he was elected, without opposition, to high office within his local union. At the recent UAW convention, Ken and his fellow trade unionists had helped elect his friend and mentor Emil Mazey to the UAW International Executive Board and, in the process, remove one of the most corrupt union leaders that the United Automobile Workers union, or UAW, had ever known. Then, at the same convention, they all worked to elect Walter Reuther as president of the UAW. The UAW convention was a monumental change for the organization, a change that certainly was to make a major difference in the future of the union. Quite a feat.

His thoughts moved to just a few days ago. As editor of the local's newspaper, he had written a scathing editorial attacking the Briggs management for their arrogant approach and attitude toward Briggs workers. Yes, he reflected, the past five months had been very good.

He turned and looked at his crowded desk. Stacks of papers were awaiting his attention, but he decided it was late. Doris was at home, and he could deal with them on Monday. He smiled to himself. Well, some of these things could not wait until Monday. He decided to sneak in during the weekend. Suddenly, he remembered that he was to meet Art Vega and Steve Despot, his friends and political colleagues from the local, at Cupids for a cup of coffee.

He leaned across his desk and crushed out his cigarette in the ashtray full of cigarette butts. He picked up the half-empty pack of Chesterfields—his second pack of the day—and placed it in his shirt pocket. As he walked out of his office, he automatically reached up and shut off the lights, closing his office door as he headed down the hallway to the steps, the sounds of his heels echoing through the building. Had he glanced back at his office door, he would have read KEN MORRIS etched on the glass in block letters, with RECORDING SECRETARY below it. On the first floor, he saw Cliff Russell mopping the hallway floor. Ken wished the big African American a good night and a good holiday weekend. Cliff responded, wishing Mr. Ken and Mrs. Doris a good weekend.

Ken walked out and felt the cool air on his face. He turned the corner onto Fairview Street and walked to his 1937 Ford. He looked at the beat-up Ford and decided that he seriously had to consider getting a new car, yet he knew that was impossible. His seventy-five dollars a week salary prohibited such a purchase. The car needed to last a couple of more years. He had bought the car not even a year earlier, during his last several months in the Army Air Corps, while stationed in South Carolina. It was a wreck then, but with war mobilization and new cars out of production since 1942, any car was a good car. After his discharge the previous December, the 1937 Ford had taken him and Doris from South Carolina to her mother's house in Nebraska. That December 1945 drive was tough. Ken shivered as the thought of watching pavement pass below them through the flimsy floorboards and feeling the bitter cold air rush up against his legs during that drive flashed through his mind. That had been one rough trip. He never wanted to see snow or feel cold like that again.

He climbed into the car, started the engine, and rolled the window down a bit to let some fresh air into the vehicle. The window did not work very well. Ken had to hold the window in place with one hand as he cranked the window knob in a clockwise motion with his other hand. Once the window operation was completed, he released the touchy clutch with his left foot, put the car in gear, and headed east on Mack Avenue.

He always drove slowly by the Briggs Manufacturing plant, just a few blocks down from the Local 212 office. The Mack Avenue Briggs plant was the main factory of the Briggs empire. Ken had been hired at Briggs in 1935, almost eleven years earlier. He was just a kid then, twenty years old, and desperately in need of a job, any job. Now, in the spring of 1946, Briggs had just retooled the plant after four years of war production and was back building automobile bodies for Chrysler, Hudson, and a few other car companies. The plant was huge, employing nearly fifteen thousand people, and that did not include the other Briggs plants located around Detroit. The Mack Avenue plant, however, was a monster; long and narrow, it was five stories tall and nearly a half mile in length. There were few like it in the auto industry. Ken studied the building as he slowly drove by. Even though he was a top officer in the union representing Briggs workers, he could not go inside the plant. Five years earlier, he had been fired from Briggs and was therefore prohibited from entering any Briggs plant unless he received special permission from the company's management.

He soon came to Conner Street and turned left, past the ball diamond on the northwest corner. After a few blocks, he instinctively turned right onto Warren Avenue and then immediately made another right into Cupids, the drive-in restaurant he had come to love. On most nights before going home, Ken would have a cup of coffee with Danny Masouris, who co-owned Cupids with his brother. Danny was a great diversion. Ken never had to talk about union politics with Danny; they just talked about things. It was a great way for Ken to decompress after long pressure-packed days.

He joined Art and Steve at a booth and ordered a cup of coffee. The three talked about issues and gossip regarding the local and the UAW from the previous week. After his second cup of coffee, Ken rose to leave, and the two other men needled him about walking out of the restaurant without paying the bill. Ken gave it to them right back and mockingly picked up the tab and paid the bill. All laughed and wished each other a good weekend.

By the time he left Cupids, evening had darkened the sky. It started to rain again on the short drive home. He just had to cross Warren Avenue and turn into the Parkside public housing project. Returning from the war, Ken knew they were lucky to find their apartment, and it was a good home, but still, he knew that he was leaving Doris alone more than he should. Life had been relatively easy on Ken during the five months since his return to Detroit and the UAW, but it had to be hard on her. Returning to Detroit had been a homecoming for him, but for Doris, everything was new and strange. It was Detroit, a tough industrial city, and she knew no one at first. Still, Doris had a winning personality and had already made great friends. Doris knew Ken's ambitions and knew that as long as he was part of the UAW, he would be away for endless hours. He turned into the alley just behind his apartment. As he drove through the alley, he saw a man in the alley raising his arms as he ran in front of Ken's car. He thought it was strange but didn't think much about it as the man moved out of Ken's sight. Perhaps he was celebrating the anniversary of the auto industry a bit too much.

He parked the car in its normal parking spot and opened the door. He reached down with his right hand to crank the window shut, and with his left hand, he pulled the window up and simultaneously kept the glass pane in place. Then he heard and sensed a movement from behind him. The attack was so sudden that the shock consumed his body, forever eliminating the terrible pain from his memory as a metal pipe, or blackjack, descended on the back of his skull, fracturing the skull and leaving a scar that remained with him the rest of his life. With a dizzying sensation, Ken collapsed to the ground and the pummeling continued. A smashing blow to the forehead cracked his scull in a second place, leaving another permanent scar. Multiple strikes continued against his arms, legs, and body. Within a matter of seconds, the beating was over, and two men in hats and overcoats ran down the alley, leaving Ken lying in a pool of his own blood. The men had never said one word.

Inside their apartment, Doris was waiting for her husband. Dinner was just about ready. They had talked about trying to catch a movie, but by the time they had dinner, it might be too late. She knew that Ken was stopping for a cup of coffee with a couple of the guys, but tonight she was apprehensive. Earlier in the day, an older man had come to the door, asking if Ken Morris lived at the address. Doris, without really thinking about it, answered yes, but she thought it unusual. It was a strange, unsettling experience.

As she waited, with the radio playing some music in the background, she heard a scratching at the door. Somehow Ken was able to drag himself to their door. Doris opened the door, looked down on the ground, and saw her husband collapsed on the front stoop, withering in agony while blood seemed to be everywhere. She screamed and then knelt to help her husband. Some neighbors heard her scream and rushed to the apartment. Someone said, "Get some blankets." She and a man managed to get him to the bedroom, and she called the police. In shock, Ken's body was shivering and shaking. He drifted in and out of consciousness, but he remembered the police arriving.

The police called for an ambulance, and in the moments before it came, Ken could remember the police questioning Doris. The officer asked, "What does your husband do?"

"He's the recording secretary of Local 212," the twenty-three-year-old brunette shakily responded.

"Oh my God, another union matter," he said, almost dismissing the crime that just occurred. The officer then asked, "Little lady, where are you from?"

Through her tears, she mumbled, "I'm from Nebraska."

"Well, little lady, why don't you just get out of here and go straight back to Nebraska. Don't stay around this place."

Ken blacked out again, and his next memory was in the hospital. Amazingly, his good friend Bill Mazey found out about the beating and was at Saratoga Hospital, on Gratiot Avenue, immediately after Ken's arrival. Ken regained consciousness and saw Bill before he saw Doris. The memory does funny things. Ken knew he was in bad shape, and his first thought when he saw Bill was of a Local 212 member who had given him half a dollar as a deposit for his union dues. He reached into his watch pocket and pulled out the coin, saying, "Bill, turn this over to someone."

Ken then recalled someone from the prosecutor's office in the room. He heard comments between the prosecutor, doctors, Doris, and Bill. The prosecutor wanted him to swear to something, and he heard, "… being almost beaten to death—could be fatal …"

Ken lay there, becoming less aware of the commotion around him, wondering why. Why would anyone do this to him? Union politics could be tough, but not like this. He didn't have any enemies, and he had just been elected by acclamation, so *why* was he a target? Could it have been the editorial against Briggs? But that made no sense either. He had a right to say what he believed. It was guaranteed by the US Constitution, so why? Why would someone do this? Who was he a threat to? The sedation covered the pain as he drifted off into space.[1]

Four days after the beating, a *Detroit News* photographer snuck into the room and, without permission, took a photograph of the beaten man. The photo showed Ken sleeping in a hospital bed. The head and shoulders photo showed both eyes badly blackened and a huge gash stretched diagonally across his forehead. He was in bad need of a shave, and his right arm was bent toward his head and heavily wrapped with tape. The caption in the paper read:

> One of the beatings of officers of Briggs Local 212, UAW-CIO, which will be investigated by grand jury, is that of Kenneth Morris, recording secretary of the local. Morris was photographed in Saratoga Hospital, where his physician reported he is suffering from a fractured skull, fractured right leg, cuts, and partial paralysis of the face due to a nerve injury.[2]

Ken, sedated heavily that first week in the hospital, thought of many things as he floated in and out of consciousness. He kept wondering why anyone would do this to him. *Why?* Other thoughts rolled in and out of his mind. He thought of home, of Pittsburgh. Ken thought of his Pittsburgh buddies and how their trip to Detroit in 1935 had changed his life. Most of all, he thought about Briggs, the auto industry and the subsequent building of the UAW.

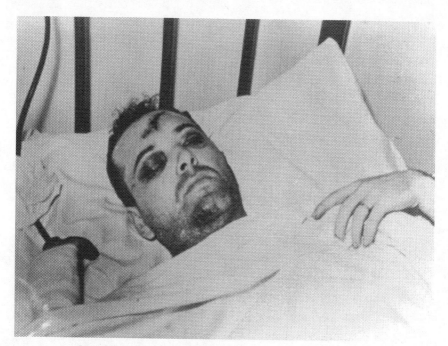

Ken Morris in *Detroit News* photo, taken June 3, 1946

PART I

THE JOURNEY BEGINS: 1935 TO 1939

CHAPTER 1

HE BROKE HIS FATHER'S HEART

Dad never spent a lot of time reminiscing about his early life, but stories were told about his life in Pittsburgh, and my older brother, Greg, and I listened with great intensity. More often than not, these stories were told as we were driving with him someplace, usually to or from one of his meetings or events on a Saturday or Sunday. He told us of his caddying experiences and how his love of golf evolved. He enjoyed high school at Oliver High in Pittsburgh. From him, we learned that his high school was located across the street from a cemetery, and he often recited their favorite football cheer: "Kick 'em in the wishbone; kick 'em in the jaw; throw them in the tombstone—rah, rah, rah."

THE JOURNEY BEGAN ONE COLD April morning in 1935 at a truck stop just north of Pittsburgh. Morris left home at 5:00 a.m., and it took some time for the spring chill to work its way out of his thin body. He had no way of knowing then that this journey would lead him to a life that he could never have fathomed that April morning. He and seven other guys were heading for Detroit. From there, they were going head to Chicago, St. Louis, and Denver, finally ending up in California. They planned to be gone at least a year, or at least that's what Morris told everyone.

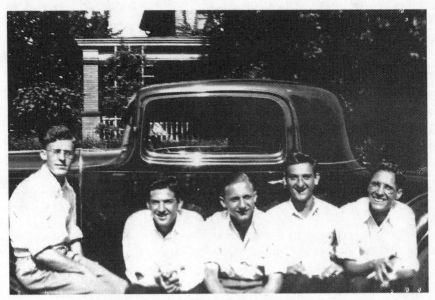

Ken Morris, second from left, in roughly 1935. He is probably with his traveling salesmen partners.

Most of the guys hitched a ride to Detroit, where they would meet at a location known as Grand Circus Park. One fellow had a small black Ford coupe; two of the fellows crammed suitcases and material for their work into that car. Everyone else had to find his own ride. It was an adventure, to be sure. But it was more than that. These were Depression kids. Life was hard. To help with household expenses, Morris gave almost every penny he made to his stepmother. Even so, he felt he was not giving enough to the household—that he was a weight on the family and it was time to move on.

. . . .

Morris Katz and his family lived on the north side of Pittsburgh, a working-class multiethnic melting pot known as Woods Run. Their house was a three-story building, with a shoe repair shop in the storefront portion of the structure, a kitchen and living area right behind the shop, and his parents' bedroom behind that. His father, Louis, rented out the second floor, and the boys stayed on the third floor. The boys were Harry, born in 1908 in the old country; Morris, born in New York City in 1915, and Saul, also born in New York, in 1916. Another brother and sister, a set of twins, were born later, but they died as small children, perhaps a result of the great flu epidemic of 1918–19.

Morris enjoyed being a kid growing up on McClure Street. He fondly told stories of playing ball, sneaking into the local movie theater, and being protected by his older and extremely tough brother Harry. Tragedy struck when Morris's mother died when he was ten years old. The boy was very close to this strong woman, both in body and spirit, and she had encouraged Morris to learn and read every book in the nearby library. Among her last words to him was a plea to stay in school and get an education.

His father was a good provider. A Jew from Poland, Louis Katz left his homeland in 1913 to avoid conscription and seek a better life. A shoemaker by profession, he ran a successful shoe repair store. To be successful, Louis knew that he had to move his trade and family into diverse non-Jewish neighborhoods that needed his services. Woods Run was full of Poles, Italians, a few Irish, and many eastern European working people who could afford to use his shoe repair services and occasionally buy a pair of new shoes. This strategy worked well until the Depression hit; then life became hard.

After several years of trying to raise Morris and his brothers, Harry and Saul, as a single parent, Louis took a new wife, Freda. She was young and new to the United States. She had lived through Russian pogroms and escaped anti-Semitic persecution when she came to America.

Freda was extremely young when she married Louis and was not prepared to be a mother of three wild and willful young boys. Decades later, she talked about how ignorant she had been in trying to cope with her new stepsons and a new country. She knew she made mistakes as a mother and a wife, but she did the best that she could. Morris, in particular, had a difficult time adjusting to his new stepmother. The family soon grew when Freda gave birth to her only child, Jacob.

By 1930, everyone in Woods Run seemed to be feeling the Depression. The three older boys helped the family survive economically. Every spring, summer, and fall, Morris caddied at the Shannopin Country Club, not far from Woods Run. At the golf club, he learned about life, businesspeople, and golf. He made good money, almost all of which went to his stepmother.[3]

Kids were often expected to drop out of school by sixteen and help provide for the family. Louis's oldest son, Harry, dropped out, so Freda expected the same from Morris and Saul. Morris watched in dismay as his younger brother, Saul, left Oliver High School and enrolled in a trade school in his junior year. Morris knew his brother loved Oliver High. Saul was president of his class and involved with sports. Although he enjoyed his time at school, he did the "right" thing by the family. Morris displayed what would be a lifelong stubborn streak and stayed at Oliver.

Morris also loved high school. He stood five feet seven inches but seemed taller due to his huge head of wavy black hair. His high school yearbook was full of details about a life he rarely talked about as an adult. Out of 105 graduating seniors, he was one of 18 who graduated with honors. With his ability, he should have gone to college, but in his family's economic position, that simply was not an option. He took practical classes such as accounting and shorthand. He was the only boy in his shorthand class. His teacher told him that if he became a male secretary, he could learn to run a business from the inside and eventually be the man who ran the company. He participated in all kinds of school activities. He was active on the Oliver High newspaper staff, a member of the yearbook staff, president of the reading club, and chair of the class ring committee. He acted in his senior play, ran some track, and even started a boys' cooking club. Morris, the Oliver yearbook stated, wanted to be a successful manager and eventually own a large business.[4]

Morris graduated from high school in 1934 and could not find work. The accounting and shorthand classes seemed worthless. After several months, he saw an ad in the newspaper that read, "Wanted, earn good money working for Hoyt Products." He took the streetcar to the Hoyt offices in the Commonwealth Annex of downtown Pittsburgh. A man explained it all to him. A simple job, it relied on salesmanship through door-to-door sales. He signed up. Morris and a crew of young men began meeting and heading out to local towns, usually company towns, in Western Pennsylvania. They'd knock on a door and a tired housewife, often a Polish immigrant, would answer. Morris said he and his friends were representing Hoyt and selling everything for the home, from hair tonic and shoelaces to cleaning fluid and other household things from a list of over two hundred items. As the woman was about to shut the door, Morris quickly learned to say, "I'm working at this temporarily, and I'm getting points. If I get enough points, I'll be able to have a scholarship to go to school." Or sometimes as that door was closing, he said, "I must get three hundred orders, and then I will get a steady job." Either line often worked, although the steady job line seemed more effective. Either way, the housewives listened and doors often opened a little wider. Morris enjoyed this job, as he loved meeting new people.

The young man learned to understand his customers. He had many Polish immigrants on his various routes through Charlevoix, Aliquippa, Ambridge, and many other towns. He also found that Hoyt was often the only competition to the company store, the only place in town where people could shop. Thus Hoyt provided competitive if not better prices for their wares. He learned to say his opening lines in Polish to help keep that door open. He also learned that the doors closed faster when he used his own name, his Jewish name. He found that when he used a name like Ken Morris, instead of Morris Katz, sales increased. With a new name, he brought more money home.

Morris also saw the workers, the men who dragged themselves home after their shifts. They'd often be filthy from their work in a mine or factory, and their wives would have a hot tub of water sitting on the kitchen floor, ready for a bath so the workers could clean up before dinner. From time to time, he heard talk about a strike. Sometimes he overheard someone whispering the name John L. Lewis, the president of the United Mine Workers. Sometimes the housewives quietly said, "No, I can't buy today; we have to save every penny if there's a strike." When there was talk of a strike, Morris never pressured his customers.

After about a year of this, one of the guys said that they did not have to stay in Pittsburgh. They could do this anywhere and in any large city. They needed to find a local wholesaler or distributor. From that conversation, the boys hatched a plan together and decided to see the United States. Again, the plan was to start in Detroit, known as the "City of Champions" since the Detroit Tigers had just won the World Series, the Detroit Lions had won their football championship, and the

Red Wings had won hockey's Stanley Cup. Detroit was also the home of Joe Louis. It was, of course, the home of the automobile industry as well. Detroit was a city of opportunity—it was in the west.

Morris told his dad about the plan. Louis thought his son was nuts. He had heard about boys and young men roaming the country. He did not want his son to be one of those bums. While Morris didn't bring a lot of money home, he was helping the family, Louis told him. His father forbade Morris from making the trip. Morris did not say anything. But he thought, *Well, goddamn it, I have a right to go.* So on that April morning, he found one of his buddies, and hooked up with a trucker headed for Detroit. It wasn't hard; the driver wanted the company. He left without telling anyone in his family.

He and his buddy were squished into the cab of the truck, and after a full April day of that, he looked out at the road between Toledo and Detroit. They could see the tall buildings of Detroit coming into view on the horizon. Pittsburg was history. So too was the name Morris Katz. From now on, he would be Ken Morris ... and the best salesman possible.[5]

. . . .

The boys successfully met up at Grand Circus Park. What a place! Detroit seemed three times the size of Pittsburgh. Within this park and along Woodward Avenue were newsstands, movie theaters, and men giving political speeches on soapboxes. This seemed to be where all the action was. The soapboxers were great. All kinds of people were standing on their boxes and talking about the problems of the world. These men sold communism, socialism, Marxism, or their own political solution to address the problems of the world. In most cases, small crowds gathered to listen. What the hell—they were men out of work and had nothing else to do. Ken enjoyed the buzz these men and their audiences created, and he was to spent much of his free time listening to these characters.[6]

Ken and some of the boys found a place on Alfred Street, just off Woodward Avenue and only a few blocks from Grand Circus Park. It was a rooming house on a street of great old Victorian homes that had been cut up into flats and rooming houses. The boys soon hooked up with a distributor and began selling their products door-to-door. But things were not as simple as they had seemed in Pittsburgh.[7]

The sales did not develop as the boys had hoped. In Detroit, people had more than just a company store from which to purchase their goods. Selling door-to-door was nice, but customers were not as plentiful. It became tough to pay the weekly rent and the upkeep on the car. Soon the only married man returned home with his car. Then another got homesick. Within a matter of weeks, Ken was by himself. He was too stubborn to return home, for he had told too many friends that he would be gone for a year. He sent a letter to his dad, saying that he was in Detroit and was all right. He told him that he was going to earn his own way for a while, so Louis did not have to worry about feeding him. He did not contact his father again for a long time. He broke his father's heart.

CHAPTER 2

BRIGGS SLAUGHTERHOUSE, THIS STOP!

We knew that Dad had hitchhiked to Detroit, that he and some friends were planning to see the country as door-to-door salesmen. Perhaps it was because we were so young, but he never talked about bad times. Sure, he talked about the problems of finding work. He talked about roaming around the city and listening to the soapboxers. If anything, he gave us the impression that he was in a new city looking for opportunity, in spite of the Depression.

THE SIGN WAS HUGE. ANYONE who walked or drove down Woodward at Alexandrine Street could not miss it:

BREAKFAST

Three Eggs/Toast/Potatoes

10¢

Over the next few years, Ken had many meals at Tree's Restaurant. He always tried to keep a dime in his pocket, for there were many days that this ten-cent breakfast was his only meal for the day.[8]

He tried to continue his door-to-door effort, but doing it as a one-man company just did not work. His mode of transportation was streetcar, electric bus, or bus, but these transportation options limited him. He needed to get to the more isolated neighborhoods, but the trips were too difficult without an automobile. If he could not get there to sell his goods and, perhaps more importantly, deliver the products he sold, he was not going to be successful. He did meet a few other door-to-door salesmen, but their various companies did not need more salesmen. They were laying off their own employees.

By the beginning of June, desperation was sinking in. He avoided his landlord. Finally, the man confronted Ken one night in June and told him to pay his rent … or else.

His ten-cent breakfast was becoming too expensive. He was behind on his rent and had no prospects whatsoever of paying July's rent. Ken made a tough decision, a dishonorable decision. He decided to sneak out of the rooming house, but how? He had a fairly large suitcase full of his clothes, shoes, and all the other stuff he had packed for their trip around the county. To make matters worse, it seemed the landlord was always around now that he was behind on his rent. One night when the landlord was away, Ken snuck out. To avoid looking suspicious, he left his suitcase behind, squeezed two shirts and three suits onto his body, and walked out. He never looked back.

Now what was he going to do? He'd heard of a flophouse down near Jefferson Avenue. A homeless facility run by the Mariners' Church, it was called Mariners' Hall. Mariners' Hall was simply a hall with rows of beds laid out in neat rows. It had a large bathroom with a couple of showers. He was a step above being homeless, being a hobo. Occasionally, there were odd jobs, but nothing permanent. Someone, either one of the fellows or the people who ran the place, seemed to know where a day's work could be found. It was a day here and a day there. Some days he went to the plants, but they weren't hiring. It seemed you had to know somebody to get in at the big plants. Ken was discouraged but never thought of quitting. He was not heading back to Pittsburgh.[9]

. . . .

Besides looking for work, Ken remembered another experience from his Pittsburgh days. Ken liked to act. He had gained some experience acting in stage plays while in high school. The acting bug bit him hard in those seemingly carefree days. After high school, he had kept an eye open for other acting opportunities. One of his Hoyt sales friends had mentioned that he knew of a Pittsburgh troupe that needed actors. Two former professors from the University of Pittsburgh ran the acting group. A man and a gorgeous woman—either the man's wife or live-in girlfriend; Ken never knew which—ran the acting group. They had gained citywide notoriety because both had been discharged from the University of Pittsburgh for being Communists. That didn't bother Ken, as the two were extremely nice and encouraging people. He just wanted to act in plays. Ken's first production with the group was a play by Clifford Odets, *Waiting for Lefty*. Ken was the taxi driver, and the play was about a taxi worker's effort to organize a union. They rehearsed constantly, and Ken loved it. As the taxi driver, Ken's character played a lead role and was the man who bargained against the company (a prophetic role for the future labor leader).

Ken remembered a woman coming up to him after one performance and saying, "Boy, I watched this play in New York. You were far better than the fellow who had the same role there." This was heady stuff for a young man not long out of high school. He had fun. The acting group was known as the Little Theatre Group, and to be a member, he joined the players group. Later, Ken's father told him that he had read that the group was connected to the Communist Party. Ken wasn't surprised, but he didn't care. Just before he left Pittsburgh, the professor suggested he look up the Little Theatre Group in Detroit. He was sure Ken would have fun acting with that group.

In Detroit, Ken had plenty of time, more free time than he would have for the rest of his life. He walked all over the city. One Saturday afternoon, while walking near the City College Campus (now Wayne State University) on Cass Avenue, he saw a sign on a house reading "Little Theatre Group." Ken's eyes brightened as he thought about the last words the professor had said to him. He walked up the front porch steps and knocked on the door.

The door opened slightly, and a man asked suspiciously who he was. The tone of his voice made Ken think it was the 1920s and he was knocking on the door of a speakeasy. He felt he needed a password to get in.

Ken identified himself. He said he had just moved from Pittsburgh, where he was an actor with the Little Theatre Group there. The door opened, and Ken entered. The Detroit Theatre Group never welcomed Ken into their group as the Pittsburgh group had. Ken did not understand the cold reception until years later. The Detroit group must have thought he was a government agent sent to inform on Communists. Still, in spite of the cool reception, he was so lonely that he continued to stop by that house.

After his third or fourth visit, one of the guys said there was going to be a picnic at Belle Isle, sponsored by the local Communist Party. They wanted to perform *Waiting for Lefty*. He asked if Ken wanted to reprise his role as taxi driver. Ken eagerly accepted.

Two weeks later, they performed the play on a nice summer day at Belle Isle. There were a few missed cues, but the audience seemed to enjoy the performance. Ken received some compliments, but it wasn't the same as Pittsburgh. These people were not friendly, he thought. They were arrogant SOBs, and he decided he didn't want anything more to do with them. No one asked him to join the group or the Communist Party, and that was fine by him. Years later, he thought about what would have happened if these people had been friendly and encouraging like the professor and his lover. If that had been the case and he was asked to become a Communist, would he have done it? He felt he probably would have. Why not? He was lonely and would have enjoyed new and welcoming friends. At that stage of his life, the nineteen-year-old young man never thought about the politics of being a Communist. Had they been the right kind of people, with welcoming personalities, who knows what might have happened in Ken's life?[10]

. . . .

On a night in early August, some of the regulars at Mariners' Hall were having one of their typical bull sessions. One pulled out an article he had ripped from the *Detroit News*, reporting that Detroit's population had risen to 1.6 million people, an increase of over 120,000 people in eighteen months. He read, "Detroit is leading the nation back toward prosperity and in certain respects has itself already arrived." The guys laughed; they certainly were not part of that prosperity.[11]

Another fellow, a real wise guy, a know-it-all type, told them that the state fair was coming and that he heard Chevrolet might need some people to work at their exhibit.

The next morning, Ken and a couple of the guys walked up Woodward to the Chevrolet administrative building. It was early; the soapbox orators weren't even out yet. There were so few people on the street that Ken worried his old landlord might see him. Word that Chevy was hiring had clearly reached the public, for a line of people waited outside the building. Eventually, his turn in line came, and he was hired. He had his first real job in Detroit—mopping floors at the state fair's Chevrolet exhibit. Work started at eleven o'clock each night. His first real job in Detroit lasted nine days. For the first time since arriving in Detroit, he was able to put some real dollars into his pants pocket. It only cost him ten cents to get there and back via the streetcar. After work, he usually stopped at his ten-cent breakfast spot and then walked back to the hall to sleep. He was pocketing almost a dollar a day.

The state fair began on August 30 and closed on September 8. The end of the fair's run came quickly, much too quickly. Still, Ken felt good. With some overtime, he had been able to save about fifteen dollars. He was thinking of moving out of Mariners' Hall, but he reminded himself that he shouldn't get too cocky.

In a twist of fate, while Ken was working at the state fair, the American Federation of Labor (AFL) began a convention at the Fort Shelby Hotel, just a few blocks from Mariners' Hall, to start a union, the United Automobile Workers. At the time, Ken had no idea that one day he would become intimately involved with this union, its conventions, and its politics. All this was a different world from the one in which Ken lived.

One afternoon in early October, that same wise guy was holding court with the guys. He announced that he had started work in one of the Dodge plants, probably Dodge Main, over near Hamtramck. He had a Dodge badge to prove it. Ken asked him how he got that badge.

Wise Guy told him what to do. He told him of a place known as the Free Employment Agency, just off Michigan Avenue. He told Ken to see a white-haired fellow named Mr. Christie and ask him for a job. Wise Guy added that if any problems occurred, to ask to see a man named Culver.

Wise Guy's advice had worked once; maybe it would work again. The next morning, Ken walked down to Michigan Avenue and turned left toward Navin Field, the home of the Detroit Tigers. He headed to the building that housed the Automobile Manufacturers Association—the trade association. Ken walked into an impressively large room with deep dark wood, and there was one man sitting behind a counter. Imagine, a huge room with only one man in it. Ken walked up to the man, assuming he was Mr. Christie. The man looked up and with a somewhat irritated voice told him that they did not open until nine o'clock.

Ken thought that this fellow was not in a good mood and immediately decided that he was not the man to talk to. Ken asked if Mr. Culver was available.

The white haired man's demeanor softened a bit, and he reached over to his intercom, flicked a switch, and announced to the voice on the other end that a young man was here to see Mr. Culver. Ken heard a gruff voice say to send him up.

Ken walked up a flight of stairs to a large office. A man sitting behind a desk invited him to sit down. Mr. Culver then proceeded to give Ken one of the most amazing performances that he had ever heard from a human being. Ken did not remember the specifics, but the man talked endlessly about the Depression, jobs, and the need to support manufacturing companies. He paused as he finished and focused on the young man, surmising that the young man was looking for a job. He then proceeded to tell Ken how times were tough. He pulled out charts showing high unemployment and low productivity. And after some twenty or thirty minutes, he asked what he could do for the young man.

Ken said he was looking for work. Culver said he could not offer him a job.

Ken walked dejectedly out of the office and back down the steps.

He'd thought that he might have a chance since Mr. Culver had spent so much time talking. Another opportunity lost.

Once again, he entered the large room with Mr. Christie at the counter, but this time the atmosphere had changed. There was noise echoing through the room and a long line of men waiting to see Mr. Christie. Ken got in that line, and when his place in line came up, Ken stepped to the counter.

He told Christie that he had just come from Mr. Culver's office. Before Ken could finish, Christie nodded and reached down to give him a job application. Ken took it over to another counter to fill it out.

The application had "Briggs Manufacturing Company" handwritten at the top of the page. There was a card clipped to the application. It directed him to be out at Briggs by eight o'clock the next morning to apply for a job. Ken thought this might be his big break.

Back at Mariners' Hall, Ken didn't say much. Later that night, he did tell Wise Guy about what had happened. Wise Guy told Ken that Briggs was the toughest auto plant in Detroit. He said they built auto bodies for Ford, Chrysler, Dodge, Hudson, and others. Wise Guy added that his fellow workers at the Dodge plant said if you can't get a job, you go to Briggs.

The next morning, he left Mariners' Hall before seven o'clock. He took the streetcar down Woodward and transferred to the Mack Avenue line. He asked the driver where Briggs was, and the man said he would announce it. After a while, Ken heard the announcement: "Briggs slaughterhouse, this stop!"[12]

Ken jumped to his feet and saw the gate that had Briggs Manufacturing Company marked on it. Behind the gate were a number of buildings, but one building was huge and dwarfed all the rest. It was five stories high, but from Ken's vantage point, it was not the height that struck him but its length. It seemed to stretch forever. This was the Briggs Mack Avenue plant, the epicenter of the Briggs Corporation.

He was sent to the personnel office, where a clerk looked at his application. They nodded and gave him another one. This one was more official and had the company's name printed at the top. As he wrote down his name, he paused for a moment. Ken Morris. It wasn't his official name, but it was the name he had used for the past six months. The name stayed.

He completed the application and was hired on October 9, 1935. He was to report to work at the Mack Avenue press room at ten thirty that night.

He walked out of that personnel office feeling lighter than air. He had a job ... a job in an auto plant. He was going to make some money![13]

CHAPTER 3

NO ONE WORKS ME LIKE A DOG

One time while driving in the 1955 Plymouth, we asked Dad about his first job in Detroit. He quickly responded, "I worked two weeks as a janitor at the state fair. That was an important job; I needed the money." Later we asked about how he was hired at Briggs. He said, "It was the Depression. A group of people stood outside in the cold, and the foreman would come out and size people up. If he liked the way you looked, he might ask if you knew how to operate a press. When my chance came, the foreman looked at me and said, 'can you operate a press?' I needed a job and didn't hesitate. I said sure, and that's how I got hired." While that is not the exact way he was hired at Briggs, the point was the same: during the Depression, desperate people did whatever it took to get a job, any job.

THE PLANT WAS DIFFERENT AT night. He arrived sometime after ten o'clock, and the atmosphere was changed from that morning. There were fewer people around, the dim light cast dark shadows throughout the plant, and the noise from the plant seemed more pronounced. He was told to report to the press room. Walking through the plant was terrifying to the young man. He had never been inside a building like this. The machines were huge and not clearly defined in the haziness of the dark night.

He found his way to the superintendent's office. There were six or seven guys in the office, all being hired. The superintendent, without a word of welcome, looked him up and down and said, "You know how to operate a punch press, don't you?"

Without a moment of hesitation, Ken lied and replied, "Yes, sir."

A few moments later, he was escorted onto the plant floor to a press where several men were working. The press was huge; it punched the quarter panels for car bodies. Ken looked up at the machines and thought, *How the hell am I going to operate these things. Oh my God, what am I into now!*[14]

Since his shift started at eleven o'clock, Ken had a few moments to study the machine, the buttons, and the process. A group of workers had gathered near the new employee, waiting for their shift to begin as the afternoon shift was finishing up work. Ken intently watched the fellows working. He had to figure out what he was going to do.

The terror he felt inside must have shown on the outside. Soon someone came over and gave him some heavy work gloves and an apron. Then a couple of fellows took pity on him and explained how the machine operated and which buttons he had to press. Another worker said that he would be his partner. He said they would take a flat piece of sheet metal and place it in the press; then they'd press the green button and the huge press would slam down and stamp the metal into the quarter panel. The heavy press shaped the sheet metal into the quarter panel; the two workers would lift the part off the press and stack it off to the side. The more quarter panels produced, the greater the chance of receiving their full wage; if they did not meet their production quota, it would be reflected in their paychecks.

The task required perfect timing. The men wanted to work as fast as possible in order to be fully paid, so a split-second rhythm evolved between the team. One man hit the green button. The press slammed down to stamp out the part, and the men removed the newly formed panel. Then the men would lay down the next flat piece of sheet metal. While one man was centering the piece, the other man hit the green button, slamming the press down. Hands, fingers, and other appendages had to be out from under the press before it came down or their limbs would be crushed. Split-second timing was required. This was their job for eight hours a day, with a half hour lunch break. If a man became tired or got sloppy during the shift, a lost finger, a flattened hand, or a scarred face could be the result. So it was as the weeks rolled by.

When they made their production quota, and if they worked forty hours a week, Ken made just over seventeen dollars per week. On an annualized basis, this amounted to about nine hundred dollars per year. Of course, this assumed forty-hour workweeks, which were rare. They worked based on need, so they often worked just three or four days per week. And then there were plant shutdowns for model changeover; weeks or months went by without any income. Thus Ken's pay was much less than he had anticipated. But he was single and not used to receiving any kind of paycheck. He got by, but he sometimes wondered how married men with families survived.

Within the first couple of weeks on the job, Ken was working with a fellow who had a full-time job at Packard. There had been a layoff at Packard and the fellow needed money, so he hired in at Briggs. This was a temporary position until he went back to the Packard plant. Ken found that many men who were laid off at other manufacturers used Briggs as a stopgap employer. The fellow from Packard hated Briggs and talked about how primitive the working conditions were as compared to other auto factories in Detroit. He complained about the bad air, the SOB foremen, having no breaks with the exception of lunch, and more. The drinking fountain was twenty feet away, but a worker could only get a drink of water before the start of the shift, during the lunch break, or after the shift was over. The Packard man called it barbarian. There were, of course, no bathroom breaks and no relief people of any sort. It was archaic to this guy, but it was the norm for Ken. Ken had nothing else to compare it to.

One evening, about an hour or so into the shift, the Packard fellow said, "No one is going to work me like a dog. I quit." He threw his gloves onto the floor and walked out. In the meantime, the operation still had to move. Ken felt obligated to try to keep the process going on his own. After a short while, the foreman came by and said, "Keep up that job until I get a replacement." Ken somehow kept that press going. Being such a little man, the job was nearly impossible, yet he succeeded in keeping his station operating. Finally, after about three hours, someone showed up to help him. It was the roughest three hours of physical labor of his life. Of course, since his production quota was not met, Ken's pay was docked in the next paycheck.[15]

Whether it was because of this experience or something else, the night superintendent—the supervisor whom Ken had met on his first day—took a liking to Ken. The superintendent was a quiet man who didn't want to be bothered during his shift. He expected everyone to complete his work, and he expected his foremen to make sure everyone on the line completed his quota. The superintendent began seeking out Ken to do extra jobs or errands. He often pulled Ken out of production work to do other jobs around the press room, which was fine with Ken—after all, he was off the line working odd jobs for the superintendent and receiving full pay. No one liked production work. Before the lunch break, the superintendent often gave Ken two bits and told him to get him a pork chop sandwich. Ken went off the premises to an all-night cafe and got that sandwich almost every night.[16]

Ken was making his seventeen dollars a week, but sometimes, if there was overtime, he could pull in upwards of twenty-five dollars a week. He moved to a boardinghouse near Woodward and Mack avenues. He loved the area. This was where the action was. There were clubs and ten-cent dance halls. Big bands played at the Graystone and Arcadia ballrooms. This was the place where people gathered, where young people came to congregate. It was fun, especially now that he was making some money.

The weeks turned into months, and work became a regular routine. From his boardinghouse, Ken jumped on the Mack Avenue streetcar and was at work within thirty minutes. He punched in to work and did whatever work was assigned to him. While he became knowledgeable about his department, the remainder of the vast plant was a mystery to him.

Briggs was a huge place, with varying cultures and subcultures. There were many different departments: a trim department, an assembly department, a cushion department, a foundry, and much more. Besides the five-story main plant, there were the other Briggs plants in Detroit. These included the Hamtramck plant, where small parts were manufactured; the Meldrum plant, where high-end bodies for Lincolns and Chryslers were made; and the Highland Park plant, the plant where the Model T had previously been made and was now rented by the Ford Motor Company to Briggs, where they made Ford bodies. There were three shifts, and Ken worked on the shift that had the fewest people, an atmosphere Ken liked. Ken's overtime work occasionally overlapped into the morning shift. Everything was so different when the morning shift began. The light of day seemed to change the colors of the plant. As they came in to start the new shift, the men seemed fresh and more alert. After seven thirty or eight, more of the Briggs white-collar staff were on the premises, both in the plant and housed in other buildings on the property. There was more life in the place.

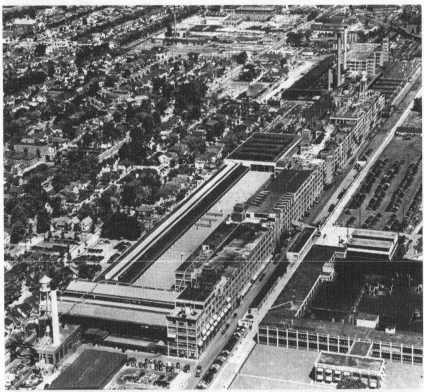

Briggs Mack Avenue plant, about 1954. The plant stretched about a half mile.

When they left the plant around seven in the morning, Ken saw lines of men outside. Sometimes one of the foremen would be walking out with the production workers. One day a foreman told the group of workers to look at that line of job applicants. He added that if Ken or his coworkers wanted to complain about their jobs, just look—there were dozens who could fill a vacancy. Ken felt a shiver of fear run down his back. He did his job. He didn't complain. Why did this man, a foreman, have to lord his power over him? In Ken's world, it was the foreman who had all the power. He could fire a person without any reason. Ken saw it happen. A foreman could send a person home without pay. Occasionally, Ken worked the day shift. He saw that Briggs brought in extra workers but did not have specifically assigned work for them. If, after four hours, there was no need for the worker, then the foreman sent the worker home—without pay. This made no sense to Ken.

As Ken became more acclimated to the plant, he began to notice older men, men without an arm, a hand, some fingers, or perhaps hobbling from a permanent foot injury. These men were "pity" employees, men who had suffered accidents in the plant but were kept on the payroll, at much-reduced wages, to carry buckets of bolts or other pieces of equipment needed by the workers on the line. In all likelihood, it was the company's way of avoiding workers' compensation costs.

One day Ken got a glove out of the tool crib. As he put his right hand into the glove, he felt something preventing his finger from sliding in. He shook the glove and someone's finger fell out. Ken took the finger and the glove back to the tool crib. The man running the crib gave him another set of gloves and threw the finger into the garbage can.

Ken and all other production people in the plant were paid by piecework. In order to achieve his forty-three cents an hour, he had to produce a minimum amount of work when he was at the punch press or suffer a deduction in pay. Sometime after the start of 1936, probably in February, Briggs offered a great deal for the production workers. They said that workers would be paid for nine hours of work in eight hours, if they produced the equivalent of nine hours of production. Eight hours of work for nine hours of pay. This was a good deal. After a couple of weeks, the company sweetened the pot. They offered ten hours pay for eight hours work. The men, especially the younger ones, jumped at the idea.[17]

Ken remembered one of the older men on the job, a heavyset fellow, shaking his head at the young workers and saying, "You boys are making a mistake." He went on to explain that the company was going to lay everyone off soon for retooling. At that time, the company routinely figured out new production quotas, and all the extra work was calculated into the production output for the next year's model.

Money was scarce. Some of these guys were college graduates looking for jobs elsewhere. Others had ambitions of their own. Many had families to support. They figured they were short-timers and not going to spend a career on the production line. They needed the money. Who cared about next year?

Production was high as they rolled through March. Then in April, the layoff came. All the castings in the plant had to be changed to reflect the new model designs. Ken and the others were released from the plant. The foreman said that if they were lucky, they would receive a telegram from Briggs in a couple of months, calling them back to work.

. . . .

Ken was out on the street again, but this time it was different. This time he had some money in his pocket. He had been able to save just over a hundred dollars in six months. He cut expenses and looked for a job to help him get through what might be a long summer, but he felt confident he could get by.

Ken still had not made many friends. The workers in the plant were great but mostly lived separate lives outside the plant. Many were married or stayed close to their own ethnic groups. Ken came to know a young man named Walter Smith. Walter worked at a White Tower hamburger place on Woodward. Walter and his brother and sister-in-law rented an apartment back on Alfred Street, near John R Street. Ken became their roommate. The apartment was next to the Colonial Theatre. From here, they were only a few blocks from Woodward and very close to Paradise Valley and the Black Bottom neighborhoods. Detroit, like most places in America, was a segregated society. In Detroit, the area where many of the city's black population lived was Paradise Valley, an area slightly east of John R. The main street of Paradise Valley was Hastings Street. Ken enjoyed walking through this area of town. He liked the atmosphere, the sounds, the smells of home cooking, and the music.

Ken found a temporary job, again selling door-to-door. This time he was selling magazines, traveling all around the state, even to Chicago. He never made as much money as in the plant, but he enjoyed being outside and meeting people. When back in Detroit, Ken enjoyed the summer. He and Walter occasionally went to a Tiger game (at the newly renamed Briggs Stadium), played some golf with a set of Walter Hagan golf clubs that Ken bought for $14.95 at Hudson's Department Store, or went to a movie. Ken loved movies.

He found himself heading back toward the plant, but not for work. He enjoyed watching sandlot games at Mack Field. The old African American baseball team, the Detroit Stars, had recently folded, but there was plenty of good sandlot baseball to be seen at Mack and Fairview streets. He liked his new apartment and his life, and he waited for a call from Briggs.

In August, Ken was in Chicago selling magazines. Walter Smith contacted him and informed him that Briggs had sent the telegram. He was to be back to work by the next Monday. By the time Ken got the message, he had only two days to get back to Detroit. He hitchhiked back and returned on Sunday, just before he was to report to work. He was glad to be going back to work. He wasn't making any real money, and his savings had been depleted weeks earlier. He was ready to go back to the plant, but this time things were different. Production was up, and the sound of union organizers was in the air.[18]

Chapter 4

I'll Be Back, You Sons of Bitches, and Organize This Plant

Dad had a very old unopened bottle of French wine that he'd received from a top management person at Briggs. He was very proud of the old bottle, which I think was from the eighteenth century. It surprised me. Why would a Briggs executive give a dreaded union man such a gift? Dad said that despite many differences, he formed many good relationships with Briggs management. Good people were good people. Later, he talked about the time one spring when a top executive offered him and some of his buddies a weekend job to prepare his large sailboat for the upcoming sailing season. The guys worked all spring, scraping, sanding, and varnishing that boat. As an extra reward, the owner let the guys take the sailboat out on Lake St. Clair one Sunday afternoon. The day started off sunny and warm. One of the guys seemed to have a knack at handling the boat, and Dad was having a great time. Then a weather front moved in, and soon the winds were howling. The sailboat was leaning, with the mast nearly horizontal to the water. Dad thought they were doomed. Fortunately, the storm moved on and they were able to limp back to the Detroit Yacht Club on Bell Isle. Soon Dad felt solid ground underneath his feet. It was decades before he was on a sailboat again.

These stories indicate that while workers and management had major differences, Walter Briggs hired good and decent men who did, in fact, build a great company. The men on the line felt that Briggs produced a good product. While their labor policies and the men who enforced them were shortsighted, many, if not most, management people were decent and hardworking individuals.

LONG BEFORE KEN MORRIS DREAMED of coming to Detroit, two families found their way to Detroit, and those families left their imprint on the city and the automobile industry. These two families and the forces behind them participated in a strategic chess match over labor peace on the east side of Detroit from 1936 to 1953.

. . . .

Walter O. Briggs was born in 1877, in Ypsilanti, Michigan. Briggs grew up in a modest middle-class family, with his father working for the Michigan Central Railroad as an engineer. When Briggs was fifteen, he sought and found employment with the Michigan Central Railroad. The boy started as a common laborer but moved up in the company to become a foreman. Briggs left after eleven years and became a foreman at a local cement company, the C. H. Little Company.

In 1904, Briggs made a career move that eventually brought him great wealth. One of his boyhood friends, Barney Everitt, convinced him to come to work in Detroit's bourgeoning automobile industry. Everitt ran an auto trim factory that took body shells from various auto manufacturers and primed them for final assembly. This was a novel and successful approach to automobile manufacturing, basic outsourcing. Briggs was able to learn the business inside and out. In 1909, Everitt decided to invest with two other entrepreneurs, Bill Metzger and Walter Flanders, to found the E-M-F automobile company. To raise capital for this new company, Everitt sold his auto trim company to Briggs. The E-M-F Company was successful early on, and it eventually evolved into the Studebaker empire.

Briggs, like his competitors the Fisher brothers, took automobile body making into new territory. Within ten years, the Briggs Manufacturing Company, as it was renamed, was doing much more than just trimming and painting bodies for car manufacturing. After World War I, Briggs began producing car bodies to manufacturer's specifications. Thus a client such as Ford, Hudson, Paige-Detroit, Chalmers, or E-M-F simply told Briggs what their designers needed as a body, and Briggs' staff completed the design and manufactured the product to the company's specifications. Briggs became known for developing innovative design and manufacturing techniques.

After World War I, Briggs was convinced that a closed automobile body could be developed for the industry. Most of the auto companies believed that such a design was not feasible and was cost prohibitive, likely costing an extra thousand dollars per vehicle. Briggs convinced Hudson to try his idea on their Hudson Essex model. The design not only proved a great success but also enabled Briggs to deliver the product at less cost than the traditional open-body vehicle. By the early 1920s, the Briggs innovation in body design and manufacturing made him an auto baron in his own right. This innovation made him an enormously wealthy man by the time he was forty-five years old.[19]

. . . .

Walter Briggs was a gruff and difficult man; colleagues considered him tough but fair. One associate said of him:

> [Walter Briggs was] scrupulously and unfailingly honest. I don't suppose there is anyone in all Detroit which is more anxious for a man always to get every cent that is due him in a transaction. At the same time he is equally insistent upon a square deal for himself. He's intolerant of a man who tries to "put one over." In other words, he wants to be exact in his dealings.
>
> I have known men to be frightened of him, not because he was cross or unreasonable—though I admit he can be severe on occasion—but rather because they were acutely conscious he knew so much more than they knew about their own particular jobs.[20]

People who worked with Briggs knew him as direct and straightforward in his business dealings. They knew he made quick and intuitive decisions. And he was a man who liked to win. Briggs found another way to win in addition to making high quality and innovative automobile bodies during the 1920s.

Henry Ford received great fame as the creator of the $5 a day wage in 1914. Under Ford's new wage system, employees received their base salary of about $2.30 per day. Then a profit sharing bonus of $2.70 was added for each employee; however, Ford arbitrarily made deductions of the $2.70 profit-sharing bonus. Ford created a Ford Sociological Department that created a code of conduct for Ford employees, and department staff visited employee homes to make inspections. If a family took in a male boarder or if an unmarried employee did not have a savings account, the profit-sharing bonus was reduced or eliminated. If an immigrant family sent money to family relatives in the old country, the bonus could be eliminated. All was at the discretion of the sociological inspector. Of course, some also believed that the $5 dollar a day wage was an effort to keep unions out of the plant, particularly the Industrial Workers of World (IWW). In 1914, the IWW was making a major attempt to organize Ford, and the $5 dollar a day wage eliminated their threat to the company. About 30 percent of Ford workers never received the full $5 a day.[21]

To help cut his labor costs, Henry Ford liked outsourcing his work, and he loved outsourcing to Briggs. Briggs paid the lowest industrial wages in the state. The Briggs Company's low labor costs dramatically cut Ford's total labor costs. Later, the Chrysler Corporation and other major car companies learned that by going to Briggs, they received an excellent product and reduced their total labor costs. This created a bonanza of work for the Briggs Manufacturing Company. As the years passed, Briggs' profits grew and their clients evolved. In 1936, Briggs supplied Ford with 66 percent of their automobile bodies; by 1939, the number had fallen to 27 percent. Briggs was now providing bodies for Chrysler, Packard, and Hudson.[22]

Walter Briggs had many interests. An incredibly active man during the first half of the twentieth century, his wealth enabled him to indulge these interests.

He married Jane Elizabeth Cameron on November 22, 1904, the same year he started in the automobile industry. From this marriage sprang a family of four daughters and a son. The children were Grace, Elizabeth, Walter ("Spike"), Susan, and Jane. Jane reminisced that her father was tough on her older siblings, but all the children adored their father. Jane also admitted that as the last child, she avoided many of these tough challenges since she was the baby of the family and therefore got off easy.

Around 1913, Walter was looking for a nice apartment for his family. As Briggs recalled:

> I wanted to rent a high-grade, good-sized apartment for my family. As I have a large family, I required a large apartment. At that time my children were young—some of them in infancy. Little did I know what I was coming up against when I started out. Invariably the first question asked by apartment house managers was "Have you any children?" Answer: "Yes." Question: "How old?" Answer: "Two years—but our baby is exceptionally quiet!"
>
> After which, without apology or explanation, the manager would bite my head off: "That's what they all say. Nothing doing. These fine apartments were not built for troublesome babies. We don't want any of your bawling or squalling brats around here." And with that, we were almost pushed out on the street. Such was my experience with all of them.

Twelve years later, in 1925, Briggs righted this wrong by investing five hundred thousand dollars in a sixteen-unit apartment building. The apartment house was on Covington Street, directly across the street from beautiful Palmer Park, in the Merrill-Palmer subdivision near Woodward Avenue and Six Mile Road. This was a unique facility. First, only families with children under five years old could rent. Second, rents were nominal. And third, each apartment was soundproof so children could make as much racket as they wanted without repercussion from other neighbors.[23]

Briggs may not have been able to find a home of his choice in 1913, but by 1915, he moved his family to the most exclusive street in Detroit, Boston Boulevard. The house was and still is a beautiful Tudor mansion that was plenty big enough for Briggs and his family. Boston Boulevard was a street full of the who's who families of Detroit, including Fisher, Winkleman, Kresge, Racham, Grinnell, Couzens, and Henry Ford (who actually lived a block over on Edison and moved out to his Fair Lane estate in Dearborn as Briggs moved in).

Briggs had other residences as well. The family enjoyed a weekend getaway mansion in Bloomfield Hills. For summer vacations, they traveled to their retreat on Bois Blanc Island, a large undeveloped island adjacent to Mackinac Island in Lake Huron. In the winter, they traveled to Palm Beach, Florida, to enjoy another mansion and a 236-foot yacht. Walter and his children led the privileged life that few could even imagine.

Briggs faced a personal health crisis in the 1920s. His daughter Jane wrote:

> [W]hen I was a child, [Dad] had a bad case of tonsillitis. His [doctor] said the tonsils had to be removed. The operation was delayed until the fall of 1928 because we went to England, where the Briggs Limited was building the British Ford [facility].... I have always been told that because Dad's tonsils were removed when they were very infected, the infection went to his legs, and I remember episodes of terrible pain he experienced for a number of years. Finally, when [the pain] stopped, his legs were useless.[24]

In spite of these problems, Briggs was active in his community. He served on the boards of the Detroit Symphony Orchestra, the Detroit Zoo, and other social and religious groups.

If Briggs had one passion outside of his family and work, it was baseball. As a young adult, he attended Detroit Tiger games whenever possible. At the time, Briggs worked six days a week and the only time to see the Tigers was on Sunday. Detroit blue laws forbade the playing of baseball in the city, and the Tigers moved from Navin Field to their Sunday ball field southwest of the city, out on Dix Street in Springwells Township. "Those were the days!" Briggs reminisced. "George T. Stallings and Jimmy Burns owned the club, and there were always more fights on Dix [Street] on Sunday afternoon than you'll see in the big leagues in five years. The players fought and the spectators fought and the gatekeepers fought the groundskeepers. Most of the customers got well ginned before going to the park. The fights started before the game [and] continued during the game and long after."

In 1920, Tigers owner Frank Navin needed some capital for his team and took on two partners, Briggs and John Kelsey. Each received 25 percent ownership. Kelsey died in 1928, and Briggs purchased his shares, thus becoming half owner. Navin and Briggs were great friends and had an understanding: if either died, the other would have a six-month option to buy the team. Since Briggs was not a healthy man, most close friends and observers assumed Navin would exercise the option. In 1935, however, Navin unexpectedly died, and Briggs immediately exercised his option and became full owner of the Detroit Tigers. By 1938, Navin Field was expanded, modernized, and became Briggs Stadium. In Detroit, Briggs became more recognized for his ownership of the Tigers than for his manufacturing company.[25]

By the late 1920s, Briggs gave up his day-to-day management of the Briggs Manufacturing Company. He spent his time running his banks, investments, and the Tigers. He also began spending winters in Florida, often sailing on his yacht.[26]

In the mid-1930s, Briggs's son, Spike, had graduated from Georgetown University. Spike shared his father's love of baseball and wanted to help run the team. Briggs said no. If the boy was to work for him, he had to start out in the factory. He started working in the Mack Avenue plant. "Dad wants me to learn to run the plant," the boy said, "But I'd rather run the ball club. Maybe I will someday." By most accounts, he was a nice young man, but as time evolved, he drank too much and needed his father's hand to guide him.[27]

There were embarrassments. Like many of his generation, Walter

Briggs was a racially prejudiced man. African Americans could work for him, but only in the foundry, the paint shop, or at other menial jobs in the plant (one of these workers was Turkey Stearns, the great Negro League baseball player). Through baseball, his attitudes were visible to the public. At Briggs Stadium, blacks sat in a segregated corner. In 1958, the Tigers were the second to the last team in the American League to integrate. This was six years after Briggs had died.[28]

While Briggs was focusing on other pursuits, he turned the running of the day-to-day operations of his manufacturing empire to professional managers. One of them was Dean Robinson, who had married Briggs's oldest daughter, Grace, in 1926. Dean Robinson was to become a major family player in the drama that evolved between Briggs and the UAW. While still a teenager, Robinson joined the Naval Air Corps during World War I. He later graduated from Yale and joined his father back in Detroit at the family's lumber company. In 1933, he was hired by the Briggs Manufacturing Company as an interviewer in their employment department and, like his brother-in-law, Spike, was fast-tracked through the corporate ladder.[29]

A mysterious person was hired to handle personnel and labor issues after a terrible strike in 1933. This was Fay Taylor, who some said had been a strikebreaker for the Pinkerton Detective Company. Regardless of where Taylor came from, he became the face of the Briggs Manufacturing Company to the workers at Briggs, much like Harry Bennett was for the Ford Motor Company. His toughness and shrewdness forced the workers to be equally tough and shrewd.[30]

. . . .

Sometime in 1953 or 1954, Jane Briggs Hart was sitting in a Florida airport with her mother as they waited for a flight to Detroit. Jane, by this time in her early thirties, was a strong and independent woman who was an accomplished pilot, a liberal Democrat, and married to Phil Hart. In the coming years, Phil Hart served Michigan as a lieutenant governor and as a distinguished US senator (1959 to 1976). Jane looked around the airport terminal's waiting room and spotted a friend sitting across the way, also heading back to Detroit. She had known and liked

Emil Mazey, the secretary-treasurer of the UAW, for years through her and her husband's activism in liberal Democratic Party activities. She tapped her mother on the arm and said, "Mom, would you like to meet Emil Mazey?"

The older widow raised an eyebrow and replied, "Why, yes. Yes, I would." The two women walked over to meet the second in command of the UAW and the man who seemingly single-handedly organized the Briggs workers into the UAW some fifteen years earlier.

They greeted the forty-year-old man with dark and thinning hair, who was reading a newspaper. After an initial greeting, Jane said, "Emil, I would like you to meet my mother."

Emil, with a big smile on his face, stood up, showing a little more paunch then he liked to admit, and greeted the wife of his old adversary warmly.

The tart response from Mrs. Briggs reflected years of frustration with Mazey and the UAW: "Well, young man, I just want you to know that *you* have been *the* subject of many discussions at our dinner table."

Jane Hart and Emil Mazey laughed, but not the stern-faced Mrs. Briggs.[31]

. . . .

In 1913, Walter Briggs moved into his mansion on Boston Boulevard; in that same year, Emil Mazey was born in Saskatchewan, Canada, to Hungarian immigrants Lawrence and Wilma. Lawrence and his two brothers had left Hungary several years earlier to avoid conscription into the military. These antiwar feelings were embedded into young Emil for his entire life. Emil had three brothers and a sister.

By 1915, the family had moved to Detroit's east side, a figurative million miles from the Walter Briggs mansion on Boston Boulevard. Lawrence eventually found work at Briggs, where he was steadily employed from the 1920s until his death in 1946.

Emil, the second of five children, loved and looked out for his brothers and his sister. He felt a keen sense of responsibility for all of them. He became extremely close to his younger brother Bill, and they became commonly linked with the labor struggles of the 1930s and

1940s. Emil also looked out for his baby brother Ernie. Ernie eventually created his own path in the labor movement, a path that led to family disappointment.

Emil went to school at Holmes Elementary and then attended Barbour Junior High School. He had to have been a good student, for he was accepted to Cass Technical High School, the premier high school within the Detroit Public Schools. The boy had a stutter, which sometimes affected him even as an adult. Through willpower, he conquered the stutter and became an effective and persuasive speaker. He learned to play a number of musical instruments, but his favorite was the violin. Emil wanted to be a concert violinist, a love he picked up from his Hungarian family. To help support himself and his family, Emil made money as leader of a small band. He made enough money to provide an allowance to Albert, Bill, and Ernie.

As the Depression deepened, Emil had to put away his dreams of being a concert violinist. He switched his high school curriculum from music to industrial pattern reading. Obviously, this was a huge change in career paths. Like young people everywhere, Emil had dreams, but his dreams of being a concert violinist came up against the reality of being a blue-collar kid growing up in Detroit. It is possible this change of school curriculum changed the young man's outlook on the world, particularly with regard to the Depression and economy that afforded working people less opportunity to participate in the American dream. Another possibility was Emil's uncle. An unemployed Socialist who lived at the family's home, he gave the boys a home education on the superiority of socialism over other economic and political systems of the world.[32]

Emil graduated from Cass Tech in 1931, when Michigan's unemployment rate was a whopping 52 percent. There were no jobs for concert violinists or pattern readers. Emil knew he had to work, but through his years of learning, watching and listening, he also knew he wanted to organize workers into unions.[33]

Emil spent hours at Grand Circus Park, Cadillac Square, and along Woodward Avenue, listening to political activists and dreamers on their soapboxes (just as Ken Morris would discover several years later). These passionate and persuasive men preaching socialism, Marxism, communism, and other "isms" captured the interest of the young man. He soon was attracted to speakers from the Proletarian Party, a political group that had spun off of the local Marxist organization.[34]

• • • • • • • • • • • • •

Within ten years of the start of Henry Ford's assembly line, there had been efforts by unions to organize workers in Detroit. The International Workers of the World (IWW), or the Wobblies, began unsuccessful efforts to organize autoworkers about the time Emil and his family moved to Detroit. The Communist Party, through the Auto Workers Union (AWU), picked up the mantle in the 1920s and early 1930s. The Socialist Party, the Progressive Party, and other Marxist groups all supported efforts to organize autoworkers. America's largest labor organization, the American Federation of Labor (AFL), initially had little or no interest in organizing autoworkers. Their member unions were interested in organizing craft unions. In Detroit, these independent, and sometimes radical groups were never strong in the plant and certainly no real threat to the auto barons. One year, in 1933, the Auto Workers Union made a huge effort to organize an auto manufacturer, and it just happened to be against the Briggs Manufacturing Company.

By 1933, Briggs and his company were commonly known for anti-worker attitudes and policies in Detroit. An explosion and fire in the late 1920s at the Mack Avenue plant killed twenty-one workers. Many Detroiters, not just autoworkers, blamed the poor and unsafe working conditions in the Mack Avenue plant on Walter Briggs and his company. Working conditions did not change as the Depression deepened. In 1933, the Communist-dominated Auto Workers Union (AWU), led by Marxist president Phillip Raymond, helped organize a strike against Briggs. While the AWU may have put the strike structure in place, the workers in the plant ultimately decided if such drastic action was necessary. After Briggs instituted wage cuts, Briggs workers became desperate. As one man's letter, sent to Mayor Frank Murphy after the 1933 strike, stated, "Workers would be nuts to strike during the worst unemployment in history unless they had no other choice." Desperate they were.

As later documented in a commission Mayor Murphy created after the strike, workers had to deal with the following:

- Wages as low at $2.94 for a two-week period
- People reporting to work and waiting hours for assignments, then told to go home with no pay
- Working conditions that forced people to breathe foul air with emery dust and particles of solder and metal floating through the air, causing workers to spit up blood week after week and then disappear, never to be heard from again

There was the instance of a man working on a press like Ken Morris did four years later, a two-person operation. Something went wrong with their timing, and the press slammed down on the man's hands. When the press lifted, the shocked worker was standing with his hands hanging like strips of crushed skin and bones. It was a late shift, and there was no medical personnel in the facility. A supervisor called the police. A patrol car came, and the officer said, "It will be five dollars, boys." The workers in the shop indicated that no one had that kind of money, and the officer replied, "We can't move him unless you give five dollars." It took a half hour, but a collection was gathered, and once the five dollars was paid, the man was taken to the hospital.

In January 1933, the Briggs strike began. As local newspapers refused to cover the story, the public was not initially aware of the work stoppage. In time, the newspapers grudgingly covered the event—after the threat of having their offices picketed by strikers.

The AWU was not alone in the organizing effort. The union had the support of all the left and liberal leaning organizations in the city. Emil played a small role in this strike through his activity in the Proletarian Party. He helped make picket signs and assist in other activities, beginning to learn the skills that would make him a successful labor organizer and strike leader.

The strike was both a success and a failure. It was a success in that Briggs was shut down and Ford, Chrysler, Hudson, and other companies felt the effects of the work stoppage. Ford had to shut down production, something that had never happened before. About ten days into the strike, a federal mediator, Mayor Murphy, and the Ford Motor Company pressed Briggs to settle and get back to work. The strike ended. The AWU was in tatters, as it faced terrible media attacks, and eventually factionalism broke out within the ranks. Many Briggs workers, including Emil's father, were fired. Those that could prove they were not union activists, like Lawrence Mazey, eventually went back to work. Some wage cuts were restored, but there was no union recognition. The strike had been broken, but Briggs cemented its reputation as the worst place to work in Detroit.[35]

After the strike was over, the federal mediator, Robert Pilkington, said that the Briggs workers had "good and sufficient reasons to rebel against conditions imposed on them."[36]

. . . .

Emil Mazey went from job to job. First he worked at Detroit's Gulf Refining Company and then at the Rotary Electric Steel Company. He was quickly fired for union activity at both of these places. As he later said about his Gulf Refining experience, "I urged the fellows to form a union ... and they said they would stand behind me if I got fired. I got fired for union activity early in 1935, and they were so far behind me [that] I couldn't find them." He later found work with an organization known as the Unemployed Citizens League, which tried to find food for unemployed workers. When he wasn't working, Emil helped pay bills by playing violin, saxophone, and clarinet in his east side band.

Emil left the Proletarian Party. They were nice people, but they seemed to be talkers rather than doers. He focused more on the Socialist Party. In April 1936, he took a job at Briggs, joining his father and his brother Bill. Emil started out in the experimental department as a helper. He was transferred to the cushion department. Unlike his apolitical father, however, Emil had another agenda besides work. Emil contacted the Communist-led UAW Local 155 and volunteered as a nonpaid UAW organizer. And he began organizing a series of sit-down strikes in the Mack Avenue plant.[37]

Four years after the 1933 Briggs strike, the workers saw conditions worsen, and the time was ripe for a guy like Emil Mazey. Yes, the plant was somewhat safer and cleaner than in 1933. Now if a man lost a finger, first-aid treatment was available, but the fundamental safety conditions had not improved. Worse yet, as Ken Morris discovered, the company was speeding up production without an increase in wages. Sit-down strikes were now taking place inside the Mack Avenue plant. In most cases, these appeared to be unplanned work stoppages and occurred when a specific problem in a department came to the surface. Emil saw that it only took a little spark of encouragement for a strike to begin, and he often provided that spark. Men simply stopped working until the dispute was solved. Once the dispute was solved and the company raised wages or corrected a safety problem, the production started back up. After a few days, the company figured out who the leaders were, and they were fired.

Ken Morris, working at his press and talking with the other workers on the line, was aware that something was happening, but so far nothing had affected his department, and he had no idea who these union people were. They heard about a sit-down or other work stoppage, but not much more.[38]

These strikes were like a mosquito bite on Briggs rear end. They were bothersome and embarrassing. In December 1936, *Time* magazine wrote an article on Walter Briggs. The story referenced "an epidemic of departmental sit-down strikes" the previous November. A few weeks later, Briggs chief manager William Patrick Brown wrote the magazine, denying any labor problems. Yet *Time*, in an unusual editorial response to the letter, still took issue with Brown and stated, "[The] U.A.W. claims there were 51 'sit-downs' in 50 days" at Briggs' Mack Avenue Plant.[39]

Actually, by the time the *Time* article was written, Briggs felt they had solved their labor problems. On December 1, 1936, four burly men walked into the cushion department, where Emil worked. Without fanfare or ceremony, the men escorted Emil to the personnel office, where he was fired for union activity. In retrospect, Emil was surprised that it had taken the company spies so long to finger him as the guy talking union. Still, it was his job, and company guards were bullying and embarrassing him; he didn't like it. The men dragged him to the Mack Avenue gate and threw him onto the street.

Emil picked himself up off the street and, with a slight stutter and a raised fist, yelled, "I'll be back, you sons of bitches; I'll be back and organize this plant."[40]

. . . .

The next morning, Emil's mother woke him up. She was so pleased, as she had just read in the paper that all Briggs employees were to receive a Christmas bonus. Emil, with tears in his eyes, had to tell his mother that he had been fired.

Later that day, Emil's father came home. He and Bill had been fired even though Bill had been at home with pneumonia and hadn't been at work all week. The company even fired someone named Robert Mazey, a man of no relation but branded with the wrong name.[41]

It looked like a long and cold winter for the Mazey family.

CHAPTER 5

THIS IS A GODDAMNED SELLOUT

I was always aware of the burley Richard T. Frankensteen. He was part of the great "Battle of the Overpass," and his photos with Walter Reuther during the UAW attempt to organize the Ford Motor Company are known worldwide. Plus, for a boy, the name "Frankensteen" simply captured my imagination. One day I asked Dad about him. He indicated that he didn't have any problems with Frankensteen, but that the big man simply belonged to a different political faction—not the Reuther Caucus—and that he eventually moved out of the UAW when he realized he could go no further in the organization. He eventually became a labor mediator. Later, I learned that the relationships between Dick Frankensteen, Walter Reuther, and others were much more complicated.

IN JANUARY 1937, A TWO-STAGE juggernaut hit the Briggs Manufacturing Company and shook management to the core. First was the success of the UAW in Detroit, Flint, and elsewhere; plus the actual union organization of Briggs by the UAW. Second was that within ten years, Briggs would change the focus of their priorities from being an innovative company producing a quality product to a company whose priority seemed to be the destruction of a strong union. Ultimately, this change in priorities led to the company's downfall.

As significant events often begin, this one did not begin with some awe-inspiring strategy or through stupendous leadership skills. Instead, typical of strikes in the 1930s, this event happened when the Briggs workers became fed up with management and staged an impromptu sit-down strike. The big difference between this strike and the 1933 strike was that organized labor provided support when the Briggs workers decided it was time to organize a union. Moreover, based on the new federal law, the Wagner Act, this strike was legal.

The first strike action to doom management was not at the huge, unwieldy Mack Avenue plant or the Highland Park plant. Instead, it was at the Meldrum plant—the country club plant within the Briggs empire. Located about a mile west of the Mack Avenue plant, near East Grand Boulevard, the Meldrum plant was the factory where Briggs made bodies for the upscale Lincoln Zephyr, made by Ford, and other high-end models for Dodge, Chrysler, and Hudson. Here, workers were allowed time to work on their product; they were given better machinery and felt they were skilled workers as compared to the production workers at Mack Avenue or Highland Park. Unknown to men like Emil Mazey, however, there was worker dissatisfaction at the Meldrum plant, and some workers had already made initial contact with Dick Frankensteen, president of the Dodge Main UAW Local 3 and a member of the UAW Executive Board.[42]

. . . .

Dick Frankensteen was born in Detroit, and he grew to be a burly six feet two inches tall, weighing 250 pounds. He was an all-city, all-state, and all-American football player and received a scholarship to play at Dayton University. Besides being a great college athlete, he was voted by his classmates at Dayton as the most likely to succeed. Immediately after college, he married and became a schoolteacher in Ohio. He wanted to coach high school football, but that plan went haywire due to the Depression, and he found himself laid off and without work. Back in Michigan, he took a job at the Dodge Main plant in Hamtramck, where he had worked summers during college.[43]

Just before Frankensteen returned to Dodge Main, one of the

first major pieces of President Franklin Roosevelt's New Deal passed Congress. The 1933 law was the National Industrial Recovery Act (NIRA). The NIRA provided many benefits to American industry, but it also provided workers with the legal right to organize into labor unions and bargain collectively. While the NIRA provided no enforcement power to protect these rights, and eventually the US Supreme Court declared the law unconstitutional, the section containing these new labor rights reemerged in 1935 as the National Labor Relations Act (or the Wagner Act). The new Wagner Act expanded the NIRA section on worker rights and created the National Labor Relations Board to enforce the law. Labor unions and activists believed a new day had arrived and the world had become more just. Some major corporations tried to find ways to comply, while others simply ignored the law.[44]

The Chrysler Corporation developed a paternalistic strategy to comply with the new law by forming Work Council Plans (WCP). The WCPs were groups of workers in each plant that met with plant management on a regular basis to address worker concerns. This might have been a good plan if the company let these councils be more than a company-controlled union. Nonetheless, young Frankensteen became active in his WCP while working at Dodge. At forty-nine cents an hour, Frankensteen could not provide a decent standard of living for his wife and their first child. He shared the economic reality felt by workers throughout Detroit. At a meeting held by his WCP committee with the company, Frankensteen made a presentation discussing his concerns and the types of problems faced by so many of his fellow workers in the plant.

A company executive responded, "We do not control the cost of living. We have nothing to say as to what the price of butter, eggs, or meat may be. We do not regulate rents. We cannot tell if your wife is as frugal as some other wife, or whether someone else's wife is more frugal. We cannot control the spending habits of people. All we know is that we pay a going rate, comparable to those of our competitors. We are a competitive market. We cannot pay more than our competitors if we hope to sell cars and stay in business and provide jobs."

Frankensteen thought hard about these words. It was obvious that the company looked at workers as nothing more than commodities, like steel or energy, not as human beings. To become more than a commodity, Frankensteen reasoned, workers had to create their own methods for wages and benefits to improve. Frankensteen concluded that the company was essentially providing an unintended invitation for workers to organize into strong unions if they were to improve their lot.

By 1935, Frankensteen and several others had organized the Automotive Industrial Workers Association (AIWA). This new union bargained with Chrysler, the company hoping it could control this independent little union. The new union charged twenty-five cents for monthly union dues and had close to forty thousand members. The AIWA watched as the American Federation of Labor organized the UAW in 1935. Frankensteen and his colleagues stood on the sidelines, as they wanted no part of a union affiliated with the AFL—an organization dedicated to organizing skilled rather than unskilled workers. Then, in 1936, the UAW left the AFL and became part of the newly formed Congress of Industrial Organizations (CIO). The AIWA, which was paying Frankensteen a salary as president of their organization, merged with the UAW-CIO. Frankensteen was still president of the Dodge local, but he also became a citywide organizer for the UAW and a member of its executive board. This was a win-win for the small AIWA.[45]

. . . .

On January 7, 1937, neither Frankensteen nor his Meldrum plant contact, Ralph Knox, had any knowledge that a major event was to take place at the Briggs Meldrum plant. As at the Mack Avenue plant, there were rumblings and frustrations inside various departments of the Meldrum facility, and the company was firing workers for union activities. On this particular January day, Briggs fired an employee for union activity. The workers in his department demanded the return of their colleague to his job. The company refused the demand. Instantly and without warning, several departments decided to sit down, and the Meldrum plant was shut down. The Briggs strike was on. The company sent the other workers home, saying there was a shortage of parts, but most workers knew the company line was a ruse. Additionally, the Briggs sit-downers were no doubt emboldened by the actions taking place sixty miles to the north in Flint, where the famous two-month Flint Sit-Down Strike against General Motors had been going on for two weeks and was receiving national press recognition. At the conclusion of the two-month strike, the UAW won recognition from the largest automobile company in the world, GM—something no one had predicted.

Ralph Knox went to Frankensteen, who, as president of UAW Local 3, easily agreed to provide support for the strike through his Local 3 membership and as member of the UAW Executive Board. Frankensteen knew that organizing Briggs would be an incredible victory for the new UAW and thus encouraged his Local 3 membership to support the battle. At Local 3, he had created a "flying squadron." This group of young men served as a UAW force providing support to workers on picket lines or involved in strikes. The flying squadron often served as the only defense the workers had against private company police forces or the local police department.[46]

Just after his firing at Briggs a month earlier, Emil Mazey was hired by the UAW as a ten-dollar-per-week organizer. The union assigned him to organize Briggs. He spent the rest of December and that first week in January talking to workers who had shown interest in the union—usually in the privacy of their homes. After the strike began, Mazey entered the picture. He worked with Frankensteen to help support the strike effort. He led the effort of providing food to the workers inside the plant.

As the days turned into the first week, the labor organizers sensed that time was running out. Even with the support of Local 3, the company was convincing more and more men to quit the sit-down strike and come out of the plant. The company continually discharged more workers as its spies identified union activists and supporters inside and outside the plant. Initially, eight hundred of the two thousand Meldrum workers took part in the sit-down strike. Briggs promised wage increases to some workers and then threatened legal action against others. Ultimately, management fired 350 workers. After ten days of the sit-down strike, there were only six actual sit-down participants inside the plant. With the use of fear and intimidation, it appeared that Briggs management was going to break the strike.[47]

The strategy now changed, and the decision was to bring the men out of the plant and close the facility through mass picketing. The sit-down had been successful in closing the plant and stopping production; if the strategy changed to mass picketing, the effort needed to be extremely effective if they were to keep the plant closed. The strategy was to quadruple the number of picketers. The union organizers had to maintain mass picketers around the plant, with special focus on the plant gates, every hour of every day. The objective was to ensure that no product, no parts, and no scab workers broke the picket line. The strike needed someone who could organize this mass picketing effort.

They turned to Emil Mazey.

. . . .

Meanwhile, less than a mile away, the Mack Avenue plant was still working. The communication between the two facilities was poor, and Mack Avenue workers didn't know what was going on up the street.

All through November and December of 1936, Ken Morris and the other workers in their department had heard rumors about sporadic sit-down strikes in various Mack Avenue departments. At the start of the new year, Ken and his coworkers also knew that the Flint Sit-Down Strike against GM was continuing. A few workers were aware that Ford's supplier of brakes, Kelsey-Hayes, had been organized in December. There was something in the air; the workers felt that now a labor stoppage might not lead to their personal ruin after all. They were empowered.

By the third week in January, Ken and the guys in his department finally had heard that Meldrum shut down. One January morning, Ken and his carpool buddies decided to drive by the Meldrum plant to see what was going on. They did not see any pickets, but it was clear the plant was closed. The guys talked in the car about joining the union. They all thought it was the right idea.

About this time, Ken transferred to the day shift, and one of the guys told him there was a union hall at a storefront on Mack Avenue. After work that day, Ken walked down Mack and saw a placard in a window that said, "UAW." Ken paused for a moment, knowing that if he walked in that doorway, his life could change forever. He knew he could lose his job, he could be blacklisted, and his new life in Detroit could be destroyed. Still, he thought, he was young, usually broke, and maybe, just maybe, the union might make a difference.

He walked in the union hall and signed up. As he left the small office, he felt good; he had a sense of satisfaction and pride. He felt that his father, who had always favored the plight of workers, would be proud of his decision. Later that week, Ken was at the National Bank on Mack and St. Jean cashing his paycheck. He saw a guy from the union depositing a huge wad of cash money. It had to be union dues, and based on the stack of bills, there had to be a large number of UAW members from Briggs. Ken realized that he was not alone.[48]

Emil Mazey organized the mass picketing effort at the Briggs Meldrum plant, which led to the UAW organization of Briggs.

Emil Mazey organized the mass picketing effort as no one had done before. He pulled in the Local 3 Flying Squadron and other sympathetic groups from Detroit and beyond, including August "Gus" Scholle, who headed the Glass Workers Union in Toledo and became a great friend of Ken's.[49] The strike had already been going on for a week and a half, and all could feel a sense of conclusion, one way or another.

The mass picketers shut down the plant tighter than a drum. Mazey's picket lines were as successful as anyone had ever seen. With production down for more than a week, Briggs management was feeling tremendous pressure from Ford, Chrysler, Hudson, and other companies to whom they supplied auto bodies to get back into production. On Monday morning, January 19, from inside the plant gates, the company shot tear gas canisters at the picket line. Pandemonium broke out, but Mazey's picket line held. The picketers threw the canisters back inside the plant gates. Then the Detroit police came. They fired tear gas canisters at the picketers, and the picketers threw the canisters right back. The police tried to break the lines by force, but the strikers, who outnumbered the police, stood their ground. At one point, the picketers, led by Mazey, charged the police, and the police backed away. The police department had had enough, and they brought in the mounted horse division. The police on horseback pushed the strikers away, and then suddenly, from seemingly out of nowhere, someone handed picketers handfuls of ball bearings, which they immediately threw to the ground, at the feet of the mounted horses. The horses panicked and soon became useless to the police as they were slipping and sliding along Meldrum Street. The police retreated again.

The strikers learned a lesson. When they outnumbered the police and stood their ground, the police backed away. The union won the battle. The company stood and watched as first its men and then Detroit's "finest" lost skirmish after skirmish.[50]

Mazey recalled this day somewhat differently years later. He simply said, "We beat the hell out of 'em!"[51]

. . . .

Later that day, Frankensteen was back at the Local 3 union hall, stretched out on a bench and trying to catch some sleep. In the early afternoon, the phone rang. It was Harry Bennett calling for Dick Frankensteen.

· · · · · · · · · · · · ·

Harry Bennett was one of the most powerful and feared men in Detroit. He worked for Henry Ford and ran the Ford Service Department (formerly the Ford Sociological Department), which housed the largest private army in the world. This private militia was not composed of fresh-faced recruits; instead, these were tough men who had often been on the wrong side of the law. Henry Ford seemed to love Harry Bennett. He was the tough street-wise guy that Ford's only son, Edsel, was not. From his office in the basement of Ford's administrative building in Dearborn, Bennett got things done; he solved problems for Ford by whatever means necessary. If he couldn't solve them legally, he solved them through other means. Henry Ford never asked what the other methods might have been. He didn't care.[52]

Henry Ford would sell his soul when it came to production and profit at his company. If production in his plants was threatened, even by a dreaded labor union, a pattern seemed to develop. He instructed Harry Bennett to step in and address the matter, even if it meant clandestine contacts with the union. Just a month earlier, the UAW West Side Local, headed by Walter Reuther, was striking Kelsey-Hayes, the maker of Ford brakes. Ford production was threatened, and Ford, through Bennett, wanted something done—but not at Ford's expense. Bennett had one of his men, John Gillespie, step in to get that strike settled. The same pattern was repeating itself at Briggs.

(Incidentally, one of the men that sat across the negotiating table from Reuther at the Kelsey-Hayes negotiations was Chester Culver, the head of the Detroit Employers Association. This was the same Mr. Culver who had lectured the unemployed and homeless Ken Morris back in 1935 and indirectly helped him find his job at Briggs.)

· · · · · · · · · · · · ·

A blurry-eyed Frankensteen picked up the telephone, and after a word or two of introduction, Harry Bennett said, "I would like to have you meet with my man John Gillespie on the Briggs situation."

Frankensteen had heard of Gillespie. He knew him to be a corrupt state Republican Party hack who had lost a fortune with the arrival of the Depression. Frankensteen said, "I'd be glad to meet with Mr. Gillespie if it [means] some action on the Briggs situation."

Bennett said that Gillespie was on his way to talk to him. Not much later, Gillespie drove by and asked Frankensteen to join him in his Lincoln. Frankensteen knew of Bennett's and Gillespie's reputations, and to help ensure his safety, he told the guys at the local where he was going. He climbed into the back seat of the Lincoln with Gillespie as the driver pulled the car away from the local.

Once the car started moving, Gillespie said, "You know, Mr. Ford is a great believer in good wages. Now, he will do nothing to enhance the union or to build the union. He will do nothing toward any kind of union recognition. But if it is wages or the working conditions that are improper, then Mr. Ford wants those things straightened out. As you know, Mr. Ford has an interest in the Briggs plant. They make our bodies. What is it you want at Briggs?"

Based on Gillespie's comments, Frankensteen realized that the loss of the Lincoln bodies must have been affecting Ford's bottom line: production. Thinking as fast as he could, he replied, "First of all, we want the return to work of all the people who have been fired. We want every one of the [two hundred and fifty to three hundred] people returned to their jobs. Secondly, we want ten cents an hour increase."

Approaching the Briggs administrative offices, the car stopped. Frankensteen thought he would be taken up to meet with the Briggs management, which would have been a first for the union leadership, but Gillespie told him to remain in the car, saying, "I'll be back in a little while."

About an hour later, Gillespie returned and climbed into the Lincoln. "Well, okay," he said.

"Okay, what?" Frankensteen replied.

"Okay, we are going to return the people. Have them all report to their jobs tomorrow. They will report back and there will be a ten-cent increase."

Frankensteen returned to the local and called a meeting of the strike leadership. He explained that he had told Gillespie what he wanted, and Gillespie had delivered on each item Frankensteen had raised.

Mazey became enraged when he heard the explanation. Mazey pulled his lean body up from the chair and fumed, "This is a goddamned sellout." He noted that there had been no negotiation with Briggs. There was no recognition of the union. He said that maybe they were going to get them back in there and then oust everyone. They'd done it before. Mazey sat down as several of the men in the room nodded in agreement.

For his part, Frankensteen was just as livid at young Mazey. "If you can't organize the Briggs plants with an increase in wages and a return of all these people who have been fired, then you are the lousiest staff of organizers that I ever heard of in my life, and you don't deserve to have a union. As far as I'm concerned, we do not need the Ford Motor Company to organize for us; we can do it ourselves, providing we can get our people back in the plant."[53]

The issue was fairly simple. Frankensteen thought the union should declare victory with the wage increase and the reinstatement of the fired employees. Mazey wanted more. He wanted an officially recognized union because he believed that, based on past performance, Briggs would let things get back to normal and then fire strike instigators. They had done it in 1933 and during the many mini-strikes held in 1936.

That night, a rowdy crowd of over a thousand Meldrum workers met at the east side Germania Hall, and the tired and scared workers quickly ratified the understanding.

In the meantime, Briggs had been assessing their position. They had taken a terrible public relations hit during the 1933 strike. In December 1936, *Time* magazine indicated that the Briggs Manufacturing Company had successfully reformed its labor policies since the 1933 strike. Watching the battle scene outside their plant, they saw that continued clashes with these picketers was not going to be successful, at least not in the short term. It was time to keep their top client, the Ford Motor Company, happy. Their new challenge was to look for better times to deal with the union.

A January 20, 1937, *Detroit News* article captured what happened next, the role Bennett played and the cold war between Briggs and the union. The article appeared on page two, as it was competing with the second inauguration of President Roosevelt. The story states:

Briggs Plant Re-Opens at Full
Capacity as Union Accepts Offer

With men laid off during recent weeks recalled to work, the Briggs Manufacturing Company's Meldrum [Avenue] plant, closed Tuesday by a demonstration of 2,000 union sympathizers, reopened at full capacity today....

Union Briggs workers accepted the company offer to rehire men laid off. Acceptance was recommended by Richard Frankensteen, organizer for the United Automobile Workers Union, who directed Tuesday morning's demonstration in which police had used tear gas in an effort to disperse the pickets....

The settlement of the dispute was announced by Dean Robinson, personnel director of the Briggs Company, after a telephone conversation with Harry H. Bennett, personnel director for the Ford Motor Co. The Briggs plant manufactures bodies for the Lincoln-Zephyr division of Ford Motor and a few special bodies for Dodge cars.

[Robinson's statement read:]

"No specific demands have been made to us by any organization or committee of the men relative to any grievances or specific condition.

"However, there has been a misunderstanding relative to a number of employees who have been recently laid off because of lack of material. This situation has now been corrected. Therefore we will open our plant tomorrow morning at full capacity, rehiring all employees who have been laid off during the past several weeks."

Frankensteen issued the following statement in reply to the Robinson statement:

"In the statement issued by Mr. Dean Robinson ... he states that no special demand has been made to them.

We assure Mr. Robinson that that condition soon will be changed with regard to their laying men off for the 'lack of material....'

"Our prime interest is in the return of those discriminated employees.... On the basis of his statement ... I will recommend to the workers of Briggs that they vote acceptance, for there is nothing in the statement which forbids us from again registering an official protest at any time. We are primarily interested in keeping the wheels of industry humming, under conditions of decency and rights.

"When the 'misunderstanding' mentioned by Mr. Robinson is cleared up, we hope that he shall not provoke further 'misunderstanding[s].' I consider this a victory, for we have proven that 'misunderstanding[s]' with regard to our organized workers must be righted."

Bennett said the demonstration was called because "the union men claimed 33 men had been fired by the company because of alleged discrimination against anyone with affiliation with the UAW...."

"I suggested to Robinson," Bennett said, "that the situation could be remedied if he would put everybody back to work...."

It was the second time in less than a month that Bennett's intercession caused the settlement of a labor dispute in Detroit's automobile plants. After eight days of a strike at the Kelsey-Hayes Wheel Corp. plant last December, Bennett telephoned the officials of the company and warned that the Ford Motor Co. would remove its brake machinery from the plant if the strike was not settled before Christmas Day. A settlement followed immediately.[54]

The innuendo and half-truths of this article are notable and demonstrate how Detroit newspapers were concerned about how they reported labor disputes. The term "strike," for example, is not used. The article is also full of face-saving comments by all concerned. The basic story of the workers accepting the agreement and returning to work is accurate, but the lead sentence gets the story wrong. These workers were not "laid off"; they were fired for legally participating in union activity. The next sentence implies that this was a one-day work stoppage due to a demonstration, when in fact the strike had been going on since January 7. Dean Robinson wanted to avoid the union issue by insisting that no demands were made to them "by any organization or committee." Well, if Briggs refused to meet with the union, how could demands have been made? Robinson insists that the layoffs were a result of a lack of material. There was probably no one in the city of Detroit who believed that statement.

Among the 350 people returned to work were Emil Mazey's father and brother (as well as the nonrelated Robert Mazey).

CHAPTER 6

GOD, THESE GUYS ARE TOUGH

Our mother understood that Dad had another wife before her. She used to say, "Your father is married to the UAW first and to me second." There was much truth in that statement. The UAW activists were committed to their union, and they learned that the only way to maintain that commitment was to be at every meeting and union activity possible. On top of that, from 1946 until his retirement, Dad was elected to his job. He had to demonstrate to his constituents that he was there for them. Mom understood that that meant her husband was away nearly every night and on weekends. She knew that if Ken were to spend any quality time with their boys, the boys simply went with him to Saturday or Sunday meetings or events. Her only challenge to her sons was simple: she told them to "behave and not make a scene." This was a difficult challenge for two brothers. It was during the early days, the 1930s, that Dad's courtship with the UAW began. The courtship and marriage never ended. It began with Local 212.

THE STRIKE WAS OVER. EMIL Mazey now had the tough challenge that Frankensteen put to him: he had to get Briggs to recognize the UAW as the employee collective bargaining agent through a legal contract. He worked like a man possessed to complete this job.

On February 14, good news arrived. The UAW had officially chartered the Briggs local. From now on, they were Local 212 of the United Automobile Workers of America, affiliated with the Congress of Industrial Organizations (Local 212, UAW-CIO).

By this time, Mazey had recruited thousands of new UAW members. One of the first symbols of victory and the demonstration of solidarity with other UAW locals took place in early February. General Motors was still at war with the Flint sit-down strikers. On February 3, a court ordered the UAW to vacate the GM plants. The GM strikers sent a telegram to Governor Frank Murphy, indicating they were going to stay in the plant, which meant that Murphy might have to use the National Guard to evict them—something the nonviolent Murphy wanted to avoid at all costs. The UAW scheduled a mass demonstration in support of the strikers. Some five thousand men and women came to Flint to support the exhausted and scared sit-downers. Emil Mazey brought two hundred Briggs members, including Ken Morris, in support. This appeared to be Ken's first active role with the UAW.[55]

From this point on, Ken remained active in the UAW for the next seventy-one years. He grew to admire Emil Mazey's leadership, charisma, honesty, and organizational skills. He also began to work closely with Bill Mazey. The Mazey brothers took Ken under their wings. In Ken and many others, they saw raw recruits who represented building blocks to help build Local 212 and the UAW. While there were sometimes significant disagreements over the years, until the day he died, Ken always thought of himself as a "Mazey man."

. . . .

In mid-February, Dick Frankensteen and Emil Mazey presented their list of demands to Briggs. These included improved wages, hours, general working conditions, grievance procedures, and official recognition of the UAW as their bargaining agent. The company dragged its feet and avoided meetings. They thought they could buy off the workers and avoid a union.

By mid-February, Ken Morris, on the day shift, knew something was up inside the Mack Avenue plant. One day around nine o'clock, a know-it-all foreman named Silver came up to the guys in Ken's area and announced, "Fellows, all of you are going to be getting fifty-five cents an hour across the board." All the workers liked this, but they knew it was not due to the Briggs Company's sense of generosity. Everyone knew that any generosity by Briggs was an effort to stymie the new union. The word spread. It turned out that foremen throughout the plant were delivering the same message. At ten o'clock, Silver again turned up with an announcement: "Whoops, the wages have been raised again. You are all going to be getting sixty-five cents an hour." The company was talking serious money. Just before noon, Silver returned and announced that everyone would receive seventy-five cents an hour. He said that the Briggs Company had decided to pay the same rates as Chrysler. The guys knew that Briggs' generosity had more to do with busting the union than being good guys. Still, for workers making 43 cents an hour, this was all good news. Wow, thirty dollars per week—a 75 percent increase in wages! It looked like the UAW could deliver, even before an official contract was negotiated. The men in the factory smiled silly smiles of satisfaction and relief.[56]

Even though the wage increase had been granted, Briggs did not sign a contract. The UAW needed to get Briggs to the bargaining table. One night there was a sit-down in the press shop. Ken, being on days, missed this activity, but it was serious, and it stopped production. The workers wanted a contract, and they wanted the UAW to be recognized. Finally, Briggs agreed.

At seven o'clock in the morning, as the night shift was leaving, an impromptu assembly of workers from the Mack Avenue plant took place outside. A young Mack Avenue worker named Jess Ferrazza came out of the plant and saw a skinny guy with a brown shirt, jacket, baggy pants, and slicked-backed black hair addressing the crowd from the top of a truck. Emil Mazey was announcing that the UAW had reached an agreement with Briggs: Briggs agreed to recognize the union. The strikes were over. A huge cheer went up in that parking lot on that cold February morning.[57]

A handout was distributed to the workers, announcing their achievement. It read:

Notice of First Union Gains—Feb. 17, 1937

Automobile Workers

The following agreement has been obtained for Briggs employees through the efforts of the United Automobile Workers of America:

(A) Wages:
The Briggs Manufacturing Co. have agreed to establish and pay rates as follows:

1. Effective Wednesday, Feb. 17, wage increases which we have asked for will go into effect
2. Equal rates of pay for same work
3. Time and a half for over 40-hour week.
4. 5% additional increase for all men and women on night shift.
5. Proper adjustments of speed-up.
6. Minimum wage for common labor, 56 cents/for new men for a period of six months and then 75 cents. Minimum wage for new women, 55 cents; for a period of six months and then 65 cents.
7. Rates of pay in Briggs will correspond to rates of pay in Union Shops!

(B) Proper Handling of Grievances
1. Your union has been given recognition by the Briggs Manufacturing Co.
2. The management is willing to deal with your department shop stewards on departmental grievances.
3. On grievances that cannot be settled by Department Shop Stewards, the Management will meet with your plant Union Steward's Committee on the points at issue.
4. If the plant Union Committee and management cannot arrive at a conclusion, your International Union Representatives will meet with the management.

If they cannot arrive at a conclusion, the entire problem will be referred to a Closed Union Meeting for your action

Important Announcement from Your Union

The Briggs management is cooperating with your Union to the fullest extent to establish proper conditions of employment. They have met with your committee and agreed, jointly, on the procedure to be followed. Plant rules will be agreed to by the Union and the management and must be followed by all workers.

We are not a mob—we are an organization. We have recognition. We have procedure—Let's follow it!

JOIN YOUR UNION AT ONCE

RICHARD T. FRANKENSTEEN
Organizational Director of
United Automobile Workers
[of] America
Emil Mazey
Organizer in Charge of Briggs[58]

Mazey and Frankensteen were exuberant. They had won their battle. The tone of the notice was positive, cooperative, and substantive. Mazey and Frankensteen opposed any more strike activity. They were party to a signed contract, and now it was their obligation to see that the union members lived up to their end of the contract. They wanted the workers to accept the collective bargaining process.

Again, the problem was Briggs. The company refused to settle on the fine details of the contract. Fay Taylor, the labor relations director who masterminded Briggs's labor relations policy through the mid-1940s, led this effort. He emerged as the chief adversary to the Local 212 negotiators. It took until April 17 for the Briggs Company to sign the contract with the UAW. During this two-month period, numerous wildcat strikes occurred. It appeared that the only way to get Briggs's attention was to stop production through work stoppages; which over the next ten years was something the Briggs employees, much to the frustration of Mazey and most Local 212 leadership, never forgot.

Nonetheless, Briggs was organized. Local 212 was established. A contract was signed. Now it was time to build a union.[59]

. . . .

The new members of Briggs Local 212 and Emil Mazey had decisions to make. His sole ambition six months earlier had been to organize Briggs. With the UAW firmly established at Briggs, Mazey had to make some career choices. The local was organized, and it had thousands of members. It soon grew into the largest local in the UAW. One of the first orders of business for the new local was to elect officers. Who would be the new Local 212 president, and was Emil Mazey running for that office?

Mazey was torn. On the one hand, he knew he could do the job as Local 212's president. He was smart, had his own loyal supporters inside the union, and had great organizational skills. These organizational skills had been demonstrated consistently during the past four months. He could give a coherent and persuasive speech; he could organize strike activity and picket lines; and he had learned office skills for the International UAW. On top of that, ever since the Briggs security police had unceremoniously thrown him out of the plant in December for union activities, he had become a martyr and hero to thousands. He felt he could win the election as the Local 212 president.

On the other hand, when the Local 212 charter had been finalized just a few weeks after the Meldrum strike, the majority of Local 212 members were from the Meldrum plant, not the Mack Avenue plant. This was a distinct disadvantage to Mazey. Adding to Mazey's internal conflict was another fact: he enjoyed being an organizer for the International UAW. He always had distaste for the internal politics of the International UAW, but representing the International UAW in organizing plants was fun and was what his life was all about. A union organizer led a rough-and-tumble life. He might be called many things, but no one called a union organizer of the 1930s a union bureaucrat. By spring 1937, plants were being organized everywhere in the industrial Midwest. Mazey felt he could make a great contribution to labor's cause by staying with the International UAW.

Under the UAW charter, Mazey could organize workers throughout Michigan, work for the International UAW, and still be the International UAW's representative to Local 212. Further, as long as he paid his Local 212 dues, he was a member of the local and could participate in the local's meetings. Mazey knew he could count on his loyal following in Local 212 if any issues came up, so he felt he could still have great influence with the local, even if he stayed with the International UAW. He chose to stay with the International UAW and organize. Besides, the other person running for president was Ralph Knox, someone Emil thought he could work with and influence regarding policy issues.

With Mazey's decision final, Ralph Knox indeed became the first president of Local 212. Knox was the worker and union supporter at the Meldrum plant who had sought out Dick Frankensteen for assistance just before the January sit-down strike. In those early days, the momentum of the UAW and Local 212 was on the move. Nothing was going to stop them. The contract was being negotiated. Local 212 moved forward in educating workers on what labor unions were all about and, in the process, hired a Transportation Workers of America organizer named Bill Lamson to be its education director.[60]

· · · · · · · · · · · · · ·

These were great days for Ken Morris. It was as if a new life had begun. Before January, he spent his days working eight to twelve hours in the plant; going back to his apartment; going out to eat and maybe catch a movie; and then returning home. Except for the people he lived with, he seemed to have no close friendships. How things changed in a matter of weeks. He started hanging around the local, a place that became his home away from home. Emil and Bill Mazey took him to Flint for the great demonstration in support of the GM Sit-Down Strikers. He began doing odd jobs around the local. He volunteered for any activity. Perhaps most important of all, he began attending labor education classes conducted by Bill Lamson at the Meldrum local union office or across the street in the basement of a church. As the new Local 212 education director, Lamson found a very willing student in Ken Morris.

Ken loved these classes and deeply admired Bill Lamson, a tall, lean good-looking man with a friendly demeanor. Ken had no grounding in labor history or its activities. At the plant and now at the Local 212 office, people would throw around terms like AFL or CIO, and Ken didn't really know what they meant. Normally, he played along as if he knew, as he did not want to appear stupid. But with Lamson, it was different. When Lamson threw out a term, Ken often raised his hand to ask what that term meant. Rather than rolling his eyes, Lamson instead smiled softly and responded to the question. He might say that the AFL stood for the American Federation of Labor and then explain the federation's history as an organization that generally organized craft workers, skilled workers that might be cigar makers, electricians, carpenters, plumbers, and so forth. He'd then move on to describe the importance of the CIO, the Congress of Industrial Organizations, and how it organized all the skilled and the unskilled workers in one factory. Lamson explained that the CIO was not interested whether the man in the plant was a skilled employee or a janitor; it wanted the entire plant organized under one union. Lamson explained these things, as well as socialism, communism, capitalism, and so much more. Lamson was no one's fool. He could tell by looking into the eyes of Ken's fellow students that they too wanted to learn this information but were too shy to ask.

Ken went to as many meetings as possible, volunteering and meeting new people. He learned to judge people. At his early membership meetings, there were always a couple of guys, usually big men, who stood up and just gave the company hell. They talked about the problems in the plant, added a few profanities, and talked loudly about closing down the plant. Ken had never heard such brave talk and thought, *God, these guys are tough.* He loved the fact that they said they were going to take on the company come hell or high water.

As Ken continued to attend these meetings and volunteer at the local, he began learning. These fellows, with all the bravado and tough talk, were usually full of bluster and, perhaps, too much beer. He learned that the key to union leadership was substance and follow-through. A committee member had to learn to write a grievance. A local union president had to be able to persuade, read, and be an organized individual if he was to lead an organization of thousands of people. While the burly men should not be written off, they were more often blowing off steam rather than raising substantive issues.

Ken volunteered for committees. His high school interests began paying off. He knew shorthand, and that meant he could take minutes at meetings. He found himself part of the Local 212 newspaper staff, and by the end of the year, he was listed as the paper's assistant editor.

Ken had found a new life and, in actuality, a new family of sorts. As the year moved forward, however, that new life and the very existence of Local 212 were threatened by incompetence and misfeasance.[61]

. . . .

Local 212 president Ralph Knox turned out to be a disaster for Local 212. No one had really known Knox, and while it took some time, the active membership began to understand that they'd made a terrible decision in electing him as the first president of the local. Emil Mazey considered his support of Knox one of the great blunders of his career.[62]

Knox was from the Meldrum plant, which employed about two thousand workers, and as the local union grew, it became a less significant power base from which to run for local union office. The Mack Avenue plant employed about fifteen thousand people in the late 1930s, and as Local 212's membership grew, most of the new membership came from the Mack Avenue plant. Knox seemed constantly paranoid of Mazey and Mazey's growing Mack Avenue plant's political strength. As time passed, the Mack Avenue plant was simply so large that other Briggs plants never could compete with its voting block of workers. If this had been Knox's only problem, the situation might not have deteriorated so quickly.

Briggs was a place where a cross section of cultures literally rubbed elbows every day. Knox demonstrated early on that he had no use for African American participation. It could be that there were not significant numbers of African American workers at the Meldrum plant. On an overall basis, about 17 percent of the workforce at Briggs was composed of African Americans, largely confined to one department. This reason alone was enough for Mazey to end his support of Knox. Mazey's career consistently demonstrated an interest in the inclusion of African American workers within the local. This may have been a risky political position to take, for large portions of the Local 212's membership were white Southerners who had migrated to Detroit looking for jobs in auto factories, but it was a position Mazey firmly held.

More than race issues started the schism between Mazey and Knox. Emil wanted to build a union. He felt the local ought to be supporting union activity wherever it might be. Knox and his white Southern base had issues with Mazey's position on race, his activist labor organizing approach, and his Socialist roots. Whether it was a specific strategy or just plain ignorance, Knox chose to take the position that all "isms" (as in socialism and communism) were the same and were all bad. He used communism and socialism interchangeably. Knox's priorities seemed to be more on promoting the local's athletic teams than processing grievances. This misplaced sense of priorities irritated Mazey and his supporters to no end. While Mazey always supported recreational and other social activities in the local, such activities were not the reason that workers organized a union and therefore should not be the top priority of a local union president.[63]

At first, the Local 212 leadership or its executive board found ways to compromise and get things done, such as setting up committees, hiring Bill Lamson, and even addressing athletic activities for the members. As the weeks passed, however, cooperation between the two factions continued to deteriorate.

From a political view, Knox then did a stupid thing. The Mack Avenue plant had been arguing for stronger representation on the executive board. The argument had merit since the vast majority of the Local 212 membership now came from Mack Avenue. Knox agreed to a change. This ended up giving Mazey, the Mack Avenue hero, more power on the executive board.

Knox had other problems that ultimately resulted in his demise. As an administrator, he was incompetent. The Mazey forces, for example, were able to control the Local 212 newspaper, which described Knox as a "treacherous and lecherous" person, implying he was a womanizer. His approach to hiring office help was unique. He was paranoid that Mazey spies might apply for secretarial jobs. To avoid that problem, he took out ads advertising the need for female piano players. His argument was that piano players and typists both played keys. Apparently, the typing at the Local 212 office was in rhythm![64]

By June, Knox realized that Mazey, an International UAW representative, was controlling his board. He sought help from the UAW president, Homer Martin (who had his own political problems). Knox asked Martin to remove Mazey from his job and remove the Mazey people from the Local 212 executive board. In fact, Martin did remove Mazey as the UAW International representative and replaced him with another capable UAW International representative, Richard Leonard. In addition, Martin, who was leading a purge of UAW staff people he perceived as his enemies, vanquished Mazey to Pennsylvania. Rather than being moved out of his home base of Michigan, in early July, Mazey sent a blistering resignation letter to Martin, which now gave him time to address the problems of Local 212.[65] The Mazey forces, still in control of the Local 212 executive board, were outraged. This was a huge tactical mistake for Knox. Not only did the local's executive board oppose the action, but many regular workers in the plants also complained.

By July, the rank-and-file members of the local were fed up. All they wanted was stable local union leadership. Mazey, much closer to the regular workers than Knox was, noticed this discontent. Emil Mazey's career was full of bold moves, and one of his first such actions came at the July Local 212 membership meeting.

Skipping the local's executive board, Mazey and his supporters proposed a resolution to remove Knox and to replace him and his vice president with the recording secretary, a fellow named Leslie Kaines. The motion passed.

This created chaos in the local. The International UAW chose not to recognize the removal of Knox. The practical result was that there were two recognized presidents of Local 212, Knox and Kaines.

The International UAW was forced to address the nightmare at its largest local union. The number two person at the International UAW was George Addes, the secretary-treasurer. Addes proposed a solution of restoring Knox to his former position, with the understanding that he would immediately resign and return to the plant. After the resignation, Local 212 was to hold new elections. Knox agreed to a version of this, but countered the Addes proposal by requesting his local union salary be paid through the end of the year. The Mazey forces agreed.

On November 22, 1937, the International UAW sent a letter to Fay Taylor, Briggs's personnel director, stating that Ralph Knox "relinquished" his positions as president of Local 212 and was returning to the plant.[66]

Knox, not to be outdone, left his position and tried to form another union at Briggs. His competing labor organization went nowhere. In the years to come, Knox accused Mazey of being a Communist and someone who could not be trusted. Knox would spend years trying to destroy Emil Mazey.

On December 2, 1937, Emil Mazey was elected president of Local 212 by a two-to-one margin. He was now independent of the International UAW, and just one year after being thrown out of the Briggs plant, Emil was the president of Local 212, the Briggs local.

At the first membership meeting of the local after Emil's election, a resolution expelling Ralph Knox from Local 212 passed unanimously. The resolution included this language: "Ralph Knox [is] expelled ... for a period not to exceed ninety-nine years." To this day, official histories of Local 212 list Emil Mazey as the first Local 212 president; Ralph Knox vanished from Local 212 records.[67]

In the same election that elevated Mazey to the Local 212 presidency, there was a contest for fifteen delegates to the Greater Detroit District [Labor] Council. Twenty-nine people ran for the position. Emil and Bill Mazey were among the candidates elected. Ken Morris was a candidate but finished eighteenth. This was Ken's first effort to run for elective office in the local. This narrow loss did not deter him from local union activities.[68]

. . . .

At roughly this same time, another labor-management battle was taking place on Detroit's east side. In this case, the company was the Detroit Stove Works, on Jefferson Avenue, just west of the Belle Isle Bridge. (The Detroit Stove Works became the Michigan Detroit Stove Works in 1927 but shall be referred to in this narrative as the Detroit Stove Works.) In this case, the relationship between the president of the company and an employee—a known gangster—would haunt the UAW, particularly Local 212, for years.

Santo ("Sam") Perrone is another man who came to Detroit with nothing. He arrived from Sicily at the age of seventeen and became involved with gangsters during the early years of Prohibition. In 1920, police arrested Perrone for murder but released him due to lack of evidence. Perrone and his brother began working at the Detroit Stove Works in the early 1910s, where Perrone developed a personal relationship with young John Fry, who went on to become president of the company in the 1930s and 1940s. Their relationship was so good that in 1930, when Perrone was arrested for violating Prohibition and served six months at the Detroit House of Corrections, Perrone had no problem returning to his old job. Perrone was a born intimidator. He found ways to get to people and scare them to death if they did not do what he wanted. He became a nemesis to working people that tried to organize into unions.

In April 1934, the workers at the Detroit Stove Works attempted to organize a union. The company president, John Fry, needed help stopping the union and turned to Santo Perrone and his brother Gaspar. Within days, the Perrone brothers broke the strike by staging riots on the picket line and viciously attacking a strike leader near his home. The strike was soon broken. Immediately afterward, Gaspar was awarded a private contract within the foundry of the Detroit Stove Works. Sam received a scrap hauling contract. The two contracts were worth approximately sixty-five thousand dollars annually.

In 1936, the Perrone brothers were arrested for being in possession of untaxed or illegal alcohol (Prohibition having been repealed) and sentenced to Leavenworth. While in prison, Fry allowed the brothers' wives to run their husband's two contracts. While the brothers were in prison, the UAW organized the Detroit Stove Works.

With the support of John Fry, who was now on the Detroit Police Commission, the Perrone brothers were paroled in 1939. The brothers immediately led a battle against the UAW local union leadership. They used intimidation, physically attacked local union leadership, smashed windows, and performed other forms of violence against the unionists. The terror worked, and the union leadership was not strong enough to fight back. The UAW local was broken, and the Detroit Stove Works was again a nonunion shop.

Santo Perrone continued in his scrap hauling contract for many years. He bought a gas station across the street from the Stove Works, at Jefferson and Canton. He conducted much of his business there or next door at Helen's Bar, which was located at Jefferson and Helen streets.

Perrone developed a unique power base. He had relationships with Detroit's notorious Mafia families, but generally dealings were at arm's length. Perrone was essentially a free agent, a muscle man who could be hired to do anything. He was a bad and dangerous man who selected which illegal operations he undertook.[69]

CHAPTER 7

HOMER MARTIN COULD MESMERIZE AND CAPTIVATE AUDIENCES

One weekend day, Greg, Dad, and I were coming back from a meeting in the white 1958 Dodge. My recollection is that we had heard Walter Reuther talking about the early days of the UAW. For some reason, Dad started talking about a man named R. J. Thomas. I asked, "Who is he?" Dad said he was the UAW's president before Walter Reuther. I was dumbfounded and said, "I thought Walter was the UAW's first president." Dad laughed and said, "No, a man named Homer Martin was the first president, followed by R. J. Thomas." Again, I was astonished. This was brand-new information, and we asked more about Homer Martin. Dad simply said, "Homer Martin was a bad UAW president."

AS THE STRUGGLES OF LOCAL 212 took place, the International UAW was having its own leadership battles. One early Local 212 member argued that these internal distractions, added by the momentous issues surrounding World War II, held back the union for ten years.[70] The first and most significant phase of the internal struggles occurred because of the UAW's first elected president, Homer Martin. Beginning with the efforts to form a truly national UAW in 1935, the union (which became an international union as the UAW organized

Canadian autoworkers) became a hotbed of internal political bickering and backstabbing. Many key and controversial UAW activists at the International UAW headquarters were instrumental in forming the foundation, shaky as it might be, for the first ten years of the UAW. Emil Mazey and Ken Morris were not directly active in this factional fighting, but they did have to choose sides.

. . . .

As noted earlier, the beginnings of the labor movement in the auto industry were erratic. Efforts to organize plants usually ended in failure until strong support organizations developed, providing the necessary tools for a union to grow. A union needed an internal infrastructure that included a strike fund, organizers, a research staff, a public relations office, and an education department. These elements of support began coming together in 1934 and culminated in Detroit in August 1935, when the American Federation of Labor (AFL) organized its first convention of autoworkers—at the same time Ken Morris was mopping floors at the Michigan State Fair.

The AFL was essentially a federation of craft unions. It organized by trades, not by individual plants or industries. Such trades included carpenters, cigar makers, plumbers, pipefitters, and typographical employees. This federation of skilled unions enjoyed its share of success. Between 1890 and 1917, when the AFL was extremely active in organizing craft workers, union wages rose from seventeen dollars per week to almost twenty-four dollars. The workweek was shortened from fifty-four hours per week to forty-nine hours. Yet by refusing to organize unskilled workers, African Americans, and women, the AFL was leaving about 70 percent of the workforce out in the cold.

As the Great Depression swept over the country in the early 1930s, it was not clear whether the US economic system—capitalism—was going to survive. The national unemployment rate averaged 21.4 percent between 1932 and 1936.[71] The unemployment rate, plus the loss of wage power for those who did work, worried the country's establishment. Anthony Badger's *FDR: The First Hundred Days* points out that many in the US business and political establishment looked around the world and were terrified of what might happen in the United States. They saw the social unrest in Germany and the Soviet Union, where revolutionary "isms" were changing the traditional power structures. While unions were perceived as terrible, socialism and communism were worse. If the workers were to have something, the power elite (including President Roosevelt) would rather legalize unions than face more dreadful alternatives. Thus, with the passage of the National Industrial Recover Act (NIRA) in 1933, the President's New Deal supported a worker's right to organize.[72]

In 1935, the AFL decided to organize the auto industry. At downtown Detroit's Fort Shelby Hotel, the convention delegates debated many issues during their convention. One major issue concentrated on how much independence this new union should have from the AFL. This contentious convention resulted in the formation of the AFL's United Automobile Workers of America, with the AFL's leadership appointing, rather than electing, Frances Dillon as president. An appointed president rather than one elected by delegates infuriated many, if not most, of the convention delegates. Many activist UAW members never fully accepted Dillon as the first UAW president.[73]

One active person in attendance was a man from Kansas City named Homer Martin. Homer Martin was an autoworker at Chevrolet and a Baptist minister. He had acquired two great skills in life. He earned his initial fame as the national hop, skip, and jump champion when he was twenty-two-years old (in today's world, this is known as the triple jump and is a summer Olympic event). His second great skill was that of an orator. He could mesmerize and captivate audiences. He spoke in a persuasive manner, often going from a stage whisper to a thunderous persuasive point. Audiences rose out of their seats as he expertly played their emotions. He was a "gifted agitator[;] he made men feel that in organizing a union they were going forth to battle for righteousness and the word of God."[74] This slim man with his slicked-back hair and horn-rimmed glasses was known as the "leaping parson."[75]

Also attending and watching this convention carefully were several AFL leaders who had been advocating the organization of the auto industry. John L. Lewis, the charismatic president of the United Mine Workers, led this group. From their perspective, they saw the AFL as an old-fashioned labor organization primarily interested in organizing skilled workers into craft unions. If the AFL failed in the effort to organize autoworkers, Lewis and the others were going to pull out of the organization and form a new group with the objective of organizing the millions of workers the AFL ignored.

Within a year, the AFL's experiment in industrial unionism failed. Lewis's Mine Workers and several other unions bolted from the AFL and formed the Congress of Industrial Organizations (CIO) in 1936. The UAW experiment in the AFL abruptly ended because most active members saw no future in an organization focused on craft workers instead of all workers in an industry. In 1936, the UAW-AFL opened its convention in South Bend and reorganized under the CIO. The UAW-CIO delegates elected Homer Martin, the leaping parson with the magic voice, president of the new organization.[76]

. . . .

Neither Ken Morris nor Emil Mazey participated in the 1936 South Bend convention, but these actions affected their lives. As the UAW met at South Bend in 1936, Ken was on layoff from Briggs, selling house goods door-to-door. Mazey, still looking for a place where he could organize a union, had just begun work at Briggs. Emil Mazey was a direct beneficiary of the new UAW-CIO. When working at Briggs and trying to incite workers to strike, he had reached out to stronger UAW local unions for help. Then, after being fired from Briggs in December 1936, the UAW-CIO hired him as a union organizer. The newly organized union provided the backbone of support that Mazey needed at Briggs, as well as support for workers and labor organizers throughout the country. Union organizers such as Mazey and brothers Roy and Victor Reuther (who were both crucial in organizing the GM strike in Flint) were available to help organize because the UAW-CIO was there to support their efforts.

The UAW-CIO attracted young idealists from around the country to help the new union. Under the CIO's guidance, the UAW's infrastructure grew fast. These activists, usually young men and women, saw an opportunity to change the world. In most cases, they were not against the United States or its government but saw this new union as a way of improving the social and economic realities within their country.

The incubator for many CIO activists who came to Detroit was the private Brookwood Labor College, located in Katonah, New York. Brookwood, founded in 1921, was the only college in the country that focused on educating young people on labor issues. Besides educational programs, Brookwood offered many programs and conferences, which spread its influence throughout America. Brookwood students might be liberals, Socialists, Communists, Marxists, or other radicals. At Brookwood, however, a unique learning environment was created so that graduates seemed to look beyond whatever social or economic philosophy they may have held before they entered the school. By the time they left, they were fledgling labor leaders, dedicated to the union to which they would eventually become attached. The Reuther brothers, George Edwards, and many others who played a significant role in the UAW were affiliated with Brookwood. More activities than just training young labor leaders seemed to take place at Brookwood. Many labor leaders met future spouses there, including Roy and Fania Reuther and Victor and Sophie Reuther. Brookwood closed down by 1938 due to lack of funding.[77]

Homer Martin, looking for UAW staff whose loyalty he could count on, turned to a man from New York named Jay Lovestone. Lovestone, a former leader of the Communist Party of America and still quite radical, provided Martin with advice and young staffers. Lovestone, never a UAW member, hoped to use the UAW and Martin for his own political purposes. Martin seemed to appreciate the man's savvy and political insights, especially since Lovestone became an opponent of the Communist Party of America after 1929. The Lovestone staffers were often at odds with Brookwood graduates and other perceived left-wing supporters, many of whom seemed more loyal to John L. Lewis than to Homer Martin.

This resulted in an International UAW headquarters fraught with bureaucracy and internal politics. Yet some UAW leaders saw a great positive influence in these young men and women who staffed the UAW. Many were brilliant negotiators and researchers. Dick Frankensteen recalled one man who could analyze bargaining issues, take complex issues apart, and explain company proposals so that all of their implications were clear to a bargaining committee. Top officers of the union knew that these staffers could see implications in complex proposals that they might not catch. These staffers, smart and so well educated, may never have worked inside a plant but made a huge difference at the bargaining table. Sometimes they were much more radical than the typical guy on the assembly line, yet they were simply invaluable to the new union.[78]

. . . .

In early 1937, after the Briggs strike, Emil Mazey made the decision to stay with the International UAW and continue organizing plants. He had been able to help organize Briggs with little interference from the Hoffman Building—the downtown headquarters of the International UAW. He assumed that same independence was to continue as he organized workers throughout Detroit.

As 1937 moved forward, Homer Martin became less secure as UAW president. Dick Frankensteen reflected that Homer Martin "was a lot of things to a lot of people. Those who knew him best found that he would make a public speech saying one thing, but in private advocate for something else. Homer was thought to be, by the men closest to him, a demagogue and without the power to really weld together an organization." Frankensteen's bottom line was that Martin was simply "not a strong leader."[79]

During the Flint GM Sit-Down Strike, Homer Martin's lack of leadership was evident. In fact, UAW organizers Roy Reuther, Robert Travis, and others were the ones who filled the leadership void. Then, as the strike came to its conclusion, CIO president John L. Lewis led labor's effort to settle. Martin seemed never to recover from his failures in Flint and seemed to become paranoid over the influence of the Reuther brothers and any other potential competitors. Martin soon labeled all his enemies as Communists, whether they were Socialists, Communists, or, for that matter, Catholics, another significant political block in the union.[80]

In July 1937, Martin fired Roy Reuther as a UAW organizer. Shortly after, Martin tried to transfer Emil Mazey to Allentown, Pennsylvania, probably as a favor to Ralph Knox. Mazey refused. It is not clear which came first, Martin's firing of Mazey or Mazey's resignation. Nonetheless, Mazey's resignation letter focused on two points. First he raised his concerns about Local 212. He wrote:

> I asked you to make a thorough investigation of Local 212. You promised to make this investigation, but did not consider it serious enough.... I feel that the [UAW] Executive Board did not try to honestly solve this problem that was presented to them.... The actions of the Executive Board have all the earmarks of a political maneuver for the coming convention. Your own remarks clearly prove this contention when you stated to me that if I took part in the affairs of Local 212, of which I am a charter member, that you would fight me.

Mazey went on to warn Martin that the upcoming UAW convention in Milwaukee should be of concern to the shaky president:

> These actions will be fully answered at the coming convention and the "spoils system" which you use to such good personal advantage will be added to the historic relics of the past.[81]

Mazey, of course, returned to Local 212 and orchestrated the ouster of Knox and the rise of his leadership at Local 212 and the UAW. Rather than worry about the politics at the Hoffman Building, he focused on developing a power base and a place of security at Local 212.

CHAPTER 8

MY GOD, HE WRITES IN SHORTHAND!

One Saturday while we were driving to or from a meeting, Dad was talking about the Local 212 Flying Squadron and some of the run-ins they had had with Detroit police or company security guards while on picket lines during the 1930s. Greg asked if Dad ever had to use guns. He thought for a moment and said, "No, I never had a gun, but I can remember a time or two when some of the fellows carried shotguns."

EMIL MAZEY WAS IN CHARGE of his world at the beginning of 1938. He'd left behind the turbulent and unproductive politics of Homer Martin and the International UAW. He was now president of his own local union, the largest within the UAW. His objective was to organize Local 212 into the best and most capable local within the UAW. After Ralph Knox, the local was in disarray. Leslie Kaines, the local's recording secretary and interim president, had done a great job trying to pick up after Knox, but he was essentially a caretaker. Now it was time to get things moving and shape the local to Mazey's vision.

To run an efficient operation, Mazey knew his local needed more than picket organizers or speechmakers. He needed people who could file grievances, maintain paperwork, collect and record the monthly union dues of members, work on committees, and fight for the UAW—both at

Local 212 and in assisting other locals in organizing. He began putting competent supporters into key positions. Ken Morris, for example, soon became the press department's union committeeman. Mazey hired new office help; he needed secretaries who could type, take dictation, and file—not employees that played the piano. Perhaps all was not work, for one of the new secretaries, Charlotte Monser, became Emil Mazey's wife within the year.[82]

Mazey wanted something else. A year earlier, he'd watched how Frankensteen's Local 3 Flying Squadron provided such crucial support during the Meldrum strike. The Local 3 Flying Squadron was composed of tough men prepared to go to any picket line or other union activity to support the UAW. Emil wanted Local 212 to have the same ability. He wanted a group of men who could be a force in assisting the UAW's brothers and sisters in organizing plants. If Local 212 were to be a tough and militant local, it would need a tough, aggressive support group.[83]

Mazey also needed people to help collect union dues. There was not a union shop or a check-off system in the 1930s. Collecting union dues was not as simple as a deduction on a paycheck—that would come later. In the beginning, plant stewards, of which Ken was one, collected the dues from each worker. Many, if not most, paid promptly. Others did not; about 20 percent of the members chose not to pay their dues. Even though these people received all the same wage increases and access to the union's grievance process, they seemed to feel above paying their dues. Some simply wanted no part in the union, and some did not want to pay more money from their own pockets. Others wanted to participate in union activities but didn't seem to want to pay their union dues. These people may have withheld their dues because they simply did not support the elected leadership of the local. Getting these people to pay was always difficult.

Of course, the issue of forcing people to join a union was controversial and remains so to this very day. From labor's point of view, the argument of paying union dues was essentially the same principle that Abraham Lincoln used during the Civil War. Lincoln argued that the United States could not be broken up into separate countries or individual states. Each state and each individual was part of the United States and as such enjoyed the same benefits and privileges as provided by the US

Constitution. He argued that the United States had to stay one united country. From a labor perspective, everyone in the plant was receiving the same rights, privileges, and protections as every other worker. All workers were receiving the same benefits; therefore, it only made sense that they should all belong to the union and pay their fair share in union dues. It might be different if people who did not want to belong to a union did not get the same benefits and protections, but that was not the case in the 1930s (nor is it today).

Thus each UAW local tried its very best to collect dues from all workers, as union dues were their lifeblood. As the local's steward in the press room, Ken normally collected the monthly dues. Occasionally, a member of Local 212's Flying Squadron joined Ken on these visits, mostly to give him or other stewards additional support. These teams may have made a difference. In many cases, Local 212 supported regularly scheduled union dues drives designed to create peer pressure and public education regarding the need for employees to pay their union dues. Regardless of what strategy was used, there were always some who simply would not pay their union dues.

Mazey asked one of his key supporters in the Mack Avenue plant, Art Vega, to spearhead forming the Local 212 Flying Squadron. Vega agreed. An organization meeting of the Local 212 Flying Squadron was planned.

As with everything else, Ken volunteered for the flying squadron. He walked into the initial meeting and was no doubt one of the smallest persons in the room. Ken was never regarded as a muscle man or a tough guy within his local or the UAW; he simply volunteered for everything. At that initial meeting, Art Vega asked for a volunteer to take the minutes of the meeting. Ken stepped forward. As he was taking notes, someone looked down and saw he was using shorthand. The fellow exclaimed so the whole group heard, "My God, we've got somebody who writes in shorthand."[84] Ken was already using his high school skills as the assistant editor of the *Voice of Local 212* newspaper. He'd now gained a reputation as someone who took verbatim notes.

About two hundred men signed on and became part of the local's flying squadron. Members who had cars were a priority. Ken again volunteered; he did not have to be a tough guy to drive a car. A few months earlier, Ken had bought a car and then learned how to drive. As a flying squadron member with a car, Ken became a captain. When there was a need, Art Vega called Ken at his new residence, a boardinghouse on St. Jean Street, just a few blocks from the Local 212 offices. From that time on, Ken always lived near the local.

When Vega's call came, Ken quickly put on a white shirt, grabbed his black flying squadron jacket, put on his army-style Flying Squadron cap, and rushed down the stairs to his car. Meanwhile, Vega then called the first fellow Ken was to pick up, usually Pat Caruso. By the time Ken picked up Caruso, Caruso had called the next person, and so forth down the list. Literally, within minutes of the time Ken received his call, a car full of men were on their way to assist at a picket line or in whatever activity for which they were needed. Of course, Vega called all his captains, and the process repeated itself throughout the flying squadron ranks. This calling tree turned out hundreds of supporters within fifteen minutes, and soon Local 212 became known as having one of the best flying squadrons in Detroit.[85]

Rarely did Ken witness violence. The presence of the flying squadrons was usually enough to provide the support necessary for a picket line, and the company police or the Detroit police usually backed away. However, two strikes in 1938 did get out of control and become full-fledged riots.

. . . .

Local 212 was the strongest UAW local on Detroit's east side. Detroit is divided into east side and west side geographic areas—anything east of Woodward is considered the east side, and anything west of Woodward is the west side. On the city's west side, Local 174, or the West Side Local, was the dominant UAW local union of that area. The president of the West Side Local was Walter Reuther, who also served on the UAW's Executive Board. Local 174 was an amalgamated local, which meant that it represented more than one company. As the West Side Local, Local 174's jurisdiction was many manufacturing companies located west of Woodward. By 1938, Local 174 represented manufacturing companies of various sizes, one of which was the Federal Screw Works company located at 3401 Martin Avenue, south of Michigan Avenue and west of Livernois Avenue.[86]

By 1937, the US economy was beginning to show signs of recovery. This positive news stopped when a recession hit in mid-1937 and continued into 1938.[87] On a Monday in late March 1938, Federal Screw, with the tacit support of the Ford Motor Company and Harry Bennett, made a unilateral decision to cut wages, completely ignoring its contract with the UAW. A strike immediately ensued. To further complicate and escalate matters, the following day Federal Screw brought in strikebreakers. These were nonunion workers, often called scabs, hired to take the place of the union workers.[88]

Strikebreakers, or scabs, are dirty words in the labor movement. In many cases, these workers were simply trying to find employment to support their families. From a labor point of view, however, they were replacing union workers and weakening labor's effort to have decent wages and working conditions in a plant—thus they served management's effort to destroy what the labor union had gained through collective bargaining. Further, whether workers are organized or not, there is usually a sense that one's job is his or her job. Strikebreakers, therefore, further insulted workers by taking their jobs.

Reuther tried to open up discussions with Federal Screw, but the company refused to talk with UAW leadership. Reuther knew he had to stop the company from breaking the union, and this meant stopping the scab workers and closing down the plant. And it meant keeping the wages at the agreed-to levels. If one company succeeded in unilaterally cutting wages, others would follow, and that spelled the end of the UAW. Of course, the company might have approached the union and indicated that the economy was in a downturn and they needed some help. In 1938, labor-management relationships were not that sophisticated, and companies like Federal Screw did not believe reopening the contract was an option—their choice was to break the union.

Reuther knew that Detroit police officers were providing the strikebreakers with protection—escorting them to and from the plant. Federal Screw management was in fact working with acknowledged Detroit antiunion Mayor Richard Reading and the police commissioner to gain police protection of the plant and the scab workers. Reading

Mounted police lead strikebreakers to the Federal Screw plant

had promised to end strikes in Detroit (he was also a corrupt man who later served prison time for pocketing illegal funds from a bookmaking operation in Paradise Valley.) Taking on Reading and the Detroit Police Department was a problem for Reuther, and he called for help from UAW allies throughout Detroit.

On a cool Wednesday morning, the Detroit police escorted about forty strikebreakers from their cars parked on Livernois Avenue down Otis Street, a side street lined with small homes surrounded by picket fences. Many Federal Screw workers lived in these modest homes, and they were outraged at their employer and the scabs who were taking their jobs. They yelled epithets as the men walked the four blocks to the plant. As the day progressed, supporters from UAW and other locals from around the city began gathering along Martin Street, marching up and down the street, the plant on one side of them and the neighborhood homes on the other. The Briggs Flying Squadron arrived, and Ken parked his car near Michigan Avenue. His team jumped out of the car and quickly moved to the plant, some four or five blocks away.

Detroit police attack Federal Screw picketers

By four o'clock, the day had warmed, with temperatures approaching sixty degrees, but on Martin Street, the temperature was much hotter. Some five thousand picketers fully encircled the plant. The police entered the plant. Word worked its way through the picket lines that the police were coming out with the scabs. Just after four, the police, including fifteen mounted police officers, began escorting the scared union busters down Otis Street, to their cars parked on Livernois. No one really knew what happened, but soon picketers were scuffling with police. Then police began swinging their billy clubs and arresting people. Some picketers started throwing stones, bricks, and sticks at the police officers.

People, boards, bricks, and stones seemed to be flying in all directions. Ken retreated toward Michigan Avenue. People from the neighborhood invited picketers into their homes for sanctuary and assisted injured picketers, but Ken was not injured and did not need their help.[89]

Ken kept moving and soon found himself on the other side of Michigan Avenue behind some storefronts. Not far away, he saw a gathering crowd. It was a friendly group listening to someone standing on top of a car making a speech. Ken moved in that direction until he was able to hear the speaker, using a West Side Local sound car, captivating the crowd. He was standing next to some people on the outer edges of the crowd. Ken remarked to the guy standing next to him that the man on the microphone sure knew how to give a speech. Ken asked who the speaker was. The fellow turned to Ken and said that was Victor Reuther. What a talk Victor was giving! Victor talked about the rights of workers, the sacred meaning of a contract and how union busters could destroy the UAW. It was one of the best speeches Ken had ever heard. After the talk, Ken rounded up his team and headed back to the east side.[90]

The *Detroit Free Press* reported that forty people were seriously injured and hospitalized that day. Of those injured, thirteen of them were police officers. To the surprise of many, no deaths were recorded. Ten men were arrested, including a Teamster activist named James Hoffa, who must have heard the call to help workers on the picket line from his Teamster office near Briggs Stadium.

The next day, Homer Martin and Walter Reuther appeared at the Detroit City Council, protesting police brutality. Reuther reiterated his desire to work with the company to address its economic problems, but until an agreement could be worked out, the plant was closed. Within a week, the union and the company negotiated a new contract. The UAW, through strong leadership and a united front, had won.[91]

. . . .

A similar strike, but with subtle differences, occurred about two months later at the American Brass Company, located on West Jefferson Avenue near the Ambassador Bridge. The UAW did not organize American Brass. A CIO union, the Mine, Mill, and Smelter Workers, had organized the plant. The workers had been in a sit-down strike in one of the company's buildings since mid-April due to unilateral cuts in wages. On May 26, the Detroit police evicted the strikers. Walter Reuther and the West Side Local called for the various flying squadrons to come out and support the CIO strikers at American Brass. The Local 212 Flying Squadron was on its way.

Upon arriving at the scene, strike officials assigned them to a plant entrance, one that seemed a bit out of the way. They were given picket signs, but these signs were different—the picket handles, or boards, were made of two-by-two boards, much heavier and stronger than the one-by-two-inch boards normally used. Ken noticed the weight of the stronger boards and realized that strike organizers had learned from the Federal Screw strike. These two-by-two boards could stop unruly police officers if they got out of hand.

Besides the presence of Detroit police, the company had hired private detectives. From the picketers' standpoint, these men were no better than Harry Bennett thugs who were there to knock the hell out of them. The picketers were not there to harm the factory but to support the American Brass workers.

Ken had never seen so many police officers in his life. While they were picketing at the side entrance, a police car pulled up. *Bam!* Suddenly, there was a haze in the car. A tear gas bomb had exploded inside it. Ken was sure the blast killed or at least blinded one of the officers. Ken, of course, realized that he and his union brothers and sisters were to be the recipients of the tear gas. Before he could spend any time worrying about the officers in the car, someone fired tear gas bombs from the plant roof at the union sound car on Jefferson Avenue, and all hell broke loose.

Police and mounted police attacked the strikers and their supporters. The picketers, including Ken, ripped the placards from their two-by-twos and soon had their own weapons to protect themselves. Pandemonium broke out as men, women, and police were running everywhere. The strikers, without hesitation, fought back. Some grabbed bricks from a construction site. Others used their two-by-two boards. Nightsticks, stones, bricks, and boards filled the air, with horses trampling and pushing men to the ground. The police were too strong, and the picketers started retreating from the plant. Picketers too injured to walk were helped by their union brothers. These injured picketers were packed into friendly cars and taken to the UAW's Hoffman Building on Woodward Avenue, where a medical team was waiting (the union had learned from the Federal Screw strike to have medical assistance nearby). Ken was stung by a club that hit his left ear, but with the adrenaline of the moment and compared to so many others he knew he did not need medical care.

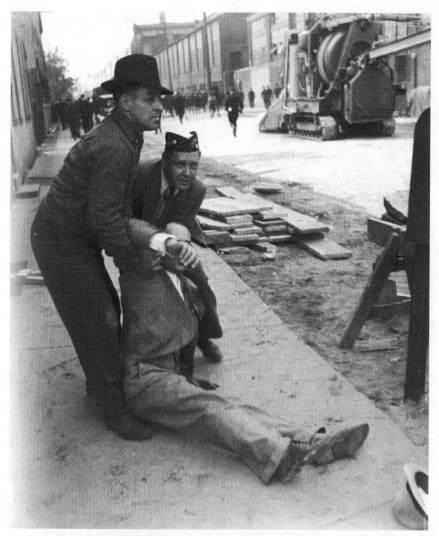

**Men help injured person. Note that one man is
wearing a Briggs Flying Squadron cap.**

Near the end of the battle, Ken was running and saw a policeman knocked to the ground. He watched the officer get to one knee, pull out his revolver, and begin to aim it at one of the picketers. In one smooth motion and without thinking about potential consequences, Ken took his two-by-two and swung hard at the police officer's arm. *Whack!* He heard the thud and felt the arm crumble. Ken did not stop to look, but he was sure he had broken the officer's arm. As he moved out of the immediate area, things quieted down. He found his buddies and returned to the local.[92]

. . . .

In early 1938, Emil placed Ken on the Local 212 Education committee.[93] Ken was already close to Bill Lamson, the local's education director, and now their friendship deepened. Lamson was a Socialist and began taking Ken to Socialist Party meetings. It was here that Ken met Victor and Sophie Reuther, Roy Reuther, and many other important people in his life.

Many of these new acquaintances became lifelong friends of Ken's. George Edwards became more than a friend; he eventually became Ken's attorney. Edwards was from Texas. His father, George Sr., was a civil rights attorney and a Socialist in Dallas, Texas. George Jr. went to Southern Methodist University, Harvard, and at about the time Ken met him, he was studying law at the Detroit College of Law. Like the Reuthers, Edwards attended Brookwood College and was part of the cadre of young people who came to Detroit. Along with Walter and Victor Reuther, he was one of the original organizers of Local 174.

Edwards eventually phased out of the UAW in the 1930s and devoted himself to public service. He later became a Detroit Common (city) Council member, president of the Common Council, a candidate for mayor of Detroit, and district judge, where he championed a juvenile court. Later, in the 1950s and 1960s, his judicial career continued to develop.[94]

Gus Scholle was another one of the remarkable people who helped develop the industrial labor movement in Michigan. A bit older than most of the young firebrands, Scholle was born in 1904. He became involved in labor's cause with the Glass Workers in Toledo. As the CIO evolved, there was a great desire to find competent and tough labor leaders. CIO labor leaders identified Scholle as one such man and sent him to Michigan to organize. He helped Emil Mazey organize his picket lines during the strike at the Meldrum plant in 1937.

Scholle was a man's man, with an intellect that surprised his adversaries. He became president of the Michigan CIO and eventually the president of the Michigan AFL-CIO. In the 1950s, he was appalled by the way the Michigan Republican Party gerrymandered legislative districts so that the more urban regions had fewer legislators than rural regions on a per capita basis. He became a crusader for "one man, one vote." His case was ultimately joined with others, and the US Supreme Court ruled against blatant gerrymandering and in favor of the one man, one vote concept. Ken developed a deep and personal friendship with Gus Scholle.

These people fascinated Ken. They opened up a new world that represented more than the rough-and-tumble life of Local 212. They were some of the intellectual elite of labor and social thought in Detroit. Ken was so impressed that he became a member of the Socialist Party … for about six months. While the Socialist Party did not move him, these people did. They were the ones who helped him grow intellectually and spiritually.[95]

CHAPTER 9

YOU MAY SHOOT SOME OF US

While in our white 1960 Chrysler, we once asked Dad when he first met Walter Reuther. I don't remember if he knew the exact date or not, but I remember him saying that he met May Reuther before Walter. May, he said, was an extremely nice person and worked as her husband's secretary. Dad said that often when he had business at the UAW International's office on West Grand Boulevard, he usually visited with and had wonderful conversations with May. He felt that they had a good friendship—not necessarily better than the one he had with Walter, but a friendship that was uniquely their own.

IT IS IMPOSSIBLE TO TELL a story of the early UAW without talking about Walter Reuther. In 1998, *Time* magazine picked Walter Reuther as one of the top one hundred most influential people of the twentieth century.[96] The redheaded labor leader negotiated amazing benefits for his members, benefits that became commonplace for Americans throughout the United States. But he was much more than a labor leader. Walter Reuther once said, "If it were just a question of winning six cents an hour, I wouldn't be interested. I will be dissatisfied as long as one American child is denied the right to education ... as long as one American is denied his rights.... I'll do all I can to dispel the corruption of complacency in America and seek a greater sense of national purpose."[97]

In the late summer of 1960, Walter traveled to Hyannis Port, Massachusetts, to meet with Senator John F. Kennedy, the man nominated as the Democratic Party's candidate for president. Kennedy wanted the redhead to bring forward his best ideas regarding how to build a better America. Reuther spent hours at home in Rochester, Michigan, in his den, preparing for the meeting. At one point in this preparation, he looked up from his work and said to his young daughter Elizabeth, "This is my favorite pastime. I'm an idea man." His agenda with the future president included civil rights, health care, unemployment, and a concept he and others had been talking about, the Peace Corps.[98]

These ideas captured Walter Reuther. He was a planner and visionary, but he was more than that. He was an implementer too.

Walter's ideas were numerous and global in their vision. He negotiated pensions, health care, and wage increases. Long before the start of America's entry into World War II, Reuther came up with an idea to convert American automobile factories into military production facilities to fight Nazi terror. He said American factories could build "500 planes a day," an idea vehemently opposed by the auto industry. Yet when war came, that is exactly what President Roosevelt ordered and Detroit became the Arsenal of Democracy.[99]

After Reuther became president of the UAW and negotiated innovative labor contracts, he began to address many of the social ills around him. In the late 1960s, many people in the UAW heard their first environmental speech at Detroit's Cobo Hall as Walter discussed the evils of our poisoned air and water.[100]

It was in the arena of the national civil rights movement where Reuther may have shined the most. He was an avid supporter of the American civil rights movement and particularly supported the efforts of Dr. Martin Luther King Jr. He marched with King at demonstrations throughout the South, and under his direction, the UAW was a major financial supporter of Dr. King's efforts.

Reuther was one of the key organizers of the 1963 March on Washington.[101] He, along with six others, delivered a speech that hot afternoon at the Lincoln Memorial. It was a fine speech, but it was overshadowed by Dr. King's "I Have a Dream" speech. Standing on the steps of the Lincoln Memorial was Walter's assistant, Irving Bluestone. As Walter walked up to the podium to give his speech, Bluestone overheard a young African American woman say to her friend, "Who is that man?"

Her friend replied, "Why, don't you know? That's Walter Reuther; he's the white Martin Luther King Jr." The compliment was one of the best Walter Reuther ever received, and he beamed with pride whenever he retold the story.[102]

Yet before he could do all these things, and before becoming one of the most influential Americans of his time, Reuther had to fight his way through the maze of UAW politics to become its president. Along his route to power, gangsters and thugs physically assaulted and threatened him. Then, once he became the UAW president in 1946, he had to battle his way through shotgun pellets to maintain his life's ambition. Along this journey to win the UAW's presidency, Reuther had to make endless political choices if he was to get the votes necessary to reach his goal. Some were great political decisions; some were bad decisions.

Ken Morris, Emil Mazey, and many members of Local 212 had to live with one of his bad decisions.

. . . .

Walter Reuther came to Detroit from Wheeling, West Virginia, in 1927. Three years earlier, he dropped out of high school to become an exceptional tool and die worker in an effort to support his family. As a tool and die maker, he developed molds and redesigned machinery in the plant so that an assembly line could make its product flawlessly. It was the most skilled job a person held in a plant, and such a worker was a true artisan. At age nineteen, he decided that it was time to try to improve his lot, so he and a buddy traveled to Detroit.

Reuther's first job in Detroit was with the Briggs Manufacturing Company. As a skilled employee, Reuther was making eighty-five cents an hour, twice the wage of an unskilled worker. He stayed twenty-one days at Briggs. His stay was short not because the company wanted him to leave but because Reuther, as a gifted tool and die maker, felt his creative talents would never be fully utilized at Briggs. He wanted greater challenges and quickly moved on.

He learned that Ford was hiring tool and die leaders at its Highland Park plant. A tool and die leader was an experienced tool and die maker who led a team of fifteen to twenty men in resetting the huge complicated presses that reflected a new model year design of an automobile. Tool and die leaders were generally mature men in their forties or fifties, not some kid not yet twenty years of age. When the young redhead applied for the leader position, he could hardly get in the door, but after great persistence, he convinced a key supervisor that he was capable of doing the job. Reuther hired in at $1.05 an hour. Within a few years and even after the Depression hit, Reuter's skill at his craft became obvious, as his hourly wage had grown to $1.40.[103] As his brother Victor said, this put him into the "aristocracy of labor."[104]

As a gifted worker, there is no question that had he stayed at Ford, he was going to be very successful, perhaps becoming one of the top craftsmen in the company ... or in whatever undertaking he might pursue. Reuther wanted more. Like many young people, he might not have known exactly what his future would be, but he knew it had to start with more education. Working nights, now at the Rouge complex in Dearborn, Walter attended Dearborn's Fordson High School during the day. He embraced classes such as algebra, geometry, German, English, and science. He was literally up day and night and still found time to organize and be president of a new club.

The new club, the 4C Club, was comprised of older students working their way through high school. Everyone had to apply to be a member of the club. On the application, there was a line for applicants to write about their life goals. Walter wrote, "I realize that to do something constructive in life, one must have an education. I seek knowledge that I may serve mankind."[105] The club, composed primarily of European immigrants and first-generation children of immigrants, raised money to help disadvantaged students and sponsored films and lectures. One member was Merlin Bishop, who became a great friend and colleague of the Reuther brothers.[106] Merlin's brother, Melvin, occasionally participated in these activities. In time, Melvin Bishop was to play an extremely controversial role in the history of Local 212 and the UAW.

After Walter and Merlin Bishop graduated from high school, they went on to the College of the City of Detroit, or City College (today's Wayne State University). In 1930, Reuther's kid brother, Victor, made the journey to Detroit, and the three became roommates. The Depression had hit Detroit hard and Victor was not able to find a job.

Walter and Victor Reuther had grown up in West Virginia, the sons of a Socialist father. Valentine Reuther was an immigrant from Germany and taught his sons—Ted, Walter, Roy, and Victor—the principles of socialism. The boys grew to appreciate and believe in the same goals that George Edwards was learning from his father in Texas.

Reuther had been so busy working, attending school, and even making some modest land investments that he had not focused on political or Socialist Party activities while in Detroit. Perhaps it was Victor's arrival, or perhaps it was just coincidence, that when the two brothers arrived at City College they became involved in many progressive activities.

The two young men organized the Social Problems Club in the early 1930s; the club reviewed and debated major issues affecting the student body and the community around the college. They talked, but they also took action, including a move to integrate the City College swimming pool. The club later affiliated with the League for Industrial Democracy, a national college club whose charter members included Upton Sinclair, Clarence Darrow, Jack London, Walter Lippman, and Ralph Bunche.

The club also documented, with photos and prose, Detroit's Hoovervilles (shantytowns of unemployed people often on the edges of cities or near railroads), prostitution, and crime. Walter, Victor, and Merlin Bishop explored and photographed the underbelly of Detroit's culture and society.[107]

In 1932, Roy Reuther joined his brothers. He had been laid off from a job in West Virginia, so it seemed natural for him, the middle brother of the three, to move to Detroit. The brothers campaigned vigorously for Norman Thomas, the 1932 Socialist Party candidate for president. They knew he could not possibly win, but they believed he was fighting for the Socialist principles and programs that America needed to adopt if it were to get out of the worst depression in history.

Ford management knew that Reuther was a fine craftsman with

a great future in their company, but being an active Socialist did not fit well with the Ford Service Department, run by Harry Bennett. A few weeks after the November election, Walter entered the huge Ford Rouge plant and reached for his card to punch the time clock to enter work. Much to his surprise, instead of a time card in his slot, Ford management had placed a pink slip, thereby discharging him. None of Walter's supervisors could explain the firing to him; they just implied that it came from higher management. While he did not know it at the time, Walter was blacklisted at automobile plants throughout Detroit.

While Henry Ford did not like Socialists or Communists working for him, he was not averse to cutting a business deal with the Soviet Union. By 1932, Ford was phasing out the Model A. Ford sold the presses and dies to the Soviets, who were building a factory in the city of Gorky. Reuther was offered employment—if he wanted to move to Russia. Walter and Victor had often talked about a European trip. The offer to work in Gorky gave them that opportunity. The two young men decided to go on the great adventure that took them to Europe, the Soviet Union, and Asia. In later years, this trip proved extremely controversial for Walter and Victor Reuther, but in 1932, the young men saw it as an opportunity of a lifetime.[108]

In January 1933, the Briggs strike had started at Highland Park. At the time, Roy was working as an electrician at Briggs, and he was a part of the strike. All three men volunteered to help on the picket lines. This is when they first met young Proletarian Party activist Emil Mazey. On a cold winter day immediately after completing their shifts at the Highland Park picket line, Walter and Victor said their good-byes to Roy. It was two and a half years before the brothers were together again.

Roy Reuther stayed on that picket line. During a scuffle a few days later, police brutally pushed Roy into the spike of an iron fence, leaving a terrible wound and a scar reminding him of the 1933 Briggs strike for the rest of his life.[109]

Roy and Merlin Bishop stayed in Detroit, eventually becoming instructors for the Federal Emergency Relief Administration (FERA). This federal program was initially created by the Herbert Hoover administration and continued during the Roosevelt administration as part of the New Deal. The program was essentially a forerunner to unemployment insurance compensation and public works programs. The FERA offered education classes for the unemployed in addition to relief and public works programs.

Thanks to FERA, Merlin Bishop taught in Detroit and Roy Reuther in Flint. Both men maintained and built contacts with grass roots workers in the plants who wanted to organize unions. Roy Reuther was an excellent teacher. He taught Flint workers labor history, public speaking, and other important lessons. He eventually moved on to Brookwood College in New York as an instructor for future labor leaders. During these years and for the remainder of his life, Roy was known for his warmth and humanity. Besides being devoted to Walter's and labor's cause, Roy was known as the most approachable Reuther brother. Of the brothers, he was the one people could talk to about an issue or problem that they might not be willing to take to Walter or Victor.[110]

Walter and Victor Reuther returned from their around-the-world trip in the late fall of 1935. After some campus lecture tours, the two brothers found themselves at Brookwood, visiting Roy and the school's president, Tucker Smith. Besides being a labor college, Brookwood's other mission was teaching pacifism. Victor took a Brookwood job lecturing around the country about the dangers of war.

Walter became active in labor activities. He traveled to Detroit and then marched in picket lines in Akron, Ohio, where Goodyear workers had begun one of the first successful sit-down strikes, and then returned to Detroit. At this time, Brookwood was considering opening up a Detroit campus and wanted Walter to run it. This proved to be a defining moment in Walter's life. He loved the idea of running a labor college. To do this, however, would take him out of what all three brothers considered the action of organizing the unorganized. Brookwood was trying to train labor leaders, not organize workers into unions. If Walter took the Brookwood job, he would be an academic, not an organizer. Walter needed to decide whether he wanted to be an academic leader or a labor leader. Both Victor and Roy (and possibly Walter's future wife, May Wolf) convinced Walter to be part of the labor movement.[111]

**Harry Bennett's men prepare to attack Walter Reuther
and others at the Battle of the Overpass**

After returning to Detroit, Walter also discovered that Ford had blacklisted him. He could not get a job anywhere. The outstanding tool and die maker could not even find a job on an assembly line or as a janitor in any Detroit factory. Instead, he tried to educate and organize working people as a self-appointed activist. In a short time, he developed a relationship with a small west side local union, the Ternstedt Local 86. Timing is everything, and right about this time, the UAW was holding its second convention in South Bend. Walter, being the only Ternstedt worker interested and prepared to pay his way to South Bend, attended the convention as a Local 86 delegate. It was at this 1936 UAW convention that the union broke away from the AFL, joined the CIO, and elected Homer Martin as president. The UAW essentially recreated itself, and Reuther was right in the middle of several key convention issues. He was a frequent speaker at the convention and involved in several debates on the convention floor. By the end of the convention, he had made a significant impression, and the delegates elected him to the UAW Executive Board.[112]

As 1936 ended, all eyes of those interested in the future of the labor movement turned to Flint. There, the fledgling UAW took on General Motors, the giant of the automobile industry, in the famous Flint Sit-Down Strike. Roy and Victor, who had returned to Detroit, became UAW organizers. Roy was working for the International UAW and was sent to Flint, territory he knew well from his FERA days. Victor worked at the Kelsey Hayes plant, where he, Walter, George Edwards, and Merlin Bishop organized that plant in early December. Roy and another UAW activist named Robert Travis were the chief strategists of the Flint Sit-Down Strike. Shortly after the strike began, the International UAW asked Victor to join Roy in Flint. Victor quickly moved into Roy's Flint apartment, where he became famous operating the union sound car that rallied workers repeatedly to support the union during numerous battles with police and company security.[113]

January 1937 was probably the most hectic and significant time in UAW history. Walter played a supporting role in the Flint strike, but he was spending most of his time trying to organize the west side Local 174 into a huge power base. Of course, while all this was going on Emil Mazey and Dick Frankensteen were organizing Briggs. Union activity was breaking out all over Michigan. This activity might not have been successful without the support of the International UAW and the CIO, but the support of the rank-and-file workers in the plant made the difference. They started the Flint strike, they risked their jobs for the union they wanted to create, and they staffed the picket lines or stayed in the plant—all at great personal risk. By the spring of 1937, the UAW and other unions organized plants throughout Michigan and the country.

In May of 1937, Walter Reuther and Dick Frankensteen were involved in one of the most famous battles in labor history, the Battle of the Overpass at the Ford Motor Company's Rouge plant in Dearborn. Dick Frankensteen, the International UAW's point man in charge of organizing Ford, and Reuther, as president of the Local 174, organized a mass leafleting campaign. UAW locals, including the Local 212 Flying Squadron, participated. Before the organized leafleting began, Reuther, Frankensteen, UAW organizer Bob Kantor, and UAW east side regional

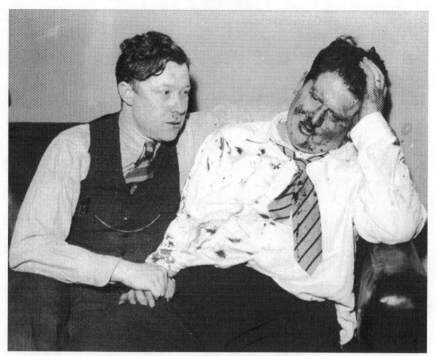

Reuther and Frankensteen immediately after the Battle of the Overpass

director Jack Kennedy posed for photos on the overpass connecting the Rouge plant to a parking lot. Originally built by Ford, the overpass was considered public property, as the company had leased the bridge to a local public transit agency. Harry Bennett sent his Ford Service thugs out to remove the men from Ford's "private" property. The four labor men, with Reuther and Frankensteen specifically targeted by the Ford men, were beaten and forcibly removed from the bridge. Reuther and Frankensteen were dragged down each step of the overpass's stairway.

It was a public relations disaster for Ford, as a *Detroit News* photographer captured the beating of the labor leaders. The photos of the attack and its immediate aftermath were published around the world. This attack on Walter Reuther made him one of the most recognizable labor leaders in Detroit and the country.[114]

Walter went through 1938 as a key UAW leader, but he was a long way from being the UAW president. Still, after the April 1938 Federal Screw strike, his reputation as a strong militant leader was further enhanced. These actions demonstrated that he was not afraid of a company, the

Roy, Victor and Walter Reuther at 1937 UAW convention

company's security, or the police. He had repeatedly demonstrated his militancy and, as a result, was finding more supporters. At the same time, he was also making enemies.

. . . .

On April 9, 1938, not even a week after the successful conclusion of the Federal Screw strike, Walter and May Reuther (Walter married May Wolf, a teacher's union organizer, in March 1936) hosted a small birthday party for Victor Reuther's wife, Sophie, in their second-story apartment on La Salle Street, just south of Davison Avenue. Also in attendance were Victor, Roy, George Edwards, Frank Marquart (who eventually became the education director for Local 212), Tucker Smith (the president of Brookwood), a UAW member and supporter named Al King, and several others. May ordered Chinese food.

Their discussion centered on UAW politics. George Edwards was in the process of ridiculing some of the Jay Lovestone people who were supporting Homer Martin when there was a knock on the door. Assuming it was the food, Victor and Sophie moved toward the door. As

Victor opened the door, two men burst into the room with guns drawn. They told everyone to put their hands up in the air.

One of the men, the bigger of the two, said, "All right, Red, you're coming with us."

Their intent was to kidnap Walter. Everyone realized that this was deadly serious; if Walter left with these men, he might never return. George Edwards said, "You're not getting him out of here. You may shoot some of us, but you won't get out yourselves."

That seemed to create some uncertainty between the two thugs. The shorter man went over to Walter, pulled a blackjack out of his pocket, and began beating Walter, who slumped to the floor with his hands raised, trying to ward off the blows. A lamp was broken and a glass coffee table smashed, but Walter was able to grab the blackjack and pull it out of his assailant's hands. Then Sophie threw a wine bottle at the gunman, creating more confusion. In the turmoil, Al King slipped out a window and leaped from the second story of the apartment. He was able to shout for help. The gunmen got worried and left.

The police were called, and the incident was public. Initially, some of Walter's detractors said this was just a Reuther publicity stunt, but within days of the attack, the assailants were identified and captured. The Ford Motor Company, under John Gillespie, had recently employed one of the assailants. Gillespie was the same man Harry Bennett had sent to get Dick Frankensteen to settle the Briggs strike, and he negotiated for Bennett during the Kelsey Hayes strike as well. A jury quickly acquitted the intruders, but there was no doubt in the minds of the people at the party that this was a Harry Bennett hit.

Years later, after the UAW had organized Ford, Walter received a telephone call asking for a meeting. The call was one of the assailants. The man apologized for the attack. He indicated that he was following Harry Bennett's orders and hoped there were no hard feelings. Walter did not accept the apology.[115]

. . . .

Walter Reuther moved through 1938 continuing to be immersed in UAW factional battles. Near the end of the year, he learned some devastating news. Homer Martin had begun secret negotiations with Harry Bennett. If successful, Harry Bennett would essentially be in control of the UAW. Martin must be stopped … but how?

CHAPTER 10

HOMER MARTIN HAS TO BE STOPPED

Many times while driving the streets of Detroit in the late 1950s and early 1960s, we heard that two people were essentially wicked and hurt the working men and women of the UAW. The first was Homer Martin. The second was Harry Bennett. Bennett was Henry Ford's right-hand man who ran the company's service department, which was the company's paramilitary operation. We learned that Harry Bennett used every trick in the book to beat the UAW and anyone or anything that Henry Ford did not like. He hired thugs, worked with the underworld and may have been involved in murder. To a young boy, he did not seem like the kind of person that Henry Ford, the inventor of the assembly line and the founder of Greenfield Village, would hire. The only thing that could be worse than Harry Bennett and Homer Martin is if they teamed up to work together, which is exactly what they did.

THE FIRST TWO YEARS OF Homer Martin's UAW presidency had been disastrous for the UAW. His lack of leadership, as exhibited during the GM Sit-Down Strike, was obvious to many. His suspicion of colleagues such as Walter Reuther and UAW staffers such as Emil Mazey, Victor Reuther, Roy Reuther, and many others raised questions about his own loyalties. His apparent paranoia over different ideas and other factions in the UAW also spread a sense of unease.

In 1936, the UAW's membership was 27,000. After the successful organization of General Motors, Chrysler, Briggs, and many other companies, the 1937 UAW membership surged to 232,000. By 1938, however, the membership dropped to 144,000.[116] Something was wrong. To be sure, the 1937–38 recession put many people into a position of choosing work (and the company) over unions. Still, the primary answer pointed to the leadership at the International UAW headquarters. Workers did not want to belong to a union if all they saw were internal power struggles, factionalism, and other problems within their own organization.

By mid-1937, the constant bickering with UAW Executive Board members was public knowledge and devastating for the union. At one board meeting, Martin grew so frustrated with a debate between himself and Walter Reuther that he physically attacked Reuther to end the discussion.[117] Many on the board became disenchanted and evolved into his opposition. Ambitious men in their own right, some board members felt they had the leadership skills and the necessary constituencies to take Martin's place. Chief among them were Walter Reuther and Dick Frankensteen. Martin's various attacks, verbal and otherwise, offended other UAW members. The Communist-hating Jay Lovestone became more of an influence with Martin during these times. Many UAW Board members viewed Lovestone's reputation and his influence with concern. Among union officials with Socialist and Communist backgrounds or those whose political base included Communists and others from the political left, Lovestone's influence with Martin was an anathema.

As 1937 turned into 1938, local unions such as Local 212 continued their efforts to organize. These men and women inside the UAW's locals were the heart of the UAW. Many, such as Emil Mazey, tried to stay out of the political quagmire at the International UAW headquarters, but the factionalism at the top led to factionalism inside the locals. There was no doubt that after Mazey became president of Local 212, he was in firm control. Yet in a local the size of Local 212 (with about 20,000 members), there were always political factions that led to challenges. Many of Mazey's opposition were former Ralph Knox supporters and aligned with Homer Martin. Others in the Local 212 membership were sympathetic to the Communist Party and were on Mazey's political left. And of course, some people were just opposed to Mazey, a young man who sometimes seemed too sure of himself. Nonetheless, Mazey worked hard to create an independent local, develop a strong flying squadron, address the day-to-day grievances of the Local 212 membership, and avoid entanglements with the International UAW.[118]

. . . .

In late August 1937, the UAW held its third convention, this time in Milwaukee. By this time, the union had broken into two specific caucuses or political parties. There was the Progressive Caucus, led by Homer Martin and Dick Frankensteen. Then, to counter the Progressive Caucus, the Unity Caucus was formed, headed by a loose-knit and fragile alliance of Socialists, Communists, and other anti-Martin groups. Martin's poor leadership skills and paranoia over other competent labor leaders created the Unity Caucus, as various UAW factions were convinced that Homer Martin was destroying the UAW. For many UAW officials, it was unthinkable to sit by and watch the destruction of the one organization that had finally become effective in organizing industrial workers in the automobile industry. Thus the Unity Caucus brought rival groups together because of their distaste and distrust of Homer Martin—being anti-Martin was the common denominator of the Unity Caucus.[119]

The Martin-led Progressive Caucus lashed back at this opposition by simply referring to anyone in the Unity Caucus as Communists or "Reds." Such a charge was persuasive to many regular UAW members who did not know Unity Caucus leaders. Unity Caucus leaders such as the Reuther brothers, George Edwards, and Emil Mazey were openly called Communists or Reds.[120] The great irony, of course, was that each of these people had paid his dues as a union front-line leader. They acknowledged their Socialist leanings, but as trade unionists, they led the battles to organize the UAW. Martin had never really led an organizing fight. Walter Reuther, Victor Reuther, and George Edwards fought to organize Kelsey Hayes. Roy and Victor Reuther gained national attention by leading the GM Sit-Down Strike. And Emil Mazey led the fight to organize Briggs and then formed one of the most effective flying squadrons in the union. These men may have been Socialists, but they were not Communists; their loyalty was first and foremost to the UAW (unlike Communist members who were required to take their orders from the Communist Party organization). Much of the membership who knew them understood this; still, Homer Martin was the incumbent president and held all the institutional power. The result of all this was a union split wide open.[121]

The 1937 Milwaukee convention might have torn the UAW apart. It was John L. Lewis, the great bushy-eyebrowed labor leader from the United Mine Workers and the founder and president of the CIO, that held the UAW together. He was near the zenith of his power and had such magnetism that when he came to the convention, both sides listened. Lewis saw the infant union falling apart, and he preached compromise and unity. He argued that there had to be a place at the UAW Executive Board table for all sides. At the end of the convention, Martin's Progressives held sixteen UAW Executive Board spots; the Unity Caucus held eight. Frankensteen and R. J. Thomas, from the Jefferson Chrysler local, became new vice presidents.[122]

Within weeks of the Milwaukee convention, Homer Martin broke the fragile agreement between the Progressive and Unity caucuses over the issue of wildcat strikes at GM plants in Pontiac. He then had Lovestone followers take over the editorial content of local union newspapers like the *Voice of Local 212.*

At about the same time, Martin fired a number of Unity Caucus international staffers, including Victor Reuther, Robert Kanter (who was with Walter Reuther and Frankensteen during the Battle of the Overpass in May 1937), and Stanley Novak. These well-respected UAW leaders had led some of the toughest strikes in the UAW's short history, and they were affiliated with the Unity Caucus. Many of these staffers were replaced by men and women supported by Jay Lovestone, the former Communist Party advisor to Martin. From a local union standpoint, solid international staffers were replaced by young ideologues. Martin also announced that leadership of the Ford organization effort was shifting from Walter Reuther to his ally on the UAW Executive Board, Dick Frankensteen.[123]

. . . .

The Unity Caucus soon experienced a shattering internal blow from its own membership. Trust between the Reuthers, Mazey, and other Socialists with the Communist members of the Unity Caucus was shaken forever by what was known as the "double cross" at the 1938 Michigan CIO convention.

In the early spring of 1938, Dick Frankensteen lost his influence with Homer Martin, another sign of Martin's insecurity. At the same time, the Communist faction of the Unity Caucus was growing apprehensive over the power of the Reuther brothers and began wooing the influential Frankensteen. At the first Michigan CIO convention held in Lansing, Walter Reuther was a potential candidate for president but withdrew his candidacy with the understanding that the Unity Caucus would support Victor Reuther for secretary-treasurer. Frankensteen and the Communists within the Unity Caucus, however, cut their own deal in support of another candidate, and Victor was badly defeated. Reuther, Mazey, George Edwards, and others (including Ken Morris) were furious at this double-cross by the Unity Caucus's Communist faction and vowed to end their relationship with it. Yet they could not break up the Unity Caucus, again because their common adversary was Homer Martin. They knew that to save the union, Homer Martin had to be stopped. This action by the Communists left a bitter taste in the mouths of the moderate or more right-leaning members of the Unity Caucus.[124]

. . . .

With Frankensteen on the outs with Martin, Martin's strength on the UAW Executive Board diminished. Frankensteen was making a bold move for leadership of his union. He knew that Martin's time had run out, and in all likelihood, a new UAW president would be elected in 1939. He wanted that position over Reuther or anybody else, and he believed that his new friendship with the Communists might make the difference.

The Frankensteen split with Martin was extremely public. On May 25, 1938, the *Detroit News* reported that Homer Martin dumped Frankensteen as head of the Ford organizing effort and then appointed the five area regional directors, including Walter Reuther, to head the Ford organizing drive.

Martin then implemented a desperate strategy to get rid of his opposition on the UAW Executive Board. At the request of John L. Lewis, the UAW Executive Board held its June 1938 meeting in Washington, DC. Lewis hoped to negotiate peace in the critically important autoworker's union. Martin, apparently feeling deep anxiety regarding his opposition, made an executive decision to suspend five UAW Executive Board members: Wyndham Mortimer, Dick Frankensteen, George Addes, Ed Hall, and Walter Wells. Martin argued that he had to purge these elected union officials in order to fight Communists. In sympathy and support of the Unity Caucus members, Walter Reuther and several other board members chose to join the suspended members and walked out of the board meeting.[125]

. . . .

When Reuther returned from the Washington board meeting, first his wife and then his brothers and others such as George Edwards castigated him on his decision to support those from the Communist left wing who had double-crossed the Socialists in Lansing just a few months earlier. These people had had it with the so-called Unity Caucus and their so-called Communist allies.[126] Later in the year, in an effort to demonstrate his own independence and to become more mainstream, Reuther resigned from the Socialist Party and began to purge the Communist influence from Local 174. He did this not as Martin did—by simply dismissing the Communist supporters. Instead, Reuther waited for the next local elections and did not support their reelection to posts within the west side local. In other words, he used the tools of democracy instead of those of an autocracy.[127]

During the summer and after Martin had suspended the board

members, John L. Lewis placed the union under CIO receivership. Lewis and the top CIO leaders felt it was crucial to keep the union together until its next convention, in 1939. Lewis appointed two top CIO leaders, Philip Murray and Sidney Hillman, to oversee the affairs of the UAW. Lewis also reinstated the expelled executive board members, and an uneasy truce existed.[128]

Then Homer Martin pulled out of his hat a strategy that might have been brilliant for him personally but a disaster for the UAW. The strategy ultimately backfired and cemented Martin's ruin as a UAW leader. Martin began negotiating secretly with Harry Bennett about the organization of Ford workers by the UAW. Martin believed the successful organization of Ford would make him a hero with the union membership and unbeatable at the next convention.

Harry Bennett realized that there was not much chance of Ford winning the National Labor Relations Board (NLRB) unfair labor practices case the UAW had filed. He knew what his company thugs had done to keep the union out of Ford. He saw a way out of his labor problems by taking advantage of a weak Homer Martin and a weak UAW.

Beginning in the summer of 1938, Bennett had his man John Gillespie convene a series of secret meetings with Homer Martin. As the months progressed, Bennett, through Gillippse, outmaneuvered Martin by negotiating items that were essentially giveaways by the company, but Martin felt he had negotiated big wins for the Ford membership. Bennett's big issue was to get the UAW to drop its NLRB case against Ford in exchange for Ford recognition of the union. By November, Martin had negotiated a deal with Ford. Under the deal, Ford would only recognize the UAW if Martin maintained his presidency of the UAW. The deal also required the UAW to leave the CIO and return to the AFL.

When Martin informed the UAW Executive Board of his secret negotiations with Ford in the fall of 1938, the board balked. Board members saw this as secret negotiations with the most despicable of all men, Harry Bennett. They saw that Homer Martin had essentially negotiated a relationship that simply created a company union, and the UAW, in effect, would lose its independence. The Bennett/Martin deal was repugnant to the UAW Executive Board and the UAW rank and file.[129]

Years later, in his book about his years with Henry Ford, Harry Bennett admitted that after Martin lost his power in the UAW, he and Henry Ford felt "guilty" about old Homer and felt they should help him out. Bennett wrote that he found Martin work and the Ford Motor Company bought him a completely furnished house in Detroit. Homer Martin was essentially on the Ford payroll.[130]

．．．．．．．．．．．．．．

As 1938 ended, the internal UAW governance was in shambles. Martin and his Progressive Caucus had lost its power. The Unity Caucus was fractured. Local leaders such as Emil Mazey were watching their union disintegrate. John L. Lewis knew that Homer Martin had to be eliminated.

And the manufacturers? They loved it. They again felt confident that the UAW-CIO would implode. They knew that unions were here to stay, but they saw a new opportunity to see a weaker, less militant union replace the UAW-CIO.

CHAPTER 11

MARTIN HAS RESORTED TO RED-BAITING AND GANGSTERISM

During our drives, Dad usually had the radio on. He listened to WJR, "The Great Voice of the Great Lakes," a station known for news and old-fashioned standards. Perry Como, Frank Sinatra, Doris Day, eh! Soon the culture wars took over, and I made sure I got into the car first and punched the radio station button to WXYZ or CKLW, to listen to rock and roll. I got to hear about ten seconds of a song before Dad switched back to WJR and the Andrew Sisters. I did not realize then the power of WJR. Its massive radio signal truly did reach out to Michigan and much of the Midwest. I knew that Walter Reuther announced his five hundred planes a day concept on a national radio hookup that probably included WJR. I had no idea that our good friend Emil Mazey used the same WJR to reach Local 212 and other UAW members regarding the battle between the Homer Martin faction and the UAW-CIO faction.

AT THE START OF 1939, the International UAW was in disarray, but Local 212 was one of the strongest and best-organized locals within the union. As the year played out, Emil Mazey and Local 212 proved to be major actors in ensuring that the UAW-CIO maintained itself as a viable labor organization. It was also the year that Ken Morris established himself as a Local 212 leader.

The uneasy peace between the Homer Martin forces and the CIO forces fell apart. Martin's support on the UAW Executive Board dwindled to just five. The CIO forces, led by George Addes, Ed Hall, Walter Reuther, and now R. J. Thomas, had had enough of watching Homer Martin cozy up to Harry Bennett. Then there was his Red-baiting and his infatuation with the AFL. The anti-Martin faction moved out of the International UAW Griswold Building headquarters, and the UAW turmoil continued.

The two factions of the union split forever. Homer Martin left the UAW-CIO to form his own autoworkers union. He argued that he still enjoyed the majority support of the regular members. He felt he was forming a more middle-of-the-road union that was removed from the radical politics of the CIO. Meanwhile, the UAW-CIO argued that they had the more seasoned UAW leaders and represented the trade unionists in the factories. Emil Mazey, Ken Morris, and other key leaders of Local 212 stayed with the UAW-CIO.

. . . .

In the 1930s, the real power in the UAW was at the grassroots local union level. This was particularly true during this period of internal strife inside the UAW. As 1939 began, Emil Mazey and Local 212 demonstrated how a single local union helped save the UAW-CIO.

In late January, Mazey, frustrated with the factional fighting of the International UAW, decided that he had to communicate directly to the regular members of his Local 212 and the UAW in general. With the approval of the Local 212 executive board, he did what was common for powerful and often wealthy people of this period to do in order to reach the public—he bought radio time. He addressed the entire city on WJR on January 23 to explain to everyday UAW members what all the factionalism was about and why it had to end.[131]

Mazey began his talk by explaining that the purpose of this address was to help Local 212 members and UAW members across Michigan understand the factional problems in the UAW and the steps necessary to protect the union. He then slammed Homer Martin:

> Homer Martin and his "rump" group of four [UAW] Executive Board members have lent strength to the enemies of organized labor and to the employers. In collaboration with Ford officials they are attempting to set up [dual unions] in the automobile industry.... Martin has resorted to the most vicious union-busting tactics known in the history of the labor movement, Red-baiting and gangsterism. Martin's most recent cry of "communist" and "red" has been leveled at the International Executive Board. If the Board members are Communists at the present time, it would stand to reason that they must have been Communists when they were members of a Martin Executive Board Caucus only a few short weeks ago.... Martin has recently organized caucuses within Local 212 and is attempting to break up our union by calling its officers "communists".... The La Follett Committee in its many lengthy reports brought out conclusively that red-baiting was the successful method used [by] stoolpigeon and spy agencies in their efforts to stymie the growth of labor organizations.... The manufacturers and reactionaries have given Martin considerable support in the past few days because of his company union policies.

Mazey then linked Homer Martin to the UAW's number one enemy, Harry Bennett:

> [Martin] has been publicly applauded by such notorious union-busters as Harry Bennett, the head of the Ford Service Department, who viciously assaulted and attacked UAW members who were peacefully attempting to distribute Union literature at the Ford River Rouge Plant on May 26, 1937.... It is difficult to believe that a loyal union leader could possibly be so naïve as to trust

a man who had used every method known in labor history to stave off unionism at Fords.

Mazey concluded by discussing the need to address UAW unity in the future and look to the UAW Convention a few months away:

> In this difficult period, we must maintain the solidarity of our organization in the shops; must rally the support of all union members, despite disrupters and company stooges. An important task facing our union is preparing for a convention to be held in Cleveland, beginning March 20, 1939. At this Convention we can take steps to guard against the recurrence of factionalism and dictatorship in our union.

Emil's address laid out the problems of the UAW civil war on a national level. Now the battlefront took place in union halls and local union elections across the country.[132]

. . . .

Everyone knew that Ken Morris was a hard worker who continuously volunteered for all types of activities. He had always been a shop steward and had been the assistant editor of the Local's newspaper since its inception. Now Ken was running for local-wide office in the February election. The results were described in the February 19, 1939, *United Automobile Worker, Local 212 Edition*, probably written by Ken:

> Local 212, the most powerful unit of the [UAW], in its recent election of officers held on February 6th and 7th, once more placed strong, militant and aggressive leaders at the head of the organization … Emil Mazey; incumbent took the lead in the presidential race….
> Ken Morris, Assistant Editor, became a candidate for the position of Guide in the opposition to the incumbent "Kid Paducah." [Ken] started to gain slowly over a field of four candidates and was more than three hundred

(300) in the lead when the voting was completed in all the plants except Mack Avenue; from that time on he piled up a two to one lead over his nearest opponent, thereby enabling him to receive the handshakes of congratulations from all his opponents.[133]

While Ken soft-pedaled his election as guide, there is little doubt that it was extremely important to him. In 1935, he came to Detroit with nothing but a new name and a suitcase. In less than four years, he had gone from being a nobody at a huge manufacturing facility to winning an election of the entire Local 212 membership. While it was not clear exactly what a guide did, except bring guest speakers to the podium during union meetings, it was a local-wide position that placed him on Local 212's executive board. In addition, Ken was also elected a delegate to his first UAW Convention—another local-wide election. His hard work; his volunteering for any assignment; and his skills at typing, shorthand, and handling grievances had all paid off. Ken was a bona fide leader of Local 212 and felt tremendous satisfaction at this acceptance.

At about this same time, Ken learned what it was like to be part of the Local 212 leadership team. One day during those long winter months of 1939, Emil Mazey contacted Ken and asked him to accompany him to a meeting with the UAW's secretary-treasurer, George Addes. A dark-haired Syrian from Toledo, Addes was a strong autoworkers activist since the early 1930s. A truly respected labor leader, he enjoyed support from across the UAW, but his most significant base of support came from the Communist elements inside the UAW. Addes was not a Communist, but this element could approach him on any issue and therefore reciprocated with their loyalty.

The Addes meeting took place in the booth of a drugstore on the ground level of the Hoffman Building, off Woodward Avenue, just north of downtown. Addes told the Local 212 men that the International UAW-CIO had no money and no funds to finance the upcoming convention in Cleveland. Mazey, who had guessed the purpose of the meeting, had a solution in mind. Unlike many other local unions, Local 212 had a high percentage of actual dues-paying members, and this made them financially secure. The work of the union stewards, the flying squadron members, and the numerous "union dues" drives had proven effective, thus Local 212 could help the International UAW union. Mazey offered to provide the International a six-month advance of monthly dues of Local 212 members. This large sum of money helped fund the International UAW through the convention and provide payroll for staff. Local 212, and several other big UAW locals that provided similar advances, made the difference. Without their financial support, the UAW-CIO might well have collapsed and Harry Bennett and Fay Taylor would have been negotiating with Homer Martin's UAW-AFL.[134]

. . . .

One Friday evening in February, Ken Morris, acting in his role of a captain of the Local 212 Flying Squadron, received a telephone call. Local 235, the Chevrolet Gear and Axle plant, needed help. On Saturday, the local was going to have a membership meeting, and the Local 235 leadership received word that Homer Martin and his entourage were planning to crash the meeting. Local 235's membership meeting was taking place just prior to their voting for delegates to the UAW-CIO Cleveland convention, and there was great concern that Martin and his AFL contingent would successfully disrupt and hijack the meeting.

Local 235 was located on the east side, just off Harper Avenue. Like the Briggs local, it was a huge plant, but unlike the Briggs local, its politics were a bit less certain. Would the local stay in the UAW-CIO or choose to follow Homer Martin and the UAW-AFL? About a half hour before the Saturday meeting was to begin, eight cars of the Local 212 Flying Squadron showed up at the hall. Some thirty-five men dressed in black jackets, Local 212 army-style caps, and armbands walked into the partially filled hall. As they entered, there seemed to be a great sense of relief from the Local 235 membership. Ken Morris did not feel as if they were trying to intimidate or strong-arm anyone to take a position. Instead, he felt the Local 212 Flying Squadron was providing a sense of security and safety to the members of Local 235, and the proof of that was in the positive comments and good-natured kidding that went on between the Local 212 Flying Squadron and the Local 235 membership.

The Local 212 Flying Squadron members positioned themselves in small groups throughout the hall. When the hall was filled to capacity, the Local 235 leadership began the session. On the podium preparing to speak were anti-Martinite UAW Executive Board members Dick Frankensteen and Ed Hall. The head of the newly formed Michigan CIO, Adolph Germer, was also waiting to speak.

A disturbance broke out at the main entrance to the hall as Homer Martin and his entourage of heavyset men pushed their way into the meeting. As the Local 235 sergeant at arms pushed back, with the assistance of the Local 212 Flying Squadron, Martin said that as president of the UAW, he was requesting to speak at the meeting. Word of the request got to the podium, and the chairman of the meeting asked the crowd, "Should we let Martin in?"

Someone in the audience moved to let Martin in but said that his henchmen needed to stay at the door. The membership adopted the motion. Martin made his way forward, and ignoring the motion, his men followed. The Local 235 men, aided by the Local 212 Flying Squadron, repelled Martin's bodyguards and pushed them out of the hall.

Martin walked to the podium carrying a briefcase. Based on past experience, there was probably a handgun in the briefcase or stuck in his belt. Martin stepped up on the stage, and from the crowd came catcalls and other jeers. Frankensteen, Hall, and Germer spoke. Then Martin had his turn at the microphone, and in the midst of jeers from the loud and noisy crowd, he became frustrated and started the old argument that all those against him were "Reds." As he finished his comments, he shouted into the mike, "All good union men, follow me!" and he headed toward the exit door. A few of the more conservative men in the hall, men who were good union members who obviously were not happy with the way the meeting had been conducted, rose to leave, and some others seemed uncertain of what to do.

At that moment, a young man named George Merrelli, who had been aligned with Martin and the conservative Catholic forces inside the local, moved quickly to grab a floor microphone near the front of the hall. He yelled into it, "Don't go out, fellows! Stay here—stay with the CIO!" Thanks to those few but effective words, only a handful of men left with Martin. The CIO was a clear winner that night, and the

Local 212 Flying Squadron had helped create an environment where the meeting could move forward. It was the first time Ken Morris saw George Merrelli, but sixteen years later, their rise in the UAW would be in partnership.

For now, two big UAW locals on Detroit's east side demonstrated that Martin was out of UAW leadership and that the UAW-CIO appeared to be the dominant and favored organization of the people. But questions continued. Who would rise to leadership in the Martin vacuum, and what effect would all this have on the collective bargaining process?[135]

. . . .

Just a little west of Detroit's Grand Circus Park sits the abandoned Moose Hall, a building that from the outside has not changed much in nearly seventy years. It was here, in early March 1939, that some people believed a new UAW would be born. These people hoped this new UAW was to take the place of the more militant UAW-CIO. This was where Homer Martin planned to reaffiliate the UAW with the AFL. The real question was whether the regular members intended to support the man who was still technically the head of the UAW.

As both the *New York Times* and *Time* magazine reported, the Homer Martin convention was disorganized and poorly attended. Top UAW leadership had refused to join him, instead opting to stay with the UAW-CIO. At best, there were 350 delegates claiming to represent the UAW membership, yet no top International UAW or local union leaders attended. The Martin convention was a flop, yet he maintained an illusion that his UAW was still the bargaining agent to auto industry employers.[136]

. . . .

The 1939 UAW-CIO Convention in Cleveland essentially determined the leadership of the UAW throughout the war years. The power behind the scene was again John L. Lewis. Representing Lewis at the convention were Sidney Hillman and Phil Murray. Hillman was the well-respected leader of the Amalgamated Clothing Workers of America, and Murray was president of the United Steel Workers. Both men served as vice presidents of the CIO. At the Cleveland convention, both men usually holed up in their hotel rooms, monitoring the proceedings. Their assignment was to make sure this regenerated union would not blow itself up with new internal fighting.

There was a new spirit in the delegates that streamed into Cleveland. These were primarily young men and a few women who felt they had vanquished an evil force from the UAW. Homer Martin was gone, and the feeling was that the UAW could grow without the internal strife from the past. But also, in one quick moment, the internal politics of the UAW changed. With Martin and his very conservative forces out of the UAW leadership, the political center of the UAW moved left. Socialist and Communist forces had more sway than ever before, and sharp conflict continued. This could be seen in Local 212, where the majority of the delegates were pro-CIO. But now what? Who would these delegates vote for? It appeared in Local 212 that about 60 percent of the delegation was comprised of Mazey forces, which now meant more centrist support for people like Walter Reuther. However, about 40 percent of the local were even further left. They tended to support George Addes, the effective yet left-leaning leader whose support came from the Communists within the union.[137]

The convention was long, eleven days, and meetings took place from early morning until late at night. Ken had never experienced anything like it. There were meetings of each of the committees; in particular, the Constitution Committee met continually. They recommended many changes in the UAW constitution, with a special emphasis on limiting the power of the UAW president so that no future president could arbitrarily dismiss other UAW Executive Board members. Of course, it was one thing to agree to a concept but quite another getting the concept down into constitutional language. This took time, as many self-appointed wordsmiths questioned each proposed word and sentence being offered and then offered their own language, which created more debate.[138]

The convention met at Cleveland's civic center, but the hot spot for action was the convention's nearby headquarters, the old Hollenden Hotel. Ken and the Local 212 delegation stayed across the street at the Olmstead Hotel. There were delegates, particularly in the evening, walking the streets and chanting "CIO … CIO." Some chanted for their favorites for president; George Addes's and Walter Reuther's names could be heard on the Cleveland streets.[139]

It was during this convention that Ken Morris became part of a new caucus. This caucus was to become a major force in the union and eventually the majority political organization within the UAW to this day. The names evolved over the years—initially it was the "Right-Wing Caucus," then the "Reuther Caucus," and today it is the "Administrative Caucus." Why the Right-Wing Caucus? These were the centrists of the UAW, and they were politically right of George Addes and his left-wing supporters. The leaders included Walter Reuther; Emil Mazey; Bill Marshall, president of the Chrysler Jefferson plant's Local 7; Tracy Doll, the president of the Hudson plant's Local 154; and many other leaders. It was a force to be reckoned with but at the time was not the majority force within the UAW.

There was serious talk about Walter running for president. But it was George Addes, supported by the strong contingent of Communist or Communist-leaning delegates, who was probably the strongest potential candidate. Then there was R. J. Thomas. Thomas was known as a "meat and potatoes" leader. He enjoyed playing poker at night, smoking a cigar and having a drink, rather than attending a caucus discussing UAW policy issues. On more than one occasion, Ken was with some of his buddies as they moved from one hotel room to another. Drinks and food were available in these hospitality suites. Occasionally, he ended up in a room where R. J. Thomas, Dick Frankensteen, and others were playing poker. Ken was amazed at the amount of money on the table.[140] He could not imagine people risking such money—apparently, Ken's fiscally conservative nature showed at an early age.

Interestingly enough, Dick Frankensteen's name was not mentioned as a serious candidate for UAW president. His influence in the UAW had ebbed. To be sure, Frankensteen continued to be a powerful force in the UAW, but not as a presidential candidate. He tried to run as a candidate on the Addes slate for vice president but ultimately lost his vice presidency and became a board member and a regional director in the Detroit area.

One evening around 11:00, during the latter part of the convention, about fifty to sixty members of the Right-Wing Caucus were meeting in the Olmstead hotel. Local 7's Bill Marshall was chairing the meeting when someone came into the room and announced that Sidney Hillman was meeting with the commies and telling George Addes why he couldn't run for president. Someone else yelled, "Hey, let's go over there." With that, the meeting was over, and the room emptied as the delegates headed across the street to the Hollenden Hotel.

The group moved into a large ballroom and a couple of hundred people were part of an ongoing meeting in a corner of the room. As Ken and the group moved forward, he recognized people who he knew were identified as belonging to the Communist element of the union. Some were good guys; some were people he didn't want anything to do with. Nonetheless, this was the first time he saw them all in a public meeting. Normally, these men objected to strangers busting into the room. Instead, the room was dead silent, except for Sidney Hillman, the surrogate for John L. Lewis, who commanded respect from all factions within the union. Hillman was explaining why their candidate, George Addes, was not to be a candidate for UAW president.

Hillman spoke in a strong voice, with a touch of broken English. He said that the UAW simply couldn't have splinter groups if it was to survive. The CIO worried that an Addes election might make Martin's UAW-AFL more attractive to moderate labor activists. Therefore, he, John L. Lewis, and Phillip Murray could not support the candidacy of George Addes. And for that matter, he added, looking in the direction of those who had just arrived from across the street, they would not support the candidacy of Walter Reuther. Instead, the CIO leadership supported a more neutral candidate, R. J. Thomas. Their announcement not only crushed the Addes caucus members, but it was also a mighty blow to the Right-Wing Caucus.

The meeting was over, and the members of both caucuses silently filed out of the room. John L. Lewis had effectively spoken. There were no more chants in the street for George Addes or Walter Reuther. R. J. Thomas became the new UAW president. Addes continued in the number two spot, as the union's secretary-treasurer. Walter Reuther moved up to become vice president in charge of the General Motors Division.[141]

CHAPTER 12

CLOSE THE GATES; WE'RE ON STRIKE

The news was on while we were in the 1960 Chrysler one day, which meant we were listening to WJR or WWJ. A report indicated that city cutbacks were being introduced and there was to be a dramatic reduction of Detroit's mounted police unit. I said that was terrible, as the horses were so great to look at during parades and other events. Dad looked at me and said I had it wrong, that the police used the mounted police unit for crowd control. He said, with a touch of bitterness in his voice, that the mounted police were used to break up picket lines by crushing and stepping on people. He added that in 1939, many men and women who participated in a Local 212 picket line that encircled Briggs Stadium were pushed to the ground by Detroit's mounted police. From that point on, I had a very different view toward police and the horses they rode.

EMIL AND THE BRIGGS LOCAL union leadership returned home with the hope of renegotiating their contract with Briggs and continuing with building their union. Emil was excited by the convention and excited about a provision John L. Lewis had just won from the mine companies. It was called the union shop, a guarantee that the company would recognize one union and even automatically collect the union dues. Emil thought if they could win this at the collective bargaining table, it would be a grand-slam home run. Imagine not having to run around trying to collect union dues from each plant worker—what a time saver.[142]

They started negotiations with Fay Taylor, who threw the labor leaders an unexpected curve ball. The Briggs man told the collective bargaining committee that the company could not negotiate with them because he did not know if Local 212 represented the majority of the workers. He said that a Martin committee had contacted them and said they represented the workers. Additionally, Briggs refused to negotiate grievances, per the contract, and serious worker complaints began piling up.[143]

Emil and his committee were surprised but not deterred. They knew there were some Martin supporters in the plant, but nothing close to a majority. To try to address the issue, they made up index cards with a statement asking the workers to indicate whether they supported the UAW-CIO as their union representative. Each member favoring the UAW-CIO signed the card. At the next meeting with management, Emil presented Fay Taylor with thousands of cards. Taylor did not recognize the cards, so Emil asked to talk to Mr. Brown, the president of the company. A few minutes later, Brown came into the room. Emil rose and shook hands with the smaller man, and then they sat down to discuss the issue. Brown said he could not accept the cards, as they could have been obtained by Mazey stewards under threat of coercion and intimidation.[144]

Emil and the bargaining committee recognized that negotiation was fruitless. They jumped into their cars and drove over to the International UAW headquarters, now located in a building at 281 West Grand Boulevard, across from the General Motors Building, and met with R. J. Thomas. The committee explained the situation and requested strike authorization.

R. J., in his shirtsleeves and chewing on a cigar, said, "Now look, fellows, you know we don't have any money in the UAW. We are broke; there are no dues coming in. While I might tell you to go ahead and strike, there is no help we can give you."

Emil responded, "We are not asking you for any finances. We have a little money in our treasury, and we have the manpower. All we want is the International UAW's approval to strike Briggs."

Thomas replied that if all the Local 212 members wanted was strike approval and no financial commitment, it was fine with him.[145]

. . . .

Negotiations had stopped, and Local 212 knew that a strike was coming, but they needed a spark, an emotional issue to ensure the membership would follow leadership. The company conveniently gave them one by firing several workers for union activity. Emil demanded their reinstatement. The company refused. The expiration of the contract was May 11, and that day came and went. As the days passed and further negotiations failed to materialize, anticipation of a coming strike was on everyone's mind. The only question was *when*.[146]

Just before nine on the morning of May 22, Ken Morris was working in the press room. He was well known by both management and the workers. Ken was interrupted and told he had a phone call waiting for him. It was Emil, who said, "Shut her down."

Ken, prepared for this instruction, grabbed a small piece of wood as a club and proceeded to walk off his job. He saw Roy Snowden, one of the strong labor men in the plant, and told him to pass the word: "The plant is going to have a sit-down. We are going to have a sit-down, and we are going to stay inside the plant." He then walked by his superintendent and greeted him with a hello. The superintendent, a friendly man, knew instinctively what was going on and did nothing to stop the union guy. Ken, with another fellow, walked outside to the plant gates and told the men, "Close the gates; we're on strike."

Unlike the Flint Sit-Down Strike from two years earlier or the original Briggs strike, this was much more of a *gentlemanly* sit-down strike. The workers stayed in their departments. Superintendents and foremen appeared to stay in the plant. There was no apparent violence, threats, or other forms of coercion used by union or management. Ken stationed himself outside by the guard's hut, making sure the plant entrances were sealed. He knew that Emil and others were talking with Fay Taylor. After a while, a long black limousine pulled up. The guard came to Ken and said, "It's Walter Briggs. He would like to go up to his office." Ken, knowing there was really nothing the old man could do, told the guard to let him pass. From the backseat, the big smiling face of Walter Briggs went by with a nod and a hand wave. He was taken to a special elevator reserved for him, probably because he did not want others to see his disabled form being taken out of the car.

After a few hours, all realized that the strike was going to be long and nasty. Briggs was nervous about the safety and protection of its equipment. The company and Local 212 struck a side deal: the workers would leave the Briggs plants with the assurance that Briggs would not import scabs to start production. The workers filed out of the plant. With the exception of one incident, the stabbing of a worker, which was never fully explained, there was no record of violence. Pickets were set up, and Ken found that he was coordinating much of the strike activity.[147]

The 1939 Briggs strike had begun, and it was a unique strike. In essence, it had three sides. One side, of course, was management, led by Fay Taylor as the chief negotiator for Briggs. The other side was the UAW-CIO, led by Emil Mazey. Then a third side developed, representing the UAW-AFL, or the Homer Martin forces. This was among Homer Martin's last feeble but still dangerous efforts to stay in control of autoworkers.

Within days, the city of Detroit felt the ripple effect of Briggs going down. Soon Chrysler was without the necessary body parts to build cars—then Ford and other companies. First it was fifteen thousand people out of work, then forty thousand, and soon seventy thousand people were idled by the Briggs strike. In 1937, when the UAW struck Briggs, there was only small mention of the disruption in Detroit's local newspapers.[148] The 1939 Briggs strike saw daily front-page coverage by the *Detroit News,* the *Detroit Times,* and the *Detroit Free Press.* Emil was under enormous pressure from the press, the company, and UAW leadership—not to mention his workers who were on strike—but he never seemed to blink.

The most important activity was maintaining picket lines around all of the Briggs plants, including their brand-new plant way out on the northeast corner of Outer Drive and Mound Road. Ken put together brigades of volunteers making picket signs and ensuring that adequate food and other necessary supplies were available for the picketers. Nights would be lonely for these picketers, especially for those out at the Outer Drive plant—a relatively undeveloped area of Detroit.[149]

Soon, Martinite men began harassing the picketers late at night. Normally, a union only had to worry about the Detroit Police Department, company security, or hoodlums hired by a company to break a strike. It was now the splinter group of the UAW-AFL that was physically attacking UAW-CIO picketers. Their objective was to scare the UAW-CIO members and break the strike. Picket line violence occurred nightly during the strike. The Martinites had roving cars that came upon Briggs picketers. Altercations occurred. On other nights, the Local 212 Flying Squadron members retaliated. Battles late at night put men on both sides in the hospital. It was a violent strike, with many believing that the Martin supporters started most altercations, but to be sure, the Local 212 Flying Squadron responded with equal or greater force.[150]

The strike committee was worried. Picketers were being attacked, and the company was not showing signs of weakening. On top of this, Briggs was meeting at the Book Cadillac Hotel with Homer Martin.[151] Would Briggs really recognize Martin over the CIO? A new strategy was needed. At a meeting with local leadership, someone pointed out that Walter Briggs's money and power came from the Briggs Manufacturing Company, but his fame and popularity came from being the owner of the Detroit Tigers and Briggs Stadium. Many people of Detroit did not relate Walter Briggs to a car company—and certainly not to the unfair labor practices for which his company was famous inside the labor movement.

Emil Mazey's team made a decision to hit Walter Briggs where it hurt, an informational picket at Briggs Stadium on Saturday, May 27. On that day, the Detroit Tigers were playing against the St. Louis Browns, a game sure to attract a good crowd. The strike committee had only days to put their plan into action. Assignments given to members included receiving police permission to picket, printing up new picket signs attacking Briggs's unfair labor practices, contacting other local unions seeking support, and much more. Ken took the assignment of operating the boiler room coordinating all strike activity. He worked all night on Friday, making sure that signs, assignments, and other necessary elements for the demonstration were ready.

On Saturday morning, volunteers arrived early and received their assignments. Ken gave them instructions. They were told that this was an informational picket and to avoid either intimidating or obstructing paying customers, to keep the entrances and exits of the stadium open, and to avoid confrontations. An hour before the opening pitch, some two to three thousand picketers encircled the stadium. The crowd was good-natured, with union songs being sung and friendly banter between the baseball fans and picketers.

At roughly this same time, Emil Mazey was in a meeting with the Detroit police chief and the county prosecutor. They told him that it would be illegal for the march to begin. They said that it would be a secondary picket, and that would be illegal. Emil responded by saying that the police had already granted approval for the demonstration. It is not clear exactly what happened, except that their plans continued. It is entirely possible that there simply was not the time to stop a march that was already beginning.

What happened next and who started the disturbance first was never clear. Nonetheless, the *Detroit News* called the informational picket a riot. As the pickets continued their peaceful picket line, mixed in with the approximately eighteen thousand people who attended the game, the mounted police moved in. A police inspector announced that if the group did not disburse, the police would charge. A moment later, one of the demonstrators yelled, "Pull that cop off his horse." Everything went downhill from there. Women demonstrators stuck the horses with hairpins. Demonstrators and police knocked one another to the ground. After the battle, Detroit Lieutenant Hugh Meyers said that he had told the union members they could picket and added, "I did not know until the mounted men arrived that the picketing had been banned." After the hour-long melee, police arrested eleven picketers, including Bill Mazey. The story was all over the front pages.[152]

With so much bad publicity, plus feeling the economic pain of the strike, Briggs decided to come to the table. And as in the 1937 Briggs strike, Ford decided that their production lines had been down too long and it was time to put an end to the strike.[153] Fay Taylor announced that

Local 212 activist Joe Ferris being arrested by Detroit police. A few days later, Ferris was shot by a Homer Martin supporter.

he was prepared to "horse trade" over some of the grievances. Emil Mazey announced to the press that Local 212 was not concerned about horses but would come to the table to negotiate about human beings.

. . . .

Just after the Briggs Stadium incident, a group of Martin's men attacked the Local 212 picket lines in Highland Park. Local 212 vice president Joe Ferris and a car full of UAW-CIO men jumped into a car and chased a carload of Martin's men. They followed the sedan down Seven Mile Road and then over to Eight Mile Road, where at Oakland Boulevard, the two cars collided. The men in the Joe Ferris car jumped out and began banging on the Martinite car, smashing the windows. Then a man in the Martin car began to fire a handgun. An AFL supporter named Joe Green, president of UAW Local 203, shot Joe Ferris in the leg. Three men in the Martinite car were from out of town and were cited by police for carrying concealed weapons. The police also found three blackjacks in the car. Later in court, one of the men said they were in Detroit to "help Homer Martin settle this strike."[154]

. . . .

Nine days after the Briggs Stadium demonstration, with the strike still on, Local 212 member Frank Klimmer was brought before the Detroit Recorder's Court. He had been arrested during the Briggs Stadium melee for disturbing the peace. During the course of the trial, a Detroit police officer testified against his own police department. Lieutenant Hugh Meyers of the special investigation squad testified, "I gave my permission to these people to picket there as long as they did not block the entrances or exits to Briggs Stadium. They were walking up and down the sidewalks peacefully. There was no disturbance until the police charged. I saw the mounted men coming down the street. I went out into the street, put my hands up, and shouted, 'Whoa! What's going on here?' A sergeant in charge of the men told me, 'I have orders to clear Trumbull Avenue.' Then the police charged the crowd."

The police were red-faced. The charges against the demonstrators were dropped. Shortly afterward, Lieutenant Meyers retired from the police force.[155]

Just as the trial ended, Briggs settled with Local 212. On June 6, the membership ratified an agreement with the following provisions:

- Local 212 of the UAW-CIO was the exclusive bargaining agent.
- Employees unfairly discharged would be rehired with back pay.
- Briggs was to pay for shop committee members to attend weekly committee meetings.

There were other improvements, but Emil Mazey did not get a union dues check-off system. Still, this was a tremendous contract—the best in the auto industry.[156] Further, the period of Martin, the UAW-AFL, and dual unionism was rapidly closing.

It was also agreed that the National Labor Relations Board would hold an election to determine which union should represent the Briggs workers. The Local 212 UAW-CIO did not want Briggs management ever again to claim that they did not know who represented the workers in the plant. The results of the September election were as follows: UAW-CIO—13,301 votes, UAW-AFL—1,052 votes, and No Union—978 votes.[157]

. . . .

In UAW history, the 1939 Briggs strike is not considered the key strike ending the Homer Martin era in the UAW. That honor goes to the GM Tool and Die strike, which occurred a few weeks later. That action, once and for all, ended Homer Martin, the UAW-AFL, and dual unionism. Perhaps the significance is because this was a strike against General Motors, the largest automaker in the world. That, coupled with Walter Reuther's leadership in the strike, elevated it over the Briggs strike in historical significance. Regardless of one's perspective, there can be no doubt that Walter and the rest of the UAW hierarchy learned from the Briggs strike that the auto manufacturer's effort to, in effect, support a company union via the UAW-AFL was not going to work. Because of the Briggs strike, Reuther and the UAW leadership knew the CIO was the majority of their workers; they just had to convince GM management of that fact.

Meanwhile, back at Local 212 and Briggs, Emil Mazey and his supporters had every reason to feel satisfied. During 1939, their local had made a difference between independent unions or company unions at Briggs and in other automobile plants. They were mostly young men and, after these events, probably felt a bit cocky.

At the same time, Fay Taylor sat at his desk. In his mind, he had not lost a war, merely a battle. Mazey was his problem—Mazey and his supporters. Eliminating them would be the key to eliminating the power of Local 212, or so he thought.

PART *II*

IT'S ALL JUST OUT OF REACH:
1940 TO 1946

CHAPTER 13

MORRIS STEPPED OUT OF LINE

Greg and I always attended the Labor Day Parade, which marched down Woodward Avenue. We joined Dad and marched with the Local 212 delegation. We enjoyed the camaraderie and marching with all our Dad's friends, but as a young boy, I envied the teenagers who carried the American and UAW flags at the head of the delegation. These two older fellows were the sons of Morris Hood Sr., Ken's good friend from the early days of Local 212. These two young men later became powerful legislators in Lansing. Sometime in the mid-1980s, I was at a reception and talking with one of Morris Hood's sons, Ray. I told him about marching in the Labor Day parades. With a big smile, he told me that he and his brother, Morris II, always carried the flags. My response was that I was jealous of both of them because I wanted to carry a flag, but I was too small. Ray laughed and took me over to repeat the story to his brother, Morris Hood, Jr. Today there is still a family member of Morris Hood Sr. serving in the Michigan Legislature (Morris Hood III).

IF EVER THERE WAS A heyday for Local 212, it was the period between 1939 through 1941. The local's contributions to the building of the UAW into a strong organization were without equal. Local 212 was the largest local in the UAW, and in that capacity the local made new gains in the world of collective bargaining and in the treatment of all workers in the Briggs plants.

The Briggs Manufacturing Company, led by crafty labor relations director Fay Taylor, was out to get Mazey and Local 212. Taylor's tactics included discharging workers for various infractions and then forcing the union into the lengthy grievance procedure process. Speedups of production put increasing pressure on workers. At times, the workers rebelled and various departments walked off the job. Briggs led the industry in wildcat strikes from the late 1930s into the late 1940s. Unknowingly, these unauthorized strikes ultimately played a huge factor in the future of Ken Morris and others. In most cases, Local 212 officials never authorized such work stoppages—they were in violation of the contract. In fact, it was usually the local leadership that helped settle the wildcat strikes by negotiating or working out the problem with management. Workers at all levels in the plant knew the power of a work stoppage at Briggs. After all, in 1936, Emil Mazey used this technique to create support for a union, until Briggs discovered Emil, fired him, and unceremoniously threw him onto Mack Avenue. Unfortunately, Emil's use of wildcat strikes became a culture at Briggs, and no one in the union could effectively resolve the problem. Thus, evidence suggests that Emil and other Local 212 leaders wanted to abide by their contract, but individuals in the huge plants staged work stoppages when *they* felt the need to do so.

From Fay Taylor's point of view, Mazey and his union supporters never addressed the problem seriously and therefore were at fault. From the local's point of view, management usually triggered a problem in one of the plant's departments and the workers simply did what they knew best: they stopped production. Briggs, being a supplier company, was always vulnerable to strikes; not only did the union know it, but so did the rank-and-file members in the plant. Even though Mazey and his supporters rarely approved of wildcat strikes, Fay Taylor and the company used these wildcat strikes to blame union leadership for encouraging such activities in the plant. Fifteen thousand workers in any factory, such as the Mack Avenue plant, proved to be extremely difficult for anyone to control. The union did not want to capitulate to Briggs discharge of employees and felt their members should not be treated as slaves by Briggs management; Briggs felt the union was protecting bad employees and wanted to treat the employees as they always had.[158]

In some ways, the wildcat strikes proved to be the eventual demise of Local 212 as a powerhouse in the UAW and the downfall of the Briggs Manufacturing Company.

. . . .

Race relations were always a difficult issue in automobile plants. A plant, after all, was a microcosm of the United States, and as such, racial issues often became an issue in many UAW plants. In the 1930s, African American workers had no idea if the union was going to include them in any gains or instead continue to treat them as a microcosm of US society, excluding the black working class. Addressing the issue forthrightly presented challenges to labor leaders for decades. Some unions and UAW locals were slow to address these issues. In many cases, corporations used black workers against the UAW during organizing drives. This was particularly true during the effort to organize Ford. Yet because of Emil Mazey and his leadership team, Local 212 was ahead of most other UAW locals of the time. Sometimes the challenges to battle racism were large battles about equal pay for equal work; sometimes they were small, more symbolic battles. Nevertheless, Emil led Local 212 in being one of the most progressive local unions in the area.[159]

By 1941, as war production increased, there were approximately twenty-two thousand workers at the Briggs Mack Avenue plant, of which approximately 10 to 15 percent were black.[160] African American workers' job assignments were usually relegated to stock handlers, wet sanders, sprayers, or janitors—tough, hazardous, and demanding work. From Local 212's inception in 1937, Mazey fought for equal pay for equal work for all men and women. In the case of African American workers, significant gains in wages occurred, and eventually full integration in the shop became standard. Before full integration, some of the job classifications traditionally reserved for African Americans showed tremendous wage increases between Local 212's 1937 inception through the beginning of the war effort. In 1936, wages for spray men, wet sanders, or spot sanders was 43 cents an hour; by 1940, the hourly rate for these jobs was $1.13. These wage improvements were real and made a huge economic improvement in the quality of lives of people assigned to these job classifications.[161]

There were other symbolic but no less significant changes that occurred. Emil Mazey always made sure that African American workers had at least one member on the Local 212 board. As a 1957 article in the *Michigan Chronicle* points out, "That may not sound like much of an accomplishment today, but 20 years ago, when men of various nationalities were not so accustomed to working together, this in itself was a major accomplishment. It was real pioneering. It meant a Negro in leadership."[162]

The Local also negotiated equal seniority for all workers. In the past, African American workers were often the first to be laid off and the last to be rehired. Under the seniority system, not only did that policy become outdated, but black workers also found that because they had seniority rights, it was easier to gain access to jobs that they never before had a chance to acquire.[163]

Local 212 had its own support staff. As mentioned previously, Emil Mazey met and married one of them, Charlotte. Emil felt he had to practice what he had been preaching and decided in 1938 to integrate the administrative office of the local. Mazey had a problem with this objective. The women in the office refused to work with a black worker. Emil, always known as someone who could turn on his charm, decided to take the office staff to dinner and persuade the women that a change in hiring policy was a good thing. His persuasive powers were not what he thought. The women still refused to work with a black woman. Emil had enough. He told them that either they accepted the change or they could find a new job. An African American woman was soon hired.[164]

The demographics of Briggs workers were diverse. Many white workers came to Detroit from the South, looking for work. This Southern workforce encouraged institutional racism at Briggs. There were unwritten rules about how things should be. At a January 4, 1941, Local 212 general council meeting, Emil held a discussion on the history of black workers in America, from slavery to the present. During the meeting, Morris Hood, an African American worker, was sitting next to Ken Morris. Hood worked in the Highland Park plant and told the members he was trying to transfer into the tool crib department. He explained that some workers in the plant were opposed to the transfer because of his race. The local immediately passed a resolution condemning the action of those opposed to Hood's transfer and supported Hood's effort to get the new job.[165]

Years later, Hood recalled that one of his proudest moments was when Local 212 paid his way to Houston to attend, as a delegate, the national NAACP convention.

Perhaps one of the best summaries of Local 212's early activities with African American workers came from *Black Detroit and the Rise of the UAW*, which states:

> Under [Emil Mazey's] leadership Local 212 developed an unusually favorable reputation among black workers. It had not only eliminated discrimination at social functions and from the very beginning included a black man on its board of trustees, but also been the first to employ a Negro office secretary (appointed over the opposition of white secretaries) and successfully fought to abolish racial pay differentials for equal work. In the view of Mazey, a Socialist, it was important for blacks, exploited by employers in the same way as white workers, to join and participate actively in the union; but equally essential was the reeducation of biased white workers and the abolition of racial discrimination.

To its credit, Briggs seemed willing to make such changes. Change moved more quickly at Briggs than other workplaces because of the continuous progressive leadership of Local 212 elected officials. These men ran for election in a plant that had more Southern whites than black workers yet generally maintained their principles for the betterment of all.

. . . .

Ken Morris continually grew as a committeeman and a man learning about the labor movement. He spent time with Bill Lamson. He worked on the Local 212 newspaper, served on committees, and continued to develop friends and networks inside the UAW and throughout the Michigan labor movement.

Sometime in the spring of 1940, Briggs fired Ken. The reasons for the firing are unclear, but Emil was extremely unhappy with Ken and felt that Ken had exceeded his authority as a Local 212 official. While out of work, Ken still maintained his activities and membership at the local. During this period, the UAW was making an active effort to organize the Works Progress Administration (WPA). The WPA was the largest employer in America and continued to be until the start of World War II. It appears that Ken did some organizational work for it. Then, beginning in September, Ken began work for the City of Detroit elections office. He initially worked on voter registration and ballot tabulation. These were temporary duties, as Ken waited to get back to Briggs.[166]

At a Local 212 membership meeting in June 1940, resolutions were placed on the table regarding the upcoming negotiations with Briggs. One motion was to "accept the new contract and go on record supporting our local officers in their efforts to obtain the reinstatement of Ken Morris."[167] Another motion from the flying squadron criticized local officers for not being able to get Morris back to his job. The flying squadron members further stated that they were opposed to ratification of any contract without Morris's return to employment.

Ken attended the 1940 UAW convention as a delegate. R. J. Thomas appointed him to the convention's education committee, where he became the committee's secretary. According to Emil Mazey's convention report in the local's newspaper, Ken presented the committee's report to the full convention.[168]

In December 1940, Emil reported to his general council that contract negotiations had been completed, and among the successful items negotiated was the reinstatement of Ken Morris with full seniority.[169]

These must have been trying months for Ken. He learned that even though he had lost his job at Briggs, he could earn a living. He learned that he had excellent networks that could lead to a staff position at the International UAW, the CIO, or a job in local government, but such positions held little interest for him. He identified himself as a Local 212 man, and he wanted to get back into the plant. Perhaps the local was where his friends and security lay, or perhaps it was the best place to further his political ambitions—one will never know. Nonetheless, he was back in the plant and happy to be back. He learned to be more cautious in his dealings with management.

. . . .

These were relatively stable years for the UAW and Local 212. Still, other issues, real or imagined, emerged. Working people, like everyone else in society, like to gossip. Emil's wife, Charlotte, having worked at the local before they were married, now volunteered her services in the Local 212 office. Malicious word spread around the local leadership and the plants that Emil had put his wife on the local's payroll. While there was no truth to the rumor, something like this was poison to a man running for office every year. Emil and his supporters tried to quell the rumor mill. They knew that Emil and his slate would feel the effect of the false allegation at the local's upcoming election.

Walter Reuther, George Addes, and Emil Mazey at 1940 UAW convention

Emil could be brash. He could exaggerate, and in this time of relative prosperity, perhaps he was a bit overconfident. These traits combined with a major issue that had been simmering with the local membership for several years. The issue was seniority. The UAW's effort at making seniority an operative factor in automobile plants did more than just about any other factor in providing workers with dignity and security. The issue that plagued Mazey would be what kind of seniority system Briggs used: company-wide or plant-by-plant seniority.

Briggs had seven plants. The major ones were the huge Mack Avenue plant, followed by Highland Park, Outer Drive, Meldrum, and the new Eight Mile Road plant, just east of Mound Road. Each plant was its own community, and many, if not most, of the workers wanted a plant-wide basis of seniority. This meant that if a worker was laid off at, say, the Meldrum plant, that worker only had rights to be rehired on a seniority basis at Meldrum, usually in the same department. He or she did not have rights to move to the larger Mack Avenue plant or the other plants in the Briggs empire. This ensured a more homogeneous environment, as strangers were not coming and going from plants; instead, friendly faces remained in plants. At the same time, workers from other Briggs plants were not able to use their seniority to "bump," or replace, employees at other plants.

Others believed that a company-wide seniority system was the best. This protected all employees by placing them under the company umbrella so their seniority could be used at any Briggs plant. The International UAW Executive Board supported the company-wide concept and so did Emil Mazey. The problem was his regular members in Local 212. They had voted in a nonbinding recommendation, 6,467 to 2,188 in favor of plant seniority. To compound problems, the Highland Park plant was being phased out. The plant-wide seniority system won in all the plants save one: the Highland Park plant, where the company-wide system won by 99 percent. These workers were terrified of losing their jobs and were more than happy to bump other workers with less seniority in order to maintain employment.

This company-wide approach to seniority also meant that African Americans and women were less likely to be shut out of moving into other plants and departments. Under this company-wide approach, a system was created that allowed people to experience upward mobility in the plant before and during the war.[170]

Emil fought with the company to ensure that Highland Park employees be the first hired at the new Eight Mile Road plant. The company apparently wanted simply to hire new men, probably men that were not identified with the UAW. Fay Taylor said that Emil needed to give other young men some of the same opportunities that had been afforded to other Briggs workers. Emil's response was cold: "We haven't had any opportunities." In the end, Emil supported company-wide seniority, and the Highland Park workers kept their jobs, but Emil took another big political hit, especially at his largest base of support, the Mack Avenue plant.

Local 212's next election was in January 1941. As mentioned, Emil could be brash and arrogant. So much so that he made enemies. Some members of the International UAW Executive Board thought he should be taken down a peg. That happened when Emil told his Local 212 constituents that he had the support of UAW president R. J. Thomas. Emil may have believed he had the UAW president's support, but in fact it had not been given. Thus the support Emil counted on was publicly repudiated, giving his opposition more to campaign against.

Emil was in trouble, and so was Emil's slate of candidates. On Emil's slate for reelection to the Local 212 executive board was Ken Morris, but now Ken was running for election as recording secretary, which would place him in charge of the local's records and make him editor of the newspaper. This was a major step up the leadership ladder in the Local and the UAW. Emil, Ken, and the entire slate fought hard, but winds of change were in the air.

Emil and his slate took a beating. In the race for president of the local, Emil and his opponent, Joe Ferris, were in a dead heat. Neither had a majority (over 50 percent of the votes cast), and there was some question regarding the Local 212 charter about what would happen next. Rather than create more controversy and turmoil, Mazey agreed to step down with a compromise candidate, Harry McMillan, taking his place. At the membership meeting where he stepped down as president, the membership gave him a standing ovation and passed a resolution urging the International UAW to hire Emil as an organizer.[171]

The International UAW hired Emil. Due to his reputation of successfully working with African Americans, Emil was placed in charge of organizing black workers at Ford. Some African Americans took offense at Mazey's new position. They were upset that a white organizer was brought in to organize black Ford workers. In spite of these concerns, Emil excelled at putting together a structure to organize Ford and played a significant role in the ultimate UAW organization of the company.[172]

Ken and other Mazey supporters continued their active involvement with Local 212 and other UAW activities. The Mazey supporters became the minority party in Local 212, but it did not diminish their support for or their desire to fight for their local union.[173]

CHAPTER 14

ARE YOU SAYING I'M FIRED?

To the best of my knowledge, I never heard the name Melvin Bishop until February 1983, at Dad's retirement dinner. The dinner guests packed one of the convention rooms at Detroit's Cobo Hall. Governor James Blanchard and many other dignitaries were there. Many longtime friends and family members attended. Dad's speech, which was too long as usual, went back to the early days. He always tried to teach and remind people about the early days of the UAW to capture their imaginations. Here, for the first time, I heard a new story. It was about a shady UAW official named Melvin Bishop who didn't like the Emil Mazey and Ken Morris crowd at Local 212. He told how Bishop had him fired from Briggs, but that later, much later, Dad had the satisfaction of taking Melvin Bishop's place on the UAW Executive Board, a position he held for twenty-eight years. Who was this Bishop guy? I wanted to find out.

BRIGGS MANAGEMENT WAS NO DOUBT elated to see Emil Mazey out of Local 212 leadership. Still, its problems with production persisted as wildcat strikes continued, if not increased.

These work stoppages were not generally major strikes. They often started as disagreements in some part of a Briggs plant between a foreman and a set of rank-and-file workers over a process, an attitude, or an action that took place in one of the departments. When a disagreement or issue flared up, workers simply stopped work, sometimes walking off the job. Just as when Emil Mazey had been president of the local, Local 212 committeemen stepped in to settle the problem and production continued. These strikes were more a nuisance than work stoppages in the traditional sense. That said, they affected the company's productivity, and Briggs had a right to be angry and frustrated. In some instances, other auto manufactures did not receive their products from Briggs; their facilities had to be shut down, laying off thousands of Detroit autoworkers. It is sad that the company and Local 212 never came to a joint solution to the problem. The real issue was trust. The company did not trust union leadership, and the union and regular workers did not trust Briggs.

By 1941, conversion of auto plants to war production was being required by the US government, and like the auto companies, the government did not want any slowdowns.[174] As a result, Briggs management had a unique ally—a man they had always considered their enemy—in their effort to maintain and increase production at the expense of the worker. Their new ally was Franklin Roosevelt.[175]

The war in Europe had started in September 1939, and the president came to realize the need to convert domestic-production facilities into war-production plants. But this president was a friend of the autoworker, and rather than fight with the UAW and other labor organizations, he tended to work with them. R. J. Thomas, George Addes, Walter Reuther, Dick Frankensteen, and others were invited to the White House to discuss the importance of war production. The president made it understood that any reduction in production was not the "American" thing to do. After Pearl Harbor, the president convinced the UAW and other labor organizations to enter into a no-strike pledge. Therefore, work stoppages at Briggs were more than a mere problem to the Briggs management; they became a huge problem and embarrassment to the leadership of the International UAW.

The UAW and other unions received a great benefit in return. The government did not oppose workers being organized. Most plants, particularly in the North and West, were either organized or relatively easy to organize, and union membership grew. In 1939, the UAW had a membership of 156,000 men and women. That number increased to 461,000 by 1941. By 1944, at the peak of war production, the UAW membership would top off at one million members, a number not seen again until 1950.[176]

. . . .

In 1941, a new player entered the picture at Briggs. This was the newly elected UAW east side regional director, Melvin Bishop.

All kinds of people were in the labor movement. These people were a mix of leaders, ideologues, and working people. Many were ambitious and some opportunists. There was nothing wrong with being ambitious or an opportunist, but unfortunately, a few in the UAW took the wrong path as UAW officials. One of these men, who enjoyed the early support of the Reuther brothers, was Melvin Bishop.

Bishop was born in Illinois in 1909, and he and his brother, Merlin, came to Detroit looking for work in the 1920s. While working at Ford, he and his brother began attending Dearborn's Fordson High School. There, the two brothers met Walter Reuther. By the early 1930s, the three Reuther brothers were great friends with Merlin. At one point in the early 1930s, the Reuthers were roommates with Merlin as they attended Detroit City College. The relationship with the Reuthers and Merlin was much closer than the one they had with his brother, Melvin.[177]

While Walter and Victor were on their trip to Russia in 1934, they learned that Roy, Merlin, and other young Socialists met numerous times to discuss politics and unions at the Socialist Party headquarters in Detroit. Merlin and Roy eventually attended the Brookwood Labor College together. In time, Merlin became a respected labor leader in the UAW. He played an important part in the GM Sit-Down Strike. He was also the first UAW education director and eventually became a UAW assistant regional director on the east coast.

His brother, Melvin, remains much more of a mystery. It appears that Melvin was also active in the Socialist Party movement, as demonstrated by the infamous "Vic and Wal" letter. In the long and cold winter of 1934, Victor Reuther wrote a letter from the American Village in Gorky, Russia, to Melvin and his wife, Gladys Bishop. The letter described life in Gorky and how impressed the two brothers were with the industrial facilities and how well the workers were treated. The final lines of the letter were:

> Let us know definitely what is happening to YPSL [Young People's Socialist League], also if the Social Problems Club at City College is still functioning and what it is doing. Carry on the fight.
>
> Vic and Wal [*sic*]

Melvin shared this letter with others. Over time, the letter appeared in different publications, and to the bane of the Reuther Brothers, the letter got into the hands of their enemies.

As Victor Reuther's *The Brothers Reuther* points out, there were at least five different versions of the ending of this letter in the twenty years after the original letter was sent to Bishop. One fictitious ending stated, "Carry on the fight for a Soviet America." In later years, Melvin Bishop said many things about what the letter actually said, but he never produced the original copy. As such, various versions of the letter with the ending "Carry on the fight for a Soviet America" popped up over the years, used by enemies of Walter Reuther. This letter was cited as proof by the never-ending quest of right-wing organizations that Walter Reuther was a Communist. It took an investigation of the US Senate to clear this matter up in 1958.[178]

Something happened to Melvin Bishop between 1934 and the 1940s. He was active in the UAW, though not on the same level as his brother. And he became a loud and profane man who physically assaulted union members and, in one case, beat and kicked a disabled UAW veteran. As Melvin Bishop's career evolved in the 1940s, it proved to be a black mark on the UAW-CIO.[179]

. . . .

The position of UAW regional director was becoming a greater force inside the UAW. As such, it is important to understand how the organizational structure of the union evolved. At the 1939 UAW convention, the union reorganized into more structured geographic regions, with Michigan having more regions than any other state. The International UAW structure was essentially finalized. At the top was the UAW president. Directly underneath the president was the number two power position in the union, the secretary-treasurer. Below these two positions came the UAW vice presidents; the number of vice presidents evolved during the years, but they generally served as directors of union-wide departments such as head of the GM, Ford, or Chrysler departments. Underneath vice presidents were the regional directors. Regional directors were essentially "governors" of their geographic boundaries of assigned local unions and responsible for coordinating and implementing UAW policy with the local unions and membership inside their regional boundaries. The regional directors also joined the UAW president, the secretary-treasurer, and the vice presidents on the International UAW Executive Board. Sometimes two regional directors, or codirectors, were named if the region was extremely large. This was the case with the two regions in the Detroit area: there were codirectors in both the east side and the west side regions. Local 212 was an east side local. Yet both the east side and the west side regions initially voted for the same regional director positions. Thus delegates to a UAW convention from the east side actually voted for both the east side and west side regional directors. This created significant problems in the east side region, not rectified until after World War II.

Since he was a west sider from tool and die Local 157, Melvin Bishop was an unusual selection for an east side regional director. He was new to many of the local union leaders on the east side of Detroit. Some remembered him from the 1939 and 1940 UAW conventions, where he had been the chair of the Competitive Shop Committee. At the 1940 convention, he spoke to the convention and said that he had been one of the first people fired by UAW president Homer Martin during the 1938 and 1939 factional battles. His election at the 1941 convention did not seem controversial, as local union independence was at its height during this period. Times were changing, however, and the International UAW became stronger and developed greater control over local unions, such as Local 212. The codirectors of the east side region were Leo Lamotte and Melvin Bishop. Bishop had Local 212 under his jurisdiction.[180]

Still, it is hard to understand how a west side local union leader received jurisdiction of locals on the east side of Detroit. Bishop, although tied to the Thomas-Addes left wing of the UAW, also appeared to have the support of Walter Reuther, the power broker of the west side. Of course, Melvin Bishop and particularly his brother, Merlin, had a long history with the Reuther brothers. Did Reuther have a hand in trying to put a friend into the east side?[181]

Local 212 and other locals may have supported him simply because Walter was for him and wanted an ally on the UAW International Executive Board. Three years after Bishop's election, Emil Mazey bitterly stated in a letter written while serving in the army during World War II, "I haven't all the facts about the Reuther-Bishop deal but [offhand] it strikes me as the lowest level of political opportunism I have ever seen. The position was evidently sold to a lot of people that Reuther stood a chance to lose his job so Bishop would have to be supported to save dear Walter." Later in the same letter, Mazey added, "I can still remember Reuther telling one of our caucuses about Bishop being a singer in a 'hollyroller [sic] tent church.' I can still hear Reuther referring to Bishop as a screwball and a nut."[182] By 1944, when Mazey wrote the letter, he had many reasons to be bitter about the selection of Bishop, but in 1941, the future was not so clear.

Immediately after Bishop won his election at the August 1941 UAW convention in Buffalo, New York, another wildcat strike erupted at Briggs. A frustrated R. J. Thomas told the Local 212 leadership to leave Buffalo at once and get the plant back to work. Ken Morris, taking his first airplane ride, and other Local 212 leaders flew back to Detroit to work out the problems. They immediately resolved the issues, and the plant was back to work within hours.[183]

This new wildcat strike was enough for R. J. Thomas, who had recently been contacted by the Briggs Manufacturing Company regarding the wildcat strikes. Thomas, no doubt, was also thinking about the no-strike pledge meetings with the Roosevelt administration. To him and other International UAW leadership, it did not seem to matter who was president of Local 212, for the strikes continued. When Mazey was president, wildcats occurred. Now Mazey was out, and the new president, Harry McMillan, was in. The wildcat strikes continued.

Thomas felt that more aggressive action was necessary. He placed Local 212 under receivership of the International UAW, with Melvin Bishop in charge as administrator. Thomas may have told Bishop to take care of those "dead end kids," the term which was often used to describe the young Local 212 leaders, and get them under control.

Regardless of Thomas's strong emotions about the wildcat strikes, to remove a local union's officers from elected duties and insert an International UAW representative into the day-to-day business dealings of a local was and is highly unusual. This action deeply offended the Local 212 leadership and its members. These people felt that Local 212 had helped make the International UAW a stable and strong union and that they were dealing with an obstinate company. The action practically guaranteed more strikes.

To address the problem of wildcat strikes, Bishop did something that many Local 212 members could simply not forgive: he began working with Briggs's labor relations man, Fay Taylor. Workers were soon being fired from Briggs for being involved in unauthorized strikes or other serious offenses. Often the firing slip stated that the UAW regional director (Bishop) approved the dismissal of the individual. Now, in almost an unbelievable turn of events, an International UAW official was working with a top official of a major corporation to discharge workers, even those who were considered good union members.

After a while, a pattern emerged: the people being fired were more often than not supporters of Emil Mazey or the Mazey political faction of Local 212. In most cases, the fired Mazey men protested, claiming they had nothing to do with the particular work stoppage. Bishop saw Mazey as a threat, perhaps because of Mazey's success in the now completed job of organizing Ford, or perhaps it was because of his strength in Detroit UAW politics. Bishop was even overheard saying that he knew the Mazey group was responsible for the strikes and that he would "clean them out." Whatever the reason, Bishop feared Emil Mazey, and he feared Mazey forces inside of Local 212.[184]

Between April 1 and October 1, 1941, the Mack Avenue plant experienced twenty unauthorized wildcat strikes. The department or line committeeperson often led the strikes. Of the twenty wildcat strikes, two were led by people affiliated with Mazey (or Green Slate); five of the wildcats were led by nonaffiliated local leaders; and thirteen were led by the political group known as the Social Club, or the Mazey opposition. In other words, those involved in the clear majority of strikes were the Mazey opposition, yet Bishop went after Mazey people. Furthermore, after firings or discipline, Bishop continually tried to help the anti-Mazey forces return to work and provided little or no assistance to Mazey supporters.[185]

After the August UAW convention, with Bishop newly assigned as administrator over Local 212, Ken participated in many meetings with the new regional director. He observed that the man was cavalier toward many of the workers; that he was working with Fay Taylor and the Briggs personnel department; and that he seemed more interested in making examples of individuals, often from the Mazey faction, than in getting to the root causes of the strikes. As the weeks progressed, Bishop verbally mistreated the Mazey supporters in local union meetings, accusing them of inciting the work stoppages, even though all evidence indicated the opposite.[186]

. . . .

The issue of company-wide versus plant-wide seniority continued to plague workers and the UAW. These seniority issues caused many of the wildcat strikes at Briggs. Personnel decisions are part of management responsibility, and the contract with Briggs was clear: workers were to move from one plant to another when layoffs or personnel adjustments were required. The problem occurred because this transfer by seniority process was new to the recently negotiated contract and not understood by the Briggs workers. Neither the company nor the union did an adequate job of explaining the change to employees. Often, when someone was scheduled to be transferred from one plant or one department to a new position, workers in the new department simply stopped work and did not accept the new worker. They were damned if some new person, perhaps of another political group, perhaps an African American or someone of a different ethnic group, or just simply a new face, was going to "bump" one of their buddies. Usually when this happened, the Local 212 committeemen successfully worked with the immediate floor management to develop a solution to the issue. Regardless of the reason, the regular workers seemed ready to risk their jobs by refusing to accept new workers in their departments.[187]

On September 30, two wildcat strikes occurred in the Mack Avenue body shop over a worker bumping into one of the departments. The company management told UAW committeemen Joe Vega and Don Snively, who were from another department, to go settle the strike. The two committeemen, both Mazey men, were unsuccessful in resolving the problem. Briggs then fired the two committeemen for not getting the men back to work. The fired committeemen and other men from the shop left the plant and headed to the Local 212 offices. Local president Harry McMillan and Ken Morris made speeches pleading with the men to return to work, reminding them that they had a contract and that leaving their jobs would not solve their grievances but only make it more difficult for them to retain employment. Vega and Snively also addressed the wildcat strikers. Even though they had just been fired, they said not to worry about them, but that they should get back to their work assignments and keep the plant running. By this time, however, Briggs management had already closed down the plant and sent most of the workers home. The *Detroit Times* and the *Detroit Free Press* had front-page stories about the work stoppage and reported that it had forced the Plymouth plant to shut down, sending over eleven thousand workers home.

Bishop told reporters, "So far as I'm concerned, if we have to remove every man in the plant in order to settle this thing, we are going to do it." Both he and Briggs management indicated that the problem was a result of a group (implying Mazey) who wanted to create chaos in the plant. The next day, the number of Detroit workers idled tripled, as thirty-seven thousand autoworkers from Dodge, Briggs, and Plymouth plants were sent home.[188]

The next morning, October 1, Ken Morris went to work in the press room of the Mack Avenue plant at his usual time of seven o'clock. About fifteen minutes later, one of the plant supervisors called him into his office. The man told Ken that there was another wildcat strike, or more accurately, a work stoppage, in the body shop one floor above the press room. Ken, who had stopped many wildcat strikes, suggested that the best way to address the problem was to wait until the body shop's steward, a fellow named Pat Ryan, came to work at eight. Ken told the Briggs supervisors that he really didn't know anyone in the body shop and that Ryan would probably get things resolved in a matter of minutes. It seemed to Ken that there was an understanding of the strategy discussed, and he proceeded to return to his work area. A few minutes later, another supervisor came up to Ken and asked him to follow him. Ken dutifully responded.

As they walked along, the management man said, looking down at the floor, "You should head down to the local offices."

Ken, not sure what he meant but smelling a rat, said, "Are you saying I'm fired?"

"Yes." The two men walked to the personnel office, where Ken was handed his discharge papers. The discharge paper had a box that indicated the reason for the firing, and Ken looked down and was astounded. The box stated that the discharge had been made at the request of the UAW regional director. (Years later, in 1946, Morris would come across a letter that Bishop had sent to Briggs indicating that he, Bishop, had investigated the issue of wildcat strikes and that Morris was one of those responsible for them.)[189]

Other problems soon developed. The men involved in the work stoppage on the floor above heard of what had happened to Ken. They were furious and were advised by their steward to go to the Local 212 hall on Mack Avenue. Bill Mazey, the shop committee chairperson for the Mack Avenue plant, was working at the Local 212 office. As the men flowed into the local's auditorium, Mazey tried to determine the facts. Bill was concerned that these workers not be put into a position where they would be fired because of the unauthorized work stoppage, which was in direct violation of the contract. He strongly urged the men to return to work immediately. At a point of frustration, he accused the department's steward, probably Pat Ryan, of being weak and a coward by letting the men strike and walk off the company property. The steward stepped over and slugged Mazey across the face, cutting his eyelid. As the two squared off and began to fight, other men stepped in and separated them. Mazey, with his eyelid squirting blood every time his heart beat, held a handkerchief to his face and pleaded with the workers to return to work; otherwise, under the Briggs contract, they would likely lose their jobs. The workers, who had become subdued during the fight, were gaining newfound respect for Mazey as he kept looking out for their best interests even though his eye was bleeding profusely. They quickly talked to each other and voted to return to the plant. The newspapers reported that six men were fired, but the number who lost their jobs in the two-day period was closer to fourteen.[190]

There was no question that the Briggs men who violated the contract were at risk of being fired. The issue puzzling so many was that Local 212 officials who had nothing to do with the work stoppages were being fired for no cause. In fact, in many cases it was these union stewards who were trying to get people back to work. In almost every case, when a superintendent fired a committeeman and was asked why, the superintendent simply implied that these were his orders, with Morris, Vega, and Snively being chief examples. Even more puzzling was that the International UAW did not object to this clearly unfair management approach.

At least two of the three men fired, Morris and Vega, had been discharged before. It appeared that in the previous two firings, there might have been some justification for the company decision. Yet in both cases, the men had been returned to work as a result of negotiations between the union and the company. The three were optimistic that they would be returned to work, especially since they all had absolutely nothing to do with the work stoppages. No matter how hard Local 212 officials tried, the company did not budge. And Bishop? He never tried to get the men reinstated.

On October 16, a meeting was held at the International UAW offices at 281 W. Grand Boulevard, near Cass Avenue and Milwaukee Street. In attendance from the International UAW were President R. J. Thomas, Secretary-Treasurer George Addes, and Regional Director Melvin Bishop. From Local 212, there were many, including Bill Mazey, Joe Vega, Ken Morris, and Joe Ferris. Also in attendance, at the risk of losing his job on the International UAW staff, was Emil Mazey. The Local 212 men had a copy of a speech that Bishop had given on October 14, just two days earlier, at a meeting with Local 212 members. In his speech, Bishop indicated that Local 212 leadership had never been very good and that he was not going to let a minority of men (as in the Mazey forces) dictate what would happen at the Mack Avenue plant. The Mazey forces were extremely upset with the speech and demanded the meeting with Thomas. Thomas seemed more interested in the hard copy of the speech than the content of the document.

Referring to the speech and the shorthand notes that accompanied the typed text, Thomas asked, "How did you get these?"

Ken Morris said, "That's my shorthand. I took the speech down and typed it up."

R. J. marveled at the twenty-six year old's skill and said, "Well, you know, my wife isn't too happy over the fact that I need a [female] secretary to travel with me from time to time. Why don't you come work for me as my traveling secretary?"

Ken was so mad that Thomas was changing the purpose of the meeting and not dealing with the Bishop issue that he uttered one of his more nonpolitical statements, "I wouldn't work for you under any circumstance."

As the meeting continued, the Local 212 delegation pointed out that under the UAW constitution, an administrator can be placed over a local union for only sixty days. Bishop's sixty days had expired. Thomas agreed to withdraw the administratorship. However, he asked the local to cut its number of paid positions from eight to three. The Local 212 delegation agreed, but they wanted something more—new local elections to be held in late November, several months earlier than the normal election. Thomas agreed to that as well.

As the meeting broke up, Thomas told Bishop to get busy on negotiations and get the discharged cases back to work, saying, "But that doesn't mean the men that might be found guilty of the wildcats." Thomas turned to the Local 212 members and asked if they concurred. They did.

Ken Morris and the others left the meeting feeling that much had been accomplished, and Ken in particular felt that he would be returning to work soon since he had had nothing to do with the strikes.[191]

. . . .

Meanwhile, life in Local 212 continued. Ken Morris was still editor of the newspaper and remained active. Needing a paycheck, Ken began working for another east side UAW activist and friend, Charles Edgecomb, at the Labor's Nonpartisan League. Edgecomb was also running and was elected to Detroit's Common Council, and Ken was active in his campaign.[192]

As agreed in the meeting with R. J. Thomas, the election was coming up in November, and Emil Mazey and his supporters, known as the Green Slate, wanted to take back control of the local union. Emil Mazey could have run for president of the local, but there was a feeling he might be too much of a lightning rod. A compromise candidate, Joe Ferris, emerged in Mazey's place. Ferris was a longtime vice president of the local from the Highland Park plant. He was the man shot in the leg during the 1939 Briggs strike. Also running on the Green Slate was Bill Mazey for vice president; Ken Morris, running again for recording secretary; and Don Snively, running as trustee.

Bishop's slate of candidates ran on the Social Club Ticket. These candidates argued that they would rid the local of the Mazey influence. They also were politically astute enough to claim independence from Bishop and to argue for the reinstatement of Morris, Vega, and Snively.

The election turned out to be close. It also demonstrated that being a martyr on an election slate made a difference. The election for president was close enough to require a recount, and Joe Ferris, the man shot two years earlier, was elected. Bill Mazey lost his bid for vice president by five votes. Ken Morris, the discharged worker, was easily elected as recording secretary, and Don Snively and other Green Slate candidates won in other offices. So the Mazey name was indeed a bit of a lightning rod. Bill Mazey lost, but the Local 212 membership was also making a statement that it wanted Bishop and his people out of the local union politics.

· · · · · · · · · · · · ·

The new local union leadership was no ally of Bishop. He had had good union men fired, he was too close to Briggs management, he ran an anti-Mazey campaign, and by involving himself in local politics, he was violating International UAW policy, which directed International UAW officials to stay out of local politics. Local 212's executive board passed a resolution on December 5, 1941, to send Joe Ferris, Ken Morris, Joe Vega, and Don Snively to a December 11 meeting of the UAW International Executive Board in Buffalo, New York. Their assignment was to protest Bishop's high-handed activities regarding Local 212 and to get the UAW Executive Board to join in the fight to have Morris, Vega, and Snively reinstated as employees of Briggs.

Ken prepared for this hearing as if he were trying a case before the Supreme Court, and in a sense, he was. He and fellow Local 212 officers were appearing before the top policy and decision-making body of the UAW. The night before the board meeting, Ken and his Local 212 delegation of President Joe Ferris and Don Snively brought Walter Reuther into Ken's hotel room. Ken, leading the discussion, laid out the facts of their argument. Reuther seemed interested in their problem, but was noncommittal.

Between the time of the December 5 Local 212 resolution and the December 11 board meeting came December 7, 1941. The December 7 attack on Pearl Harbor undoubtedly reduced the significance or the focus of the Local 212 issue before the UAW Executive Board.

On Thursday, December 11, the Local 212 men went before the UAW Executive Board. Local 212 president Joe Ferris deferred the presentation to Ken Morris. Ken proceeded to review the wildcat strikes for the board. He first dispelled the assumption that Mazey forces within the local led the wildcat strikes at Briggs. He pointed out, by reviewing each work stoppage, that Mazey opposition groups led fifteen of the twenty wildcat strikes. He further demonstrated how Local 212 committeemen, led by Mazey forces, tried to get the men back to work in accordance with the contract. He documented that Bishop wanted to destroy the Mazey support inside the local by any means necessary. The board did nothing.

In March 1942, at an International UAW Executive Board meeting in Chicago, R. J. Thomas stated his position and the decision of the board. The minutes from the meeting:

President Thomas addressed the members of the committee of Local Union No. 212. He frankly stated to the committee that in his opinion, the committee had very little respect for their International Executive Board.... There had been too much trouble in the Briggs Local; not only before the administration [by Bishop] but also after ...

In the past [the] Briggs Local has been most disrespectful to its superior officer [Bishop]. He also pointed out that this Board had been extremely courteous in allowing them to appear ...

[The Local 212] charges against Regional Director Bishop could not be considered. It was unfortunate the Local took advantage of their dislike for Brother Bishop by making it public.... Differences of opinions should not be made public gossip. Such action is not evidence of good unionism on the part of Local Union 212 officers and only tends to blacken the organization in the eyes of the public ...

President Thomas chided the members of the committee for their very childish attitude. They must realize they are no longer children—they have grown up and must act accordingly. It is not good unionism to go around carrying grudges and slandering people's [characters].

Thomas's final comments referenced the fact that Detroiters often referred to Local 212 members as the "dead end kids."

Melvin Bishop had won the battle, but the war continued. The UAW Executive Board, including R. J. Thomas, George Addes, Dick Frankensteen, Walter Reuther, and others, knew that the Local 212 men were solid UAW members. But none of these board members were ready to rock the boat against one of their fellow UAW Executive Board members—after all, they might need them later in their effort to either maintain their positions or move up the UAW political ladder. The Local

212 leaders and membership would have to deal with the iron hand of Melvin Bishop on their own. It would be a lonely battle.[193]

Ken Morris and his association with Briggs continued for the rest of his life, but he was never reinstated as a Briggs or later Chrysler employee (Briggs was bought by Chrysler in the 1950s). In 2007, Doug Fraser said that, even forty years after the incident, he, as president of the UAW, checked with high-ranking Chrysler executives to see about Ken's reinstatement. Fraser argued that Ken was clearly a responsible trade unionist and in fact worked well with many of the Chrysler executives, but the company men refused to reinstate him.

At the end of 1941, Ken Morris had finally been elected to one of the top positions of the Local 212. His leadership and acceptance by the local union membership could not be denied. Yet to compound problems, the United States was at war, and as a young single man, he had two options: being drafted or volunteering to join the military. On January 17, 1942, Ken enlisted in the US Army to begin a new chapter of his life.

CHAPTER 15

I'LL CUT THE BULLSHIT; BISHOP GOT REELECTED

I don't recall too many conversations with Greg, Dad, and I regarding his time in the Army Air Corps. When we talked about those years, it was usually when Mom was with us, often on a trip to Nebraska or some other place. Dad was twenty-six years old when he enlisted, and he was to become a sergeant. Only in researching this book did I realize how important his time in the Army Air Corps was to him and, of course, our mother. He did his share of marching while in the service. It was not uncommon for Dad to have the three of us marching in step from the underground parking lot at Grand Circus Park to one of the hotels in downtown Detroit on our way to a meeting or other event. I can still remember marching and Dad saying in cadence, "You have to keep on to your left, your right. You have to keep on to your left. Sound off: one, two. Sound off: three, four. One, two, three, four; one two … three, four." And so it went.

KEN SPENT HIS FIRST TWO weeks in the army sitting at Fort Custer in Battle Creek. He moved on to complete basic training at the army's Jefferson Barracks, located just south of St. Louis, Missouri. Little is known of these months except that his military records indicate he was hospitalized for pleurisy (a form of pneumonia) in February 1942. He also received many letters from friends and colleagues containing welcome news from Detroit.[194]

The UAW activists who served in the military viewed the war as a terrible disruption, not unlike tens of thousands of Americans who dropped what they were doing to enlist in the armed forces. Ken's unjust firing was constantly on his mind, and he continually thought about the politics of his local union and of the UAW. The longer he was gone, the more out of touch and removed he was from UAW politics, which ate at his mind and heart. He was starved for information because he wanted to remain relevant in his local union and the UAW. Ken knew that the more he was out of sight and mind, the odds of reversing his unjust firing or of being a political force in his local union diminished by the week. His strategy was to keep his name in front of the Local 212 members.

At Jefferson Barracks, he received at least ten letters. These letters reflected the friendships Ken had developed with a variety of people. Art Vega, his friend from Local 212, updated him on Local 212 politics and gossip. Patrick McManus, the Local 212 financial secretary, sent Ken receipts for his union dues and additional information on Detroit activities. Bill Lamson, his trusted teacher, mentor, and friend, sent him letters about gossip and his new post of running Detroit's civil defense air raid system. Lamson was, for the time being, exempt from the draft because he was married with a small son. Bill Dufty, a union organizer and gifted writer (and who would become an author and a husband of actress Gloria Swanson), also updated him on labor activities. Ken even received a letter from R. J. Thomas, who told him that even though he was in the army, his case would not be forgotten. Jess Ferrazza wrote and told him about Melvin Bishop's efforts to stack the new Briggs plant with only his supporters and about Bishop's continued unethical association with Fay Taylor.

In early March, Ken received letters from Art Vega, Eddie Levinson (the author of 1938's *Labor on the March* and the education director for the UAW), and a woman named Midge (possibly a Local 212 secretary) regarding recent news coverage of Melvin Bishop. The regional director was again in trouble with Local 212.

Local 212 leadership was not satisfied with the "do nothing" February decision of the UAW Executive Board regarding Melvin Bishop and the firing of the Local 212 activists. Longtime and well-respected Local 212 financial secretary Pat McManus wrote an open letter to the Local 212 membership that appeared in the local's newspaper. The letter, addressed to the UAW Executive Board, preferred charges against Melvin Bishop through a clause in the UAW constitution. The local sought to have five members of the UAW Executive Board bring charges against Bishop. If this did not work, the local had another option: a vote against Bishop by a majority of the local unions from the east side region. McManus's February 28 scathing letter cut no slack with the powerful UAW regional director. McManus charged the following:

1. Bishop violated the UAW constitution in the firing of several men [these men were not Morris, Vega, and Snively].
2. Bishop "sold out" the UAW by writing Briggs and closing out the cases against Morris, Vega, and Snively.
3. Bishop conspired with Briggs by ignoring the UAW contract on seniority and placing his political buddies in the new Briggs plant, known as the Roosevelt plant on Connor Avenue.
4. Bishop used his own slush funds in the November Local 212 election. This was in direct violation of UAW policy.
5. Bishop also tried, before the December meeting of the UAW Executive Board, to get the former Local 212 president Harry McMillan to lie about the recent firings to the board, adding that Bishop called R. J. Thomas "unprintable" names.

The letter received coverage in the Detroit daily newspapers.

Ken was ecstatic to receive this news and on March 10 sent the following exuberant telegram to Local 212 president Joe Ferris:

SAW CLIPPING STOP CONGRATULATIONS GLAD
MEMBERSHIP FOUND BISHOP OUT STOP AM ALL
THE MORE POSTIVE OF OUR ORIGINAL FRAMEUP
… CLEAN UP LOCAL ILL THEN BE HAPPY STOP
MY CONGRATULATIONS TO MEMBERSHIP FOR

THEIR ACTION SHOWS SOLIDIFIED LOCAL STOP
BISHOP IS NO DOUBT WORSE THAN MARTIN
EVER COULD BE STOP MY ADDRESS 8-6 LUBBOC
FIELD PVT KEN MORRIS [sic][195]

But his euphoria turned to disappointment when Ken learned from
other letters that the UAW Executive Board did nothing on the issue and
east side local leaders preferred to wait for the next UAW convention
to oust Bishop.

. . . .

After six weeks of basic training, Ken became part of the US Army Air
Corps and was shipped off to the 500th School Squadron's Advanced
Flying School at Lubbock, Texas, on March 6, 1942. During the war,
hundreds of US Army Air Corps airfields were built in the Midwest
and Texas for the purpose of training young men to fly. Staffing and
running these bases were major undertakings. In February, the Lubbock
Army Flying School opened and began training military pilots for
bombers, fighters, and transport aircraft. Ken played a support role in
this mission. His ability to type, take shorthand, and follow through
on paperwork (all the Local 212 grievances had paid off) made him a
unique and valuable commodity at the new and rapidly growing airfield.
Ken became a competent and even influential clerk whom his superiors
consistently relied on during the war years.

Soon after he arrived in Lubbock, Ken wrote a letter to his Local
212 friends, which appeared in labor newspapers throughout Detroit.
He wrote, "Even tho there are no drinks sold in this town—Prohibition
since 1917—we manage to get dizzy on cokes and aspirins. Tell the
boys I need Raleigh cork-tipped, stamps, paper, razor blades, my dream
Packard, a new radio[,] and a blonde with a mole on her lip ..." Through
various letters, he received assistance with all his needs except for the
Packard and the blonde.

Ken worked as a clerk in an engineering squad at the air base. He
impressed his superiors. On May 1, he was promoted to corporal. Two

weeks later, on May 16, he was moved up to sergeant. By August 1, he was again promoted, this time to staff sergeant.

Letters continued to find him. Gus Scholle, the Michigan CIO coordinator, wrote him about labor issues, political concerns, and chasing women. Bill Lamson wrote from his front porch on Detroit's Holmes Street about life in the Office of Civilian Defense and sent him a new brochure put out jointly by the AFL and CIO, encouraging labor unity during the war. In a letter a few weeks later, Lamson wrote about his successful civil defense trial blackout effort in Detroit and the tri-county region. George Edwards, recently elected to the Detroit Common Council (again, today it is the Detroit City Council) and originally from Dallas, wrote a letter on council stationary. Edwards encouraged Ken to visit his parents in Dallas and provided their address and phone number.

In the spring, Ken received an April 18 *Detroit News* article entitled "The Picket Line Brings News Photographer National Prize." The article was about *Detroit News* photographer Milton Brooks, who received a national award (and later the first Pulitzer Prize in photography) for a photo taken at a 1941 melee during the UAW strike against the Ford Motor Company. The photo shows members of the Local 212 Flying Squadron reacting to a Ford thug. In the photo, Jess Ferrazza is shown giving a dropkick to a doubled-over Ford Service man being held by other Local 212 Flying Squadron men. As Ferrazza delivers the full force of the dropkick, at least five other men are simultaneously pummeling the Ford man. At the same time, Roy Snowden has a bat raised and is about to swing the bat down on the Harry Bennett man. A vicious picture, it always irritated labor leaders because it made labor union members appear to be hoodlums. (Thirty years later, Jess Ferrazza acknowledged to this writer that he had lived with the photo for most of a lifetime, but what the photo did not show, Ferrazza reminded, was what the Ford Service men were doing to him and his buddies a few moments before the snapshot was taken. This observation is consistent with photographer Milton Brooks' comments, which accompany the Pulitzer photo at the Newseum located in Washington, DC).

First Pulitzer Prize photo shows Jess Ferrazza and Briggs Flying Squadron men rallying after being attacked by Ford Service men at 1941 Ford strike

In late May, Pat McManus wrote Ken a letter expressing deep disappointment in Joe Ferris's leadership. McManus compared him to Hitler. He also expressed frustration with the fellow appointed to take Ken's spot as recording secretary. Because of these growing frustrations, he wrote, more men in the plant were returning to the Mazey faction.[196] About the same time, Bill Lamson wrote to congratulate Ken on his sergeant stripes and to say that Ferris had completely turned against the Mazey faction at the local.

. . . .

In spite of dreaming about Detroit, Ken worked hard. One lieutenant wrote that Ken Morris did a superior job "in suggesting new methods for accomplishing work, inaugurating new systems for doing work simply, installing new filing systems, and developing new forms." He further wrote that other squadrons at the air base adopted Ken's development of "Oil Consumption Percentage" charts. The lieutenant added that Ken's leadership skills and work habits were beyond question and recommended him for officer training school.

During the sweltering month of August, Ken received what had to be a disappointing letter from Art's brother, Joe Vega—one of the three men Bishop had fired from Briggs. The letter was brief and to the point:

> Well I'll cut out the bullshit and tell you as far as I can what you want to know. The [1942 UAW] Convention was very lousy as far as I am concerned. (Bro) Bishop got re-elected along with LaMotte. Our case is still pending. I think we may be re-instated [at Briggs] after the war. I don't think it would be a good idea for you to write to the Briggs Co. The old machine [the Mazey faction] elected 12 out of 13 [delegates] and the company did not like it. [Fay] Taylor told McDonald that the Mazey machine had taken control of the plant again. They are calling people back to Mack but none of our people of course. Seniority does not mean a thing.

This letter may have brought the Detroit home front back to Ken. In September, he received leave time and headed back to Detroit. He found a room for two dollars a night and proceeded to find all his friends and renew relationships. One suspects that he was proud of his stripes and his success in the US Army Air Corps. While in Detroit, no doubt in his army uniform, Ken visited Fay Taylor at his Briggs office. Ken inquired about getting their jobs back, and Taylor indicated that it was not likely. Joe Vega had been right: Taylor did not want any Mazey men in his plant.

. . . .

As 1942 ended, Ken received letters from Emil Mazey and Bill Lamson. Both letters informed him that Gus Scholle had married Socialist Kathleen Jones, which appeared to surprise no one. Mazey was still at the Ford Department and wrote that the UAW and Ford had finally concluded their contract.

In January 1943, Ken's first letter was from Emil Mazey. The firebrand had agreed to run again for the presidency of Local 212. He felt that the members were fed up with Joe Ferris and the time was ripe for his return to the local.

During this time, the idea of attending officer training school became stronger in Ken's mind. Encouraged by his commanding officers, Ken spent the later months of 1942 and the early months of 1943 readying his application (in triplicate). Ken needed to provide information about his background, including the official documentation on his name change, and he had to provide reference letters of recommendation. These letters of recommendation speak volumes regarding the respect that Ken Morris generated from the men he served under during the previous nine months. Sergeant Morris demonstrated ambition, the desire to serve, and an ability to work with men from all walks of life.

In February 1943, he was transferred to Bryan, Texas, where a brand new air base was being constructed. Bryan was a small town of about twelve thousand people, located nearly five hundred miles from Lubbock, between Dallas and Houston. He was assigned to work with a Captain Ralph O'Hair in the manpower (personnel) section.

In March, good news came from Art Vega. The Local 212 elections had been held, and Emil Mazey had won big. Emil and his entire slate took over the local. Ken was pleased, as he knew that Emil would carry on the fight against Bishop.

On April 30, 1943, Emil Mazey wrote Ken. Among other issues, Mazey indicated that he was going over the facts of the Morris, Vega, and Snively firings and was trying to figure out a strategy. He also expressed growing concerns over the Communist element that was taking root in the local, writing, "Communist Party members in the UAW are getting pretty brazen and cocky." He added, "Communist Party members in the UAW are the most reactionary forces in the union today. At the present time they are pushing the incentive pay plans, better known as 'speedup and piecework systems,' and our local has gone on record in opposition to incentive pay." Emil also railed at President Roosevelt's latest order to freeze wages as "vicious pieces of antilabor legislation."

In early June, Ken returned to Detroit on leave. He had a fine time and enjoyed being back and visiting with friends. At one point during the visit, he attended a meeting of local union members and heard former president Joe Ferris say, "That Ken Morris did his own bargaining to effect his return to the Briggs roster." At the time, Ken did not say anything, but as the days passed, the comment continued to trouble him.

When he returned to Texas, Ken wrote a letter to the *Voice of Local 212*. On July 15, the Local 212 newspaper printed the letter addressing a number of issues, but the letter was primarily an attack on Joe Ferris. Ken indicated that he was disturbed by Ferris's comment and felt an obligation to set the record straight. He wrote that the only reason he went to see Fay Taylor regarding the reinstatement of the three men was that [former] Local 212 president Joe Ferris had made no real effort on their behalf. He reminded the Local 212 readers that the three men were elected stewards in the plant, had nothing to do with any work stoppages, and were unjustly fired by the company. He concluded the letter by stating that newly elected Emil Mazey said he would take up the unjust firings and if necessary take it to the labor board, adding "which I believe is swell."

. . . .

Earlier, in April, Ken Morris received disappointing news. The army denied his application for officer training school. The official letter, dated April 19, 1943, stated that he failed to meet the qualifications for these reasons: "a. Not enough general military background. b. Civilian experience not justifiable to be of appreciable value to military service." No doubt other issues entered Ken's mind. His application had provided a copy of the 1937 probate court record of his name change from Morris Katz to Kenneth Morris. Was there an issue of character? Or perhaps someone focused on his last name, Katz. Was this an example of anti-Semitism? (Ken Morris never talked about these issues with his children. However, the initial thought of his sons, who were baptized in the Presbyterian Church and read this material sixty-five years after Ken's application, was that it was a probable case of anti-Semitism.)

Whatever the case, upon his return to Texas from his June leave in Detroit, Ken Morris got down to the serious work of preparing the new airfield. Ken again demonstrated outstanding leadership qualities in personnel work. There is delicious irony in the fact that one of Ken's greatest nemeses at this time was Fay Taylor. Had Taylor and the Briggs Manufacturing Company promoted men from the shop, men like Ken Morris, who clearly had an aptitude for personnel issues, to work in personnel and other operations, perhaps Briggs would have enjoyed a more positive and ultimately productive experience with the UAW.

From March 1943 to April 1944, Ken Morris's commanding officer was Captain Ralph O'Hair. O'Hair came to know Ken as a soldier and a friend. Ken was the top enlisted person in their first assignment together, and O'Hair later wrote that Ken Morris was "diligent far beyond the call of duty, which [has created] the high esteem with which he was regarded by the individuals in the organizations whose work he inspected. He was regarded as an advisor and as a friend by all, which was of utmost importance to the successful operation of [our] office."

Captain O'Hair recalled:

> From July 1943 to April 1944, [Ken Morris] was the mainstay ... of [my unit] which carried on orthodox station S-1 functions [in a business organization, these corresponded to personnel or human resource department work].... To say that he performed well, duties which were assigned him in [this] work[,] is inadequate. He simply lived for his work, on occasions, working until dawn the following day after a hard day's labor had already been expended. He attacked unwieldy or knotty problems with initiative and courage, and without exception, rendered a thorough, smooth performance of whatever project or task was his assignment."

O'Hair concluded a recommendation letter for Ken by writing, "[Whoever] considers him for a job, men like him are rare."

Ken's work at the base seemed overwhelming, yet he found time to socialize. Sometime in the spring or early summer, he was introduced to a brunette from Nebraska, named Doris Stone. Doris was in Bryan with some friends and on the rebound from a failed romance. Ken, never known as a ladies' man, took the initiative with the twenty-year-old. He pretended to be a man about town and asked her on a date. According to Doris, who recalled many years later, "We went to the movies, and while watching the movie, he leaned over and kissed me on the cheek. I remember thinking, 'This man is too fast for me; I'm not going to see him again.'" Ken recognized a woman who was not only attractive but intelligent and social; and even though she was from the conservative state of Nebraska, she was open to liberal politics. In late August, Ken wrote Joe Vega, seeking advice on wedding rings. On September 11, Vega responded and advised Ken to buy a white gold diamond ring.

Ken and Doris Morris

In October, they were married. Married life agreed with Ken, at least physically, as his Army Air Forces Physical Fitness Test recorded that his weight went from 145 to 160 pounds in less than a year of marriage. Doris put him on a diet to get him back to 150 pounds. At the same time, his physical fitness scores moved from very poor to good.

Military life and marriage kept Ken busy. One of his commanding officers, perhaps O'Hair, urged him to stay in Texas after the war and open an insurance company in Dallas. They would be partners. Doris was more interested in such options than Ken. Ken's plan did not change; he was to return to Detroit with his wife.

. . . .

Emil Mazey was back in charge of Local 212. Joe Vega was his vice president. Even though the wildcat strikes never stopped while Mazey was out of power, Fay Taylor believed that Mazey was behind them and that upon Mazey's return, there would be more labor unrest at Briggs. They were a company into full war production and employing over thirty-two thousand people, making parts for several types of planes used by the army and navy. One of its products was turrets for heavy bombers. The turrets had more than two thousand parts composed of everything from large pieces of aluminum to small quarter-inch gears. In addition, Briggs made the bodies for the Sherman tank and produced large steel cartridge casings. Making war products comprised 96 percent of the plant. Briggs had never produced so much product.[197]

Briggs management was aided by the no-strike clause and a federal formula restricting wages. R. J. Thomas, Addes, Reuther, and the UAW Executive Board agreed on the controls, as they saw the need to ensure the UAW's reputation as a partner in winning the war through war production. It was important that UAW workers be viewed as "Rosie the Riveter" or part of the "Arsenal of Democracy," not wildcat strikers threatening war production. At the local level, however, leaders were frustrated. They saw bargaining stagnated, stalled by federal bureaucrats, and huge profits going to the companies. It was also a frustrating time for the leadership on the UAW Executive Board—a leadership that was, on one hand, working together, but on the other hand, had members jockeying for ultimate power if R. J. Thomas faltered. Emil Mazey, much to the frustration of International leadership, led the battle against the no-strike pledge. He was publicly critical of the UAW leadership, President Roosevelt, and the Roosevelt administration.

And of course there was Melvin Bishop. Emil Mazey detested Bishop. In 1942, while the Briggs' Mack plant was closed so it could be retooled for war production, many employees found work in other factories around town. Bill Mazey and his young brother Ernie found work at the Hudson plant, just about a mile away from the Mack Avenue plant. They entered a plant full of tension. Many white workers wanted to stop production because of the employment of African American workers. Both Mazeys were part of the effort to reduce the friction and keep the plant running as new minority workers were employed or upgraded.

One day the Hudson plant manager, Melvin Bishop, and the Hudson local union president, a fellow named Germain, were walking through the plant grounds. Bishop observed the two Mazey brothers walking off their shifts and said to the plant manager, "You ought to get rid of those fellows before they get seniority."

Local 154 President Germain instinctively reacted against Bishop's comments and said that no, that can't happen, because the Mazey brothers are good union men.

A week later, a superintendent fired Bill, Ernie, and several other workers. The superintendent said he was sorry to be doing this but had to follow orders from his personnel office. There was no doubt that the UAW regional director was behind the firing.

In 1942, Bill Mazey went to the UAW convention as a Hudson Local 154 delegate and received more votes from his adopted local than any other candidates. Emil never forgot the pain his brothers went through because of Melvin Bishop.

In September, Emil spoke at a Local 212 membership meeting regarding the 1943 UAW convention to be held in Buffalo. All the local unions from the Detroit east side region were to elect two coregional directors. Emil spoke against Melvin Bishop. The *Voice of Local 212* wrote, "Mazey reminded the membership that Melvin Bishop was instrumental in having ... Jos. Vega, former Recording Secretary Ken Morris (who is now in the Armed Forces), and Brother Don Snively fired from their jobs at Briggs during the [administratorship of Melvin Bishop] of the Local. Mazey also accused Bishop of having his two Brothers, Wm. Mazey, a former Executive Board Member and Shop Committeeman of Local #212, and his brother Ernest Mazey, fired from the Hudson Ordnance Plant because they led the fight in Local 154 against giving up the overtime and premium pay provisions."[198]

Emil Mazey went to the October 1943 UAW convention and led the Local 212 delegates in the battles against the no-strike provisions and other issues. He fought the reelection of Bishop. He lost on all counts but succeeded in being a thorn in the side of Melvin Bishop and top UAW leadership. Since being elected again as Local 212's president, Mazey seemed to have been even more aggressive in taking on the International UAW's leadership.

Shortly after his return from the convention, Emil Mazey received his draft notice. He had been reclassified 1-A from his previous deferment, which exempted him because he had been married with a child before Pearl Harbor. He and the UAW appealed by citing Mazey's need to maintain war production, but the appeal was denied. Mazey always believed he was drafted because he criticized the Roosevelt administration's policies on labor. In January, the *Detroit News* reported that Emil Mazey was inducted into the army. When asked if he expected to pass his physical, Mazey told the reporter, "Sure, I expect to pass.... I feel as fit as a fiddle."[199]

The ranks of many of the UAW pioneers had been depleted because of the war. Roy Reuther was drafted in 1942, even though he had a bad heart. George Edwards enlisted, even though he had a "safe" job on the Detroit Common Council. Art Vega was drafted in 1943. In the same year, perhaps after his firing from Hudson, Bill Mazey joined the navy and expected to be shipped overseas. Bill Lamson, Ken's mentor, was apparently drafted in late 1943 (his death in 1944 was Ken's greatest loss of the war). Jess Ferrazza, who succeeded Emil Mazey as president of Local 212, was drafted in 1944 after he strongly opposed the no-strike provision at the 1944 UAW convention in Grand Rapids. In addition, Gus Scholle became part of the military. He was assigned to General MacArthur's staff toward the end of the war, and during the occupation of Japan, he helped write protections for working people into the new Japanese constitution.

. . . .

Back in Texas, Ken Morris and his commanding officers continued their work. The base began operations in late 1943, and they were satisfied with the work they had accomplished. In April 1944, Captain O'Hair was transferred, but he and Sergeant Morris corresponded on a regular basis; in fact, Ken received more letters from his former commanding officer than any other person during 1944. Ken's new commanding officers continued to provide Ken's military file with commendations. He was also busy with married life.

Conversely, Emil Mazey had a particularly difficult time in the armed services. He was convinced that his background as a labor leader and a Socialist labeled him as a subversive.

In September, Emil sent a letter to his best friend and current president of Local 212, Jess Ferrazza. His bitterness and frankness about the challenges of running for high office within the UAW were candid, as was his disgust with Melvin Bishop:

> I have never gotten very far in International [*sic*] union politics because I have been too honest and principled. But if I never hold a top position in the UAW, I will never aspire to it by making deals similar to the Reuther-Bishop affair. I still remember that Bishop fired Vega, Morris, Snively and four others.... He had my brothers Bill and Ernie fired from their jobs at Hudson.... I can still hear Reuther referring to Bishop as a screwball and a nut....
>
> I can understand how miserably Ken Morris must have felt about the Bishop deal.
>
> You know, Jess, I have always looked upon the labor movement as a vehicle to use to eliminate all of the evils of our society. I helped build and maintain a powerful union at Briggs for job security and a more pleasanter

[*sic*] job. I got fired from Briggs because I played a leading role in the building of our union…. If I ever get out of this army I will make Bishop and Briggs pay dearly for their conniving. Our union must be improved so that no member will lose his job because he exercises freedom of speech as his [conscience] dictates. I'm sorry if I have been too emotional in this letter but I have to express my pent-up feeling to someone that I'm sure understands my feelings….

I'm now in a tank outfit and am getting the old run-a-round [*sic*]. I hope that your activities in Grand Rapids [fighting the no-strike clause at the 1944 UAW convention] won't bring you closer to the army. Take a little time out and answer this letter as soon as possible.[200]

Emil Mazey was feeling a little sorry for himself and, perhaps, a little homesick. His feelings toward Bishop and his frustration with International UAW politics were clear and concise. Emil was a Walter Reuther supporter, but he knew that Walter's ambition to become UAW president required artful deal making, which Emil detested. In fact, at the 1944 convention, Walter won his reelection as UAW vice president by only a few votes. This demonstrated that Walter could take nothing for granted in his quest for the UAW presidency.

• • • • • • • • • • • •

The winds of war were moving people all over the world, but not Ken. Ken never left the United States. Ken's ambitions still burned, especially when a new opportunity appeared. For perhaps the first time since leaving Detroit, he considered another career. In April 1945, Ken applied for a position with the United Nations Relief and Rehabilitation Administration (UNRRA). The UNRRA was an effort by President Roosevelt and administered by the new United Nations to bring countries together to provide assistance to the huge refugee problem that was developing as the war in Europe was winding down.

Ken felt that his clerical and organizational skills would be useful in the worldwide effort to assist Jews and other displaced peoples. At the time of his application, the war was over in Europe and the refugee problem was widely known. It is not clear if he viewed this as a complete career change or as a means of getting into action before the war's completion. His application was not accepted or perhaps was held up by superiors at Bryan Air Force Base.

About six weeks before he submitted his UNRRA application, he received a February 25, 1944, letter from Emil Mazey, now stationed in Columbia, South Carolina:

> Dear Ken:
>
> This is an old familiar voice from out of the past saying hello and how are you.
>
> I have heard from many of our mutual friends, who had the [pleasure] of seeing you in Detroit in the fall. They tell me that you have a very lovely and attractive bride.... Congratulations!
>
> I have seen a good part of ... the [South] and frankly I think the Civil War was fought in vain; I don't think the [South] as a whole was worthwhile fighting over....
>
> I am now a tank gunner. I didn't get much chance to use my knowledge in doing office work in the army. They have made things plenty tough for me and I have been visited frequently by the S2 and GT sections of the army as well as the Provost Marshals Office [sic]. It looks like my past followed me into the army.
>
> I know that you are as disappointed about the election of Bishop as I was. Let's hope that we can clean this mess up sometime in the near future.
>
> You probably wonder what happened to your grievance Ken. I took your case up as soon as I took office in March 1943 and even Thomas [was] in on the case. The company was as reluctant as ever to reinstate you. The only course we could have followed was to take your case to arbitration because of the "no-strike pledge"

of the CIO. Frankly, Ken, I was afraid of arbitration because I didn't think you could get a square deal from an arbitrator during the war....

I am convinced that the only way to win your reinstatement under a proper basis is to be in a position to strike if necessary to get justice. I talked this matter over with many of the boys and they agree with me 100%. I hope you can see the logic in this position....

How about taking enough time out from loving your pretty wife to write to an old comrade.

Even in the army, Emil was still working on a grievance that was now over three years old.

In mid to late 1945, newly promoted Master Sergeant Morris was shipped out of Texas. He might have been stationed in California for a little while, but he ended up at the 593rd Army Air Force base in Charleston, South Carolina, where he served his remaining time in the military.

In December 1945, Ken was discharged. By this time, he had purchased a 1937 Ford Coach. This was a nearly two-ton vehicle well beyond its prime, but because of the war, no new cars had been built since early 1942. Civilian vehicles of any kind were at a premium. There was not much left of the car's floor, and the road could be seen through the floorboards. Nonetheless, Ken and Doris headed on a multiday trip of over fifteen hundred miles, from South Carolina to Doris's home in Sutton, Nebraska. Snow seemed to find them everywhere, particularly in the Ozark Mountains of Missouri. Just miles from Doris's family home in Nebraska, the old Ford stopped working. Doris's uncle rescued the two, and a local mechanic repaired the car. After a long vacation and with their freshly tuned Ford, the couple began their journey to Detroit, a journey that found Ken perhaps more ambitious than ever—and a man who wanted to settle a grievance older than World War II.

. . . .

Unknown to Ken, Emil Mazey, Walter Reuther, or other labor leaders, a series of meetings took place during these war years. Participants in these meetings included an interesting array of leadership from Detroit's manufacturing community and its underworld. Included were Harry Bennett of Ford, John Fry of the Michigan Stove Works, Dean Robinson from Briggs, and representatives from other manufacturing companies. On occasion, members of the underworld, including Santo Perrone, attended the meetings. At some point in these discussions, Perrone was told that a scrap contract from Ford and Chrysler might be available if the underworld hoodlum performed services to eliminate or weaken unions after the war.[201]

CHAPTER 16

BISHOP RAISED THE ANTE TO GET MAZEY SUPPORTERS

Except for Mom's cousin, Greg and I had no relatives in Detroit. We saw our relatives once a year, if we were lucky. The men and women who took on the role of surrogate aunts and uncles were people from the labor movement, mostly from Local 212. Dad had known these people so well before the war, and he introduced Mom to all of them upon their return to Detroit. My brother and I, of course, came to know and love them later, during the 1950s. Emil and Charlotte Mazey were warm and wonderful. Charlotte, who had blond hair when we knew her and dressed so well, was the most glamorous woman we had ever met. Dad's best friend was Pat Caruso; their bond ran deep from the bowels of the Briggs Mack Avenue plant. Pat and his wife, Vivian, were the best people Greg and I knew. There were so many others. Jess and Janice Ferrazza and Art and Betty Vega were also great friends. Moreover, what was interesting about each of them is that they talked to Greg and me as adults. They might explain issues to us, but there was never any child's play with them. Life was the UAW and the labor movement—with occasional lessons about the Lions, Tigers, or Red Wings tossed in.

THE DRIVE FROM NEBRASKA TO Detroit in 1946 could be long and treacherous, particularly in their beat-up Ford. One never knew what to expect from winter weather on US Highway 6, a two-lane transcontinental highway that connected towns and cities in the Midwest to both the East Coast and the West Coast. Doris had grown up just a few blocks from the great highway and used it on a regular basis as she went to and from the small towns of Nebraska. In the dead of winter, it took two full days to get to Detroit—if the weather cooperated. Ken and Doris fought truck traffic, slowdowns in the cities and towns along the way, and the weather.

The two had plenty of time to talk about the future. To Ken, he was bringing his wife of just over two years to Detroit. He knew he was without a job and no family to greet him. However, he did have friends, a base of political support at Local 212, and connections with many unions throughout Detroit. The labor movement was his life and avocation, and he wanted the UAW and the labor movement to continue to be part of his life. Yet there was something else. During the war years, Ken learned that he could succeed in any number of activities. He may not have made officer school, but with hard work and determination, he knew that success in whatever field he might chose was attainable.

Still, Detroit was a gritty city, and he was putting his wife in an awkward position. While the UAW and Local 212 were like family to Ken, it might not be the same thing for a twenty-three-year-old woman from small-town Nebraska. They knew housing in Detroit had been nearly impossible during the war and had not improved much in the postwar months. Ken wanted a decent place to live and contacted friends on the Detroit Housing Commission well in advance of his return. His friends put him on the waiting list for an east side Detroit public housing apartment complex known as Parkside for forty-five dollars a month. Parkside would be great for Ken. The location was perfect, about a mile from the new Local 212 building.

After many miles' worth of discussion, with the cold January air whistling through the floorboards, Ken and Doris reached an understanding regarding their future. Bill Mazey had written that after the war, he was going to get a job in a plant and go to law school. Bill, like Ken, had been impressed with the legal help Local 212 had received from the top labor attorney in the state, the burly and flamboyant Nick Rothe. Bill worked out an understanding with Rothe that after law school, an invitation was available for Bill to join the Rothe law firm. Bill was certain that such an arrangement was just as possible with Ken. Doris loved the idea of her husband becoming an attorney. Ken was not so sure. He simply was not yet ready to leave the UAW to become a labor lawyer. Ken agreed that he would run for union office, and when he lost, which was inevitable in union politics, he would find a job in the plant and follow Bill Mazey's example of going to law school.

. . . .

Ken's return to Local 212 was better than anything he could have expected. Local 212 was now located in a new building, a former two-story car dealership on the northeast corner of Mack Avenue and Fairview Street. This building became Ken's second home for the next nine years. The ex-GI felt uneasy as he made his way through the entrance of the building. He walked in a different man, both mentally and physically, than when he left Detroit just over four years earlier. The skinny kid who had left for the Army Air Corps in January 1942 was now wider, with an extra fifteen pounds on his five-seven frame. He was wearing wire-rimmed glasses, and his hair was thinning, almost unimaginable before he left. As he moved from one office to another, his heart probably skipped a beat or two as old friends greeted the returning veteran, but he also saw many new faces inside the local's offices. He recognized right away that the war had brought thousands of new people to Briggs, and one of his new challenges was to get to know these new people.

The Mazey caucus had been defeated in 1944, and as the 1946 elections approached, the Mazey group had split. The majority of the Mazey group was running under the "Pioneer Ticket," and the opposition was called the "United Pioneers." Each faction, however, had known of Ken's impending return, and each group picked him as their candidate to run for recording secretary of the local, the same position he briefly held before enlisting in 1942. By being on both slates, Ken ran unopposed. This was perhaps the most heartwarming welcome back imaginable.[202]

Even though he was a consensus candidate, he still campaigned for the job. He had a lot of catching up to do. He did not fully understand why there was such animosity toward his friend and Pioneer Ticket candidate for president, Jess Ferrazza, who had also recently returned from the military. There were other concerns as well, particularly working with and getting to know the people in the plants. There were so many new faces, including more African Americans in better jobs, and so many more women. Everyone knew that as production declined and the work force reduced, a natural friction developed between current employees, particularly women employees, and the GIs returning home from the war. The company wanted to return to the prewar status quo and lay off the newer employees, especially the women workers; but Local 212 believed they had a duty to represent all employees, including the women employees, and thus fought for their seniority rights.[203]

. . . .

Ken met with his old friends Art Vega and Roy Snowden to learn more about a troubling situation affecting some Local 212 activists. They sat at a coffee shop across the street from the Local. Ken offered each man a cigarette. Ken had heard that unknown assailants had viciously attacked Art and Roy in 1945, and he wanted to get the facts from two men he had known since the inception of Local 212. By the time the first cup of coffee arrived and cigarettes were lit, he was riveted to the story the two men told.[204]

Roy was a longtime Local 212 Flying Squadron member. He drank too much, and he was not afraid of anything. In the first assault, he said two men attacked him as he entered his apartment and beat him into unconsciousness. Before Snowden could continue with his story, Art piped in and said his beating came next. Art explained how he and his wife, Betty, had been walking down the street near his home when two men attacked and started beating him with blackjacks. His raised arms caught the blows from one of the men who was aiming the club at his head. He was lucky; he received a broken arm instead of a fractured skull. As the beating continued, Betty took off one of her high-heeled shoes and started beating one of the attackers. Because of her courage and screams, the assailants fled. Roy then told of his second beating. He was attacked walking down Mack Avenue, near his home. He was beaten so badly that his ear was almost severed.

Ken asked what the police had to say. Both men laughed and cursed at the same time. They said the police just wrote the assaults off to intra-local-union rivalry. It was true that things could get hot and heavy in local politics, but never had anyone brought thugs in to attack an opponent. The men agreed that the police were doing nothing to track down the assailants.

Then they talked about Genora Dollinger. Ken could not place her, but her name sounded familiar. Genora, the men reminded him, was a CPer (a Communist Party member) from Flint, who had been active in the Flint Sit-Down Strike. She had remained active in Flint UAW efforts and caused controversy in every plant she worked in before the war. By the start of the war, she had been blacklisted in Flint, so she came to Detroit and found work at Briggs. Vega and Snowden told how she became active in the local's education and public speaking committees. She might have been a CPer, but she had guts, common sense, and seemed fearless. The guys admired her.

Dollinger also became part of a Local 212 investigating committee regarding the Vega and Snowden beatings. The committee met with many people and concluded that there must have been a quid pro quo agreement with a local underworld figure and Briggs. They learned that local mobster and strikebreaker Santo Perrone had a son-in-law named Carl Renda, who had just gained a scrap metal contract from Briggs. Immediately after Briggs awarded the contract to young Renda, the Briggs beatings began.

In addition, the local's investigating committee felt that Melvin Bishop was involved. Art and Roy told Ken of Chet "Whitey" Kosmalski, another good union brother who had been fired from Briggs at about the same time as Ken. Kosmalski, however, returned to his job through the power of Melvin Bishop. The men said that Kosmalski had recent run-ins with Bishop and his staff. Ken made a mental note to meet with Kosmalski to get his side of the story. Ken wanted to know everything about Melvin Bishop.

The men went on and told how the chair of the investigating

committee wrote R. J. Thomas in September 1945, requesting that charges be brought against Bishop, and again, as in 1942, the UAW International Executive Board did nothing. Like the Detroit police, the board seemed to feel that the violence was just some internal squabble between local factions. According to Dollinger, she asked vice president Walter Reuther to have the UAW Executive Board propose a reward to deter any more violence, and Walter responded, "Come on, Genora, let's not get dramatic."[205]

In October 1945, Genora Dollinger was sleeping in her home with her husband. Two men broke into her home and attacked her with blackjacks as she and her husband lay in bed. Dollinger's husband, Sol, rolled over through the continuous thumps of the blackjacks and covered his wife's head and body. Until the day she died, Genora believed her husband's action saved her life. Sol then tried to rise, and although he collapsed from the beating he had taken, it was enough for the assailants, and they fled through the door. His wife was in the hospital for many weeks with a concussion, a partially paralyzed face, and a broken collarbone that left her in a cast for six weeks.[206]

Art and Roy finished their story. Ken looked at the ten or so cigarette butts in the ashtray on the table and grabbed the bill.

. . . .

A few days later, Ken met Whitey Kosmalski for breakfast at a new drive-in restaurant named Cupids. The restaurant was located on the corner of Warren and Conner, across the street from Doris and Ken's apartment in Parkside. Ken had known Kosmalski, but not well. After some initial small talk, the waitress poured a second cup of coffee, and Ken offered Whitey a Chesterfield. Ken was impressed that the man had brought a large envelope containing papers to help him with his thoughts. Whitey accepted the cigarette and began his story.[207]

Whitey reminded Ken that he had been fired about the same time as Ken, Joe Vega, and Art Snively, but after continual pressure, Bishop helped get him reinstated. After being reinstated, he still got into trouble with Briggs's management, but Bishop continued to protect him. Whitey said that he was fired again from Briggs at the start of

1945 and that Bishop had returned him to work once again. Then, just after his reinstatement to employment, Local 212 elected John Murphy as their new president. One night Bishop telephoned and said, "Whitey, something must be done with Art Vega and Roy Snowden. They are giving John Murphy too many headaches."

Whitey asked Bishop, "What do you want me to do with Art and Roy?"

Bishop's response was swift. "I don't care if you have to break their necks, but I want them to stay away from Local 212. Murphy can't do me any good politically if they continue to bother him."

Whitey added that he could not remember his exact words, but he told Bishop that the regional director had two organizers on his staff whose jobs were to control Local 212 and that he could not understand why he, Bishop, was calling a rank and file member, who was not even a committeeman.

Bishop's response was curt. "I called because Pat Ryan told me to call you." Bishop then hung up. Afterward, Whitey felt that Bishop was expecting return favors for Bishop's efforts over the years to get him back to work at Briggs.

Art Vega was beaten up a few weeks later. Whitey said, "I called the regional office, which Bishop ran, and a Mr. Hutchinson answered the phone. I asked if he had heard about Vega."

Hutchinson said, "Yes, and I'm sorry the boys missed Roy Snowden."

Whitey said he asked Hutchinson who "the boys" were.

"It's none of your business," came the response.

Then Whitey said he found out that Snowden had been beaten too. Whitey looked at Ken as he took a final drag on his cigarette and put it out in the ashtray between the two of them. He said, "I was really shocked because then I was convinced that Hutchinson arranged both beatings to please Melvin Bishop."

Whitey explained that he had been at the Local 212 hall shortly after the conversation with Hutchinson and saw Hutchinson standing across Mack Avenue in front of a drugstore with Local 212's Tony Czerwinski, part of the Mazey opposition at the local. Whitey crossed the street and asked the men if they would have a cup of coffee with him, and they agreed. After the men sat down and ordered, Whitey asked Hutchinson if he had seen Roy Snowden since Roy was beaten up.

Hutchinson replied, "I don't have to see him, Whitey. I know how he looks, and if he opens his mouth again, he will get some more. That also goes for that hunky Steve Despot."

Whitey looked up from his notes and told Ken that he knew Hutchinson would not do anything unless his boss, Melvin Bishop, approved it, and he also knew that the beating victims were Mazey men. It all stunk to high heaven because Bishop had obviously found thugs to beat up his opposition.

Whitey continued, saying he called Pat Ryan. Ryan was the committeeman who, in all likelihood, worked above Ken's department in 1941. He was the man who could not control his department, which led to the strike when Ken was fired. Now he was on Mel Bishop's staff.

When Ryan answered Whitey's call, he said, "Well, Whitey, you know someone had to shut their mouths," meaning Vega and Snowden. "They were impossible, and from now on, the same thing will happen to anybody that talks too much about Melvin Bishop or the regional office."

Whitey said that not long after that, he received a call from someone he did not recognize, who told him to keep his mouth shut.

Whitey took a drag on the third cigarette he had bummed from Ken and took a sip of coffee. He looked up and told Ken that he was "definitely convinced that Mel Bishop had Hutchinson, assistant to the UAW-CIO Region 1, hire somebody to cripple up Vega and Snowden."

Whitey had one more point to make. He said that the previous July, he had sent a statement providing all the information he had just told Ken to Walter Reuther, and he slid across the table a telegram addressed to Reuther:

DEAR SIR AND BROTHER STOP I HAVE RECEIVED A PHONE CALL WEDNESDAY MORNING AT APPROXIMATELY 230 AM STOP THE PARTY THAT CALLED TOLD ME TO KEEP MY MOUTH SHUT OR I WOULD RECEIVE THE SAME TREATMENT THAT

MR ROY SNOWDEN AND ART VEGA RECEIVED
STOP I BELIEVE IT IS TIME FOR LOCAL UNION
AND INTERNATIONAL UNION TO THOROUGHLY
INVESTIGATE THE BEATING OF THE TWO
BROTHERS AND ALSO THE THREATS THAT
I HAVE RECEIVED BECAUSE I ONLY WANT TO
PREFER CHARGES AGAINST THE PEOPLE THAT
SHOULD BE EXPOSED. CHESTER KOSMALSKI

Reuther immediately responded with a letter:

Dear Brother Kosmalski:

This will acknowledge receipt of your wire of July 25,
relative to the threatening telephone call you received....
This is a most intolerable situation and one which
cannot be condoned by the UAW-CIO if we are to
remain a progressive, democratic trade union. I would
like to suggest that all the facts concerning this whole
problem be assembled and presented to the International
Executive Board for appropriate action.

After Ken read the correspondence, Whitey said that Walter
responded correctly, but the UAW Executive Board did nothing. He
added that Reuther and Dick Frankensteen sent a letter of concern to the
Detroit police commissioner.[208] Whitey pointed out that the Local 212
investigating committee put the facts together and sent it to the UAW
Executive Board and no action was taken.

Ken looked up with a new respect at the man across the table from
him. Whitey indicated that he had to go, as did Ken, but Ken sat for a
few minutes digesting all of this new information, finishing a cigarette.
He knew that once something got back to the UAW Executive Board,
politics and relationships could take a black-and-white issue and turn it
into many shades of gray.

Ken knew that Dick Frankensteen was leaving the UAW; in fact,
Dick had already announced that he was running for mayor of Detroit.

His departure meant a shift in the balance of power inside the UAW. It could be Walter's chance to be president, but for him to succeed, he could not afford enemies. Ken was not sure where Walter stood with Bishop, but in any battle with Bishop, Ken knew that Local 212 could not count on anyone on the UAW Executive Board. He crushed his cigarette out in the astray already filled with the half dozen other cigarette butts he and Whitey had consumed.

A new friend, Danny Masouris, the owner of Cupids, suddenly interrupted Ken's thoughts. Danny and his brother, Pete, had opened the restaurant upon their return from the war. Ken and Danny hit it off from the beginning and developed a friendship lasting fifty years. Danny greeted Ken, and they talked for a few minutes before Ken paid his bill and headed for the local.

. . . .

While the politics and life of Local 212 continued to evolve, Emil Mazey was stuck in the army, stationed in the Philippines. As 1945 turned into 1946, many in the army felt they were being treated like pawns and did not understand why. They simply wanted to return home and get back to their lives. In Washington, DC, Secretary of War Robert Patterson was under great pressure to slow down the demobilization of the military. His advisors told him and President Truman that armed conflict could break out with the Soviet Union at any time, saying that the United States should not dismantle the greatest army the world had known. While this global decision making evolved into the far more serious Cold War, men on military bases around the world wanted to come home.[209] No one was more interested in getting home than Emil Mazey. The Japanese had surrendered in August, and the world was moving forward without him.

In either late December or early January, Emil met with some other enlisted men, and he argued that instead of complaining about their plight, they ought to do something about it. Soon the men organized a meeting of about six hundred soldiers. The group created a six-person committee, which elected Emil as chair. They raised nearly six hundred dollars to send cables to President Truman, members of Congress, the media, and others. Emil's group then received permission from the base commander to have a larger meeting of four thousand men, where they raised nearly ten thousand dollars. They decided to follow the same pattern of contacting members of Congress and the press. They took out ads in the fifteen leading newspapers in the States to plead for demobilization. Within days, the demobilization effort, led by Mazey, had swept through the entire Philippine Islands and was reaching troops around the world.

On January 13, 1946, the *Detroit Free Press* editorialized:

Emil Mazey, Leader!

The appearance at Manila of Detroit's [Sergeant] Emil Mazey as one of their leaders does not help the cause of soldiers overseas who joined in mass demonstrations against Secretary of War Patterson and [the delay in] returning them to the United States.

Detroit will do all right for a while more, we think, without the presence of the man whose stormy career during five terms as president of UAW-CIO's Local No. 212, the Briggs union, stamped him as an agitator and an extremist....

Our sympathies are with all soldiers who are not needed, and we favor their earliest possible return home. However they must remember national policy and the duty of men in uniform to serve under their officers' orders.

Soon after the troops took action, a congressional committee was in the Philippines investigating the demobilization issue and other issues of waste and inefficiency that the men had documented. The committee wanted to interview Emil and other men, particularly regarding the issue of waste. Emil was told the men should speak freely as any testimony was not to be used against them. The problem, as Emil saw it, was that no one bothered to tell the enlisted men that they were immune to any repercussions. Emil tried to explain to the scared men that they were before a congressional committee and needed to speak freely. Several officers and some members of the congressional committee objected to Emil talking to the men and accused him of leading the witnesses. The committee held its hearings and told Mazey they would get back to him.

Unknown to Emil, his efforts, along with the efforts of many GIs from around the globe, led President Truman to order Secretary Patterson to move forward with demobilization. Truman and his political advisors realized that American citizens wanted the troops home and were not interested in more conflict. This order, however, took time to implement.

At some point, probably in February 1946, Emil received orders to pack his gear and report to his commanding officer. He was ordered to get on a waiting airplane. Emil walked toward the airplane with a confident stride, as he was sure the congressional committee must be calling him back to testify in Washington. All the good work had paid off! The plane took off, heading east, and after a few hours landed on a tiny island called Ie Shima, located in the South China Sea, about fifty miles east of Okinawa. Thinking it was a refueling stop, he got out to stretch his legs after the bumpy landing on the unpaved airstrip. As he walked away from the plane, the copilot threw his duffel bag off the plane and shut the airplane's door. The engines started, and the airplane took off. Emil had been taken to his new assignment, a job doing nothing on one of the most remote military bases in Asia, if not the world. The military had found a way to silence the union organizer from Detroit; they put him where no one could find him.[210]

While perhaps a great oversimplification, it might be said that Emil Mazey's leadership, his use of demonstration, his organizing skills, and his courage contributed significantly to the global effort by enlisted men that helped sway the Truman administration against a new military buildup. The Truman administration learned that the American people were tired of war.

. . . .

Ken spent his final weeks before the election campaigning. He attended membership meetings, talked at plant gates with workers, and had continuous breakfast, lunch, and dinner meetings with Local 212 members, often at Cupids. Having been away for so long, he brought a new perspective back to the campaign. His time and successes in the army had made him a more confident man. Being married to Doris had also brought a new sense of perspective to Ken's life. He was more than just one of Emil's followers; he had come into his own, as a leader and a man.

Jess Ferrazza was running as an underdog, and the Pioneer Ticket was running a negative campaign. In 1943, Ferrazza had followed Emil as Local 212 president after Emil was drafted. Following the popular and charismatic Emil Mazey was difficult, and Ferrazza simply was not well received by Local 212's membership. Then there was Ernie Mazey, who was running as Jess's vice president. From Ken's perspective, Ernie was completely different from Emil or Bill Mazey. Both Bill and Emil had warm hearts and open personalities as compared to their younger brother. More troubling was that Ernie was a CPer and Trotskyite. Ken thought one could believe in whatever political party one felt comfortable with, but that trade unionists had to put their union first. He was never sure that Ernie could do that.

Longtime Local 212 activist Tom Clampitt beat Jess Ferrazza by just 155 votes out of the 4,200 votes cast. Ernie Mazey lost by a greater margin: nearly 300 votes. Except for Ken, the Pioneer Ticket took a beating. Ken was not as close to the United Pioneer people, but he thought he could work with them.

The election of delegates to the upcoming UAW convention in Atlantic City told a different story. With the assumption that Emil Mazey might be back for the convention, he had been placed as a candidate for delegate. The Local 212 membership voted for nine delegates. Emil Mazey received the most votes (1,561), followed by the newly elected president, Tom Clampitt (1,042), and then Ken Morris (909). The Mazey group had taken at least six of the nine spots.[211] Ken's homecoming was almost complete. There was just one problem yet to be resolved: he had no job.

At the March 3 membership meeting immediately after the election, newly elected president Tom Clampitt rose to say that considering the workload and the problems facing the local, he recommended placing

Ken Morris, the newly elected recording secretary, on the local's staff at full-time salary. Of course, everyone in the hall knew that Ken could not work at Briggs, and the motion passed unanimously.[212]

Ken drove home that night feeling satisfied. Ken thought that with all the Mazey candidates losing, he represented the traditional Green Slate more than anyone else at the local. Perhaps the membership saw him as someone different, someone more than just a Mazey man.

What a night. What a welcome home. After all, he had been elected unanimously to a top position of his local after a four-year absence. He had just been placed on the Local 212 payroll. He was making only $75 a week ($3,900 annually), but that would be enough to meet the $45 rent at Parkside. He had the political base he needed. Moreover, as a result of all these actions, his arrival at next month's UAW convention as a newly elected officer of Local 212 should be grand. There was just one dark thought as he pulled into the parking spot behind his Parkside apartment: Melvin Bishop. Could they find a candidate to beat Melvin Bishop in Atlantic City?

CHAPTER 17

WALTER, I CAN SUPPORT YOU; I CAN'T SUPPORT BISHOP

Sometime in the late 1960s, Dad and I were driving somewhere in our 1968 Chrysler, and I asked why the UAW was not as democratic as the Teamsters were. After all, I said, the Teamsters were a direct democracy, with each member having one vote for president, unlike the UAW, which elected delegates to a convention that represented their local union members. It was possible, I said, that at a convention, delegates might not accurately represent their constituents back home. I'm sure Dad nearly drove off the road as I said this, but his answer was firm and sure. He said that the UAW's approach was much fairer. For example, he said to take on Walter Reuther in a national election was incredibly difficult and expensive. A challenger had to be able to raise money to visit nearly every union hall in the United States and Canada, while the incumbent routinely traveled the country on union business. Yet at a UAW convention, delegates could react to the latest information regarding a candidate. Plus, the opposition could quickly put a campaign together if any front-runners faltered. If real opposition developed or things suddenly changed, the delegates could react with the latest and most accurate information, and then they could return to their home locals to defend their votes. No place was this better demonstrated than the 1946 UAW convention.

MELVIN BISHOP HAD PROBLEMS OF his own as the 1946
UAW convention approached. He was no fool. He had been active in the
UAW from its inception, and he had been the UAW east side regional
codirector since 1941. He had to deal with the toughest, most unruly
militant group in the UAW, the men and women of Local 212, and he
had found ways to squelch their arrogance and disobedience. A real
opportunity was now opening up in the top ranks of the UAW, perhaps
the greatest time for advancement since 1939, and Melvin Bishop was
determined to take advantage of his chance.

The opportunity developed for two reasons. First, Dick Frankensteen
had announced he was leaving the UAW. Frankensteen was a UAW
pioneer. He was a popular leader who had navigated his way through
the Homer Martin years. Most people thought that either Frankensteen
or Walter Reuther would be the UAW president after R. J. Thomas.
Frankensteen's departure meant a vice presidency was opening up, and
as far as Melvin Bishop was concerned, this was his vice presidency.
Second, Melvin Bishop knew that Walter was planning to challenge R.
J. Thomas for the UAW presidency. The redhead had just led a successful
strike against General Motors, and now, with Frankensteen out of
the way, Bishop knew that Walter was going to make a run. Melvin
Bishop had been part of the Reuther group, but as regional director
had gravitated to the left wing, headed by George Addes. But because
his brother, Merlin, was a Reuther man and he knew Reuther could not
take a chance on losing the support of both Bishop brothers, Melvin
Bishop believed he could run for and receive Reuther's support for vice
president.

Before the UAW convention and the election for vice president,
Bishop had some problems that needed to be addressed. As always,
there was Briggs and that damn local, Local 212. The Mazey forces
had control of their huge block of convention delegates, and that was a
problem. Normally the 212 block was a major concern, but now that he
was running for a union-wide position, the Local 212 voting block was
less of a factor. His other problems were more severe since they affected
his relationship with Walter Reuther. Bishop and Victor Reuther had
had a falling out back in 1944 that had not fully mended. That was
not good for his ambitions. He also had managed to attract Walter's

attention over his treatment of a "pain-in-the-ass" UAW veteran just a few weeks earlier.

How did he get into these fixes? Moreover, could he repair the damage with Walter?

. . . .

Melvin Bishop was a tough, profane man who did not take crap from anyone. In 1944, he and Victor Reuther, then the UAW's assistant director of the union's War Policy Division, got into a classic battle between an International Executive Board member and a UAW staffer. Most board members were reasonable people and worked well with staff. However, getting on the wrong side of a UAW Executive Board Member could destroy a UAW International staffer's career. The difference in this case was that the UAW staffer was Victor Reuther, who had a longtime record as a UAW pioneer in his own right. It did not hurt that he was also Walter and Roy's brother.

Under Victor's leadership, the UAW was hosting a major 1944 veteran's conference in Washington, DC. A steering committee was proposed to handle the details of the conference. Victor Reuther, under the signature of R. J. Thomas, sent a letter to all regional directors, asking them to suggest potential members to serve on the nine-member committee. The letter indicated that previous military service was the top criteria for selection, not UAW region or geography. Reuther never received a nomination from the east side region, so he moved forward and selected the committee for the conference. Bishop saw Victor Reuther at a UAW board meeting after the deadline to select the committee and told Victor that he wanted to nominate Norman Mathews, a well-respected UAW leader from the east side region. Officially, however, the date to submit names had passed, and Victor, through a letter from R. J. Thomas, had already notified each UAW veteran selected as a steering committee member. Bishop, on his own authority, told Mathews that he was the region's steering committee member and to attend their meetings. Mathews flew to Washington, DC, to attend the meeting, but Victor informed him that he was not on the committee and could not participate in the meeting. Mathews was humiliated.

On April 12, 1944, Bishop sent a blistering memorandum to Victor Reuther. He told Victor that he and his codirector, Leo Lamotte, were extremely embarrassed by the fact that Mathews had been denied a seat at the steering committee meetings. He reminded Victor that he had spoken to him at the recent UAW board meeting, and based on that discussion, he had told Mathews to proceed to Washington. Then Bishop complained further that Mathews should have been seated since the committee, originally designed for nine members, had only seven appointed members. Finally, Bishop was outraged that the largest region in the UAW was ignored. Bishop closed the memorandum by stating, "May I suggest that in the future, even though we may not receive better cooperation, that at least a greater degree of coordination by way of information on such matters be adhered to."

Victor responded five days later. In a remarkably frank letter to a UAW Executive Board member, Victor wrote that if Bishop had read and followed the directions of previous letters, there would have been no problem. He pointed out the first communication from R.J. Thomas stated that the committee was to be between seven and nine members and that a nomination by regional directors would not necessarily mean an appointment to the committee (Victor did not want a political committee but rather a committee of people with clear-cut military experience). He further pointed out that Bishop did not supply a name until three days after the deadline, and by that time, the committee had already been named. Victor added:

> I can also agree with you that such a misunderstanding reflects very bad organizational policy, but not on this end. I can assure you that this office has always been, and is now, very anxious to give the best cooperation to all International Officers and Regional Directors. *Cooperation, however, is a matter which grows out of joint effort* [emphasis added]."[213]

Victor concluded the letter by writing that since Bishop's memorandum had been copied to R. J. Thomas, Secretary-Treasurer George Addes, Leo LaMotte, and Norman Mathews, he was doing the same. He also indicated that he was providing these people with copies of all the communications that had been sent on the matter. Victor Reuther knew how to protect himself against Bishop.

The matter technically ended, but Bishop was sure that Victor Reuther still harbored a grudge. In 1946, this incident was a nagging concern to Bishop as he prepared for the Atlantic City convention.

. . . .

Then there was a more serious problem. In early March 1946, Bill Marshall, the former president of Local 7 and the current head of the Veterans Department, accused Bishop of attacking a disabled veteran. In this case, Marshall sent R. J. Thomas a memorandum on March 8, 1946, raising the issue:

> Yesterday afternoon Brother Robert Stone was knocked down and kicked twice while lying on the floor in the same side in [which] he had been wounded twice. This was done by an International Board [sic] member, Melvin Bishop, without warning.[214]

Marshall noted that he had no idea what the argument was about, but he knew that Bishop had to be aware of the wounds that Stone had suffered. He described Stone as a twice-wounded veteran from the European front who had spent seven months in the hospital and had recently received a medical discharge. At the time of the beating, Stone was on the waiting list for three major surgeries in Ann Arbor. Marshall concluded his memo:

> I do not know what position the International Union will take in this matter but due to the number of calls and complaints this Department has received today in which we concur that the officers of the International recognize the seriousness of this affair and should act accordingly [sic].

Marshall copied Walter Reuther and Dick Frankensteen on the memo.

That same day, Walter Reuther sent a short memorandum to Melvin Bishop, referencing the Marshall memorandum: "Since the letter refers to conduct involving you personally, I should appreciate your comments on this matter before it is discussed with the top officers."

By this time, just two weeks out from the 1946 UAW convention, Walter had probably finalized his slate for his candidacy for president. Presumably, Bishop was already on the Reuther slate. The last thing Walter needed was a member of his slate, a man running for vice president, involved in an assault on a disabled veteran.

Bishop immediately responded to Reuther's memo by stating that Marshall never asked him for his side of the story, which involved a previous meeting with Stone before the beating. Bishop argued that Walter had only one side of the story. He then added:

> Rather than attach too much importance to the statement, I am rather inclined to believe that this "one-act melodrama" was written while Brother Marshall was in one of his frequent drunken stupors.[215]

Bishop went to Atlantic City as part of Walter Reuther's slate. He was running for Walter's vice presidency position should Walter oust R. J. Thomas.

. . . .

Just prior to the start of the convention, Walter Reuther met with Ken Morris to discuss Melvin Bishop. Walter knew Ken's feelings about the regional director, but he told Ken he had to have Melvin's support to get elected. Melvin's brother Merlin was now the educational director of the East Coast region and in a close election, Merlin and Melvin's support had to be maintained. Ken told Walter that he would never support Melvin Bishop. Walter replied that he could not support Ken's position.

Ken responded, "Walter, I can support you; I cannot support Mel Bishop, and I'm very damned unhappy."[216]

• • • • • • • • • • • • • •

As the convention approached, Bill Mazey, Ken Morris and a few others from Local 212 were implementing their own plans. These men and many like them, mostly veterans returning from the service, wanted a clean and democratic union. The UAW was considered one of the most democratic unions of its time, but the returning vets were tired of people like Melvin Bishop. They did not want the UAW to run like other unions that focused more on sheer power and not the needs of their membership. They felt that the UAW was a cut above such organizations.

These Local 212 delegates had something else on their minds. They decided to put forth Emil Mazey as a candidate for east side regional director. Mazey, still stuck on the island in the South China Sea, had no idea what was going on in Detroit or that his name was being thrown in as a candidate for regional director.

During the weeks and days approaching the convention, Bill, Ken and the rest of the Mazey team approached convention delegates and local union leaders from the east side region to assess their situation. Most people felt that since Emil was not home to campaign for himself, the men from Local 212 had no chance of taking on an incumbent or winning against a viable candidate attending the convention. The Mazey team was undeterred. The team found its way to Atlantic City a few days before the opening of the convention on March 23 and set up campaign headquarters at the Chelsea Hotel. At the convention hall, delegates saw a large sign announcing Emil's candidacy, and all 212 delegates pledged to work day and night to find votes for Emil.

Bishop could not have been happy about this turn of events, but his focus was on moving up to become a UAW vice president. He apparently chose not to worry about the Mazey candidacy or not to give it much credibility. He may have thought that he was going to be the UAW vice president and that becoming the next east side UAW regional director was someone else's problem.

The convention had all kinds of business to take up, but the upcoming elections created electricity among all the delegates in the hall. Walter Reuther was taking on R. J. Thomas! With Frankensteen out, all knew that this election was too close to call. The secretary-treasurer election traditionally follows the president's election, and it was common knowledge that the powerful George Addes was an odds-on favorite to be reelected. Then the two vice presidential elections followed. Bishop was running for the first seat should Walter win his election. After the union-wide election of officers, the convention would break up into regional caucuses for the election of regional directors.

At the convention, Ken picked up a terrible cold, and a doctor confined him to bed whenever possible. Trying to sleep on the afternoon before the presidential election, he heard a knock at the door, and when he opened it, he found Roy Reuther and Leonard Woodcock standing in the hallway. Walter, apparently feeling uncomfortable with their last conversation, told them to secure Ken's vote and support. Walter knew that if Ken decided to bolt, the popular returning veteran could easily take a number of Briggs and other delegate votes with him. The fact that Walter felt he had to send Roy and Leonard to secure his vote upset Ken a great deal, and he told the two men as much. For the next hour and a half, Ken made it clear that if he made a commitment, the commitment was solid. He was for Walter but could never support Bishop.

Ken told the two men that Walter knew everything that Melvin Bishop had done to the Mazey forces at Briggs. Ken, with anger rising in his voice, said that it was Melvin Bishop, the UAW regional codirector, who told Briggs to fire good union men, including Joe Vega, Art Snively, and himself. Ken reminded Roy and Leonard that he had taken this issue to the UAW Executive Board in 1941 and no one, not Walter or anyone else on the board, had offered support to Ken or the Briggs members of Local 212. Ken apologized for not having warm feelings toward Melvin Bishop. He said he would do everything in his power to end Bishop's career in the UAW. In the end, Roy and Leonard left Ken's room satisfied that Walter had Ken's vote, but Ken also felt that the two men had a greater respect for him. Roy was already a good friend of Ken's, but Ken felt that a new depth of understanding was reached with Roy and Leonard—an understanding that would stay with them for the rest of their lives.

It took a while for him to calm down, but Ken came to appreciate that Walter was counting every vote, as he knew the coming election was too close to call. Walter did not take a single delegate for granted and did not want to risk losing any votes.[217]

By the time of the president's election, the Local 212 people demonstrated their prowess. They had a block of around 400 votes for Emil Mazey at the regional level. Moreover, this block made them an important power block in the elections for president and the vice president races.

The UAW presidential race of 1946 was a defining moment in UAW history. Walter Reuther won this race by 124 votes out of 8,765 votes cast. Walter won because he was a leader, had a vision of the progressive force the UAW could be in American society, and had successfully led the 113-day 1945–46 strike by the UAW against General Motors. While R. J. Thomas called the strike an example of Reuther's poor leadership, the rank and file saw something that they liked: leadership and vision.

Walter Reuther celebrating his 1946 election as UAW president, with brother Roy looking on

Reuther was also the head of the right-wing caucus, which really represented liberal, center, and conservative political views of the union. The Communist and extreme left forces continued to support Thomas and George Addes, but these forces were weaker in postwar America. Reuther had grabbed the political center of the union.

Reuther's 124-vote margin made him president of the UAW. George Addes was easily reelected as secretary-treasurer, so the next key race was for the first vice presidency position. This was the position Melvin Bishop claimed, but he was in for a rude awakening. In most cases when a union president from a major union like the steelworkers or the mine workers lost an election, the defeated candidate stepped away quietly and often found a decent job with the CIO or other support organizations. In this case, R. J. Thomas was not going to ride off quietly into the sunset. Instead, he mustered a coalition of his own supporters and left-wing Communist Party forces. Together these forces delivered the first major defeat for Reuther, as Bishop lost his bid for vice presidency to R. J. Thomas by 556 votes. The Local 212 block of votes along with other dissatisfied east side local unions made the difference.

Bishop, not to be denied, decided to run for the second vice presidency position. This created a problem for Reuther, as he already had a candidate, John Livingston, running against Dick Leonard. However, a delegate from Local 669 did nominate Bishop with the following opening comment:

> I want to place in nomination a man whom I greatly admire, a man whom I think is a credit to the labor movement. I don't know too much of him …, but I have learned a lot since coming to this convention.

Regardless of whether it was this rousing and conflicting nominating speech or Reuther's concern about splitting his strength in a three-person race for the position, Bishop withdrew as a candidate for vice president. As it turned out, Livingston lost to Leonard. Reuther was now president of the union, but he had no support from either his secretary-treasurer or the two vice presidents. Bishop next had to see if he could retain his position as the east side regional director.[218]

Support for Bishop fizzled throughout the convention hall when people heard how he had attacked the disabled veteran just a few weeks earlier. Did Walter pick the wrong man to support? Perhaps, but the support of the Bishop brothers may have made the crucial difference in the Reuther election. Reuther had counted every vote. In the end, however, Reuther could not bring the necessary support for Bishop, as Local 212 stood unanimously in his way, a decision its members never regretted. The Local 212 delegates' next challenge was to ensure that Bishop was not reelected regional director.

Bill Mazey, Ken Morris, and the rest of the Mazey team were elated after the major UAW elections. The battle now moved from the huge convention hall to a smaller caucus room. Here the east side delegates met to vote for their next regional directors. The east side region had two codirectors. The incumbent codirector was Norman Mathews, the same person who had been banned from the veteran's conference two years earlier. Mathew's reelection was a cinch.

Bishop wanted to retain his office, but the 212 group had done its job. After reviewing where the delegates stood, even Bishop knew that he could not win, so he decided to save himself from further embarrassment and did not run for reelection as regional director. In and of itself, this was a huge victory for the dead end kids from Local 212. The next question was whether Emil Mazey, a man not present, could win.

The delegates elected Norman Mathews unanimously, which left several candidates vying for the second regional director position. Emil Mazey received the bulk of votes from the first local union in the region. Emil's victory was academic from then on, as he won in all the east side local unions. It was a great day for Bill Mazey, a brother loyal to another brother. It was a great sense of accomplishment for Ken Morris and Local 212 members as Bishop, the man who stood against honest union leadership, was defeated. If he did nothing else in the UAW, Ken was satisfied because he helped knock Melvin Bishop off the UAW Executive Board. Bill Mazey and Ken Morris were already great friends, but this moment of solidarity between the two was a bond that lasted the rest of their lives.[219]

. . . .

It was early May, and Sergeant Emil Mazey was commanding a small group of new soldiers on Shima Island. Their assignment: picking up trash. One of the new soldiers on the island heard someone refer to the sergeant by his name, Mazey. The guy asked if the fellow heading the detail was Emil Mazey of the UAW. Once it was affirmed, the private walked up to the sergeant and said, "Congratulations on being elected to the UAW Executive Board." More than a month after the fact, Emil found out that he had been elected to take Melvin Bishop's place.[220]

As luck would have it, the army was through with Emil. By mid-May, he was shipped back to the States and by the third week of May, Emil was working at the desk that once belonged to Melvin Bishop.[221]

. . . .

Ken returned to Detroit and felt more empowered than ever. Bishop was gone, and now he wanted to focus on building Local 212.

What were Fay Taylor and the Briggs Manufacturing Company thinking? They could not have been happy to see Morris, a Mazey man, back from the war and elected to office. They certainly were not happy that Local 212 had led the effort to oust their man, Bishop, from his position of power in the UAW. Even worse, the election of Emil Mazey to replace Bishop had to be the worst nightmare imaginable for the Briggs management.

In May, Dean Robinson, now the president of Briggs, sent a letter to all employees. The letter indicated that the company was interested in sharing "greater prosperity and security for the employees." The letter talked about more cooperation in the plant in an effort to create a stronger company. Ken, thinking that the letter sounded shallow and insincere, studied the words carefully and wrote a scathing editorial in response to the Robinson letter.

Ken's editorial appeared in the *Voice of Local 212* on May 24, 1946. He went after Briggs, Dean Robinson, and Fay Taylor. In an editorial dripping with sarcasm, Ken wrote, "At last! The company cares! The impossible has happened! The company wants to do something for the workers!"

Ken's editorial said the workers were happy to cooperate with Briggs, but Briggs management had to understand that cooperation is a two way street. He wrote that Briggs "workers want an opportunity to live a decent life without being subject to constant threats of discharge!" He must have incensed Briggs management when he wrote:

> Your workers, [a] great many of them were in the Armed Forces, do not like to see Hitler's Gestapo methods used in your plants! Do you? The workers know that every time they open their mouths—every time they ask for something they believe is right—every time they mention an improvement, particularly in working conditions and safety improvement—one of your salaried men [makes] a report direct to headquarters (Mr. Taylor's office) in the same manner as they did in the factories patrolled and controlled by the Nazis in Germany during their regime. And, Mr. Robinson, your workers did their part in eliminating that set up. Remember? Why bring it [into] the Briggs' plants?

Continuing, Ken made suggestions that might actually encourage cooperation in the plant. He wrote that if workers had complaints, the supervisors and superintendents should be empowered to resolve minor concerns. He wondered if the company's policy was one of actually provoking wildcat strikes when the company implemented policies that angered workers in the plant. He wrote that the company's attitude always seemed to begin from the perspective that the worker is wrong and the company never makes mistakes.

Ken concluded by stating, "Cooperation is not one-sided, Mr. Robinson! Both sides must cooperate. If the Briggs Manufacturing Company will cooperate and give instead of always taking, we'll get along! Don't you think so, Mr. Robinson?" [222]

Ken felt good about this editorial. It was strong, but it put issues that needed to be said on the table. It further demonstrated that the ex-GI was still a militant Local 212 leader.

. . . .

Somewhere soon after this editorial was published, some discussions took place. The discussions might have been at a country club in Grosse Pointe, a bar on Jefferson Avenue, or in an office of the Briggs Manufacturing Company, but the discussions took place. This man Morris had insulted the Briggs nobility. He had accused them of being Nazis, the greatest insult of all considering everything they had done during the war. This man, this Mazey man, had attacked the company's labor policies, and whether there was a ring of truth or not, it had to be stopped. Compounding problems was Mazey's return to replace Bishop, and now this man Morris and his editorial ... It must be stopped.

Within the week, Ken Morris was nearly beaten to death, hanging on to life in an east side hospital.

PART *III*

VIOLENCE AND INVESTIGATIONS:
1946 TO 1958

CHAPTER 18

I DIDN'T THINK KEN WOULD MAKE IT

Sometime in the late 1970s, Dad; Greg; Greg's wife, Audrey; and I were driving to downtown Detroit. Along the way, Greg asked Dad if he remembered the time back in the late 1950s when he was caught playing with a handgun in our parent's bedroom. "Hell, yes," Dad replied. "I couldn't believe it. I walked in and you were standing there twirling that gun like a cowboy. I was never so scared. It was the last night that gun stayed under our roof." From the backseat, I said, "So that's what happened to that pistol." Dad turned in horror. "Jesus Christ, don't tell me you were playing with that gun, too?" I said, "Yep, I always wondered what happened to it." I couldn't believe that Greg and I had never talked about that gun before that moment. After Dad's beating, his good friend Bill Dufty had given the gun to him for protection. Dad had kept it buried behind his many multicolored pairs of socks in a dresser drawer, an easy location for two little boys to find.

FLOATING IN AND OUT OF consciousness, Ken remembered little from that first week in Saratoga Hospital. His life passed through his mind during the first couple of days, but as the sedatives were decreased, he began focusing on the question of why he had been attacked and who did it. He had no enemies at Local 212. Bishop was out of power, though still on the International UAW payroll as the director of the union's skilled trades department. Ken was sure he would not risk his job by ordering an attack. Then there was Briggs. Ken did not want to believe the company paid someone to attack him, even though the local's committee studying the previous beatings was convinced that the company had hired mobsters to attack the other Local 212 members.

The Detroit police and an assistant Wayne County prosecutor interviewed him. Ken was of little help, as he had no memory of the assailants. The Detroit police seemed to want to help, but outside of being polite to Ken and Doris, they never seemed to do anything.

Doris, who did not drive, was nearly always at his side. Usually she took the Conner Avenue bus to Gratiot, or one of the wives picked her up and brought her to the hospital. It took a week before the doctors allowed Ken to look at his wounds in a mirror—they were afraid of the emotional trauma he might experience when he saw his broken, bruised, and swollen face reflecting back at him. Even without seeing himself in a mirror, Ken knew it was bad by the reaction of his visitors. In those first few days, most visitors walked into his hospital room with good cheer and then winced in dismay when they focused on his face. They quickly recovered and talked about his recovery.

Emil or Charlotte Mazey visited almost every day. When Emil, who had just returned from overseas, saw Ken, he just became more incensed about the beating. No one knew better than Emil that being a labor leader was a tough business. On numerous occasions, Emil had been in fights, been pushed around by police, and in turn had pushed back on those police. Some rough characters had threatened him in the past. He had seen men beaten up by hoodlums and the police, but Emil had never seen a beating administered in such a brutal fashion.

George Edwards and his wife, Peg, visited. George, now the president of Detroit's Common Council and serving as Ken's attorney, visited his client. Later, George recalled that visit:

> [Ken] was conscious but very weak. When I returned to the car, I told my wife that I didn't think that Ken would make it. [But] Morris's relative youth and conditioning from his military service stood him in good stead.[223]

Others visited him, especially Local 212 stalwarts Pat and Vivian Caruso, and Steve and Emily Despot. They were constant support for both Ken and Doris.

As the sedatives decreased, the pain increased. While Ken was still in critical condition, the doctors told him it would take weeks for his initial recovery and months before he was back to normal.

The labor movement was stunned by this blatant attack on a respected UAW leader, a World War II veteran, and a man universally recognized as a good guy.

. . . .

Labor leaders and people around Detroit learned the details of the incident from the local newspapers. The first story appeared in the early edition of the *Detroit Free Press* hours after Ken was taken to the hospital on Saturday June 1, 1946:

> Kenneth Morris, 30, of 12117 E. Warren, [recording secretary] of Briggs Local 212, UAW-CIO, is in Saratoga General Hospital with injuries he received when two unidentified men attacked him as he parked his car in the rear of his home, police said.
>
> Morris told police he did not know the men. Hospital authorities said he had been kicked and beaten severely. The Briggs unit is known as one of the UAW-CIO's most militant locals.

On Sunday, June 2, the *Free Press* took a different approach as it referred to the Briggs beatings as *The Terror*:

> Briggs Local 212 has had its latest visitation of The Terror and again international officers of the UAW (CIO) as well as officials of the local are baffled.
>
> Two men—they are always two—struck down Kenneth Morris … Friday night.…
>
> The attackers, as on four previous attacks in the last

13 months, never spoke a word as they fractured one of [Morris's] arms as well as his nose, skull, and wrist.

Saturday, Emil Mazey ... said he planned to ask a grand jury to investigate the beatings.

At the same time homicide squad detectives and the Wayne County prosecutor's office were searching for two persons said to have witnessed the attack. Morris could provide no clues....

The motives for the beatings never have been clear, according to UAW (CIO) officials. The victims have been of diverse union political faiths.

On the same day, Sunday, June 2, this appeared in the *Detroit Times*:

Two known suspects are being sought by detectives as the assailants of Kenneth Morris ... who was severely beaten with an iron bar Friday night ...

Their identity became known while police were denying charges of union leaders that the department was lax in attempting to find the instigators of a series of attacks against officers and members of Local 212....

Neighbors who saw two assailants flee obtained the license number of their Packard car, [and] ownership was traced to a member of the union, police said.

The owner, detectives said, reported [that] he had loaned his car yesterday to two men whose descriptions correspond with those of the men who attacked Morris.

Police Inspector George McLellan replied hotly to charges by Emil Mazey, UAW-CIO regional director, that the "Police either were incompetent or unwilling to act."

Mazey said he would ask for a grand jury to investigate the attacks.

Police have been hampered by lack of "co-operation

from union members and victims," the inspector said. "We were not notified of the attack on Morris until three hours after it occurred. Maybe a grand jury would force them to cooperate."

George Edwards, president of common council and personal friend of Morris, conferred Saturday with officers of the local about the attack.

On June 3, the *Detroit Times* wrote that the Detroit police reported that their original theory of the attackers was inaccurate:

The clue which led police to believe they knew the two assailants who beat Kenneth Morris ... into insensibility Friday night collapsed today and the search for the pair began anew....

Morris ... is unable to describe his assailants, the inspector added, and other witnesses gave divergent accounts of the attack.

The attack, fifth in a series upon union officers and members of the Briggs union in the last 14 months ...

On June 4, Emil Mazey's plea for a grand jury investigation was successful. The *Detroit Free Press* reported:

An investigation of thug terrorism at Briggs Local 212 UAW (CIO) has been started by the Grand Jury.

It will seek to discover the forces behind five attacks and severe beatings with lead pipes administered to four Briggs local officials over a period of 14 months.

The new jury action followed a formal petition by the UAW signed by its president, Walter P. Reuther.

The union termed the beatings the work of "professional hirelings of antilabor groups," discounting a theory of intra-union trouble.

Grand Juror George B. Murphy and special

Prosecutor [*sic*] Lester S. Moll formally accepted the new probe in a meeting with union officials Monday.

"This is certainly closely enough allied to our purpose to warrant a thorough investigation," Moll declared.

The new jury twist broadened the [Grand Jury's] investigation, originally aimed at the (AFL) Teamsters' attempts to organize Detroit's independent food merchants....

Meantime, the jury moved into permanent headquarters on the nineteenth floor of the National Bank Building, where investigators will start taking formal testimony [*sic*].

The *Free Press* followed up the next day, Wednesday, June 5, with an editorial:

Decision by Judge George B. Murphy to include within the scope of his grand jury [on] terrorism that afflicts a UAW local may at first glance appear to be a digression. Efforts of the AFL Teamsters Union to squeeze tribute from independent grocers is the jury's primary business.

However, it is proper and doubtless necessary that the jury inquire into sluggings that have had officials of Briggs Local No. 212 as their victims.

In the nether world of hoodlumism there is an interlocking of affairs. Its mercenaries don't limit themselves to one cause or one general. The exploring investigator cannot predict where the trail will lead, so he cannot set limits to his probing so long as it remains in the general field under examination.

On June 6, seven days after the beating, the UAW Executive Board met in Cleveland. Jack Crellin, a man who later became the *Detroit News*'s labor reporter for decades, wrote for the *Detroit Times:*

A $10,000 reward for the arrest and conviction of persons responsible for the beatings of members of Briggs Local 212 was offered today by the international executive board of the UAW-CIO. A reward of $1,000 has been offered by the local.

After a week's investigation, the Detroit Police Department did not detain any suspects. Many in the police department believed that this was simply a case of intraunion dissension and that it was up to the union to clean itself up. Yet the attacks on Ken and the other victims were professional. There were no threats by the assailants. In Ken's case, however, unreported was the fact that two clues were left at the scene of the crime. The police found a hat and lead blackjack on the ground near Ken's Ford. These clues might lead to the criminals. Yet within weeks of their placement in the department's evidence room, the clues disappeared. Emil Mazey and other union officials wondered how this could be. Did the criminals have an inside man in the police department? Or perhaps the police just didn't give a damn.

Of course, even if the attacks were the result of intraunion politics, they were still illegal assaults of a Detroit citizen. Should not the police try to find these attackers, whoever they might be? Or was the implication that union members had to live under a different set of standards, something less than other citizens?

Predictably, Local 212 was outraged. The Local 212 president, Tom Clampitt, editorialized against the beatings and took on the issue of intra-local-union politics as the reason behind the violence. Clampitt wrote that such an argument defied logic, since Ken had been on the slate of both political factions in the local and had been elected without opposition.[224] At a June 9 membership meeting of the local, Clampitt said that the lack of motives was confusing the police department, as was its belief that all five beatings were about intraunion politics. He pointed out that this could not be the case with Ken Morris. The police department, he said, had to look elsewhere for the perpetrators. Clampitt recommended, and the membership agreed, to increase the reward money to five thousand dollars. He also moved that members be assessed fifty cents a month to pay for hospital bills and lost time of all five Local 212 members that had been beaten.[225]

At some point during the first days or weeks after the beating, the officer in charge of the investigation, Detroit Police Sergeant Albert DeLamielleure, visited Ken. He made an offhand remark that the beatings had to be part of internal strife in the local. Ken knew then that the Detroit Police Department would never find the assailants.[226]

. . . .

As the weeks passed, interest in the Briggs beatings faded. Ken continued to improve. After three weeks in the hospital, he went home to continue his recovery. Before he left the hospital, the police advised Ken to get a handgun. A few days later, he and a friend, probably Pat Caruso, obtained a .38-caliber pistol. Several days later, Bill Dufty, the writer, visited. Dufty provided Ken with a .22 caliber automatic pistol for protection. These pistols never saw action, although Ken did keep one in his desk for many years. He kept the other, the .22 pistol, in his bedroom dresser at home.

In mid-August, Ken made his first return to the local's offices, needing crutches to assist his movements. He always remembered the thirty laborious steps he'd had to climb and descend to get to and from his second-story office. As the weeks progressed, so did his recovery. New battles were now developing in the local, as the opposition became Communists and Trotskyites led by several people including Tony Czerwinski and Ernie Mazey—Emil and Bill's kid brother.

Emil Mazey did not forget about the beatings. As 1947 arrived, he grew more frustrated by the secret one-man grand jury. The grand jury had begun investigating the case immediately. Secret testimony in the matter took place in late 1946 and early 1947, but no indictments were issued. Rumors of a sweetheart scrap metal deal between Briggs and the mobster Santo Perrone existed, but nothing happened. Emil wondered in the press why Judge Murphy did not issue indictments. He publicly said that perhaps the judge was afraid to indict people working for a major company such as Briggs. Murphy's response was straightforward: "If Mazey has any information to support an indictment—whether it be a laborer or a man in the front office—we want him to come in."[227] Later, it was learned that Emil was right. Judge Murphy had some of his own issues to hide.

Mazey had strong opinions but no proof. That was supposed to be the job of the Detroit Police Department, the Wayne County prosecutor and the grand jury. Further, Emil could not understand why three top management officials at Briggs, men who knew about how scrap metal contracts were issued, had recently died. He wondered why these three coincidental deaths were not seriously investigated, but even these concerns faded as time marched on.

. . . .

One day, probably toward the fall of 1946, Ken was meeting with Sam Katz, the owner of a company called American Mailers. Katz had built his company by providing home mailing addresses and labels for Detroit area unions and other organizations. Ken had copies of the Local 212 paper, the *Voice of Local 212*, delivered from the printer to American Mailers, where the company labeled the papers with member addresses and mailed them. Because the local's membership was between twenty-five thousand and thirty thousand, this was a big account for American Mailers.

After their meeting was over, Ken walked out of Sam's office and past the big presses that folded and labeled newsprint or envelopes. As he moved forward, still limping and using a cane, another fellow walked by, obviously heading back to Sam's office for a meeting. Ken recognized Jimmy Hoffa immediately. They did not know each other well, but well enough to nod a greeting to each other as they passed.

After Hoffa walked by, he stopped and turned back to Ken and stated, "Kenny, if you want, I can find out who did this to you. I can get them."

Ken, surprised by Hoffa's interest, turned and said, "Thanks Jimmy, but that's not how we do things in the UAW. We'll find them and bring them to trial."

Hoffa shrugged his shoulders and said, "Okay, if that's the way you want it," continuing on to Sam Katz's office.[228]

• • • • • • • • • • • • •

As was his habit, Ken often worked late at night. Once, Sol Dollinger, the husband of Briggs beating victim Genora Dollinger, was meeting with Ken at his upstairs Local 212 office. Dollinger was expressing concern about rumors that the gangster Sam Perrone was involved in the beatings. He asked Ken about their safety. Ken had no advice to give him but opened the bottom drawer of his desk, where the .38 pistol was lying neatly in the drawer. Ken said, "When I get ready to leave the office, I always check through the blinds … and make sure the street is clear before I go to my car."[229]

In the fall of 1946, Ken received a telephone call. The caller did not identify himself. The voice on the other end said that if Ken didn't lay off Briggs, he was going to be taken care of. The caller hung up.[230]

• • • • • • • • • • • • •

The 1947 UAW convention was approaching. Walter Reuther had spent most of 1946 battling his majority opposition on the UAW Executive Board. At the fall convention, he was either going to be reelected or defeated, becoming a has-been labor leader. The Addes, Thomas, Leonard faction knew they controlled the Reuther faction on the UAW Executive Board, but they didn't know if they could defeat Reuther at the convention. George Addes then came up with a scheme to change the balance of power at the upcoming UAW convention. The Communist-leaning leadership of the Farm Equipment Workers (FE) had forty-three thousand members and wanted to merge with the UAW. The FE leadership saw that America was becoming more conservative, especially since the passage of the antilabor Taft-Hartley Act, and they needed the protection of a large union. The Reuther opposition knew that if a merger occurred between the two unions, in return of FE's newfound stability as part of the UAW, the Addes, Thomas, and Leonard slate was going to pick up 450 to 500 FE delegates at the upcoming convention, thus making the defeat of Reuther and his forces more likely.

At a June 1947 UAW Executive Board meeting, Reuther was surprised when a proposal to allow FE to merge with the UAW was placed as an agenda item. Reuther, visibly upset, did not have the votes to stop the proposal. Reuther supporters, however, were able to convince the majority of the board to allow a union-wide referendum to determine the outcome. The national referendum ultimately was to show which group had the support of the UAW rank and file—Walter Reuther and his followers or the Addes, Thomas, and Leonard group. This union-wide referendum was held in July and became the most significant factor leading up to the November 1947 convention. The two opposing forces sprang into action, each developing a campaign to win or defeat the FE merger proposal.[231]

At Local 212, Ken was back on his feet and back to work. The local's spring 1947 election had been a nightmare for Ken. While he was easily reelected recording secretary, the other candidates on Ken's Green Slate were defeated by the left-leaning White Slate. The election had been a nasty one, with false charges of corruption thrown at the long-serving financial secretary P. P. McManus. After newly elected president Tony Czerwinski and his team took office, the Local 212 offices were lonely for Ken.

When the UAW Executive Board adopted the FE referendum proposal, Ken, like other Reuther supporters around the country, took up the cause in opposition. The issue was not really whether one was for or against the merger of the agricultural workers; it was whether such a merger should take place right before the upcoming UAW convention, thus bringing in a new voting block and skewing the vote in favor of Reuther's opposition.

Local 212 sponsored seven meetings to debate the FE proposal. Ken, along with other FE opponents from the local, debated Tony Czerwinski and other supporters of the proposal at locations near the seven Briggs' plants. The debates were intense and became bitter. It was about Communist control of the union and whether the union would be controlled by the extreme left and Communist-supported officials or, instead, by a more centrist anti-Communist leadership. It was also about basic fairness. Under the new formula worked out by the proponents of the "deal," the director of the new agriculture department and his or her staff could make appointments without the consent of the UAW

Executive Board. Every other department director in the UAW needed the board's approval, so this broke precedent and created controversy.

Local 212 voted early in the national referendum, and the membership of the local voted the FE proposal down by an eight-to-one margin. This was a major victory for the Reuther forces in the local and a huge personal victory for Ken Morris. Just as in the 1939 vote on whether union membership supported the UAW-CIO or the UAW-AFL, Local 212 demonstrated its strength and leadership. Nationally, the FE proposal was defeated by a two-to-one margin, and Reuther went to the UAW convention confident not only of reelection but also of gaining seats on the UAW Executive Board. Ken recalled in 1979: "It was the beginning of the end of [Communists] in the UAW."[232]

The November convention was almost anticlimactic for Walter Reuther. He easily won reelection. The surprising race was for secretary-treasurer. Here, Emil Mazey took on George Addes, the man who had held the position since the inception of the union and was always perceived as unbeatable.

During the nominations for the secretary-treasurer position, Walter Reuther recognized Ken Morris. Ken, standing at a microphone near the Local 212 table, began speaking, his voice echoing through the hall:

> I rise to place in nomination the name of a man for the office of Secretary-Treasurer who needs no introduction to the delegates of this great Convention. [His] record of militancy, aggressiveness and ability which has been responsible for the organization of many plants into the UAW-CIO in 1936 and 1937 …
>
> He was elected … president [of Local 212] five times. He played a prominent role in the organization of the Ford workers and directed the wage negotiations for the Ford workers after their famous strike in 1941.
>
> His contribution in helping solidify the UAW-CIO in 38 and 39 [sic] during the abortive attempts of [Homer Martin] to split our Union has made the name of his Local Union, Local 212, a famous one throughout

the UAW-CIO. During this period no fight was too big no Local was too small when they needed the help of his Local Union [*sic*]....

I am proud to nominate Emil Mazey for the office of Secretary-Treasurer.[233]

The election should have been close. In spite of Addes's left leanings, he was well liked by the membership and an honest UAW executive. To the surprise of many, Emil's landslide election, 4,821 to 2,573, ended Addes's career in the UAW with an exclamation point. In the end, Reuther supporters controlled all but two UAW Executive Board seats. Walter could now run the union and focus on collective bargaining and social issues. And what of the Addes, Thomas, and Leonard faction? Nelson Lichtenstein's *The Most Dangerous Man in Detroit* points out that Thomas and Leonard took staff jobs with the CIO, and Addes left organized labor to run a bar.

. . . .

After the 1946 convention, Melvin Bishop was given the assignment of director of the UAW's skilled trades department. Bishop wisely did not create much publicity in this new role and no doubt was pleased to have a good position with the International UAW.

In 1946, not long after Emil Mazey returned to become the east side UAW regional director, he found a little black book, a telephone book, in a desk drawer; it belonged to Melvin Bishop. Thumbing through the book, Emil stopped at the P tab and saw the initials SP along with a telephone number. Emil had the number called and found that it belonged to Santo Perrone. Emil kept this information to himself and Jack Conway, Walter Reuther's top aide.[234]

On November 21, 1947, the police arrested several people just outside of the northern Michigan town of Comins. The charge was deer shining, the illegal act of deer hunting at night by using a flashlight or car headlights to attract deer. One of those arrested was Santo Perrone, who was staying at his northern hunting lodge. The other person was Melvin Bishop. While both denied knowing one another, the local sheriff begged to differ and made clear that they were together and obviously acquainted.[235]

The deer-shining incident was the straw that broke the camel's back, and Reuther had to take action. With the Reuther forces in full control of the UAW, Walter did what people like Ken Morris, Emil Mazey, the Vega brothers, and a host of other people in the UAW had been waiting for. In a December 14 meeting, Reuther met with and fired Melvin Bishop from the UAW.[236]

CHAPTER 19

THE DIRTY BASTARDS SHOT ME IN THE BACK

In 1960, Dad was a delegate to the National Democratic Convention in Los Angeles, the convention that nominated John F. Kennedy for president. We took a family trip to Hollywood. Along the way, Dad talked to my brother about Walter Reuther's shooting (and I, of course, was listening intently). He said the doctors told Walter that his arm would have to be amputated, but that the UAW president refused. As part of his rehabilitation, Dad said Walter had strengthened his arm by constantly squeezing a rubber ball, and that exercise had helped Walter regain the strength in his arm. When we stopped in Denver, we visited the Gates Rubber Company and Dad purchased two hard rubber balls for Greg and me to help build our arms up. Later, at the convention, I was with Dad, and we ended up in Walter's hotel suite. There were many men coming and going (probably upset over Kennedy's selection of Lyndon Johnson as his vice-presidential candidate). When I shook hands with Walter, I remember being somewhat disappointed that no rubber ball was in sight. Later, Dad said he did not squeeze the ball as much as he used to since he had made such a good recovery.

IT WAS A RELATIVELY EASY decision for Ken Morris to run for president of Local 212 in 1948. After the 1947 election disaster, Ken was the highest-ranking Green Slate officer at Local 212. But taking on Tony Czerwinski, a popular Local 212 member and the incumbent president, was not going to be easy. Ken did have advantages. He could debate against anyone; he was a local union hero and martyr; no one worked harder than he did, especially at settling grievances; and he was a Reuther-Mazey man. The defeat of the proposal to merge the Communist-oriented Farm Equipment Workers cemented Ken's leadership position in the local.[237]

Ken was confident that he could win the election, but there were other concerns. In the back of his mind, he remembered his promise to Doris: if he lost a union election, he had agreed to find a job in a plant, go to law school, and join the Rothe law firm. He also had other responsibilities to consider. He was a father now; his first son, Greg, had been born the previous July, and Ken was still making only seventy five dollars a week.

Now, two years after his return from the service, Ken was not sure he could keep that law school promise. Even if he did not go to law school, other options existed. Gus Scholle, the president of the state CIO, had approached Ken and offered him the vice presidency in that organization. Ken politely rejected Gus's offer, as he felt that staying in the local was more important than becoming what essentially was a lobbyist position in Lansing for CIO issues.[238] Now, Ken knew that such positions were available. He was confident he could find something at the International UAW headquarters, either with Emil or in some other department. No matter what happened, Ken was sure he could provide for Doris and Greg.

Since returning from the service, Ken's focus and ability to solve grievances and other problems for Local 212 members became legend. As time passed, members knew that if they had a concern of any kind, they should find Ken Morris so the matter could be addressed one way or another.

The late February election approached, and the campaign turned rough, typical of every Local 212 election. He asked his good friend, and perhaps the best man in the local at solving worker grievances, Pat Caruso, to run as his vice president. Local 212 stalwarts Steve Despot and Jack Pierson ran for financial secretary and recording secretary positions, respectively. There were charges and countercharges as the election heated up.

Just a few days before the election, the opposition released a brochure attacking Ken and the Green Slate delegates for exorbitant expenses at the recent UAW convention. Ken knew that neither he nor his people had spent lavishly, but when their hotel, meals, and travel expenses were added up, and considering the fact that they had the majority of delegates, it was a lot of money—especially from a regular member's point of view. Ken thought he was doomed.

Then a friend, probably a secretary, from Local 212's financial secretary's office gave Ken information regarding expenses of everyone in the local for the year 1947. Ken compared his Green Slate expenditures to Czerwinski's White Slate costs and was in for a big-time awakening— the expenses of the White Slate officials made Ken and his Green Slate colleagues look like cheapskates. Ken quickly made handouts of this information and passed them out at the plant gates the morning of the election. He hoped this flyer would be in time to save the election.

The Local 212 election was held on February 25 and 26. Ken won by over eight hundred votes, 4,911 to 4,090. All the Green Slate candidates swept their races, and Local 212 was now a Reuther, Mazey, Morris local. Immediately after the election, Walter Reuther swore in Ken and his slate as Local 212 officers.

Briggs had fired Ken in 1941 as being part of the militant UAW faction encouraging wildcat strikes. Even though Melvin Bishop had framed him on these charges, Briggs management perceived Ken as a militant unionist and a disgruntled former Briggs employee. The assumption, especially by Briggs, was that Ken would be very tough on the company. There is, therefore, special irony in Ken's first action as president of Local 212, the local known for their wildcat strikes. In the first edition of the *Voice of Local 212* after the election, an open letter appeared on the front page of the paper:

Wildcat Strikes Not Tolerated

Since the [Morris] administration has taken office, there have been two unauthorized work stoppages in the Briggs plants.

This kind of action is in violation of the rules established by the membership of Local 212.

WILDCAT STRIKES DO NOT SETTLE GRIEVANCES. THERE IS AN ESTABLISHED GRIEVANCE PROCEDURE TO HANDLE ALL GRIEVANCES. ONLY AFTER THIS PROCEDURE HAS BEEN EXHAUSTED CAN A STRIKE BE CALLED, AND THEN ONLY BY A MAJORITY VOTE OF THE ENTIRE MEMBERSHIP.

NO INDIVIDUAL OR GROUP OF INDIVIDUALS HAS THE RIGHT TO CALL A STRIKE WITHOUT THE CONSENT OF THE REST OF THE MEMBERSHIP.

We, the officers of Local 212, do not intend to stand idly by and let this type of action continue and wreck our union.

We have been elected by the rank and file to carry out the responsibilities of our offices in a constructive and efficient manner.

WE INTEND TO DO JUST THAT!!!!!

Don't leave your jobs unless an authorized strike is voted and called for by the entire membership.

WILDCAT STRIKES WILL NOT BE TOLERATED!!

KEN MORRIS, President
PAT CARUSO, Vice-Pres
STEVE DESPOT, Fin. Sec'y
JACK PEARSON, Rec. Sec'y[239]

The man who ran as a militant and a self-described Mazey follower staked his political future on controlling wildcat strikes. Ken's straightforward approach worked. Ken was reelected president of Local 212 six times. After being president, his UAW career continued to evolve as he became one of the most respected labor leaders in Michigan. But in 1948, the violence directed at UAW leadership was not over. In fact, it was escalating.

· · · · · · · · · · · · · ·

About two months later, on Tuesday April 20, 1948, Walter Reuther was heading home from a typical fourteen-hour day. The previous six months since his reelection and the sweeping victory of his candidates on the UAW Executive Board had been hectic. Reuther had just finished a board meeting at the Book Cadillac Hotel and stopped by his office at the UAW headquarters on Milwaukee Street before heading home. It was around nine thirty, and he was looking forward to the reheated dinner May was keeping for him.

He and May, along with their two small daughters, lived in a modest ranch house at 20101 Appoline Street in Detroit, just south of Eight Mile Road, between Schaefer Highway and Wyoming Street. The three-bedroom home sat on the northwest corner lot of Appoline and Chippewa streets. The house's driveway was actually on Chippewa Street, and normally Reuther parked his car on Chippewa Street and walked through the backyard to the back door of the house. For some unknown reason, on this Tuesday night, he parked his car at the front of his house on Appoline and entered his home through the front door. It was a decision that saved his life, as an assassin was lying in wait for him in his backyard. The plan was to fire a shotgun into his chest, killing "the most dangerous man in Detroit," as George Romney, the head of the Automobile Manufacturers Association, labeled Reuther. The assassin's opportunity appeared lost.

It was good to be home. Reuther greeted his wife, kicked off his shoes, removed his tie, and entered the kitchen. The two girls were asleep as he quickly ate the warmed food and caught up on the happenings around the house during the day. May Reuther was explaining that she believed their oldest daughter, Linda, had a slight defect in her walk. Reuther rose and reached into the refrigerator for some peaches and quickly turned to May as she was demonstrating Linda's walk. Just as he turned, the shotgun blast blew through the kitchen window. Because of his last move, he received four pellets through his right arm and one pellet in his chest, while the other pellets hit the wall behind their intended target. The last movement he made to listen to his wife saved his life.

Walter collapsed in a mass of blood and human tissue to the kitchen floor. He cried, "My God, May, I've been shot!" May immediately called the police and an ambulance. In seemingly a matter of seconds, a neighbor came, saw the situation, and ran down the street to a doctor's house. The doctor came and administered morphine. He heard Walter say, "Those dirty bastards shot me in the back. They couldn't come out in the open and fight!"[240]

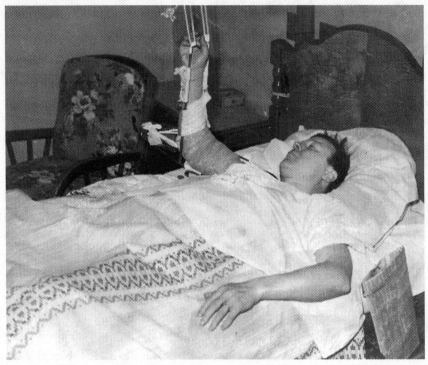

Walter Reuther recovering from 1948 assassination attempt

The ambulance, the police, and others swarmed over the house. Walter was whisked away to New Grace Hospital. The doctors told him that they wanted to amputate his right arm. Walter rejected the thought; death was preferable than continually living with the mark of an assassination attempt displayed on his body. After three hours of surgery, Walter was placed in a body cast, his right arm was placed in traction, and he was told he would live. Roy and Victor were at his and May's side during the entire ordeal.

Walter was later transferred to Ford Hospital, where the best doctors in the city told him that his arm should be placed in a fixed and useless position at the side of his body. He refused to accept the doctors' words. He said he planned to recover, and over the years and after additional surgery, his recovery was an amazing story of the human will. During the day, he continually squeezed a sponge or rubber ball to strengthen his arm. In the evenings and on weekends, he built furniture, constructed additions on homes, and through other strenuous activities made his arm stronger. He worked until tears of pain ran down his face. Through Walter's program of intense rehabilitation, much movement eventually returned to an arm that doctors had wanted amputated.[241]

. . . .

Ken Morris was attending a meeting at Local 157, on the west side, when word came of Walter's shooting. Instantly, the meeting was over, and UAW members headed across town to the New Grace Hospital, on the northwest side of the city, between Seven and Eight Mile roads. The initial thought was the need to show support for and potential protection for Walter and his family at such a terrible time. The other thought was that these men could donate blood if necessary.[242]

The mood at the hospital was somber, with most of the men not allowed anywhere close to Walter or his family. As with Ken's beating, the question that bothered everyone was who was responsible for this crime? To shoot Walter in his home was almost beyond comprehension. Did this mean the stakes had been raised from the Briggs beatings? Now, instead of inflicting beatings, the enemies (whoever they might be) were using assassination as the new tool.

Emil Mazey, as the union's secretary-treasurer, became the acting UAW president. He, along with Walter's assistant, Jack Conway, secured Walter's hospital room and home. For the rest of his life, Walter was never without a bodyguard.

. . . .

The Detroit police began their investigation. As with the Briggs beatings, the immediate reaction was to treat the shooting as an intraunion matter. But Walter Reuther was a high-profile victim, and police did investigate. The problem with the investigation was that the police, and to some extent the public, held many preconceived notions about unions. Many felt this was an underworld hit, but the Detroit Police Department struggled to accept such notions. Several years later, after a special task force was appointed to investigate the violence against the UAW, a Detroit police detective said, "Gamblers and crime syndicates have nothing to do with this[;] it's Communists."

Another Detroit police officer said:

> The shootings were an outrage, but after all, we know that Walter Reuther is a Communist, or was a Communist. He worked in Russia. When he started organizing here, he had Communist support. We know how the Reds hate a renegade, and this whole thing is simply a fight between Reds.[243]

In spite of these prejudices, the Detroit police questioned many underworld characters. They began hearing chatter about possible underworld connections. Within a matter of days, the Detroit police received a telephone tip and brought in for questioning a person of interest. He was Carl Bolton, a former vice president of Local 400, a large Ford Motor Company local from Detroit's east side (within the UAW region formally headed by Melvin Bishop). Bolton was arrested by Detroit police on April 25, five days after Walter Reuther's shooting, and charged with assault with intent to commit murder. Bolton's attorney, Joseph W. Louiselle, a well-known mob attorney, argued that Bolton had an alibi and was not at the scene of the crime. After three days, on April 28, the police released Bolton and prosecutors dropped the charges. Bolton was free but was still a prime suspect.

In the meantime, there was conjecture that Communist elements within the UAW might have been responsible for the shooting. Other possibilities included a Communist/mob alliance. Under this theory, both Reuther and Mazey had begun discussions with Ford management about eliminating gambling and other illegal activities in the plants. The numbers racket, in particular, was big business in the plant, and mobsters did not want to lose this lucrative $10 to $20 million a year income. Walter Reuther's attitude about gambling at the plant was straightforward. Shortly before the shooting, he told Ford's John Bugas, "We did not organize our union to give the people the right to shoot craps in toilets."[244] He gave Bugas the go-ahead to fire workers involved in gambling. At the same time, Communist elements that had lost to Reuther in 1946 and 1947 were desperate to maintain alliances to eliminate Reuther's power in the UAW. Was it possible that these two elements made a deal?[245]

In the fall of 1948, Carl Bolton and four others were arrested for a safecracking burglary in Pontiac, Michigan. Two of the men were John Kolodziejski and John Pantello, each a fired Ford Motor Company employee and ally of Bolton in Local 400 politics. They said that Bolton was involved in the Reuther shooting.

Later, it was learned that three days before Reuther's shooting, Bolton had asked one of the men, John Pantello, if he wanted to make a lot of money rubbing out an important man.

Pantello said, "I would do anything but that."

Bolton said, "Now, then, this offer, this is quite a little bit of money for this, and it's a good thing!"

Pantello's response was never confirmed, but he and Bolton jumped into Bolton's car and drove over to John Kolodziejski's house. Bolton said to him, "Have you thought it over? There's fifteen thousand in it."

Kolodziejski asked, "Who is it?"

"That Red, Walter Reuther," Bolton responded.

"Fifteen thousand! Is that all?"

Bolton said, "You'll get it in an hour after it's done."

Like Pantello, Kolodziejski was still unconvinced, and Bolton added, "Well, after Reuther, there will be another one to go after [in] a few days. It will be Ken Bannon."

Ken Bannon was the president of Local 400, and he'd led the Reuther forces in ousting Bolton from his position of vice president of the local. Reuther was appointing Bannon to be the director of the UAW's Ford Department, and Bannon eventually became a UAW vice president and had a long and distinguished career in the UAW.

The two men did not continue to be part of the conspiracy. The next day, April 18, Bolton returned to Kolodziejski's house and said, "I want them shotguns."

Kolodziejski went to his bedroom, where he had stored two shotguns that Bolton had previously purchased in January 1948. Kolodziejski returned from his bedroom with the 12-gauge shotguns and a bag of about twenty shotgun shells.

After receiving the weapons, Kolodziejski asked if Bolton was going hunting.

Bolton's response was quick: "I'm going out and get myself a goddamned Commie."

In September 1948, Bolton and several others were arrested and arraigned in Pontiac for burglary. On May 23, 1949, Bolton was found guilty and sentenced to ten to fifteen years in prison.

On October 8, 1948, just weeks after his arrest in the safecracking heist, a Wayne County prosecutor issued a criminal warrant against Bolton. The prosecutor charged Bolton with the shotgun assault on Walter Reuther with the intent to kill and commit murder.

While Bolton was awaiting trial for both of these crimes, other information came out. For example, at the 1947 UAW Convention, where the Reuther forces eliminated the Thomas, Addes, and Leonard group, George Addes had appointed Bolton as chief sergeant at arms for the event.

Then the shadow of Harry Bennett entered the picture. In the late 1930s, Bolton had served time in prison at the same time Bennett was on the Michigan Parole Board. Authorities learned that Bennett had interceded in a pardon for Bolton, and afterward he began working for the Ford Motor Company in Bennett's feared Ford Service Department. At some point in the early 1940s, Bolton began working at Ford's Highland Park plant and became active in Local 400 politics. In addition to becoming a vice president of the local, he was also deeply involved in running craps games and other illegal gambling activities in the Local 400 plants. Harry Bennett had been there to protect Bolton until Henry Ford II (Henry Ford's grandson, who took over the company in 1945) fired Bennett in 1945. There is little doubt that during his rise in Local 400 politics in the early 1940s, Bolton was a spy for Bennett. After Bennett's firing, Bolton seemed to have developed even stronger connections with organized crime. Once drummed out of the union, he freelanced at all types of criminal activity, and he faced trial for robbery and attempted murder in 1948.

In January 1947, the UAW discovered a problem regarding forged checks at its National Ford Council. Local 400 president Ken Bannon and others learned from Detroit police, who were investigating the incident, of Carl Bolton's criminal past and of the potential connections to Harry Bennett. Bannon, representing the Reuther forces in the local, dropped Bolton off the Reuther slate for the 1947 elections. Except for Addes's appointment as chief sergeant of arms of the 1947 UAW convention, Bolton was out of the UAW by the end of the year. At this point, he returned to robbery. He was a petty thief, but was he an assassin?

Thirteen months after the Walter Reuther assassination attempt, on May 23, 1949, police officers took Bolton to prison to serve his ten to fifteen years for the safecracking job. His trial for the assassination of Walter Reuther did not take place until 1950.[246]

. . . .

After Walter's shooting, Victor Reuther began to travel, accepting invitations to speak or attend conferences in Germany and England. As 1949 began, Victor was back at home and returning to the routine of life as the UAW's education director. After work, Victor's routine was to drive to his northwest Detroit home on Mark Twain. He always parked on the short side street to the south of his home, which dead-ended into a field. When exiting the car and walking to his home, he occasionally heard the sound of a car starting and roaring away. He did not think much about it and assumed the spot must be a good place for young people to neck.

In the spring of 1949, Victor and his wife, Sophie, received calls from the Detroit police indicating that neighbors were complaining about loud barking from their cocker spaniel. On May 23, a police officer came to the Reuther house to ask about the dog. The officer said the dog had to go, but he refused to name any neighbors who had complained about the dog. That was a rough night for the Reuther family, as Victor's two young sons had to part with one of their best friends.

Late on the evening of May 24, Victor was reading in his living room when a shotgun blast blew through his front living room window. The shotgun pellets ripped through the right side of his face and upper body, tearing out his right eye and doing tremendous damage to his face, throat, and chest. Glass, ripped from his eyeglasses, tore into his skull. The would-be assassin dropped the shotgun to the ground and ran to a getaway car, a 1939 or 1940 Mercury. Victor's wife immediately called the police and an ambulance, which took Victor to Ford Hospital, where he spent many hours in surgery. As dawn was breaking, Sophie was able to announce that her husband was out of danger. He spent weeks in the hospital going through many surgeries. His eye was gone, but he recovered and continued his career in the UAW and later in the AFL-CIO.

At Ford Hospital, Roy Reuther was asked if he was going to be the next victim. Standing and holding the hand of his wife, Fania, he responded:

> Naturally, I've thought of it. The state police have offered to post guard, and I've accepted it. I'm not going to resign or go into hiding or anything like that. We're fighting for good clean unionism. Our record stands by and for itself. After Walter was shot, Victor and I talked this over and agreed to continue the good fight. Whoever has done this represents forces that are against clean unionism. Whether they are employers, Fascists, or Communists makes no difference. This can't be fought by resigning![247]

· · · · · · · · · · · · ·

After several surgeries and weeks of recovery in the hospital, Victor returned home for more weeks of regaining his strength and spirits. This also gave him a chance to talk to neighbors about the crime. Detective

Sergeant Albert DeLamielleure ran the Detroit Police Department's investigation. DeLamielleure also ran Ken's and probably Walter's investigations. Soon after Victor returned home, still a very sick man who could barely talk, DeLamielleure came to the house and asked to speak to him privately. Sophie led him into the bedroom and left. The lead investigator pulled up a chair and asked, "Mr. Reuther, have you had any recent difficulties with your wife?"

As Victor wrote in his book, *The Brothers Reuther,* "If I had had the strength, I would have picked up a chair and hit him over the head for his sordid insinuation that Sophie hired someone to murder me."

Victor learned from the newspapers that one neighbor walking his dog the night of the shooting could give an excellent description of people waiting in a car near the Reuther home. Victor talked to the neighbor and realized that the police had done very little follow-up with this potential eyewitness. Victor brought this to the attention of DeLamielleure and suggested that perhaps his neighbor could help identify suspects. Irritated with Victor's "interference," the detective dropped off several shoeboxes of photographs to the neighbor's house.

A few days after the photographs arrived, the neighbor began to receive threatening and anonymous phone calls. The menacing voice on the end of the line said that he and his family would be in grave danger if the police received any information on the assassins. After several calls, the man had a heart attack and ultimately packed up his family and moved to Florida.

The intimidation worked, but who was making the phone calls? No threatening calls came to the neighbor before Victor's discussion with DeLamielleure—only after the police dropped off the photos.

After the night of the shooting, Sophie Reuther mentioned on numerous occasions that it was too bad they had to give up their dog. According to Sophie, that dog never would have let anyone near the window without barking loud enough to wake up the entire household. Victor casually asked neighbors if they had complained about the dog. The neighbors he talked to indicated that they had never made complaints, but Victor realized that even if they had complained, they were not, in all likelihood, going to admit to such complaints now, after the shooting.

Victor called the local police precinct station and asked if there was any kind of record of people on Mark Twain or neighboring streets complaining about a dog. The desk sergeant checked the records and said that no record of complaints existed. Victor wondered who the police officer was that came to their home the night before the shooting—was he a real police officer or an impersonator?[248]

• • • • • • • • • • • • •

Immediately after Victor's shooting, many thought about Carl Bolton, the man charged with Walter's assault. Some observers found it ironic, perhaps conspiratorial, that Victor's shooting occurred on May 24, the day after Bolton began his prison sentence for the Pontiac burglary. Was this an effort to provide an argument that if Bolton did not shoot Victor Reuther, he did not shoot Walter Reuther?[249]

• • • • • • • • • • • • •

Enough was enough. The UAW had been through Detroit police investigations, and nothing happened. Now the labor organization decided it was time to call in its own investigators. Soon help was coming via two no-nonsense investigators from Washington, DC.

Recovering from his wounds is Walter Reuther, with his daughter Linda, Governor Williams, and Emil Mazey. Photo is from late 1948 or early 1949.

CHAPTER 20

CARRY OUT PLAN R

From 1955 to 1971, Dad's office was located at the UAW's Solidarity House, the union's international headquarters overlooking the Detroit River at 8000 E. Jefferson in Detroit. On Saturdays or Sundays during the 1950s, Greg and I often accompanied Dad while he caught up on things at his office. We enjoyed these trips and the people we met. At the entrance, a guard, who after a few words with Dad, waved us by. As we were pulling up to the building, I remember Greg pointing to the west boundary of the property, where a long dog pen had been built for the two watchdogs that patrolled the sight at night. I never actually saw the dogs, which made them even more mysterious, but I knew why they were there, and I knew they were vicious. They were on the property to protect Walter Reuther.

IN LATE JULY 1949, THE telephone rang at a modest home in Alexandria, Virginia. A sixty-five-year-old man pulled himself out of an overstuffed chair, placed a file of material on a cluttered desk, and walked across the room to pick up the phone. Recovering from surgery two months earlier, physical activity was still a chore for him. He picked up the receiver after the fourth or fifth ring. He knew the call was long distance as the sound of static jumped from the receiver. The man on the other end of the line spoke loudly over the static and asked if this was Heber Blankenhorn.

It took a moment before Blankenhorn recognized the voice and determined that it was Harold Cranefield, the lead attorney for the UAW. He knew that Cranefield was calling for help. Blankenhorn was aware of the Walter and Victor Reuther shootings but had no idea of the status of the police investigation. After initial greetings, Cranefield told him that the investigation was stalled and the UAW Executive Board felt more needed to be done, as the Detroit police appeared to be dragging their feet. Cranefield said the UAW Executive Board had authorized him to see whether Blankenhorn was available to investigate the violence. The phone connection was so bad that Cranefield said he would put all the relevant information together in a letter and Blankenhorn could respond.

Blankenhorn hung up the phone. He walked over to his cluttered desk and thought about Detroit and the Reuther shootings. He continued standing as he absentmindedly looked out at Duke Street. At sixty-five years old, did he really want to take on an assignment that would pull him away from home? Then he remembered Cranefield almost pleading with him over that lousy phone connection. The UAW attorney said the union was frustrated. There were shootings and beatings of elected UAW officials, and the Detroit police showed no inclination to get to the root cause of an obvious conspiracy to silence the UAW in Detroit. They needed a man with Blankenhorn's background to supplement the feeble efforts of the Detroit police.

Blankenhorn walked back to his comfortable chair and sat down. He surveyed the room and saw mementos and photos of a bizarre and unique career.

Heber Blankenhorn started his career as a newspaperman at the beginning of the twentieth century. He worked for the *New York Evening Sun* and rose to be the assistant city editor. During World War I, he served as a captain in the propaganda section of the American Expeditionary Forces, where he became legendary in his knowledge and implementation of propaganda leaflets that led to the peaceful surrender of thousands of German soldiers. He became one of the top intelligence experts in the country. In 1919, Blankenhorn authored a book called

Adventures in Propaganda: Letters from an Intelligence Officer in France, chronicling his war years. After the war, he began working for the Bureau of Industrial Research, a nonprofit think tank that provided research for organized labor. In 1924, he wrote *The Strike for Union*, the story of the yearlong 1922 strike against the coal industry. Later in the decade, he became the publicity director for the Amalgamated Clothing Workers.

In the 1930s, Blankenhorn moved to Washington, DC, to become an aide to Senator Robert Wagner. There he helped write the National Labor Relations Act. Later he joined Senator Robert Lafollette's staff and was part of the investigating team that determined US corporations spent $80 million a year on union espionage and spying during the 1930s.[250]

At the start of World War II, Blankenhorn was asked by General Dwight Eisenhower to handle his propaganda and intelligence efforts in North Africa. Blankenhorn never cared for the FBI, particularly J. Edgar Hoover, and the feeling was mutual. Although, Ike and the army wanted Blankenhorn for duty, the FBI did not give Blankenhorn top security clearance. The FBI provided no reason for the lack of clearance. Perhaps it was from the Lafollette years, perhaps the result of personal run-ins with Hoover. Regardless, General Eisenhower had to request White House intervention in getting the FBI to move on his clearance, after which Blankenhorn applied his propaganda techniques in North Africa and Europe.[251] Back from the war, he was in Alexandria with his wife, Ann, an activist on social issues and women's rights.

. . . .

Cranefield's letter arrived during the first week of August. The letter summarized the Reuther shootings. It reviewed Walter's shooting and the charges against Carl Bolton. The new prosecutor, Cranefield wrote, doubted that a guilty verdict against Bolton could be obtained. The lawyer also wrote that the Detroit underworld was making efforts to get Bolton released from Jackson State Prison, where he was serving a long sentence for a Pontiac, Michigan, robbery, and "spirit him out of the country or have him knocked off."

Cranefield reported some optimistic news. The Detroit police, after both Reuther shootings, performed the routine of arresting "every police character in town along with some miscellaneous Reds, subjected them to questioning, and released them." Their mode of operation was to "go out and pick up the person indicated in [a] tip, bully him for a few hours, and release him." The UAW also learned that the sheriff from Oakland County (located north of Detroit) and the Michigan State Police developed a team to investigate the labor violence independently of the Detroit police. As he read the material, Blankenhorn thought that it was good news that should be explored.

The letter proposed hiring someone like Blankenhorn to manage the investigation for the UAW. In essence, the UAW saw no real coordination or effort by law enforcement to address the violence and was determined to do its own investigation. Blankenhorn was at the top of the UAW's list, and the organization wanted him to come to Detroit to coordinate the investigation. This meant working with and gaining information from the Detroit police and other law enforcement groups. The new governor of Michigan, G. Mennen Williams, a Democrat, had indicated state assistance in this effort.[252]

Within days, Blankenhorn drafted the "Plan for Centralized Investigation of Cases R." He proposed that the UAW hire two people. He would serve as director of the operation for $10,000 a year, and his assistant would be paid the salary of a UAW international representative, $4,680 per year. The assistant he had in mind was Ralph Winstead, a former Lafollette Committee ace investigator who had worked with Blankenhorn for six years. Winstead was familiar with the UAW, as he had worked with the union during a Ford strike in Dallas several years earlier.

The plan outlined two key objectives. First, all information on the case needed to be gathered quietly. Next, Blankenhorn and Winstead planned to backtrack the case and create their own networks to gather information. The plan was to develop a relationship with the Detroit police and the other law enforcement agencies in the Detroit area. They knew that getting the Detroit police to cooperate was going to be a challenge.

Blankenhorn argued that the UAW was currently spending

approximately $6,000 a month on "negative" protection by paying for guards and other security methods. By hiring an investigating team to find the root cause of the criminal activity, the UAW would be paying for "positive" protection at the cost of $3,000 to $4,000 less than the negative protection payouts.[253]

On August 21, 1949, about three weeks after the initial phone call, a letter from Cranefield arrived, stating, "I am authorized to inform you that the officers of the International Union have approved the retainer of yourself and Mr. Ralph Winstead to carry out the plan outlined by you in your memo entitled 'Plan for Centralized Investigation of Cases R.'"[254]

. . . .

The first official meeting of the new investigators took place on September 2, 1949. Governor Williams chaired the meeting of state, Oakland County, Wayne County, and Detroit officials and police detectives. Additional new faces joining the group were Blankenhorn, Winstead, Cranefield, and Jack Conway, the administrative assistant to Walter Reuther. Some of the government officials attending were Lieutenant Joseph Sheridan of the Michigan State Police and Wayne County assistant prosecutor Joseph Rashid. Governor Williams had an interest in solving the Reuther shootings. Walter was shot before Williams had become governor, but Victor's shooting had occurred on his watch. After that shooting, Williams contacted President Truman and asked for FBI intervention.[255] The FBI, however, refused to cooperate, arguing that they had no jurisdiction.

As they started, Governor Williams reviewed the case against Carl Bolton and looked at other pertinent issues. The case against Bolton was strong on innuendo but weak on facts. An informant "stated that he asked various other people among the [leadership] in the gambling syndicates as to their views on the necessity of 'eliminating' Walter Reuther, and they all said yes."

The Detroit police disagreed with the informant. They believed that the mob had no interest in eliminating Reuther since there was no evidence that Walter had tried to interfere with their activities.

(Although if Detroit police had investigated this further, they would have found that both Reuther and Emil Mazey had had discussions with high Ford officials regarding the need to eliminate gambling in the plants.) Furthermore, the Detroit police felt that the mob had more efficient methods for assassinating Reuther. In their view, a mob hit might have involved blocking Reuther's car at some secluded spot and using a machine gun to finish him off. The police had also checked out the top three gambling mobsters in Detroit, the Licavoli, Bommarito, and Lucindo syndicates, and felt they were clean.

The Wayne County prosecutor's office, led by Wayne County Assistant Prosecutor Joseph Rashid, planned to take the Bolton case to court in 1950. The UAW investigators and other members of the investigating team felt there was not enough evidence to convict Bolton, with the primary issue being that Bolton could not be identified as being at the scene of the crime. Even if he was convicted, the real problem was to find out who had hired Bolton.[256]

Blankenhorn and Winstead continued their investigations. They enjoyed working with the Michigan State Police, the Wayne County prosecutor's office, and other law enforcement groups outside of the Detroit Police Department. In time, they developed many threads of information, some more credible than others. Many of these leads simply died because they never received full cooperation from the Detroit Police Department.

. . . .

Shortly after arriving in Detroit, Ralph Winstead interviewed Ken Morris about the Briggs beatings. The work of Blankenhorn and Winstead was quiet and mysterious, and few in the UAW knew what they were doing. Ken did not know much about what they did. Years later, Ken did not even remember Blankenhorn's involvement in the case, and Doug Fraser, who at that time was an administrative assistant to Walter Reuther, said he had not been involved and knew little of the activities of the investigators. Fraser indicated that his colleague Jack Conway and Emil Mazey coordinated the investigation with Blankenhorn and Winstead. They were the UAW people most familiar with the activities of the two investigators. Still, Ken knew that the UAW felt the Detroit police had done a lousy job of properly investigating the beatings and shootings and that they, the union, had to make their own inquires.

In late 1949, Winstead called Ken at his Local 212 office. He said the Mount Clemens Police, through a tip, had picked up a person of interest who was being held in their jail. The Mount Clemens Police told Winstead that this fellow, a man named Dick Lambert, worked as the manager of Santo Perrone's country home and may have been involved in Perrone's illegal activities. Since Ken had no memory of the attackers, Winstead wondered if he could interview Doris.

Ken arranged a meeting between Winstead and Doris that evening at the Parkside apartment. Winstead pulled out a mug shot and asked both Ken and Doris if they had ever seen this man. Ken shook his head. Doris, who always tried to block that terrible night from her memory, studied the photo and said, "I know him. He came to our door and asked for Ken, and I told him, 'He's not here; he's in his office. If you want to see him, that's where you ought to go, down to the local.' So the man walked away. He was a short man ... round," she remembered.

Winstead asked if the two of them would take a drive with him out to Mount Clemens, some twenty miles north, along Gratiot Avenue. Ken and Doris agreed. They checked the availability of an elderly woman who lived in an upstairs unit to babysit their two-year-old boy and then headed off to the Mount Clemens police station. Once there, the police brought Ken and Doris to a lineup room. A few moments later, Doris was looking at a lineup of men. She instantly picked out Sam Perrone's employee and in a precise voice said, "That's the man who came knocking on our door asking for Ken." Winstead informed the Detroit police, but nothing ever happened.[257]

· · · · · · · · · · · · · ·

On December 22, 1949, a *Detroit Times* reporter received an anonymous telephone call. The caller said a bomb had been planted in a stairwell of the International UAW headquarters on Milwaukee Street. The bomb, discovered wrapped as a Christmas present, held enough explosive power to destroy the UAW headquarters and cause significant damage to the GM building, which was located across the street.[258]

. . . .

In February 1950, the Carl Bolton case went to trial. Bolton's attorney, the underworld attorney Joseph Louisell, argued that there was no proof that Bolton was at the scene of the crime. Wayne County Assistant Prosecutor Joseph Rashid argued that there was motive and enough witnesses to make a case. The real problem was the instruction given the jury. Assistant Prosecutor Rashid wanted Bolton tried as either a principal or accessory, but the judge selected the tougher standard. The judge told the jury to consider one question: "Did Bolton shoot Reuther?" The jury foreman later told the press that had the jury been allowed to consider Bolton's guilt as an accessory to the crime, the jury was much more likely to have supported a guilty decision. This was not the last time the UAW and those looking for justice had problems with a judge.

Bolton was acquitted and returned to prison to serve out his armed robbery sentence. Blankenhorn and Winstead were back to square one.[259]

None of the investigators or law enforcement officials were terribly surprised by Bolton's acquittal, but they were convinced that "Bolton was in it somewhere."[260]

. . . .

At some point in 1950, Blankenhorn received news that US Senator Estes Kefauver was planning a national investigation of organized crime in interstate commerce. Blankenhorn understood good public relations and immediately recognized that this committee could shed a national spotlight on the Detroit underworld and its connection with the auto industry and union terrorism.

By the summer of 1950, Blankenhorn was corresponding with Senator Kefauver and the committee staff. With his years of experience, Blankenhorn knew how to work with US Senators and their staffs. As

Kefauver prepared for hearings that were to take place in cities throughout America, Blankenhorn provided long memoranda detailing the web of corruption in Detroit, encompassing the Detroit Police Department, Harry Bennett, the auto manufacturers, and the Detroit underworld.

In August 1950, Blankenhorn sent a detailed memorandum to Kefauver and his committee, providing a summary of clues regarding the Reuther shootings. The investigators provided a list of ninety-five people whom they felt the committee should question, under subpoena, regarding the shootings and other crime-related activities. Among the many names included were former UAW regional director Melvin Bishop, Santo Perrone, Carl Bolton, and Harry Bennett. The listing of Bishop and Perrone was an indication that the investigators recognized culpability in the Briggs beatings.[261]

Bolton's trial was over, and many in the UAW felt they were outfoxed by the legal system. Now the issue was taking a new twist: public committee hearings before the world. The legal mechanisms would not be the same as in a courtroom. The standards of proof were different and less cumbersome in a congressional committee. Perhaps this committee was the way to unleash new information about the Reuther shootings and the Briggs beatings.

CHAPTER 21

THE JUDGE FLED TO FLORIDA

The world's largest stove, a Detroit landmark, was located near the Belle Isle Bridge, on Jefferson Avenue through the 1960s. The wooden structure, painted to look like metal, had been built in 1893 and represented the once prestigious Michigan stove industry at Chicago's 1893 World's Columbian Exposition. The company that owned it was the Detroit Stove Works, the same company that employed Santo Perrone. That information was unknown to a small boy who loved that old landmark. I often commented to Dad as we drove by that I felt the monument was a great piece of Detroit history. Whenever I made such a comment, Dad was uncharacteristically quiet and never said much. Little did I know that to our father, this landmark represented much of what was evil in Detroit. The stove eventually found its way to the Michigan State Fair. It was lovingly restored, but like too many things in Detroit, the nation's oldest state fair fell victim to state budget cuts, and the stove spent years abandoned on state fair property. In August 2011, the stove was struck by a bolt of lightning and destroyed by fire.

THE KEFAUVER COMMITTEE, OFFICIALLY KNOWN as the Special Committee to Investigate Organized Crime in Interstate Commerce, blew the top off the facade that crime was a minor role in the American business world. The Kefauver committee held hearings during 1951 in New York, Los Angeles, San Francisco, Las Vegas, New Orleans, Chicago, Cleveland, Philadelphia, Kansas City, St. Louis, Tampa, Saratoga, and Detroit to demonstrate that organized crime existed throughout the United States. During its investigation, the Kefauver committee demonstrated that the Mafia was a national organization of top criminal hoodlums throughout the United States; meanwhile, the FBI did not recognize Mafia existence until the late 1950s.[262]

US Senator Estes Kefauver felt there were connections between organized crime and legitimate businesses in the United States. One of his objectives for the committee was to demonstrate that such alliances existed. Kefauver always considered the committee's hearing in Detroit as proof that such relationships existed with so-called "respectable" business leaders of a major city.

The scope of these hearings was almost unprecedented for a US Senate committee. Instead of conducting hearings in Washington, DC, the committee conducted hearings in local settings across the country. The preparation and logistics by Senate members and committee staff was enormous by early 1950 standards.

The work of UAW investigators Heber Blankenhorn and Ralph Winstead appeared to pay off in that the Kefauver committee planned hearings in Detroit in February 1951. But upon which issues did the committee plan to focus? Blankenhorn and Winstead's background information on Harry Bennett and the significant amount of gambling and other connections between the Ford Motor Company and the underworld grabbed the committee's attention. The committee was also interested in the continual labor violence that plagued Detroit but had no hard evidence to support bringing witnesses. Then, with the Detroit hearing approaching, the committee staff received their big break.

After the Ken Morris beating in 1946, Emil Mazey had demanded a grand jury investigate the Briggs beatings. In late 1946 and early 1947, the Judge George Murphy one-man grand jury questioned witnesses. It had been nearly four years since the Murphy grand jury had concluded its work, and from the public perception, nothing had happened. No indictments had come from the investigation, and by 1950, the law authorizing the grand jury had expired. The grand jury's work was filed away in boxes and file cabinets and appeared forgotten.

Meanwhile, George Edwards, Detroit Common Council president and Ken's attorney, had run for mayor of Detroit in 1949. Edwards lost in a bitter campaign where his opponent, Albert Cobo, successfully used Edwards' labor and Socialist past and his liberal ideas (racial diversity in housing and support for public transportation) to capture labor's blue-collar votes and defeat Edwards.[263] After his loss, Edwards joined the Nick Rothe law firm (in 1950 organized as Rothe, Marston, Edwards & Bohn). Edwards met with Judge Murphy regarding his grand jury investigation and was amazed by what he learned. Judge Murphy admitted to Edwards "that he had been ready to indict Perrone, but instead fled to Florida for a vacation after being threatened."[264] Edwards, no doubt, was given this information in confidence.

As the Kefauver hearings approached, it appeared that Edwards encouraged the Kefauver staff to meet with Murphy just prior to the February 8 convening of the Detroit hearings.[265] Perhaps it was through guilt or just an effort to set the record straight, but Judge Murphy granted the committee unprecedented access to thousands of pages of secret transcripts of the closed grand jury testimony. Committee staff, working day and night as the hearing date approached, poured over the 1946–47 transcripts and other documents of the Murphy grand jury testimony. The following is a synopsis of what they learned.

. . . .

The Story of the 1946–1947 Murphy One-Man Grand Jury

The 1946–1947 Murphy one-man grand jury looked at two questions. The first was alleged payoffs by the jukebox industry to Teamster union officials, including Jimmy Hoffa. The second focus was the Briggs beatings. Judge Murphy ran all the hearings, with the assistance of several assistant prosecutors and a state assistant attorney general. An additional police officer assisted the investigation and witnessed testimony. This was detective Albert DeLamielleure of the Detroit Police Department's special investigation squad.[266] This same man had led the investigations of the Ken Morris beating and the Reuther shootings.

The Murphy grand jury began testimony on the Briggs beatings in November of 1946 and concluded testimony in early January 1947.

. . . .

The first key witness was George Herbert, and his story set the stage for the Murphy grand jury. The following is a synopsis of Murphy grand jury testimony on the Briggs beatings:

Around April 1, 1945, Herbert, a longtime employee of Briggs and a man with a sterling reputation, was working in his office. For ten years, Herbert ran the salvage operations for Briggs. Briggs used a lot of metal, and each year tons of it became scrap. In fact, Briggs earned about $1.5 million a year selling its scrap to outside contractors. Herbert's job was to find contractors that purchased the scrap at the highest price. The contractors then entered the plant to collect the material and haul it away. Over the years, Herbert developed a well-defined routine in hiring contractors to do this job. Every three months or so, the company held bid lettings for the scrap. The main reason for the continual bids was to ensure that the price Briggs received for the scrap was competitive, since market prices often fluctuated. In this specialized field, only a few companies made bids.

On this early April day in 1945, the Briggs receptionist informed Herbert that he had a visitor named Carl Renda. A few minutes later, Renda, a big man in his late twenties, and an older man named Charles Martin entered the room. Renda said that he wanted to see the bids for the latest scrap bids.

Herbert asked Renda what company he was with, and Renda replied that he had his own company. He asked Renda what experience he had in the scrap industry. Renda replied none, that he was just getting started. When asked where his office was located, Renda said he was working out of his home. Finally, Herbert asked Renda what equipment he had. Renda replied that he had no equipment. Herbert saw no reason to consider hiring a rookie in the business. The Briggs scrap business was too important.

Herbert looked at Renda, astounded that a stranger would simply walk in and demand such information. After thinking about his response and sizing up the young man, Herbert said that Briggs didn't do business that way.

Renda stared back and said that he would take the issue up with more senior management. Then he left.

Herbert shook his head and returned to work.

· · · · · · · · · · · · ·

The director of purchasing for Briggs was William Cleary, another longtime employee. In his early sixties, like Herbert, he was considered a man of impeccable integrity. Cleary passed away before the Murphy grand jury met, and he never testified. While not Herbert's supervisor, Cleary was in Briggs's top management, and he approved contracts. No vendor contract moved through Briggs without his approval. A few days after Renda and Martin had left Herbert's office, Cleary called Herbert and asked him to come to his office.

Moments later, Herbert was in Cleary's office. Cleary asked if Herbert had met Renda and Martin. Herbert, a man of strong opinions, told him he had met the men and that the young one, Renda, wanted to see the bids for the scrap contracts. Herbert made clear that he thought the men were unqualified and such actions inappropriate. Herbert testified that Cleary told him, "Give those fellows all the cooperation that you possibly can," and he was to give them all the business as directed. Herbert was stunned by the order. Briggs did not conduct business this way, and it was totally out of character for Bill Cleary to make such a demand. Still, this was Cleary's decision, and Herbert followed the directive. Herbert said that he could not give Renda all the business yet, because Renda had not made all the necessary connections with the scrap industry. Therefore, Renda received the scrap contract at the Briggs Mack Avenue plant. In time, Renda had the scrap contract for all of the Briggs operations.

Carl Renda's company started doing business with Briggs on April 10, less than two weeks after Renda had first come to see Herbert. However, the Renda contract sat on Bill Cleary's desk unsigned by the Briggs executive. He usually addressed the issues that came into his office the same day, going home with a clean desk. The Renda contract sat on his desk for weeks and then months. He told colleagues that Briggs could fire him before he signed it. There was something about the contract that he didn't like. Perhaps it was the clause that said neither Briggs nor Renda could break the contract. Perhaps it was because someone in Briggs hierarchy ordered him to just do it and get the job done. Nonetheless, Cleary became a man under a great deal of stress, and his blood pressure rose. Several months later, he signed the contract, after apparent pressure from superiors.

The current scrap haulers were outraged and stunned by Renda's company receiving this contract. A tight-knit group of mainly Jewish businesspersons conducted the scrap metal business in Detroit. They had been doing business for years with Briggs, and now they were told that an Italian kid was taking their place and that his bid for the scrap was less than their bids. This meant that Briggs was making less money for the scrap. Then, to their amazement, Renda contacted the former scrap haulers, men who had lost their biggest contract, and offered a deal. He proposed that they could keep the Briggs scrap metal business exactly as they had done before, but now they were to work for Renda and receive less money to handle the scrap. The scrap haulers, desperate to keep as much business as possible, accepted the deal. Essentially, the scrap metal was handled exactly the same way, but now there was a middleman, Carl Renda. In this role, Renda's take-home pay was up to a $100,000 a year in his new business ($100,000 in 1947 was the equivalent of $1,040,000 in 2013).

The first of the Briggs beatings occurred March 22, 1945. Two weeks later, Renda walked into Herbert's office.

· · · · · · · · · · · · ·

George Herbert followed orders and gave the job to Renda, even though the job cost Briggs $14,000 a month in losses for their scrap metal. He did not like being told to do something that was against all his instincts. Renda received the job, but Herbert was continuously on Renda's back. If something was not right, Herbert let Renda know about it. Since some of the scrap was still government scrap from the war, Herbert contacted the FBI to report that the scrap was not going to the highest bidder. Then

Herbert received word from one of the other scrap contractors. In a meeting with Renda and Sam Perrone, one of the scrap dealers heard it said that if Herbert knew what was healthy for him, he had better start cooperating, or he would be "out of Briggs or out of existence, either one."

Herbert noticed two changes in the plant once Renda was hired. He testified to the grand jury: "The Carl Renda Company was to break up any strikes that would occur [at] Briggs." However, he also noticed that strikes seemed to appear for no reason at all, that work stoppages were "manufactured strikes, created by paid men in the company for no reason." He further said, "Manufactured strikes, started by various men, [who] you would be safe to say [were] paid to start a disturbance."

When asked about the Briggs beatings, Herbert said, "Yes, we used to follow them pretty close. We first would know there was going to be a strike in a certain department, and later we would hear of the beating, so we would always put two and two together, and the common remark was 'somebody's going to get hell tonight,' because we would know ahead of time, at least a few of us would know...." Herbert was asked who was creating the disturbances, and he felt it was Carl Renda. Herbert testified that Cleary was the man between him and the higher-ups at Briggs and that he and others thought there might be UAW officials involved. He said, "I believe ... the higher-ups [in the union] are receiving part of this money [the] Renda Company is receiving.... (Of course, Melvin Bishop was the top International UAW official that oversaw Briggs issues. It was not learned until after the Murphy grand jury, that Bishop was arrested with Sam Perrone and there was a direct connection.)

Herbert testified that Renda passed out cigarettes, a difficult commodity to obtain in postwar America, to many of the Briggs union stewards. Herbert said that he raised hell with Renda and told him to stop it. Then Fay Taylor "raked me over the coals for putting my nose in other people's business and told me I was only imagining things, that Carl Renda was not giving out cigarettes, and I said, 'If you want proof, call your watchmen.'"

A few weeks before meeting with staff of the grand jury, Herbert said, "My wife received a couple of phone calls, mysterious phone calls with practically no sense of foundation of what they were talking about.

I didn't base anything on that, but I did become alarmed, when [a] car was sitting across from our house." A moment later, he testified that his wife "was hanging up clothes in the back yard … and she was hit in the head. She was knocked down, unconscious for some time." The grand jury asked when the calls and the slugging occurred. "When Mr. DeLamielleure came over, that, she says, was the beginning of her trouble."[267]

. . . .

The Murphy one-man grand jury continued with many additional witnesses, especially Briggs management officials. None of the officials could understand why Briggs would take a $14,000 a month loss on the scrap metal contract. One was George Lilygren. He was the assistant comptroller at Briggs, but shortly after the Renda contract, Lilygren left the company. Lilygren served as George Herbert's direct superior and was involved in almost every aspect of the Briggs organization. Lilygren testified that he went to see Cleary and, as Herbert's supervisor, objected to changing the scrap metal bidding process. Lilygren was equal to Cleary in authority, unlike Herbert, who was a subordinate. Cleary took Lilygren into his confidence and told him that he had received the instructions to give the bid to Renda from Dean Robinson, the president of the Briggs Manufacturing Company. Lilygren also testified that Renda's job was "to keep people in the plant on the job; that's the consideration for him getting that contract."

Lilygren had also testified that Dean Robinson spent time at Renda's hunting lodge in northern Michigan, the property owned by Sam Perrone. Lilygren felt that Fay Taylor was the one who introduced the scrap deal to Robinson.[268]

. . . .

Elgan Taylor, another former Briggs management employee, testified. He worked under Lilygren for his entire career and left Briggs not long after Renda was employed. After leaving Briggs, he and Lilygren started a consulting firm together.

Taylor testified that Lilygren "told me … that Mr. Cleary … [said] that Renda … had approached the management of the company on the proposition that if the company would sell to him their scrap, and I believe at something less than the marked price, that he in turn would offer them certain protection against work stoppages and striking and so forth."

Taylor further confirmed that Cleary did not sign a contract with Renda and threatened to resign rather than sign the agreement. Taylor testified that he believed Renda was responsible for the beatings but indicated that he did not know of Sam Perrone or his connection to Renda.

Most others from Briggs and the scrap industry either did not know of Perrone or did not know of his unsavory past. This was a time when the underworld was truly "under" the surface of normal life and many honest businesspeople did not know what was going on in Detroit's world of crime. There might occasionally be rumors or a story in the press, but these were often one-day stories that disappeared from memory soon thereafter.[269]

....

By the end of 1946, Herbert, Cleary, Lilygren, and Taylor, each of whom were employees of Briggs for more than fifteen years, had been either discharged or had left the company. Other loyal employees left the company during this same period. Herbert was fired on January 7, 1946, and was dead before the end of the year, shortly after he testified before the grand jury. The cause of death was due to natural causes. Cleary died in June 1946 of a cerebral hemorrhage, less than a year after he was discharged from Briggs and immediately after the Ken Morris beating.[270]

....

Others testified at the Murphy grand jury. Sam Perrone's testimony was short on substance. Paraphrasing his testimony: He knew nothing. A known strikebreaker since the 1930s, Perrone, when asked about the scrap deal he received from the Detroit Stove Works after its strike was broken, said, "I ain't got anything to do with any strike." Later, asked when his son-in-law Carl Renda entered into the scrap business, he responded, "I don't know. I don't remember." He did admit, however, to lending Renda thirty-two thousand dollars to help him start his business. Regarding the Briggs beatings, Perrone said, "I don't know nothing."

Perrone received more unfavorable press during this period. In 1945, a woman named Lydia Thompson was found murdered. The woman had a connection to Perrone's sister-in-law. A note was found in the woman's belongings: "If after this day you don't see me, and you don't hear from me, then go and find a man by the name of Sam Perrone and ask him where I am." Perrone was arrested, but no charges were filed. The grand jury spent many hours trying to learn more about this murder. During his testimony on the Thompson murder, Perrone simply said he knew nothing.[271]

· · · · · · · · · · · · ·

A man named Nathan Silverstine testified to the grand jury. Silverstine was in the business of selling new and used machinery and buying salvageable equipment. He found the contract with Renda questionable. During the 1920s and early 1930s, Silverstine was a Briggs employee and served as the manufacturing manager of all the Briggs plants in 1931, making thirty-thousand dollars a year during the Depression. He was fired from Briggs in 1933 because he disagreed with its labor policies.

Silverstine was asked what he had heard about the Briggs beatings. His response focused on the last beating. Referring to Ken Morris, he said, "I have heard the last boy [beaten] up, the recording secretary, is one of the quietest and [one] of the most even-brained, regular-minded fellows in the union, and I can't figure why he was beaten up. That's this recording secretary that lives over very close to Briggs, in the Parkside settlement there."

Silverstine was asked if he had an opportunity to do any business with Carl Renda. His response was frank: "They called me a couple of times. I told them where to go ... I [wanted] no part of them at all."

Silverstine knew Walter Briggs, and even though he had been fired by Briggs, he said, "Knowing Walter O. as I do, I feel that he would not [in] any way enter into [an arrangement] to control labor with a goon squad."[272]

. . . .

Dean Robinson, the president of Briggs, testified. Robinson started with the company in 1933, shortly after marrying Walter Briggs's daughter. By 1945, he had just been appointed president of the company. Ironically, one of his friends, Lester Moll, was the lead prosecuting attorney for the grand jury, which certainly was a conflict of interest. Robinson seemed the most dispassionate and emotionally uninvolved of all the witnesses that appeared before the grand jury.

Robinson was asked about his friend John Fry, the president of Michigan Stove Works, who had hired Sam Perrone to handle his scrap metal immediately after Perrone broke a strike in 1935. Robinson said, "I [have known] John for many years.... I have [discussed labor troubles] in a general way from time to time."

When asked about the Briggs beatings, Robinson said he only knew what he had read in the paper. Regarding Ken Morris, he said, "I have met him in some of the negotiations for annual contracts." When asked about the scathing editorial Ken had written right before his beating, Robinson said, "Well, we get that constantly. I don't know if he did or did not ... I don't know the timing of that. I don't know the article."

The grand jury asked if the company had conducted any investigation of the Briggs beatings. Robinson said, "Well, we have tried occasionally to do it." When asked who led such investigations, the response: "Fay Taylor."

Robinson did say the scrap metal contract was changed and given to Renda because Briggs management felt the other scrap companies were short-changing Briggs. Neither Herbert, Cleary, nor Lilygren testified that Briggs was being shortchanged by the existing scrap companies.

Then there was an interesting exchange with grand jury Assistant Attorney General Lester Moll—Robinson's friend. Moll asked his friend,

"Do you think, Dean … you could shake loose from these birds at this time?"

Robinson's reply: "Sure we could shake loose."

Moll asked, "Without any difficulty?"

"Yes, sir."

Moll concluded, "I think this might be time for a frank discussion off the record."

The sense is that this off-the-record discussion focused on encouraging Robinson to get rid of Renda and any underworld connections. Briggs retained Renda for years to come.[273]

• • • • • • • • • • • • •

Carl Renda's testimony began with a review of his early background. As a boy, his father died while in the Wayne County jail, and his grandparents raised him in Albion, Michigan. He seemed to prosper in Albion and attended Albion College, where he became the quarterback of the football team. The grand jury found it interesting that Renda remembered details of the 1941 game against Hillsdale College but did not remember many details of the William Cleary meeting in 1945. The US Army drafted Renda in 1943, but he was rejected due to stomach ulcers.

Renda saw nothing unusual in the fact that he received a contract from Briggs with no business address, no business equipment, and no experience in the industry. He indicated that he was the example of American capitalism. He took great offense from the insinuation that he received the Briggs business for anything less than good business sense of the corporation. He also claimed not to know that his father-in-law received similar business after breaking strikes for the Detroit Stove Works.

The grand jury got nothing out of Renda.[274]

• • • • • • • • • • • • •

John Fry, the president of the Detroit Stove Works, had a tough session with the grand jury. Fry, like Robinson, Perrone, and Renda, knew nothing and said nothing. Fry admitted knowing Sam Perrone from his earliest days at the Detroit Stove Works.

Regarding the scrap deal and other deals he gave Perrone, the grand jury prosecutor asked, "Well, it originally all sprang from your gratitude for strikebreaking, isn't that right?"

Fry's response showed a touch of equivocation: "No, I wouldn't say that."[275]

. . . .

The questioning of Melvin Bishop was intense and not friendly. He testified in January 1947, eight months after he lost his UAW regional director position to Emil Mazey. Bishop was serving as the director of the UAW's Skilled Trades Department, a position he served in until Walter Reuther fired him eleven months after his testimony—after learning of the Sam Perrone shining incident in Comins, Michigan.

The questioners zeroed in on the Briggs beatings and the politics of Local 212. They asked Bishop if he knew the Vega boys.

Bishop's response was short. "I know the Vega boys. We had some problems with them."

They asked about Dollinger, and he said, "I know her very well, for years.... I am afraid my vocabulary wouldn't express [my opinion of her]. I have known this gal from the early days of our union. She was very active in Flint, in sit-down strikes. She's the most active person ..."

Bishop was cut off as the prosecuting attorney asked if she was a Trotskyite. "Yes, I think so; I am not sure."

Then the questioning shifted to Ken Morris. "How about Kenny Morris?"

"Well, I don't know too much about Kenny. I know him when I see him, but ..."

"Was he an agitator, like Dollinger?"

"No, I don't think. I wouldn't say he could compete with her—no."

Bishop was asked why the Local 212 people were beaten up.

"Well, I suspected that there was division among the fellows around the union, but I tried as best I could to find out by talking to people who were friendly with them politically. I never was friendly with them politically. That's how I got myself in a lot of hot water out there from time to time, but I tried to make some checks by fellows who were on friendly terms with them. They couldn't find anything that would indicate that they were slugging it out to that extent, but there was, I understand, considerable dissension among them."

"Did this dissension bring about unauthorized work stoppages?"

Bishop's response was quick. "No. This happened more or less in the last year, that there was dissension among the whole group—what we used to call the … [Mazey] group in the local."

"You and Mazey were political enemies?"

"Well, we never ran on the same ticket."

The grand jury asked if there were two factions, the Bishop group and the Mazey group.

"I wouldn't say my group. There's some people that don't agree with Mazey."

The grand jury suggested that Bishop was being modest, that certainly he had followers, and Bishop replied, "That's right."

Bishop was asked if he had heard that a scrap contract had been given out to address labor problems in the plant.

Bishop said, "No, I have never heard anything to that effect." This was certainly perjury, since the Local 212 newspaper reported about such a contract while the Briggs beatings were taking place. Bishop most assuredly knew what had been reported in the Local 212 newspaper, which had also implicated him in the beatings.[276]

· · · · · · · · · · · · ·

One of the final witnesses before the grand jury was Spike Briggs. The committee's tone with Walter Briggs's son was different than it was with Robinson and other people involved with this sordid situation. The grand jury seemed to view Briggs as a breath of fresh air. While Robinson may have been president of the company, there seemed to be a feeling that Walter O. Briggs's son was going to be running the company and would clean it up.

Briggs had served in the Army Air Corps in the war and was

returning to take a more significant role in the family business. He was currently a company vice president and treasurer. He had personnel and labor relations under his jurisdiction.

The grand jury asked Briggs about the factional fighting at Local 212.

Briggs responded, "Well, I think [Regional Director Mazey] is trying to do a good job, getting it patched up … I believe Mr. Mazey is doing everything he can to keep the place running."

Then the prosecutor asked if labor relations between Briggs and the union were better since Mazey became regional director.

"I think it's because Mazey and I are getting along pretty well, and he is actually trying to do a good job of keeping the men at work."

The grand jury explained its belief that through Renda, Sam Perrone had been hired to address the problems with Local 212 by any means necessary and that in doing so, the process of bidding out scrap metal, a process that had been in place for eighteen years, had been voided. Furthermore, grand jury staff explained that in letting Renda get the contract, Briggs was losing fourteen thousand dollars a month.

Briggs responded, "That's bad business."

The attorneys for the grand jury then explained Perrone's background, his scrap metal deal at the Detroit Stove Works, and his strikebreaking activities.

Briggs was unaware of any of this. He seemed amazed by the whole story. The grand jury encouraged Briggs to end the Renda deal. They argued that ending the deal at this time, while the grand jury was in process, is something that people like Renda and Perrone would understand. Finally, the grand jury questioner said, "I am under the impression you may have some difficulty in getting rid of this [Renda] deal." Then the grand jury spent time with Briggs off the record, possibly encouraging him to clean up the whole mess.[277]

The grand jury concluded testimony with James Dewey, the man who was to be an impartial arbiter between the company and the union. Dewey denied any dealings with Renda or Perrone but did express great disdain for Mazey, Morris, and the rest of the Mazey faction at Local 212.[278]

• • • • • • • • • • • • •

The Murphy grand jury was to conclude without any indictments being brought forward. The testimony and other data collected by the grand jury's investigation appeared to be only hearsay evidence. The people who knew something were either dead or not talking. Perrone, Renda, Robinson, and others knew that if they said nothing incriminating and responded with as little information as possible, nothing would happen. Interestingly, Fay Taylor, the man who may have known all the secrets, did not testify. Taylor may have been seriously ill during part of the 1940s, and it is not known whether grand jury staff interviewed Briggs' top labor-relations strategist. Taylor was critical to the subject matter, and his missing testimony is a puzzle. Nothing happened to any of the people the grand jury investigated. The Briggs Manufacturing Company continued building automotive bodies for Chrysler and other automobile companies, and Renda continued to have his scrap metal contract.

Of course, after Renda started with Briggs, longtime quality employees left the company. Cleary, Herbert, Lilygren, Taylor, and several other top managers left the company or were dismissed. These employees had had no desire to leave the company and probably would not have left had Carl Renda not begun his contract with Briggs. The brain drain of this and other top talent at the company may have spelled the decline of the Briggs Manufacturing Company as a viable organization.

The grand jury investigation faded and was forgotten. Then George Edwards learned about the apparent Perrone intimidation of Judge Murphy, and Murphy decided to open up the files for the Kefauver committee investigation.

• • • • • • • • • • • • •

When the Kefauver committee staff looked at these records in early 1951, they hit a gold mine. They believed they saw how a company lost top management and made bad business decisions due to organized crime connections. They felt they could demonstrate that the connection between legitimate businesses and the underworld was real and that they were going to tell Detroit and the rest of the country the sordid story.

CHAPTER 22

BRIGGS HAS NEVER DEALT WITH GANGSTERS

I do not recall Dad ever discussing the Briggs beatings in any kind of detail. Nor do I recall Dad talking about the Kefauver committee or the Murphy one-man grand jury. I do recall that during the 1980s, Michigan Governor James Blanchard (whom Greg and I both worked for at the time) told me that while he was in Congress, our father asked him for a personal favor. He asked Congressman Blanchard to locate the minutes of the Kefauver hearings in Detroit. Dad indicated that he did not want his sons to know about the request; that this was between Jim Blanchard and Ken Morris. The 1951 document, which was printed into a thousand-page report, was obtained. In 2003, while cleaning out our parents' home of forty years, I found that document, with Dad's markings on many of the pages. More significantly than the Kefauver committee hearing testimony was the document's appendix, which contained the minutes of the Murphy one-man grand jury that investigated the Briggs beatings. It is an amazing document.

THE KEFAUVER COMMITTEE SCHEDULED ITS hearings on two very cold days in Detroit—on February 8 and 9, 1951. The hearings challenged the Detroit automobile industry's image among Detroit residents, especially as information regarding the relationship between automobile industry executives and members of the underworld became public. Many knew or believed that such relationships existed, but details of that knowledge existed primarily inside the law enforcement community or with the crime reporters of the press.

Before the Clarence Thomas hearings, before the Watergate hearings and before the Army-McCarthy hearings, there were the Kefauver hearings. On grainy fifteen-inch black-and-white television picture tubes across the country, everyday people saw live hearings of the Kefauver committee. Nothing like this had ever happened before. Television news was generally a fifteen-minute nightly occurrence; now it was unedited and live. People throughout America became aware that things were not as they seemed. This was especially true in Detroit. People learned about mobsters, high stakes gambling, jukebox industry corruption, and the efforts of one company, Briggs, to eliminate strong union leadership.

Television stations WWJ (Channel 4) and WJBK (Channel 2) covered the hearings. In a *Detroit News* article about the new type of media coverage, the Channel 4 station manager commented, "The hearings were the most terrific television show Detroit has ever seen." One door-to-door salesperson gave up on his sales efforts, as all the homemakers were glued to their televisions. He adjourned to a nearby bar and watched the hearings for himself. People asked, "Why don't the judges do something?" "What have the police been doing?" "Why are these men allowed to walk the streets?"[279]

Detroit newspapers were full of prehearing assumptions regarding what the Kefauver committee planned to cover. Rumors were everywhere. There were assumptions that the focus of the hearings was to be the Hazel Park racetrack, partially owned by Santo Perrone's son-in-law Augustino ("Tino") Orlando. There were background articles on all the crime bosses in Detroit, with references made to Perrone and Carl Renda. The only real hard news before the hearings began was the committee's effort to subpoena Harry Bennett. Bennett, fired by Henry Ford II, had retired to California. Bennett fought the committee's subpoena, saying he was too sick to travel. However, a doctor hired by the committee indicated that Bennett's health issues were not significant enough to keep Bennett from making the trip to Detroit.

• • • • • • • • • • • • • •

The UAW's Heber Blankenhorn had worked hard to provide the committee with information regarding the Reuther shootings and results of the investigation that he and Ralph Winstead had developed during the past year and a half in Detroit. Neither the press nor Blankenhorn knew whether the committee was going to address the Reuther shootings or other violence heaped upon UAW officials.

Senator Kefauver had committee members chair hearings across the nation. Senator Herbert O'Conor of Maryland conducted the Detroit hearing. It turned out that the Reuther shootings failed to be a significant part of the Detroit hearings, which must have terribly disappointed Blankenhorn. Instead, the committee focused on three criminal elements in Detroit: gambling, the jukebox industry, and Briggs—the Briggs beatings and the Carl Renda contract.

After the first day of hearings, the *Detroit News* February 9 banner headline read in heavy bold type:

DEALS WITH UNDERWORLD
DENIED BY BRIGGS CHIEF
Hoodlum's Kin Gets Contract

To the surprise of most, the hearing focused on labor violence based on the sensational information gained from the four-year-old Murphy one-man grand jury. Of course, no one knew that Judge Murphy had been threatened in 1946, and now he seemed interested in putting the testimony he received in 1946 and 1947 to use with the Kefauver committee. While committee staff had reviewed the grand jury's sensational material, Judge Murphy testified on that first day of the hearing, and he officially gave the committee the records of the secret testimony from four years earlier. He testified, "The law under which I sat has been repealed, and they, so to speak, pulled the rug out from under me, and if [the records] can be of any service to you or your committee, I do not see why I shouldn't give them to you … and I do give them to you."[280]

With Judge Murphy's permission, the committee took the unusual step of releasing information from the grand jury to the press. It was one thing for the committee staff to have access to the testimony from the Murphy grand jury, as previously described, but now the secret testimony became public. Never before had the records of a grand jury been made public, and the media loved it. The grand jury testimony became the grist of many newspaper stories in the coming days and weeks.

The underworld figures and the highly respected businessmen of Detroit maintained their code of silence during the two-day committee hearing. The attorneys for these men, no doubt, advised them to say as little as possible and to admit nothing. This might have been sound legal advice and routine for grand jury investigations, but in the glare of the television lights, these men looked as if they had something to hide. During the Kefauver hearings, just as they had during the one-man grand jury four years earlier, the men simply denied involvement, whether the questions and the accusations behind the questions were true or not. Time after time, the committee staff received incriminating pretestimony information during witness meetings. Yet hours or days later, during the actual testimony before the committee, witnesses replied differently, or if they were from another country, they pretended not to have understood the question. Those testifying were willing to risk perjury rather than admit to anything. They knew that perjury accusations were hard to prove.

What did the people of Detroit witness as they watched their snow-flecked black-and-white televisions on that Thursday morning?

The first person to testify before Senator O'Conor was Mayor Albert Cobo, followed by Governor G. Mennen Williams. Both welcomed the committee to Michigan. Williams specifically urged the committee to recommend "a way whereby the governor of a state could call for the assistance of the FBI in the solution of crimes which appear to him to be beyond the scope or resources of state or local authorities." He specifically cited the Reuther shootings and expressed frustration that the FBI did not provide assistance.[281]

Harry Bennett testified at length. Hearing Bennett testify, one might have thought he was a choirboy. Senator O'Conor asked if he, Bennett, essentially served Henry Ford as a valet or as an administrative assistant. Bennett responded, perhaps with a touch of irony, that he was really nothing more than a valet. He said it was Henry Ford's idea to hire hoodlums to work for the Ford Service Department and that "Mr. Ford" was just trying to provide a humanitarian service. The committee questioned Bennett extensively, especially as to whether or not members of the underworld received Ford dealerships. Bennett denied such deals, but Senator O'Conor did not seem to believe Bennett's responses.[282]

The steely-eyed Sam Perrone appeared several witnesses after Bennett. The questioners began by reviewing Perrone's lengthy criminal record, with Perrone predictably downplaying his various arrests. Perrone said that he had begun work at the Detroit Stove Works company in 1912 and become a core maker in the foundry. He testified that he eventually received the scrap contract from the Stove Works. When asked how he got into the line of work dealing with scrap metal, Perrone said, "Well, I figured I could make some money ... I had some people that were doing the business telling me, 'If you pick up scrap and sell it, you make money.'"

Santo Perrone awaiting questioning by Kefauver committee

The committee asked Perrone if he received his scrap contract after helping the company with labor problems. Perrone's response: "I never remember any labor trouble."

The committee then asked if Perrone heard anything about labor groups trying to organize the Detroit Stove Works while he was at Leavenworth in 1937 and 1938. Perrone: "I never heard of anything. That's none of my business." When asked if anyone had ever been beaten up regarding labor problems, Perrone's response: "I never remember any labor trouble."

The committee questioned if Perrone had ever talked to the Stove Works president, John Fry, about labor problems at the Stove Works. Perrone's response: "Never."

The Murphy grand jury testimony had occurred about ten months before Sam Perrone and Melvin Bishop were arrested for illegally hunting deer in Northern Michigan—the arrest that ultimately forced Walter Reuther to fire Bishop from the UAW. The Kefauver committee was aware of the arrests and asked Perrone if he knew Melvin Bishop. Perrone's response: "No."

When asked if Bishop and he were arrested together, Perrone said, "I don't know him." When asked to elaborate, Perrone said, "I was going to the village, and they blamed it on me for that, and I was arrested, and I had three or four guys, and they come in my cabin, and I took them to the village, and I was arrested ... because of the gaming laws ... I was arrested with a few guys. I don't know their names. I don't remember the names."

Perrone, asked how he could not know who was at his cabin, said, "I don't know. See, I don't know all of them by name. I know if I see them. If I see them, I know them. See, one guy bring another guy, and another guy bring another guy, and I happened to go to the village, and we got arrested. They figured we use lights—it was nighttime. We were going to the village, you know. They come with me, three or four guys."

When asked again if it was Melvin Bishop, Perrone responded, "I don't remember the name, see. If it was Mel Bishop or Jones or Joe, I don't remember. Probably if I see, I know the guy. I could remember, you see." One had to wonder if Perrone made an uncharacteristic slip when he referred to Melvin Bishop in the more familiar *Mel* Bishop.

When asked about whether he helped his son-in-law Carl Renda get a scrap contract with Briggs, Perrone said, "I never fixed nothing at Briggs. I don't know Briggs."[283]

. . . .

Perrone's boss from the Detroit Stove Works and Dean Robinson's good friend John Fry testified. The president of the Detroit Stove Works had a fuzzy memory of any labor problems back in the 1930s. Just as during the Murphy grand jury, he acknowledged that there had been a strike but did not recall any violence and certainly did not pay Sam Perrone to use violence against any strikers.

Fry indicated that it was a coincidence that Perrone received the Detroit Stove Works scrap metal contract just after the 1935 strike was broken.

After more questioning, Fry finally admitted to labor violence. He said that anyone around the plant, including Perrone, "should have known what was going on." After more intense questioning, when asked if Perrone had committed perjury before the Senate committee by indicating he knew nothing about any labor violence, Fry responded, "Then, yes." He further acknowledged that he would testify against Perrone if prosecutors filed perjury charges.

Senator O'Conor asked Fry how he could give a scrap metal contract to a person of Perrone's character. Fry responded that the Senator was not taking all of the considerations into account.

The chairman said, "I would hate to be one of your stockholders if that is the basis of your operation ... Frankly, it doesn't make sense."

A moment later, the Senator said, "It looks like some other motivating consideration was in operation. Now, tell us whether it was because you or anybody that had reason to fear the Perrones by reason of what they might do, or had something for which you had to pay them off, and it was a pay off?"

Fry said, "I am sure there was no fear on the part of anybody."

Senator O'Conor asked again, "Was it a payoff?"

Fry's response, "I wouldn't call it that."[284]

. . . .

Carl Renda, Perrone's son-in-law and the beneficiary of the Briggs scrap metal contract, followed Fry to the hot seat before the committee and the bright lights of the television camera. Every person appearing before the committee took the oath to tell the truth and nothing but the truth. However, before his testimony, Carl Renda never said the simple words "I do" pertaining to the oath. Instead, his attorney broke in and, after some back-and-forth discussion with the chairman, read the following statement:

> I wish to state at the outset that we have every desire to cooperate in this inquiry to the fullest extent possible.... Mr. Renda has never been charged with an offense at any time.... His personal record, both in college and in business, is perfectly clean and honorable in every respect ...
>
> Now, in fairness, I ask that the committee, at the conclusion of this testimony, either make an accusation or inform the public that there is no accusation against him, in order that any stigma that may attach from testimony here may be removed....
>
> I think that Mr. Renda ... is entitled to either an accusation or a statement that he is free of any guilt.

Senator O'Conor responded, "All right, then ...," and focusing on Renda said, "What is your full name?" Renda responded to the Senator's question and gave his name, but he never took the oath to tell the truth.

With that, the Renda testimony began. His testimony was much the same as four years earlier, but now Renda was more confident. Perhaps it was because the contract with Briggs was going into its sixth year and he felt he had earned his status as a successful business entrepreneur. Perhaps Renda was counting on the intervening years to gloss over the specifics of the memories of years earlier.

Renda explained that back in 1945, he had been a young man with no experience, who wanted to enter the scrap metal business. He denied that his father-in-law had anything to do with the business. He indicated that Bill Cleary, the deceased Briggs purchasing director, had believed that there was collusion among the current scrap owners and that Cleary wanted Renda to provide an honest and efficient scrap service to Briggs.

Renda acknowledged that he owned no trucks, had no experience, and ultimately hired the same people to do the job who had had the contract previously. He said he did not realize at the time that his bid was actually lower (and of less value to Briggs) than that of the competitors, so it made no sense for Briggs to hire him except to say that the deceased Cleary felt there was collusion by the previous bidders.

The committee asked why Briggs had hired someone to act as an intermediary, which ultimately cost the company tens of thousands of dollars extra each year. Renda replied, "They knew that I was taking care to see they were getting a square deal."

When asked how, Renda elaborated: "[By making] sure that what went on the truck was what was specified. Seeing that the accounts were well taken care of."

The committee staff said, "You looked at the trucks—in other words, you were paid fifty-three thousand dollars [in 1946] for inspecting the trucks … You were weighing them and making sure that the kind of scrap put in the trucks was the kind of scrap charged. That is an awful expensive inspector, Mr. Renda. Now, by the way, you did not, in 1946, in any way interfere with the business—that is, the scrap was sold by the fellows that took it out. Is that right?"

Renda's reply: "That is correct."

When asked why he had so few employees and was paying only sixty-nine dollars a year in Social Security payroll tax, Renda said, "I didn't have that many employees to pay Social Security."

The committee responded, "Because you were not doing anything and were taking a free ride on Briggs."

"I wasn't taking a free ride anywhere," Renda shot back. "From watching the business and taking care of it and spending so much time on it, I wound up at the Mayo Clinic on the verge of a nervous breakdown."

The committee ended Renda's testimony by asking questions about an Italian American club and the fact that Renda was president and associating with nearly every known mobster in Detroit. Renda's response to the committee innuendo was, "The fellows in the club all went out and solicited [ads for an ad book]. Those same people donate to the United Foundation and Red Cross and to many things. I don't know what implications can be taken by that, but that doesn't mean a thing. Any funds collected were distributed in a charitable way."

With that, the committee excused Renda. Renda's attorney, however, asked, "May I make a statement with respect to Mr. Renda?"

The chairman responded, "We are not going to suspend in the middle of operations to get a statement. We will take it under consideration. The next witness will be Louis Freedman."[285]

. . . .

Louis Freedman, the owner of the Woodmere Scrap Iron & Metal Company, walked to the witness table. He had testified at length to the Murphy grand jury, and now he'd provided much the same information. He said that his company had been doing scrap metal business with Briggs for twenty-five years. After he learned that his contract was not going to continue at Briggs—and no one gave him a reason for being dismissed—Freedman contacted Renda. He wanted to convince Renda to keep him on board as a subcontractor. Renda agreed to keep Freedman, but as the years passed, Renda found ways to reduce Freedman's profits to less than what they were in 1945. Why did Freedman work for Renda and make less than in 1945? Freedman said he stayed because he believed the Renda/Briggs deal was a short-term arrangement, and when Renda was out, Freedman hoped to return as one of the sole scrap contractors.[286]

. . . .

George Lilygren, Briggs's former assistant comptroller, testified. Lilygren, now living in Washington, DC, was just as straightforward with the committee as he had been during the Murphy grand jury testimony.

Lilygren specifically countered Renda's testimony. Committee staff asked him if the long-dead Cleary had ever raised concerns about scrap dealers being in collusion with each other and shortchanging Briggs.

Lilygren responded, "No, I don't recall anything like that. In fact, we had a careful system to be sure that the weights were right and the system that I worked out with George Herbert and ..."

"You think it was a pretty good system?"

"I always thought it was, yes," Lilygren responded.

Lilygren recalled that his employee, the deceased George Herbert, had complained about Renda and the scrap deal. Lilygren recounted how he spoke to Cleary about it.

The committee staff asked, "Is it not the fact that Mr. Cleary told you he had orders from [Dean] Robinson, the vice president, and there was nothing he could do about it?"

"That was my understanding, yes," Lilygren responded.

Furthermore, Lilygren testified that he was of the "opinion that there was some relief from labor troubles [as a result of the Renda contract]."[287]

The first day of the Kefauver committee in Detroit was complete. Sparks flew, and the hearing was the talk of the town. One key question was whether there was more testimony on the Briggs fiasco on the agenda. The committee did not disappoint.

· · · · · · · · · · · · ·

On Friday, February 9, the committee convened at 9:45 a.m. at the old federal building. With the television lights bright, Senator O'Conor called the first witness: "We call Dean Robinson."

There was a pause, and no one came forward. The senator again called, "Dean Robinson, of the Briggs Co." Again, there was a pause.

Committee staff said, "Mr. Robinson is under subpoena. Mr. Robinson called and said he was on his way here. I think the chair should admonish the witnesses to be in attendance and ready when called."

Senator O'Conor said, "Yes. It is essential that that be the rule, because otherwise, the continuity of the proceeding is broken." In Robinson's absence, the committee moved on to other testimony. Robinson did not make a good impression before the committee or before the people of Detroit.

Later that day, the committee again called Dean Robinson, and this time he came forward to give testimony. Wearing sunglasses to protect him from the glare of the bright and hot lights needed to provide live television coverage, Robinson, at worst, looked more the part of a criminal than that of a respected Detroit business leader. At best, wearing what appeared to be a dinner jacket, he appeared dispassionate and removed from the hearing.

In testimony, Robinson admitted that he and Detroit Stove Works president John Fry were close friends. The questioning then covered much of the same territory as the Murphy grand jury. However, when asked why Cleary made changes to the scrap metal contract, Robinson said, "We had constantly had complaints through our industrial relations department about short weight and theft of tools and other parts going out of our plant, and naturally, we thought they were being hauled out by trucks that were hauling out our scrap. We never could prove it."

**Briggs president Dean Robinson
testifies before Kefauver committee**

The committee missed the significance of this statement. Robinson talked about complaints from the industrial relations department. The deceased Fay Taylor headed the industrial relations department. His job was not to handle scrap metal; that responsibility belonged to Lilygren, Herbert, and Cleary. Taylor was not the man to address scrap issues or stolen equipment, but Robinson indicated that Fay Taylor was the man informing him of the company being shortchanged by the previous scrap metal dealers. If Taylor had a concern, he should have talked about it to the appropriate people in the Briggs management structure, which he never did. Additionally, Robinson talked about the constant problems of theft and short weights, yet Cleary, Herbert, Lilygren, or others responsible for the scrap at Briggs never reported such problems. Robinson threw the committee a slow pitch, but the committee whiffed badly.

At one point, however, Senator O'Conor expressed his frustration: "On the face of it [this scrap deal with Renda] looks absurd, to be perfectly frank with you, Mr. Robinson, and it brings us to believe that it is a pretty sorry state of affairs if American industry is brought to the point where it has to deal with hoodlums and has to deal with men [with] connections in the underworld and with criminal records in order to carry on their business."

O'Conor continued: "Now, if a man who has connections—and I am referring to the Perrones and their like—who muscled in on otherwise legitimate business, then there seems to be something that the public is entitled to know and that the Congress ought to be appraised of and take cognizance of, and that seems to be the state of affairs here [in Detroit]."

Robinson responded hotly, "We do not and never have dealt with racketeers or gangsters."

Then the committee asked Robinson if he was a friend of Lester Moll, one of the attorneys for the Murphy grand jury. Robinson responded that they were friends and that he saw nothing wrong with Moll questioning him during the grand jury probe. Robinson was reminded that at the end of his testimony before the Murphy grand jury, Moll asked if Briggs could shake loose from the Renda deal and then asked for an off-the-record discussion. The committee asked Robinson what occurred during the off-the-record discussion.

Robinson replied, "I don't recall any discussion of that."

Committee staff asked, "Do you not recall that reference?"

"I recall that, but I don't recall the discussion because I didn't know anything about it."

Committee staff pressed: "It was suggested … that you terminate the contract?"

Robinson said, "Why should we?"

"Because Mr. Renda performed no legitimate service for you?"

Robinson disagreed. "I beg your pardon—he is doing a good job handling our …"

Committee staff interrupted. "Will you tell us now once and for all: what service does Renda perform of any nature whatsoever?"

Robinson: "Well, he is serving us every hour, every day, as I told you. He is the contact man, as far as we are concerned, with any scrap that has to be moved out of certain locations, and he is called. They don't call anybody else. They call Mr. Renda, in my opinion."[288]

The committee did not seem impressed, nor did the Detroit newspapers, based on the headlines and photographs that appeared in the Detroit newspapers the next day. Robinson and Briggs were disgraced.

· · · · · · · · · · · · · ·

The next and final witness to appear before the committee on the Briggs issues was Emil Mazey. He told the committee that he was sure Briggs officials knew all about the contract with Renda. He expressed deep frustration with the Detroit police for their halfhearted effort to find the perpetrators of the Briggs beatings.

Later, Mazey talked about the broader concerns of criminal elements hired by employers:

> We have a special interest in the hearings and investigations being conducted by your committee. We are hopeful that your committee may uncover

evidence that will result in the solution of the attempt to assassinate our president, Walter P. Reuther, and our educational director, Victor Reuther, and the attempted bombing of our international headquarters.

We are hopeful that your committee may be able to expose the people responsible for the beatings administered to Ken Morris, the president of Local Union 212, the Briggs local, and other representatives of the union....

We confess to a feeling of deep bitterness against these gangster elements. During our first efforts to organize our union, we were continuously and forcibly attacked by organized gangs of hoodlums and criminals who repeatedly acted as musclemen against our people for the benefit of antiunion employers.[289]

Emil Mazey testifies before the Kefauver committee.
Note TV cameras in background.

Emil Mazey must have had some conflicting feelings about the substance of the hearings. He had to be pleased that the committee addressed the notorious activities of the Briggs Manufacturing Company. The Briggs beatings had been largely forgotten as the years passed. On the other hand, the committee did nothing to address publicly the assassination attempts of Walter and Victor Reuther. Mazey was intimately involved with the Blankenhorn and Winstead investigation. The lack of substantive questioning on the Reuther shootings had to be disappointing.

After two days of hearings, the Detroit portion of the Kefauver hearings was over. The committee continued with more hearings in other parts of the country. The anxious public had to wait until May before the committee report was released. In the meantime, the Detroit public wanted more details, and the newspapers quenched that thirst.

CHAPTER 23

IF YOU DON'T SEE ME, FIND SAM PERRONE

After Ken retired from the UAW in 1983, he spent twenty years serving as the chair of Coop/Optical, a fairly large optical nonprofit company started by the Detroit area labor movement. The company was originally started in 1960 to help working people obtain eye glasses for their families at a reasonable cost. In 2005, at age ninety, Dad's health was beginning to fail, and Greg and I were asked to clean out his Coop/Optical office on Eight Mile Road in Detroit. Upon going through the boxes and piles of materials, we came across a large very old envelope from the Rothe law firm. The contents were yellowed clippings and entire sections from the Detroit Free Press, the Detroit News, and the Detroit Times. The dates were from early 1951, just before I was born. I took these yellowing articles home, spread them out on the family room floor, and placed them in chronological order. They were the first inkling I had that the Detroit Kefauver hearings were front-page news and the Briggs beatings were a major part of the committee focus.

THE PRESS HAD A FIELD day. Newspaper stories in the Detroit dailies discussed the hearings for weeks after the committee hearings ended. Armed with testimony from the newly released 1946–47 Murphy grand jury transcripts, the newspapers had sensational revelations to write over and above what occurred during the Kefauver committee testimony.

The Kefauver committee received forty volumes of records from Judge Murphy; twenty-eight volumes of the material were given to the custody of George Edwards. Under committee guidelines, Edwards made the material available to the three Detroit daily newspapers. Edwards and a reporter from each of the three Detroit dailies worked out an agreement. The material was to stay at Edwards's law office, and each of the three reporters was given a specific amount of time with the material. Of course, George Edwards was the attorney for Ken Morris. Why the committee gave this material to Edwards is a mystery, but as Ken's attorney, he was able to review all the material from the Murphy grand jury.[290]

On Saturday, February 10, 1951, the *Detroit News* banner headline was a disaster for Briggs, Dean Robinson, and Carl Renda. In deep black ink, the headline read:

Briggs Evidence Bared
REVEAL SECRETS OF RACKETS JURY

Just below the headline was a head and shoulders photograph of Carl Renda testifying before the committee. The story then summarized the key elements of the heretofore secret Murphy grand jury.

. . . .

On Sunday, February 11, the *Detroit Times'* top headline read:

Reveal Briggs Paid $150,000 a
Year for Peace in Plants

This article keyed in on the Murphy grand jury testimony relating the extra costs that Briggs paid Renda to be the middleman of their scrap business. While the long article reviewed much of the four-year-old grand jury testimony, it pointed out that the Murphy grand jury did not indict anyone, as no solid evidence had developed for an indictment.

· · · · · · · · · · · · ·

The onslaught against Briggs continued on Monday, February 12, when the *Detroit News* headline read:

OUST FIRM CHIEF, UAW ASKS BRIGGS
Renda Deal for Scrap Denounced

That same day, the *Detroit Times* ran a similar top banner headline, only this one was in bright red ink:

Fire Briggs Head, Mazey Asks

The articles reported that Emil Mazey, Ken Morris, and others sent a letter to Walter O. Briggs demanding the dismissal of Briggs's son-in-law, Dean Robinson, and the cancellation of the Renda scrap metal contract.

Robinson issued a one-sentence statement: "We deny all the insinuations that the company was guilty of any wrongdoing."

Walter O. Briggs was in Florida and unable to be reached, but his son, Spike, the company vice president and treasurer, said he "wouldn't dignify it with a comment." Later in the article, Briggs said that a transcript of the Murphy grand jury hearings was being sent to his father. He added, "I think Dad will insist on a thorough investigation. Dad had nothing to do with any racket—if there was one. I am very unhappy that the name of Briggs has been placed in such an unfavorable light. Its reputation, name, and record in the past has been one of complete honesty. We have always operated the plant that way."

The US attorney indicated that their office planned to investigate perjury based on conflicting testimony in the Murphy grand jury and at the Kefauver hearings.

· · · · · · · · · · · · ·

As reporters reviewed the transcripts of the Murphy grand jury, they found a treasure trove of testimony on the 1945 murder of Lydia

Thompson. The *Detroit News* city edition on February 13 had a top banner headline:

Reveal Quiz on Thompson Killing

The *News* found the 1945 murder victim Lydia Thompson's note, which read, "If after this day you don't see me, and you don't hear anything of me, then go and find a man by the name of Sam Perrone and ask him where I am." The paper reported that the Murphy grand jury had questioned a private detective at length as to the connection between Perrone and the Thompson murder. In the end, as always with Perrone, there was only circumstantial evidence of his involvement. Still, it was another terrible headline.

Adjacent to the article on Perrone, the *Detroit News* had a secondary headline on the front page:

Bare More Records in Renda Deal

This front-page story did not have much hard news. The article rehashed some of the testimony from the Murphy grand jury regarding the Renda's statements in 1946 that he was a witness to be called before the grand jury.

. . . .

On Wednesday, February 14, all three Detroit dailies continued front-page headlines; however, the headlines were smaller, as the Kefauver hearings were beginning to fade after a week of above-the-fold headline stories. The *Detroit Times* headline read:

Briggs Unrest Tied to UAW Before Jury

This article reviewed the testimony of James Dewey before the Murphy grand jury. The story related how Dewey, who had no love for the Mazey faction of Local 212, felt much of the unrest might have been caused by the Mazey faction of Local 212 in the early 1940s. The article suggested that victims of the Briggs beatings were also men fired by Briggs in 1941 for supporting unauthorized strikes. Of course, the reporters had no way of knowing that the Mazey faction had actually tried to prevent the wildcat strikes. This story did not go anywhere, but it again kept the Briggs issue in front of the public.

Meanwhile, the *Detroit News* had a front-page story:

Renda's Gun Permit 'Lost' During Quiz

The story revolved around the fact that Wayne County officials could not understand how Renda's handgun permit was missing from their files. The story began to link Renda and, more significantly, Sam Perrone to the illegal alien racket.

The *Detroit Free Press* ran a story headlined:

Probe Asked in Death of Briggs Aides

The article noted that Emil Mazey, previously unaware of the testimony of the top Briggs' aides to the Murphy grand jury, again raised the issue of the 1946 deaths of William Cleary and George Herbert. Emil said, "It seems more than a coincidence that ... people who ... could shed light on the Briggs beatings and the Briggs scrap contract should all die in the same year." He asked Wayne County Prosecutor Gerald O'Brien to investigate the deaths. O'Brien agreed to look into the matter but also said there had never been any hint of foul play.

. . . .

The next day, Thursday, February 15, new banner headlines appeared in the Detroit papers. One headline attacked Judge Murphy regarding his release of grand jury transcripts to the Kefauver committee. The other story continued the linking of Sam Perrone and the Detroit Stove Works to the smuggling of illegal Italian immigrants.

The *Detroit Times* ran the front-page banner headline declaring:

SEEK OUSTER OF MURPHY FOR BARING JURY STATEMENTS

Malfeasance Charge Is Considered

The *Detroit News* ran a headline in its final edition:

State Is Balked on Jury Records

Each article reflected the outrage by the state attorney general over release of secret grand jury testimony by a state circuit court judge. As the days passed after Judge Murphy's release of his grand jury transcripts, the state attorney general's hierarchy grew more frustrated. They had no idea that this material was going to be released to the press and become the subject of sensational news stories quoting what was supposed to be secret testimony on the front page of every Detroit newspaper. They reasoned that grand jury testimony was secret and never made public. Now all credibility regarding any secret testimony was at stake. Deputy Attorney General Arthur Iverson said, "Judge Murphy was guilty of malfeasance in office and may be called before the legislature, since it is in session. His grand jury records were secret under the … law and they are still secret under the amended law.… Judge Murphy had no right to surrender those records and make them public at any time."

In addition to having Murphy impeached for malfeasance, the attorney general's office wanted the now public testimony returned to secrecy. They called on the US attorney to return the Murphy transcripts. US Attorney Edward Kane refused to surrender the material. He said he needed the information for future action by his office.

Judge Murphy's response was quick. In his mind, he was one law enforcement entity helping another. In a statement, he addressed the media:

> I turned over the grand jury records to the Senate committee at the committee's request. I did not know what use the committee would make of them. They simply asked for them in connection with their investigation here, and I obliged them.… I had no advance notion that

this action would be taken. As a grand juror, I took no oath of secrecy, such as was administered to members of the grand jury staff and to all witnesses. And in any event, the one-man grand jury law was repealed; thus, in my opinion, freeing the transcripts for use of the federal government.

The second set of headlines that day revolved around illegal immigration. The *Detroit News* ran a top banner headline:

HUNT RING SMUGGLING
ALIENS INTO DETROIT
Gang Gets $1,000 Fee from Each

Sometime just before the Detroit Kefauver hearings, federal immigration authorities raided the Detroit Stove Works and arrested twenty illegal immigrants, while another forty fled the premises. Those arrested testified that they were smuggled into Canada and later brought to Detroit by boat, through the Detroit-Windsor tunnel or over the Ambassador Bridge. At the Kefauver hearing the week before, Sam Perrone testified that he knew the workers but, of course, had nothing to do with any illegal activity.

. . . .

The media follow-up to the Kefauver committee slowed for about a week and a half, and then on Monday, February 26, the *Detroit News* ran a front-page banner headline:

Plea Sent Kefauver
ASK RETURN OF CRIME QUIZ
Reuther Shootings Reopened

The short article said that Prosecutor O'Brien requested Senator Kefauver to send his investigators back to Detroit to investigate any possible connections between the Briggs beatings and the Reuther shootings. O'Brien acknowledged that there was no proof for a connection but felt that if they spent more time on the issue, the committee could connect the dots.

One has to believe that Heber Blankenhorn was somewhere in the middle of this request. He was making one last stab at getting the committee to officially review and hopefully solve the mystery of the Walter and Victor Reuther shootings.

． ． ． ． ． ． ． ． ． ． ． ．

On March 7, the late edition of the *Detroit News* ran a small front-page headline:

Quiz Santo Perrone in Reuther Shootings

The next day, on page five, the newspaper provided a more detailed story in its early edition, with this headline:

Perrone Quiz in Reuther, Briggs Attack Is Barren

The stories told of how Perrone voluntarily went to the Detroit police headquarters, where he was questioned for two hours. While refusing a lie detector test, he went to the interrogation rooms on the sixth floor and was questioned by Detroit police detectives Albert DeLamielleure and James Blessington of the special investigation squad. Many of the questions were the same as those he had answered before the Murphy grand jury and the Kefauver committee. The hoodlum denied any knowledge or involvement in the Briggs beatings or the Reuther shootings.

The police also asked about his relationship with former UAW board member Melvin Bishop, with specific focus on their arrest for shining deer in Cummins, Michigan, in 1947. Perrone denied knowing Bishop. The article pointed out, however, that the arresting officer in Cummins said this about the men: "While they didn't say much to me, [they] appeared to be very friendly."

Perrone was asked, "Do you have any knowledge of the Reuther shooting?"

His response: "No."

He was later asked, "Do you know anything about the Briggs beatings?"

Perrone said, "No, I never heard any information about that. I never knew any of the people who were beaten."

Regarding illegal aliens, the police asked, "Did you ever put aliens to work at the Detroit Michigan Stove Company?"

"No, I never did that."

The article also said that the police had brought in Melvin Bishop for questioning two weeks earlier. At that time, he refused to answer questions regarding his relationship with Perrone without an attorney being present. Bishop, now working as a labor relations consultant, did not comment to reporters about the article.

. . . .

The final major story relating to the Detroit Kefauver committee hearings appeared in the *Detroit News* on Tuesday, March 13, five weeks after the hearings. The front-page banner headline read:

Renda Deal Cited

UAW BRANDS BRIGGS UNFAIR IN NLRB SUIT

The article said that Briggs Local 212 president Ken Morris, with George Edwards acting as his attorney, filed unfair labor relations activities charges with the National Labor Relations Board. The article cited six key allegations:

1. The Renda contract resulted in at least five violent and potentially deadly assaults on well-known members of Local 212.
2. The contract has created an atmosphere of terror and fear which

has existed as a coercing influence from the inception of the contract down to the present date.

3. By the terms of this contract, [Briggs] in effect paid $150,000 a year to secure the services of Carl Renda and Santo Perrone and the group of strikebreakers and gangsters who worked for Perrone....

4. The full facts in relation to the purpose of this [scrap metal] contract were brought before the public and the membership of Local 212 as a result of [the Kefauver committee hearings].

5. Since the release of this information, every member of Local 212 is thoroughly aware that any vigorous union activity on his part may well mark him for the special attention of the hired gangsters whose services have been bought by Briggs with the Briggs-Renda contract.

6. These alleged "services" are still available in spite of the formal demand by Local 212 that the company cease the unfair labor practice which this contract with the above-stated ramifications embodies.

The statement of facts of the suit argued that Dean Robinson and John Fry were admittedly friends and Fry "sold" the Renda deal to Dean Robinson. The suit argued that the only "asset" Carl Renda had for the scrap job was his father-in-law, Sam Perrone.

· · · · · · · · · · · · · ·

The stories continued from time to time during the coming months. Briggs refused to end their arrangement with Carl Renda. However, something was in the wind that would bring this issue to public attention once again. Unknown to all but a very few people, a small team of law enforcement officials and UAW investigators was meeting secretly, working to bring the violence against the UAW to justice.

CHAPTER 24

THEIR CASE WAS SINKING FAST

The two UAW people most intimate with the UAW's investigation of the Reuther shootings and the Briggs beatings were Jack Conway and Emil Mazey. I don't recall ever meeting Jack Conway, Walter Reuther's administrative assistant, but I had often overheard my parents talking about him. He seemed a step removed from us. But Emil Mazey was family; we spent hundreds of hours with Emil, usually at family social events but also at UAW functions. Not once did Emil or anyone else let on that he was the man helping to direct an investigation on the violence that plagued UAW activists. However, I do have vague recollections of Emil being bitter about the judicial system and the local judges that sat on the bench. Researching this book, I understand why he had such feelings.

SOMETIME IN LATE FEBRUARY 1951, shortly after the Kefauver hearings, George Edwards and Ken Morris were talking on the phone. With a sense of glee in George's high-pitched voice, Ken's attorney said that with all the new information regarding Briggs now public, it was only a matter of time before they sued the offending parties and were paid handsomely for all the suffering they had caused.

Ken jokingly said, "Do you want to buy my share of the money now?" Edwards didn't take the deal, and Ken never saw any money.[291]

. . . .

On May 1, 1951, the Kefauver committee issued its interim report, which covered the hearings in Detroit and other major cities. The committee report read:

> The most important fact uncovered in the Detroit hearings of this committee was that some manufacturers have entered into and are today continuing intimate business relationships with racketeers for the purpose of affecting their labor relationships. The sad story uncovered by the committee is somewhat complicated because it operates in two stages. The first stage is that in which the Detroit [Michigan] Stove Works, the president of which is John A. Fry, whose social respectability in the city of Detroit is beyond any question, entered into a relationship with one Santo Perrone, the obvious effect of which was to enlist the assistance of Perrone's gangster friends in Fry's labor problems.... The second stage is that in which Fry's close friend, William Dean Robinson, likewise socially impeccable and a high official and now president of the Briggs Manufacturing Co., concocted a legal fiction whereby Perrone's son-in-law, Carl Renda, obtained a contract for doing nothing, which has given him since 1946 an income ranging between fifty and one hundred thousand dollars a year, the real purpose of which was to have Perrone exert his and gangdom's influence in the Briggs Manufacturing Co.'s labor problems.[292]

The report further described the background of Perrone's relationship with Fry and the Stove Works. It reviewed the Briggs experience and summarized Carl Renda's lack of qualifications for receiving the large scrap metal contract from Briggs. It said Renda hired the same people to do the work he was supposed to do, in effect making no change in the scrap metal operation. The Kefauver report said:

> The committee regards it as obvious that Renda was being paid for something. While it was not proved by judicially admissible evidence, the inference is inescapable that what Renda ... was being paid for was the service of his father-in-law, the "muscle man," Sam Perrone....
>
> The committee's records indicated that approximately six prominent labor officers of the Briggs Manufacturing Co. were beaten in a most inhuman fashion by unknown persons in the year that followed the granting of the otherwise inexplicable Renda contract.
>
> The committee heard both Fry ... and William Dean Robinson.... **It is the opinion of the committee that neither Fry nor Robinson testified frankly concerning [their] relationships to gangsters. This committee believes that these two presidents knew of the underworld relationships which their companies had entered into in connection with their labor relations; that they had been questioned about this before a grand jury of [the] State of Michigan, in the course of which they did not speak frankly, and that they also failed to speak frankly before this committee**(emphasis added).[293]

. . . .

Just before the report was issued, Ken Morris filed a one-hundred-thousand-dollar suit against Briggs, Dean Robinson, Carl Renda, and Sam Perrone. The Ken Morris suit charged that the defendants were part of a scheme whereby Briggs provided a lucrative scrap metal contract to Carl Renda, and in return, Renda provided "industrial peace" by whatever means necessary.

Sam Perrone and his son-in-law, Carl Renda, denied responsibility for the Ken Morris beating. Their denial, in a statement provided by their attorney, Louis J. Colombo, Sr., indicated the suit be thrown out of court since the two-year statute of limitations had expired. Their statement said, "This is not an honest lawsuit. Its real purpose was not to collect damages from the defendants; its real purpose was accomplished a few days ago."[294]

This cryptic reference was acknowledgment that Briggs had finally canceled the scrap metal contract with Carl Renda, five years after the Murphy one-man grand jury and days after the Kefauver report was issued.[295]

Regarding the statute of limitations issue, George Edwards responded to the court that Morris was not able to act sooner since the Perrone-Renda-Briggs connections were not public knowledge until after the Kefauver hearing testimony earlier in the year. Unfortunately for Ken, the courts agreed with Perrone, Renda, and Briggs. The UAW took the issue to the state supreme court. The supreme court agreed with the lower court. Ken and the UAW then sought to change the statute of limitations law, which they did (even in a hostile antilabor state legislature), but the extension was not retroactive, and Ken's suit went nowhere.[296]

In May, when Briggs canceled the scrap metal contract, the *Detroit Free Press* wrote in a May 7 editorial:

> Decision of the Briggs Manufacturing Company to cancel its scrap metal contract with Carl Renda is long overdue. In all decency, the company had no other choice.
>
> The unholy alliance between Renda and Briggs was exposed at the Kefauver committee hearing in Detroit. Young Renda, a youth without any business experience, lacking even an office and telephone, was handed this juicy contract which netted him $100,000 a year because he was the son-in-law of Sam Perrone, a gangster, whose

strong-arm facilities were desired against the plant's unions ...

As long as such a contract was continued after the Kefauver charges were aired, it could only be regarded as an affront to the law-abiding elements of this city.

This might have been the end, but instead, the Kefauver committee's report provided greater incentive for law enforcement officials to continue their investigations.

. . . .

In 1951, a select group of people began meeting at the home of Wayne County Assistant Prosecutor Joseph Rashid. Besides Rashid, other attendees included the UAW's Jack Conway: Ralph Winstead, now the UAW's chief investigator; Detroit police inspector Paul Slack; and members of the Michigan State Police. Trust and secrecy were the key ingredients of these meetings. No one discussed the topics of these meetings with their family members, colleagues, or superiors.[297]

After reviewing all the clues, the group began to tie the alleged Briggs beatings' perpetrators Sam Perrone and Carl Renda to the Reuther shootings. Their evidence was circumstantial, but the more they looked, the more they found connections. They felt it was just a question of finding the key ingredient for a rock-solid case.[298]

One person absent from these meetings was Albert DeLamielleure. DeLamielleure was the Detroit police detective in charge of the Ken Morris beating. He was the detective in charge of the Walter and Victor Reuther shootings. He was also the Detroit police officer assigned as a key investigator for the Murphy grand jury. It turned out that DeLamielleure was tainted. He apparently was Sam Perrone's plant in the Detroit Police Department. DeLamielleure was a likely informant for and in all likelihood received kickbacks from Sam Perrone.

Earlier in 1951, a new police chief, George Boos, promised to clean up the police force, and DeLamielleure became one of the targets. The information on DeLamielleure may have come from Rashid's secret meetings or from other sources, but it was determined that DeLamielleure had improper relationships with Sam Perrone. DeLamielleure's wife was the assistant manager at Helen's Bar on Jefferson Avenue and Canton Street, next to Sam Perrone's Esso gas station, and it was a well-known meeting place for Perrone and his gang. Further, DeLamielleure's brother-in-law had purchased the bar, and it was later determined that the man acted as a front for the detective. Commissioner Boos deemed these actions highly improper. The *Detroit News* front-page headline read:

REUTHER CASE DETECTIVE FACES INQUIRY ABOUT BAR

In the article, Boos said, "We have received reports that the Reuther shootings were hatched in that bar. We are looking into the angle very critically."[299]

On the next day, August 24, the *News* ran a follow-up story on the front page, but lower, just over the top of the fold:

Officer Blames UAW for Inquiry on Saloon

In the article, DeLamielleure accused the UAW of linking him to Helen's Bar and the violence against the UAW. He said, "I dug deep into the Reuther cases and inconvenienced some union big shots. Maybe they were embarrassed too. I worked my head off. Maybe I was getting too warm."

DeLamielleure left the Detroit Police Department and took a job with the Teamsters (just as Melvin Bishop did after his labor consulting business failed).

Discovery of this crooked cop likely explains the missing evidence from the Morris beating. It also helps explain the threatening telephone calls that Victor Reuther's neighbors received *after* DeLamielleure paid them visits. It might also explain the police visit to Victor's home, demanding the removal of the family dog a day before his assassination attempt took place. DeLamielleure also paid Herbert's wife a visit, and she suddenly received strange phone calls and was attacked in her backyard. And of course, it was DeLamielleure who was assigned to the Murphy grand jury. Perrone probably knew what was going on regarding the investigation of the Briggs beatings and the Reuther shootings before DeLamielleure's Detroit police superiors.

. . . .

On November 20, 1951, on page 13-c, the *Detroit Times* reported that Dean Robinson, "president of the Briggs Manufacturing Co., arrived in Detroit today from London, England, where he suffered a stroke two months ago." Robinson remained ill and died in July 1958. His obituaries were front-page news, which naturally brought up the issues of the Kefauver committee and antilabor activities at Briggs. His wife, Grace, Walter O. Briggs's daughter, remarried within the year.[300]

. . . .

In late 1951, the UAW again tried to organize the Detroit Stove Works workers. Violence and intimidation again erupted at the Detroit Stove Works facilities. A brave UAW committeeman named Willie Poindexter identified Tino Orlando, Perrone's son-in-law, as a person who offered $100. Poindexter quoted Orlando as saying, "Be a good fellow; cooperate with us and get [the UAW organization drive] over with." Later, Poindexter and another man were offered $1,500 each if they left "town for two weeks."

In November 1951, Wayne County Prosecutor Gerald O'Brien arrested and charged Sam Perrone, Orlando, and several others with several misdemeanors connected to union busting.[301] Perrone was convicted in May 1952. However, Detroit Recorder's Court Judge Joseph A. Gillis placed Perrone on a two-year probation sentence instead of forcing him to do time in jail. Gillis could have made him serve the maximum six-month sentence or some portion of the sentence. Instead, even though he was convicted of a high misdemeanor, Perrone walked out of court a free man.

Tino Orlando and several other Perrone men were convicted of conspiracy to violate labor laws and carrying illegal weapons. Orlando, besides having an interest in the Hazel Park racetrack, operated Perrone's

Esso gas station on Jefferson across from the Detroit Stove Works. The defendants pled guilty, were fined $1,000, and never served jail time.

· · · · · · · · · · · · · ·

In late November 1951, Sam Perrone ended his relationship with the Detroit Stove Works. Just weeks after the UAW's Local 212 organized and signed a contract with the Detroit Stove Works, the November 26 *Detroit News* reported that Perrone, in a letter to the company, stated, "For the last ten years, I have been falsely accused of and falsely arrested for all the crimes in the calendar. In order not to give my persecutors any further damnable excuse to disgrace and degrade my loved ones, I hereby notify you to cancel, at once, my cartage and scrap iron agreement."

· · · · · · · · · · · · · ·

The Rashid group continued making connections between the Briggs beatings and the Reuther shootings. The connection was Sam Perrone and his henchmen. The problem continued to be finding proof and reliable evidence. The other problem was the international border. Many of the Perrone gang lived in Windsor, across the Detroit River, separating Detroit and Windsor. It took only a few minutes to cross the border by bridge or tunnel. In legal terms, however, the difference was much more significant. Even if the Canadian, Ontario, and Windsor authorities agreed, arresting someone in Canada for a crime committed in the United States often proved daunting and full of legal issues.

One of the first men questioned regarding the 1948 Walter Reuther shooting was Sam Henderson. Henderson fully convinced Blankenhorn and Winstead that he had nothing to do with the shootings, and he became a source of information for law enforcement officials and the UAW. He eventually was paid for his expenses by the UAW as an assistant to Ralph Winstead. Winstead had become head of the UAW investigation when Heber Blankenhorn retired back to Alexandria, Virginia.[302]

As the Rashid investigation continued, they finally got a break. The investigators found a composite drawing that police made based on descriptions Victor Reuther's neighbors had provided of a man in a suspicious car before the shooting. The drawing strongly resembled Clarence Jacobs, a known member of the Sam Perrone gang.[303] After the 1948 Walter Reuther shooting, a response to a "secret witness" query in the *Detroit News* suggested a Clarence Jacobs was involved in the assassination attempt. A link was made.

In November 1953, Henderson contacted a Canadian named Donald Ritchie. Ritchie was an ex-con with connections to the Perrones. Ritchie was also the nephew of Clarence Jacobs.

Henderson found Ritchie in a Canadian jail. At that time, Ritchie told Henderson, "I know what you want but see me when I get out." Later, Ritchie said he had great interest in the reward but did not want to deal with the red tape involved in collecting the full amount. Instead, he wanted a payment of $25,000. Ritchie was sure that if he cooperated with the authorities, he faced retribution from Perrone or Perrone associates. If murdered, Ritchie wanted the reward to be given to his common-law wife.[304]

According to an A. F. Mahan, Jr., article in the *Lansing State Journal*:

> The UAW, it turned out … signed a $25,000 contract with Ritchie.… The UAW agreed to put $25,000 in escrow in a Windsor, Ont., bank. Ritchie was to get $5,000 after making a statement to [Wayne County Prosecutor] O'Brien and after the issuance of warrants based upon it. An additional $10,000 was payable when those named in the warrants were bound over for trial, and another $10,000 if they were convicted. Then two years later, if he were still alive, Ritchie was to get the rest of the UAW's $100,000 … reward; otherwise it would go to his wife.[305]

Working without the knowledge of Prosecutor O'Brien, the UAW developed an elaborate scheme to move $25,000 to Canada. They found a Canadian attorney, Donald Morand, to handle the funds intended for Ritchie and then got Ritchie to turn himself in to Prosecutor O'Brien. Emil Mazey was responsible for getting the funds and transferring them to Canada. Mazey used a deception by indicating that the funds were for a property purchase. Except for a very few people, no one at UAW headquarters knew of the transferred funds because there was serious concern that Perrone might have informants inside the UAW headquarters. Emil Mazey, Jack Conway, and Ralph Winstead felt they had the key to the Reuther shootings and did not want a leak to ruin this opportunity.

While Prosecutor O'Brien supposedly did not know about the UAW payment, he and his assistant, Joseph Rashid, traveled to Windsor in mid-December to meet with Ritchie to determine whether he was a believable witness.

The UAW never obtained a statement from Ritchie for O'Brien. Their job was to deliver Ritchie to the Wayne County prosecutor and let the Wayne County Prosecutor's Office handle the questioning of Ritchie.

On December 31, 1953, Henderson brought Ritchie to the United States and delivered him to Prosecutor O'Brien's office. On January 6, 1954, O'Brien held a press conference announcing that he had solved the Walter Reuther shooting. He announced the issuance of arrest warrants for Santo Perrone, Carl Renda, Peter M. Lombardo, and Clarence Jacobs. Perrone fled and was the subject of a nationwide manhunt. Windsor police arrested Jacobs. Lombardo was in a Canadian penitentiary. In Detroit, Carl Renda was arrested and later released on bond.

Ritchie's signed confession was released to the press. It stated:

I was in the car the night Walter Reuther was shot. For about four or five years I had been working for Santo (Sam) Perrone. I made $400 or $500 a week.

In the occupation, I was—well, it just wasn't what people would call work.

Clarence Jacobs approached me for this particular job. He told me I would get five grand.

I was approached about five days before it happened and asked if I wanted to go. This conversation took place in Perrone's gas station at Jefferson and Canton. Perrone asked me several days before the shooting if I was going on the job. I said I was.

I didn't ask a lot of questions. These people don't talk things over very much. They don't explain things.

All I knew was that Perrone had once said, "We'll have to get that guy out of the way." Did he mean Reuther? Yeah.

I was living around in Detroit hotels at the time. For a while I roomed with Jacobs.

The night of the shooting, I was picked up in the gas station. The car was a red Mercury. I don't know who it belonged to.

I sat [in] the back seat. Jacobs drove and Peter Lombardo was in the front seat with Jacobs. The shotgun was in the front seat between Jacobs and Lombardo. It was a Winchester pump gun, 12 gauge.

I was there in case there was trouble. If anything happened, I was to drive the car away.

Jacobs did the shooting. He was the only one who got out of the car. I don't know how long he was gone. It's hard to remember time. Maybe a minute or two, maybe longer. I heard the report of the gun. Then Jacobs got back in the car and said, "Well, I knocked the bastard down." We took off in a hurry.

We hadn't followed [Reuther] home from the meeting he was at that night. I don't know how they knew he was in the house. They didn't tell me and I didn't ask.

I don't know what streets we took to get there or to get back. I don't know that part of the city.

After the job they dropped me back at [Helen's Bar], about 200 feet from the gas station. I don't know what they did with the car. I heard later it was demolished and junked. I haven't any idea what happened to the gun.

I had some drinks at the bar and then went and saw Carl Renda. Why? I always went in to see Renda. He said, "I have something for you."

He got a bundle of cash and handed it to me.

> I went downtown and met a girl. I stayed with her until four in the morning. Then I took a taxi to Windsor. I didn't count the money until I got to Canada. It was exactly five grand....
>
> I went to the bank the next day and made a deposit. I forget whether it was $4,500 or $5,500 I put in the bank....
>
> I didn't have anything to do with the shooting of Victor Reuther. I was in a penitentiary up in Montreal at the time.[306]

It appeared that the Reuther assassination plot was uncovered.

· · · · · · · · · · · ·

After Ritchie turned himself in on December 31, 1953, he was placed in Detroit Police Department custody. The police moved him from one hotel to another. On January 8, Ritchie was ensconced in a suite at the Statler Hilton Hotel on Grand Circus Park, with three Detroit police detectives guarding him. Ritchie entered the bathroom, saying he was taking a shower. After a while, the detectives testified that they became curious about what was taking the man so long. They knocked. No answer. They forced the door open. The shower was running ... but no Ritchie. He had escaped through another door and headed straight to Canada.

At nearly the same time, Ritchie's common-law wife met with attorney Morand. She requested $5,000 in reward money, since Ritchie had been delivered to the Detroit police, had made a confession, and suspects were in custody. Morand agreed that the conditions for a $5,000 payment had been met. An hour after Ritchie's escape, the woman received $5,000. The UAW had unintentionally paid for Ritchie's flight, leaving O'Brien and the Detroit Police Department looking like fools.

Ritchie was on the lam. He seemed to be running from the police but not Perrone. A telephone call came to a *Detroit Free Press* reporter. The caller, identifying himself as Ritchie, denied the entire confession. He said he needed money and was taking the UAW for a ride. Ritchie was eventually found by Hamilton, Ontario, police and arrested. An effort to extradite him failed, and Ritchie was released.

Prosecutor O'Brien was devastated. On January 9, he told the press, "I felt—and I still feel—[that] we have the solution.... We have a lot of evidence along the same lines [as Ritchie's confession], but he is the case." He added, "Without his testimony in court, our case collapses. We can't go through with the trial if the witness is killed or never comes back to this country." UAW leadership and Winstead felt the same. They had the man, and the Detroit Police Department had let them down again. Two of the police detectives guarding Ritchie were punished; they forfeited thirty days' pay.[307]

On January 12, Prosecutor O'Brien, Rashid, and others said they heard for the first time that the UAW paid $5,000 to Ritchie. They knew that the UAW had helped find Ritchie but expressed outrage that money had changed hands. Their case was sinking fast. From the UAW point of view, all they had done was pay Ritchie to turn himself in—his statement was entirely his own. However, to O'Brien and Rashid, it looked as if the UAW had paid a witness. They probably did not feel that the UAW had bribed the witness, but they felt it was a stupid mistake. And it was. This was a public relations disaster for the UAW.

Was Ritchie's confession a fake? It may never be known. It is known, however, that people close to the case believed it was valid. It is also known that Ritchie loved easy money. If he could get an easy $5,000 from the UAW, why wouldn't he want the additional $20,000, with more money after that? At the same time, Sam Perrone was still a fugitive. Did Perrone figure a way to get to Ritchie? There is little question that Ritchie was scared and that someone got to him, perhaps with a better offer. Perhaps the offer was his life; perhaps it was more money. As Emil Mazey later said, spending "$500,000 to catch the assailants of Walter and Victor Reuther" was an option, if it meant finding the assassins. He added, "Ritchie changed his story because he was scared [for] his life. The prosecutor must have believed it too, because he issued indictments based on Ritchie's statements."[308] Regardless, Ritchie's escape turned what had seemed a tremendous resolution of crimes against UAW leaders into an embarrassing fiasco.

CHAPTER 25

RITCHIE WAS NO SUNDAY SCHOOL TEACHER

The experiences of working with prosecutors and judges taught Emil Mazey and many others in the UAW a lesson. Politics was more than electing a president, governor, or mayor. It was about shaping the opinions of the legislative and judicial branches of government. Emil learned the importance of that. Emil, Pat Caruso, Jess Ferrazza, and Dad were longtime season ticket holders for the Detroit Lions, who played at Briggs Stadium, later renamed Tiger Stadium. I remember during election years, probably 1960 and 1962, when Dad had Sunday meetings, my brother and I would be picked up three hours before game time by Pat Caruso and head down to the stadium. There, we handed out campaign literature, usually supporting a judge, and also printed on the brochure were the names and numbers of the Lion players and those of the opposing team. It was a great idea since patrons then did not have to buy expensive programs. But still, I wondered, why all this work for a judge? Why weren't we doing something for the gubernatorial or presidential candidates? Years later, I learned what Emil already knew: a judge could just as easily rule against workers as a governor could sign antiunion legislation.

IN 1954, SHORTLY AFTER RITCHIE'S escape and his recanting of the confession, Carl Renda and Sam Perrone took the offensive. They sued the UAW, the Wayne County Prosecutor's Office (Prosecutor O'Brien and Assistant Prosecutor Joseph Rashid), the state police, and the Detroit Police Department for $4.5 million in civil damages. It took years, but in November 1957, the case came to trial in Detroit's Recorder's Court. The case was one of the longest trials in Michigan civil court history. In the meantime, Assistant Prosecutor Joseph Rashid had been appointed a circuit judge and Wayne County Prosecutor O'Brien had passed away. The two key champions in the prosecutor's office were gone: either dead or moved to a higher office. To complicate matters, a visiting judge tried the case. This was Judge Edward T. Kane, from Port Huron, Michigan. This was the same man, who as a US Attorney, refused to give up Judge Murphy's grand jury testimony to the Michigan attorney general. He was also a long time Democrat.

Joseph W. Louisell was a smart attorney who spent a career defending many of Detroit's notorious hoodlums. He was also the attorney that successfully defended Carl Bolton in the 1950 Walter Reuther shooting. His challenge in the Renda case was to prove that the secret meetings at former Assistant Prosecutor Rashid's house were not meetings to solve criminal cases. Instead, he intended to prove that the meetings were a conspiracy of government law enforcement agencies and union officials to get Carl Renda and his father-in-law, Sam Perrone. Louisell referred to the UAW reward as a UAW payoff in order to get a witness (Ritchie) to testify its way. Louisell expertly played upon the negative stereotype the Detroit press had created regarding labor leaders with the Renda jury.

Louisell further painted the UAW in a negative light by arguing that its investigation was an attempt to get around traditional law enforcement efforts. He argued that Blankenhorn and Winstead's efforts to work cooperatively with law enforcement were, in fact, efforts to manipulate the investigation. For example, the UAW had learned that it could not trust the Detroit Police Department; there were just too many bad cops in key positions. As the UAW investigation continued in the early 1950s, much of its investigation files were kept at Solidarity House, the UAW international headquarters, at 8000 E. Jefferson. In time, the Michigan State Police investigators assigned to the case worked out of the Solidarity House office since that was where the investigation's data was located. Louisell questioned the authenticity of a police investigation being run out of UAW headquarters.

Louisell's first major procedural decisions from Judge Kane may have been the most significant. Louisell dropped Sam Perrone from the lawsuit so that only Carl Renda was filing the civil suit against the UAW, the Michigan State Police, the Detroit Police Department, and others. This was a brilliant move since Carl Renda had never been arrested, but Sam Perrone had an arrest record as long as Detroit's Ambassador Bridge. In court, Louisell petitioned the judge to prohibit any reference to Renda's father-in-law, Sam Perrone. This meant the UAW and other defendants could not bring up in court or to the jury any reference to Sam Perrone or Renda's connection to the Detroit underworld. UAW counsel spent two hours arguing against such a ruling and lost. It was a devastating blow to the UAW's defense.[309]

One of the first key witnesses in the case was retired Detroit Police Inspector Paul Slack. Police Commissioner Boos had appointed Slack to the Reuther brothers' cases. He was also responsible for investigating Detective DeLamielleure and attended the secret meetings at Rashid's house. Louisell asked if the Detroit Police Department had been investigating the case. Slack affirmed that it had and that any information regarding the case was to go to Rashid. Louisell then asked if there were two independent investigations going on, one an official investigation and the other a rump investigation. The inspector did not disagree. Slack said that he heard Carl Renda's name mentioned in Rashid's house in relation to the Walter Reuther shooting in 1952, but that Ritchie was not mentioned until December 1953, just before his deal with the UAW.[310]

The next major witness in the case was Jack Conway, Walter Reuther's able administrative assistant. Louisell questioned Conway hard about Sam Henderson, the unlicensed gumshoe who worked for Winstead, and was critical in his method of locating and getting Ritchie to come forward. Of course, Louisell did not quite paint the picture this way. Instead, he painted the picture of Henderson contacting Ritchie and then bribing him into making a confession.

Conway responded, "Henderson came to our attention because he was picked up as a suspect in the Reuther case. We checked thoroughly on Henderson and found he never had anything to do with the shooting. We took him on because of his great knowledge of persons in southern Canada." Conway pointed out that Henderson was not employed by the UAW. He testified, "He was not on a salary; we paid him only his expenses."[311]

Under questioning by Louisell, Conway admitted that the $25,000 to pay Ritchie was in violation of UAW policy. He testified that a memo was written with the check, indicating that the money was to be used for "purchasing certain real estate in Canada."[312]

A week later, on December 5, Emil Mazey testified. Louisell asked Mazey why Ritchie asked for $25,000 when the UAW offered a $200,000 reward for Reuther's assassins. Mazey said, "Ritchie did not like all the red tape involved in the big reward. I thought it was a good deal" since Mazey knew that Ritchie had worked with Sam Perrone and Clarence Jacobs, "who are known criminals."

Louisell asked why Ritchie was of such interest. Mazey responded, "We knew Ritchie was no Sunday school teacher, and we knew his criminal background. We have long felt that Reuther's assailants were members of the underworld. … When he told us he was in the car the night of the shooting and could finger the assailants, we believed him."

Louisell then asked why the late Prosecutor O'Brien and his assistant Joseph Rashid were not initially informed of the $25,000 reward offer. Emil responded, "We felt this arrangement was our own. It was none of their business."

Under intense Louisell questioning, Mazey said the Ritchie money was kept secret "because we were afraid of a plant in the organization." He added that the UAW's "only intent was to solve the shootings of Victor and Walter Reuther."[313]

The UAW's chief investigator, Ralph Winstead, was scheduled to testify when the trial resumed after a weekend break. The UAW's chief investigator appeared to be the linchpin to the whole case. He had the files, the relationships, and the networks to explain all that happened. The UAW knew that he could put the case into perspective and context for the jurors. All were waiting Winstead's Monday morning testimony with great anticipation. All those involved with the case felt the trial depended on his testimony.

. . . .

On Sunday, December 16, Ralph Winstead rose early, dressed, and drove from his St. Clair Shores home down Jefferson Avenue to Solidarity House. The next day, Monday, was his testimony in the most publicized testimony of his career, and he wanted to review some of his records. His route on this cold morning took him from his middle-class neighborhood down Jefferson Avenue, which rolled into the Grosse Pointe communities, where the road became Lake Shore Drive. To Winstead's right were the beautiful mansions of the automotive elite. To his left, looking east, the Lake St. Clair horizon was a deep orange as the sun began to rise over the lake's distant horizon. Ice had already formed on the lake, and beautiful ice crystals reflected the early light.

He was soon in Detroit, passing by the east side automobile plants on Jefferson Avenue, many of which were showing signs of age and disrepair. He drove under the Chrysler overpass that crossed Jefferson at their huge Chrysler-Jefferson Avenue production facility. Just before Van Dyke road, at 8000 E. Jefferson, the sixty-four-year old Winstead turned left into Solidarity House. Since the Reuther shootings and the attempted bombing of the old Milwaukee street headquarters, Solidarity House was under twenty-four-hour security guard. Besides a security man, guard dogs lived on the property. No doubt the UAW appeared even more secretive and remote to the general public, but in the ten years since Walter Reuther's shooting, it was a necessary precaution.

Winstead made a few comments to the security man at the gate, parked his car, and entered the modern building. Walter Reuther had commissioned Oskar Stonorov, a nationally known architect from Philadelphia, to design the world-class building sitting on the Detroit River. Winstead went to his office and worked for about an hour before returning home around 8:00 a.m. After a bit of breakfast with his wife, Winstead put on some warm clothes, including ice-fishing togs, and told his wife that he was going to take a walk. She thought little of his announcement, except that he seemed upset about something. She thought that a walk might do him some good.

Winstead was an avid outdoorsman, equally at home on the water, in a forest, or walking on ice. Hiking on the ice of Lake St. Clair was something he enjoyed doing when the weather turned cold.

Ralph Winstead was never seen alive again.[314]

•   • • • • • • • • • • • • •

Ralph Winstead's disappearance stunned Detroit, but it did not slow the trial. Judge Kane demanded the trial continue. He said, "I've granted other defendants absences." The UAW was dumbfounded by this position, and predictably, Louisell was ready to move forward. To the media, Louisell said that he believed Winstead had skipped town. Louisell implied that Winstead was afraid to take the stand, saying to the press, "I think he's in Mexico." Louisell also added, "It appears to me [that] the disappearance is in furtherance of the UAW's plot to conceal Winstead's real complicity in this case."

Walter Nelson, the UAW attorney, argued to the court, "I don't know if I'm representing a dead man, a live man, a competent man, or one who has disappeared through violence." Nelson said he thought it was legally impossible to proceed under this latest turn of events.[315]

Judge Kane was not moved, and the trial continued as if nothing significant had happened. State Police Lieutenant Joseph Sheridan was recalled to the stand from the previous week. Sheridan was a thirty-nine-year police veteran and had worked with Winstead at Solidarity House in an effort to crack the Reuther shootings.

Louisell began questioning the veteran trooper, whose demeanor seemed dramatically changed from his previous testimony. Sheridan appeared extremely nervous when answering the questions, which were primarily about the time Ritchie had made his confession until he escaped from Detroit police custody on January 8, 1954. His responses were in single-syllable words or comments, such as "I don't remember," which was an answer he used to over forty questions. He said he had been sick and had been to the doctor, with his attorney, over the weekend. The doctor diagnosed his problem as high blood pressure. Sheridan's attorney asked that his client be given until after the Christmas break to testify. The judge, however, demanded that the testimony of the obviously terrified Sheridan continue. Did someone get to Sheridan?[316]

Authorities recovered Ralph Winstead's body from the icy waters of Lake St. Clair exactly one week after his disappearance. His death forever remained a mystery, while officially ruled an accidental drowning. Some suggested that Winstead might have committed suicide, a suggestion that the UAW's Jack Conway and others who knew Winstead totally dismissed. Conway stated emphatically that Winstead was not the kind of man who would take his own life. He added that Winstead was looking forward to testifying in the trial so he could set the record straight. Jack Conway agreed with the St. Clair Shores police, however, that the death was an unfortunate accident.[317]

In January, the trial continued, although it did not receive the press coverage it had during its first two months. The trial became a procedural tug-of-war, without much hard news to report. There were days, however, when key points in the trial were made by attorneys and witnesses.

On January 8, Inspector Paul Slack was back on the witness stand. He described seeing Donald Ritchie after his escape in Windsor, after Canadian law enforcement officials had captured him.

Ritchie told Slack, "I'm sorry for all the trouble I've caused you [regarding the confession and his escape from police custody]. I couldn't have gone through with this thing—I'd have gotten my head blown off."[318] Who was Ritchie afraid of? One has to believe that Sam Perrone was his chief worry.

Then Louisell questioned Detroit Police Lieutenant Claud Ingersoll regarding when the deceased Wayne County Prosecutor O'Brien first met Donald Ritchie. Ingersoll testified that O'Brien met Ritchie December 11, 1953, in a Windsor hotel room and that O'Brien listened to the financial arrangements made between Ritchie and the UAW. The police lieutenant also testified that Ritchie returned voluntarily to Detroit from Windsor. This was new information, as O'Brien had said he knew nothing of the UAW financial agreement with Ritchie.[319]

Later, Louisell questioned Ingersoll about Carl Renda. The attorney accused the police officer of being "out to get" Carl Renda.

Ingersoll denied the accusation.

Louisell raised his voice in distain and said, "Isn't it a fact that at the Ritchie hearing, you told me that Renda hasn't heard the last of this yet?"

As the *Detroit Free Press* reported, "Ingersoll rose from his chair and shouted: 'You know that's not true, Mr. Louisell. I learned when I was a rookie not ever to talk to you except from a witness stand. I know what you'll do to a statement. I learned my lesson from you years ago.'"[320]

Sergeant John O'Neil of the Detroit Police Vice Squad testified that Ritchie told him the UAW agreed to pay him $5,000 to provide testimony to Prosecutor O'Brien. O'Neil added that after Ritchie read a newspaper story on January 8 indicating that he was being held in custody in a downtown hotel, he, Ritchie, became frightened. O'Neil testified that Ritchie said, "I will have to change my name and leave the country because if I stay my life won't be worth a plugged nickel."[321] Ritchie escaped and returned to Canada that day.

Sam Henderson was the next man on the witness stand. Henderson, Winstead's gumshoe, was the man who located Donald Ritchie. Louisell asked how Henderson accomplished the feat. Henderson testified that Donald Ritchie was serving some time in a Windsor jail, but that he developed a relationship with Gordon Ritchie, Donald's brother.

Ritchie's brother told Henderson that Donald Ritchie and his uncle, Clarence Jacobs, handled jobs for Sam Perrone in Michigan.

Henderson testified that he asked the brother if he knew Sam Perrone (for some reason, the judge allowed the testimony regarding Perrone). Gordon Ritchie told Henderson that he knew Sam Perrone and that he and Perrone had broken a union that was trying to organize a stove works company in Cheboygan, Michigan, years earlier. Gordon Ritchie told Henderson that Perrone would go through "mad spells." He told Henderson that coming back from Cheboygan, "Perrone had a crazy spell. He wanted to shoot a hitchhiker just for the fun of it."

Henderson testified that Gordon Ritchie arranged a meeting on December 11, 1953 with his brother, Donald, after his release from jail. Donald Ritchie then told Henderson that he could be cooperative, but that he wanted a piece of the reward money immediately. Henderson did not have that kind of authority and immediately called Winstead.

Winstead, Prosecutor O'Brien, and Rashid rushed to Windsor to meet Henderson and Ritchie later that day.

After the $25,000 escrow payment was agreed to, Henderson said that Prosecutor O'Brien asked if Donald Ritchie knew any of the details regarding the Walter Reuther shooting.

Henderson said that Ritchie's response was solid. He said, "Well, I ought to. I was there."[322]

Emil Mazey then made arrangements to get $25,000 to a bank in Windsor. On December 31, 1953, after the initial payment of $5,000 was made to Ritchie, Henderson delivered Donald Ritchie to Prosecutor O'Brien in Detroit so he could make a statement.

Windsor attorney Donald R. Morand was called to testify and said that Ritchie contacted him near the end of 1953 to finalize his financial arrangement with the UAW. The *Detroit Free Press* reported that Morand "was convinced Ritchie had pertinent information because the man was willing to come to Detroit to testify, even though he faced arrest in another case." Morand testified, "Ritchie told me he knew all about the shooting, knew the people involved[,] and that he was there." Ritchie was something of a screwball, Morand added.[323]

Walter Reuther was called to testify. Reuther, much like Ken Morris with the Briggs beatings, remembered nothing of his attack. He had been blindsided. Walter told the court that he was not involved in the UAW investigation of the crimes against him, his brother, and other UAW members. It was too personal and something Walter wanted to get past. He testified that the assassins "were not shooting at me. They were shooting at the union." At the end of his testimony, Reuther was asked to remove his jacket and shirt. The jurors saw firsthand Reuther's scarred chest and mangled arm. It was a sobering moment.[324]

Carl Renda and his wife testified. Renda testified that he did not know Ritchie. Renda spent several days on the witness stand. He argued that the media around his arrest destroyed his ability to make a living and caused health problems. Defense attorneys planned to rebut such testimony by submitting similar newspaper stories from the Kefauver hearings that were just as harsh. However, Judge Kane refused to allow such evidence.[325]

Robert Busch, an employee at Sam Perrone's gas station, was called to the stand. In previous testimony, Carl Renda testified that he did not know and had never met Clarence Jacobs or his nephew, Donald Richie. Busch rebutted Renda's testimony by stating that he had witnessed many visits and conversations among Carl Renda, Sam Perrone, Clarence Jacobs, and Donald Ritchie.[326]

· · · · · · · · · · · · · ·

In the end, an exhausted jury of eight women and four men deliberated for eight hours in the old Wayne County Building and ruled against the UAW. They ordered damages paid to Renda totaling $400,000, far less than the $4.5 million initially brought by Renda. Charges against the law enforcement officials were dropped.

Renda hugged and kissed his wife.

Emil Mazey was angry and called the ruling a "miscarriage of justice," adding that the union would "seek remedies at once."[327]

**Attorney Louisell, Carl Renda, and Mary Renda
celebrate their victory over the UAW**

The UAW appealed the ruling. In 1961, the case found its way to the Michigan Supreme Court. The issues were again rehashed. The court was composed of three Republican justices and four Democratic justices, including Judge George Edwards. Edwards excused himself from the case since he had been Ken Morris's attorney. Another Democrat was up for a federal court appointment and did not hear the case. The result was three Republicans and two Democrats ruling on a party line against the UAW. Still, the UAW did not pay the $400,000 to Renda.[328] Finally, in 1963, the UAW and Renda settled the case out of court. The union quietly paid $13,000 to Carl Renda.[329]

The story of the Briggs beatings, the Reuther shootings, and the underworld violence against the UAW was over. Individuals were responsible for the Briggs beatings. Individuals pulled the trigger on shotguns that nearly killed Walter and Victor Reuther. Yet no one was convicted of any of these crimes; no one ever served time in prison for seven criminal assaults.

What did the main victim of these assaults think? Were the perpetrators Communists, intraunion rivals, employers, or gangsters? In the late 1960s, Walter Reuther reflected on the shootings and stated:

> Now, obviously, no human being could avoid having his own little reflections and his little speculations about these things. And I've had mine. But I've not made it a major effort.
>
> I think that there's no question about it that there was a particular period in the history of the UAW when disposing of me by assassination or any other way happened to be a common denominator that a number of people could somehow share.
>
> I think that the Communist Party shared that, because in their judgment, I was the only thing that stood between them and seizing the power of this union. They didn't think that anybody else could, in effect, coalesce the combination of forces in our union that

could stop them. Therefore, they would certainly like to see me eliminated.

I think the underworld figured that I was the kind of person who would do everything that I could to try to keep them from taking control of this union and using it for the rackets and everything else that they use unions for.

And I think that there [was] still a small group of diehard employers ... who also were willing to work with the underworld and who, in effect, shared this same common denominator: that they could weaken the union if they [got] me out of the way.

Now, I have been told, and this, [as] far as I am concerned, is only speculation, that there were several meetings at which these three elements had some contact with each other. I am in no position to tell you details because I don't know details. But I was told that.

Certainly there were some of the employers ... working with the gangsters.... There was this scrap iron deal [at Briggs], which was a payoff mechanism. No question about that. It all ties together there somewhere.[330]

EPILOGUE

*"He did more to organize unions than any
single individual. It's a simple fact."*

THE INVESTIGATIONS WERE CLOSED, THE committee
hearings completed, and the trials over. No one was ever convicted
of the Briggs beatings or the attempted murders of Walter and Victor
Reuther.

So was it a conspiracy of the people discussed in the previous pages
or something else? There are certain common denominators in the
story of the Briggs beatings and the Reuther shootings. Melvin Bishop,
Carl Bolton, Sam Perrone, Carl Renda, Detective Albert DeLamielleure,
and others were individuals with motives, and each had overlapping
relationships with the others. Perhaps a bad cop destroyed the efforts of
good cops. Regardless, in the United States, one is innocent until proven
guilty, and there simply was not enough evidence to convict these or
any other individuals. Still, as one newspaper story summed up, the
violence, particularly the Reuther shootings, demonstrated that the
people who hired the gangsters or the gangsters themselves "had come
within an eyelash and some bad marksmanship of getting a stranglehold
on the [UAW]."[331]

The Briggs beatings are forgotten. The Reuther shootings are
occasionally discussed as part of a book or newspaper story. In the end,
people's lives simply moved on along their chosen career paths.

• • • • • • • • • • • • • •

Walter O. Briggs died in 1952. Upon his death, most of the stories about Walter Briggs concerned his ownership of the Detroit Tigers, and they were positive. Some stories touched upon his company, the rise of the Briggs Manufacturing Company, and the constant labor problems. Most of Detroit remembered the name Briggs in relation to the Detroit Tigers and to the stadium he lovingly expanded and turned into one of the premier baseball ballparks in the country. Two years after Briggs died, his wife died, and the family had to sell the team for tax purposes—the government considered the ball club too risky of an investment. His daughter Jane Hart negotiated the sale.[332] Eventually, Briggs Stadium became Tiger Stadium. After the Tigers moved to Comerica Park at the end of the 1999 season, old Tiger Stadium was abandoned—just like so many old automotive factories, downtown buildings, and other structures that stood useless in the declining years of Detroit. Finally, in 2009, the old stadium was torn down.

Spike Briggs had the style, personality, and charisma to be a positive leader for the Briggs Manufacturing Company and the Detroit Tigers. Unfortunately, he simply could not function without his father. After his father's death, Spike said, "It was the first time that I had ever tried to work for anyone except Dad, and I guess I just wasn't cut out for it." He took to drink and ultimately lived what appeared to be an unfulfilled life in the Detroit suburb of Bloomfield Hills. He died of a heart attack in 1970, at the age of fifty-eight.[333]

In the early 1950s, the Chrysler Corporation decided to cut Briggs out of the body-making cycle and build their own auto bodies. When Briggs management learned what their major customer was up to, they decided to raise the price of each automobile body by $25. This created a quandary for Chrysler. Chrysler was not yet ready to begin manufacturing bodies. So instead of building a new body plant, Chrysler decided to buy Briggs out. Jane Hart again was the key negotiator for Briggs, and after an extended negotiation, the sale was completed. In 1954, the Briggs Manufacturing Company was sold to the Chrysler Corporation for $35 million. All that remained of the Briggs Company was the plumbing fixtures business. The company eventually moved its production facilities to South Carolina. Ownership shifted in the company, eventually to foreign interests, but in 2011, its senior management, under the new name Briggs' Plumbing Products, purchased the company. The management still refers to the company as Briggs.[334]

· · · · · · · · · · · · ·

The mob connection to Briggs met a less defined ending. The Detroit Stove Works was bought by the Welbilt Corporation in 1955. In 1957, the new owners closed the Jefferson Avenue factory. The Stove Works, except for a few assets, simply faded away.[335]

Carl Renda, the scrap metal dealer and son-in-law to Sam Perrone, seemed to disappear after his suit against the UAW. He moved to Florida and apparently died in 1989.

Sam Perrone continued his reign as a maverick gangster. Still not directly associated with any of Detroit's known underworld gangs or Mafia leaders, Perrone and his underlings continued to do business. When the Detroit Stove Works was sold in the 1950s, Helen's Bar at Jefferson and Canton Street shut down. Perrone moved his headquarters to his AAA car wash on Gratiot, between Seven and Eight Mile Roads. From there he and his gang extorted businessmen. Their plan was simple. A small bomb exploded at a person's business. The individual was later contacted by Perrone's people and told that the only way to stop a second explosion was to make a payoff. If a company did not pay him under the table, another, more severe, explosion was executed. Unlike previous years, honest Detroit cops were watching. The police felt Perrone was responsible, but as always, they needed proof.

Also in the early 1960s, law enforcement officials learned from illegal wiretaps that three young mob leaders, Jack Tocco and brothers Tony and Billy Giacalone, had had enough of Sam Perrone. He was an old man who listened to no one. They decided his days were over.

On a January winter day in 1964, Sam Perrone was climbing into his car on Gratiot Avenue, next to his car wash. He sat behind the steering wheel of his Pontiac and turned on the ignition. A massive explosion shook the neighborhood. Perrone should have been dead, but instead he was blown apart. The old man's leg was ripped from his body, and he suffered other serious injuries, but he lived. On a stretcher, when asked who had done this, Perrone dismissed the question and uttered, "I'll take care of the ones who did this."

Senior Detective Inspector Thomas Cochill, an unusually candid Detroit police detective, gave an interview to the *Detroit News* after the bombing:

> Perrone is an evil old man who has [gotten] rich on fear. He is a despicable person, an extortionist who preys on the fear he can instill in people. I personally believe, though I can't prove it yet, that he finally met up with somebody who stood up to him and gave him a dose of his own medicine. I'd like to bet that the very bombing Perrone got was what he was promising somebody else.
>
> This Perrone has what you could call the mystic stare. He has a squinted right eye, and he takes long hard looks at people. When he looks like that, he has a face out of a horror movie."

One of Perrone's partners said after the bombing, "I just can't believe anybody would *dare* do this to Sam."

In spite of the loss of a leg and mangled testicles, Perrone may have become active again. In 1965, Pete Lombardo was murdered. Lombardo was one of the men Ritchie identified as being part of the Reuther hit squad. Perrone felt that Lombardo was the one who turned on him and was responsible for the car bomb. Lombardo was found dead. Someone stabbed him in his rectum and testicles before he was killed by a .22-caliber revolver. Perrone was questioned by a grand jury, but no indictments were issued.

Perrone recovered from the bombing, but his significant role as a major criminal element in Detroit was over. He died in a nursing home on Christmas Day in 1973.[336]

· · · · · · · · · · · · · ·

George Edwards's career path evolved in a distinctive and unique fashion. After filing the lawsuit against Briggs on Ken Morris's behalf, Edwards left the practice of law for a courtroom. Governor Williams appointed Edwards a Wayne County probate judge in late 1951. Later in the decade, Edwards was appointed and then ran for election to the Michigan Supreme Court. In 1962, Edwards resigned from his prestigious Supreme Court position to become police commissioner for the newly elected Detroit mayor, Jerome Cavanagh. Edwards wanted to clean up the Detroit Police Department and go after organized crime in the southeast Michigan area. He remembered the Briggs beatings and Sam Perrone. Edwards was so effective that the mob placed a hit on the police commissioner.

In an October 1963 testimony to Congress on organized crime, Edwards discussed Sam Perrone:

> Just as dangerous to the continuance of the lawful and orderly society to which this nation is committed is the Mafia's intimidation of witnesses necessary to successful prosecutions of their crimes.... Santo Perrone avoided conviction ... solely because of fear of Mafia reprisal.

Edwards further testified:

> A Detroit gas station was bombed in 1961.... [We] discovered evidence that the perpetrator was Santo Perrone, a known hoodlum with a reputation for doing enforcement work for the syndicate. Part of the evidence was a witness who placed Perrone's associates on the scene at the time of the explosion. This testimony repeated at the trial would have made the prosecution's case airtight. Since we knew we were working against organized crime, for eight months we gave this witness police protection twenty-four hours a day. When he took the stand at the trial, he stated that he couldn't remember a thing.

Just when, or how, he had been reached is something
that I am not prepared to say. However, I have no doubt
that the methods of terror employed by organized crime
were a major factor in the failure of that prosecution of
Perrone.

A few months after this testimony, Sam Perrone's Pontiac was blown
up, and Perrone was lucky to survive. A telescopic .22 rifle and a *Detroit
News* October 11, 1963, story about Detroit Police Commissioner George
Edwards was found in the trunk of Perrone's mangled car. Edwards was
convinced that Perrone was planning to assassinate him.

Just before the congressional testimony, President Kennedy
nominated George Edwards to be a justice on the Sixth Circuit Court
of Appeals in Cincinnati. The Senate confirmed him in December 1963,
and he remained on the bench for the rest of his distinguished career.
He died in 1995.[337]

. . . .

The UAW became one of the great industrial unions in the world. Walter
Reuther and the UAW became a monolithic force supporting positive
social and economic change. Many, including this writer, believe the
UAW was responsible for the rise of America's middle class. Walter
Reuther's enemies were the UAW's enemies.

By 1955, in addition to his role as president of the UAW, Walter was
serving as president of the CIO. He and George Meany, the president of
the AFL, worked out a merger agreement, and the two organizational
foes merged to become one giant labor organization, the AFL-CIO.
Meany became the president of the new coalition of unions, and Reuther
was vice president. Reuther was concerned that the AFL member unions
behaved more like corporate business leaders, more concerned about
the location of the next convention than about substantive issues facing
the country's working men and women. Meany, for example, was proud
of the fact that he had never walked a picket line in his life.[338] The
assumption was that George Meany, an older man, was not likely to stay
in office very long with Reuther as his heir apparent. Instead, George

Meany outlived Walter Reuther by ten years. Reuther never had a chance to reshape the AFL-CIO.

Reuther also fought the forces of the political right wing, including the John Birch Society and forces led by Senator Barry Goldwater. These groups and individuals often talked about Reuther as a Communist or un-American. These organizations or right-wing politicians often brought up a version of the "Victor and Wal" letter sent from the Soviet Union in 1934 to their friend Melvin Bishop. This was the letter that Victor wrote, which ended this way: "Carry on the fight. Vic and Wal." However, in the intervening years, the letter's ending was forged several times. Its most famous forgery said, "Carry on the fight for a Soviet America. Vic and Wal." This was extremely frustrating to the anti-Communist Victor and Walter Reuther. Ironically, even President Eisenhower acknowledged the anti-Communist work of Victor Reuther. In 1959, Walter Reuther met with Soviet Premier Nikita Khrushchev and attacked the system upon which the Soviet Union was built. The forged "Vic and Wal" letters were a smear that defamed the reputation of Walter and Victor Reuther.

In 1958, Senator John McClellan, a conservative Democrat from Arkansas, led a new committee to investigate abuses of labor unions. These hearings were made famous by the verbal battles between Jimmy Hoffa and the committee's chief counsel, Robert Kennedy. Senator Goldwater and Senator Karl Mundt also demanded that the UAW and Walter Reuther be investigated. The investigation showed that the UAW was a clean union—so clean that Reuther even reimbursed the union for a dry-cleaning bill. The only real issue was the ongoing struggle between the UAW and the Koehler Company of Wisconsin, where a long, bitter, and often violent strike had been taking place. Both Walter and Emil Mazey, who was directing the strike activities, testified on the matter. While the strike was violent, the thrust of the testimony was that both the union and the company were responsible for the violence.

In the end, Goldwater muttered that bringing Reuther to testify and investigating the UAW had been a major tactical error. Reuther and the UAW looked too good. On another front, the investigation created a new and long-lasting relationship between Walter Reuther, committee member Senator John Kennedy, and the committee's chief counsel, Bobby Kennedy.

. . . .

Walter Reuther fired Melvin Bishop in December 1947 after the deer-shining incident in which Bishop was arrested with Sam Perrone. Ironically, the Teamsters hired him as a business agent, and Bishop ended up in Atlanta, Georgia. In early August 1958, Senator Hubert Humphrey sent a letter to Senator John McClellan, asking him to use his committee hearings on labor corruption to research the background of the "Vic and Wal" letter. The committee started the investigation by contacting the person who initially received the letter in 1934, Melvin Bishop. On August 16, 1958, Senator McClellan sent Humphrey the following reply:

> During the staff investigation of the [UAW] ... information was received concerning a letter which Victor Reuther is alleged to have written to one Melvin Bishop of Detroit, when he and Walter Reuther were working in Russia in 1934.
>
> As you may recall, this purported letter previously had been given considerable publicity. I, therefore, instructed the staff to locate and interview Mr. Bishop. They did and reported to me [that] they doubted Mr. Bishop's story about it. I then had them bring Mr. Bishop to my office, where I interviewed him at some length. I too was skeptical of his story, but I directed the staff to pursue every [clue] and lead he had given us. They did, but [they] were unable to get any confirmation from those to whom Mr. Bishop had referred as having knowledge of the facts....
>
> As a matter of precaution, and to preclude anyone's charging the committee with not having looked into it, I placed Mr. Bishop under oath and took his testimony

in an executive session. He admitted that he has not seen this letter for over twenty years, and his story concerning his disposition of it is completely contradicted by reliable information the committee has obtained.

I think it is significant that, with the established unreliability of Mr. Bishop and the fact that the existence and text of the letter were so questionable, no member of the Committee saw fit to ask Mr. Reuther any questions about it when he testified before the Committee in public hearings.

As McClellan concluded, not even Senator Goldwater was convinced that he could bring up any issues on the "Vic and Wal" letter, based on the incompetence of Mr. Bishop. Melvin Bishop vanished from that point on.[339]

. . . .

Walter Reuther continued to be a labor and social leader. He promoted many causes, especially as an ally and leader of civil rights battles during the late 1950s and 1960s. He was particularly close to Dr. Martin Luther King Jr. He addressed issues from fair employment standards to environmental protection. He advised President Kennedy, President Johnson, and other national and worldwide political figures. Reuther was also deeply involved in his hometown of Detroit. In the 1950s, he fought against the Fermi I breeder reactor nuclear plant, which in 1966 almost caused a catastrophic nuclear disaster in Southeast Michigan.[340] In the 1960s, Walter and his wife, May, were deeply involved in activities at Oakland University, including the development of the Meadow Brook summer festival that featured the Detroit Symphony Orchestra. After the 1967 Detroit Riots, Reuther was one of the founders of New Detroit, the Metropolitan Affairs Coalition, and other organizations of corporate and community leaders attempting to address the social ills of their city.

In the late 1960s, Reuther oversaw the building of the beautiful UAW education center in northern Michigan, 260 miles north of Detroit, on Black Lake. This facility became his dream—a place offering beauty, nature, and peace to help educate and train future labor leaders for the UAW. Now entering his sixties, Walter was perhaps thinking about retirement as the plans for the Black Lake educational center evolved. As UAW president, he continued to support a policy he strongly believed in: that UAW officials retire at sixty-five years of age. Reuther could easily have waived this provision but instead vigorously supported the rule for all UAW officials, including himself. He felt that to keep the UAW viable, new leadership had to continually emerge from the UAW's rank and file.

In May 1970, Walter; May; Black Lake architect Oskar Stonorov; and Walter's ever-present bodyguard, William Wolfson, took a chartered Learjet from Detroit to Pellston, Michigan, to review the construction status of the nearly complete UAW Education Center on Black Lake. The plane never made it. Just before their arrival at the Pellston airport, the altimeter malfunctioned and the jet hit some trees, bursting into a ball of fire. There were no survivors, as all bodies were burnt beyond recognition.

UAW members, activists, Detroit business and political leaders, and leaders from across the country and around the world were shocked to hear of his death. Ken Morris, whose office was at the UAW headquarters, Solidarity House, took his son into Walter's office two days after the crash. Everything in the office was in perfect order. As father and son silently observed the clean desk, with a dozen number 2 pencils stacked lengthwise in a pyramid, ready for action, Walter's top economic advisor, Nat Weinburg, entered the room. Deeply emotional, the teary-eyed Weinburg said to Ken and his eighteen-year-old son, "Look, look at that telephone." The two looked at the green telephone on the left-hand side of the desk; it had a dozen plastic buttons indicating the many telephone lines available to Walter. "Ken," he said in a grieving voice, ignoring the young man, "No one will ever know the people from around the world who called Walter seeking advice. No one will ever know ..." The young man immediately thought of the presidents, senators, and world figures that Walter knew and realized that these were the people who sought advice, ideas, and support from the man George Romney once labeled "the most dangerous man in Detroit."

Senator Edward Kennedy, in his 2009 memoir, *True Compass,* remembered Walter:

> [Walter] Reuther is remembered as the progressive president of the United Auto Workers union, but his larger legacy, all but forgotten to history, is that of a social visionary whose humanitarian concerns included but extended well beyond the members of his union.

Immediately after Kennedy was elected to the US Senate, Reuther called the thirty-year-old senator and convinced him to become involved with national health-care issues. In August 1970, Kennedy introduced his first bill calling for national health care, an effort that became his top priority in every new session of Congress until his death in 2009.[341]

Walter Reuther was sixty-two years old when he died. He would have retired four years later, in 1974. Walter was such an idea man, a visionary; one wonders how his creative energy might have affected the world had he lived. His creative genius might have addressed so many problems facing his country and the world. The next UAW president was Leonard Woodcock. After Woodcock's retirement in 1977, he became the US liaison to China and then the first ambassador to the People's Republic of China under President Jimmy Carter. What might Walter Reuther have accomplished if given the opportunity to live out a normal life?

· · · · · · · · · · · · ·

Emil Mazey remained secretary-treasurer of the UAW until his retirement in 1980. Some people claimed that Mazey chafed at being Reuther's second in the UAW. Perhaps there was truth in this. Had Reuther ever moved on to other endeavors, particularly in the 1950s or early 1960s, Emil Mazey was the obvious candidate to replace him as president of the union. He remained extremely popular within the UAW.

Emil Mazey said he may have been too radical as a young man.

In reflecting, there were a few actions from the 1930s and 1940s that he might not condone in the 1970s. However, he never regretted his arrest record for standing on picket lines. He once said of his effort to organize Ford, "I was arrested so often that I still have top seniority in the Dearborn jails."[342]

Mazey always remained true to his principles. In 1953, a young US Air Force Lieutenant named Milo Radulovich of Dexter, Michigan, was being hounded out of the air force because of so-called radical activities committed by his father and sister. Radulovich's father, an immigrant UAW autoworker from the east side Hudson plant, had subscribed to Serbian newspapers from his hometown. Radulovich's sister was an activist radical: she believed in civil rights and picketed the Book Cadillac Hotel to protest the hotel's racial policy prohibiting Paul Robeson, the legendary African American entertainer and activist, from using their accommodations.

Although it was during the height of the anti-Communist McCarthy era, Mazey found the charges ludicrous. Michael Ranville's book, *To Strike at a King*, describes Mazey's actions, which resulted in a letter to Air Force Secretary Harold E. Talbott. Ranville wrote:

> With uncommon eloquence, Mazey's pen quickly journeyed to the heart of the government's case, pointing out that action was taken against Milo because "he is the son of a man who rightfully thought that under the Constitution of the United States, a citizen has the right to read papers and books with which he disagreed, as well as those with which he agreed, and that his sister had expressed her 'right of assembly.' ... You do not charge the [lieutenant] with attempting to influence the thinking of his father. You simply charge him with being his father's son.... Would you have this citizen disown his own father because the father might not pass a loyalty test set up by Air Force standards? ... In fact, a son who does not have basic family loyalties could not

be expected to be either a good citizen or a good officer
of the Air Force."

The Radulovich case was brought to the attention of the country
by Edward R. Murrow on the CBS *See it Now* television program. This
program led to additional programs that helped lead to the downfall of
Senator Joseph McCarthy and the anti-Communist witch hunts.[343]

Roy Reuther brought the plight of the United Farm Workers to
the UAW's attention in the mid-1960s. Roy and Walter saw that Cesar
Chavez and his organization were about social and economic justice.
The Reuther brothers brought Cesar Chavez to the attention of Senator
Robert Kennedy. The United Farm Workers' struggle became the UAW's
struggle.

In the early 1970s, a young United Farm Workers organizer named
Patty Proctor Park worked in the Detroit office of the United Farm
Workers. Her primary objective was to raise support, particularly funds,
for the Farm Workers. She found no better supporter in Detroit than the
UAW and, in particular, Emil Mazey. Mazey helped her with contacts in
UAW locals and other unions throughout Michigan. There were times
when he reminisced about his early days, and Park came to realize that
Mazey identified with the Farm Workers because it reminded him so
much of the early struggles of the UAW.

Emil Mazey collected turtle paperweights. Over the years, people
from all walks of life gave them to Emil. There were always turtles on his
desk. One day Park asked Emil about the significance of the turtles. Emil
smiled and, perhaps thinking about his own life, said, "[Turtles] don't
get ahead without sticking their neck out." Later Emil found a painting
and placed it on his office wall. It was inscribed: "Consider the turtle.
He makes no progress UNTIL he sticks his head out."[344]

Emil's finest moments as secretary-treasurer of the UAW came when
the union was in crisis. During the 1948 Walter Reuther shooting and
throughout his recovery, Emil took the reins of the UAW and maintained
its stability, just a year after he had stepped into the number two position
of the union.

After Walter's tragic death in 1970, Emil again stepped up. There was little doubt that Walter was grooming UAW Vice President Doug Fraser to be the next president. When Walter's plane crashed, the dynamics of UAW succession changed. Emil thought about taking the position, but health problems forced him to appreciate that he was not up to the task. Leonard Woodcock had planned to retire with Walter in 1973, but Walter's death changed Woodcock's thinking. He and Doug Fraser, close friends, ran for the presidency. Because Walter's death occurred in the middle of his term, the twenty-five-member UAW International Executive Board had to vote for Walter's replacement. By all accounts, Emil's leadership kept the board (and the union) together during these difficult times. In the end, Leonard Woodcock beat his friend and colleague Doug Fraser by one vote. (Ken Morris, a member of the UAW International Executive Board, voted for Doug Fraser, but like Doug, Ken maintained his friendship with and loyalty to the new UAW president.)

Emil retired from the UAW in 1980 after fighting a series of health problems. In 1983, at the age of seventy, Emil died of cancer. One Saturday shortly after his death, Emil's wife and son quietly spread his ashes on the grounds of Solidarity House.

Doug Fraser, Emil's colleague and former UAW president said, "Emil rushed in where angels feared to tread. He was a pioneer. He did more to organize unions than any single individual. It's a simple fact."[345]

. . . .

When Briggs was sold to Chrysler, the membership of Local 212 became part of the UAW's Chrysler Department. Its membership declined to the point where, in 2008, they only had two thousand members. The Local 212 political party of Emil Mazey and Ken Morris was the Green Slate, and it is still the best slate to be on if running for local office.

In 1965, Emil talked about the accomplishments of Local 212:

> Before our union was established, wage rates in the
> Briggs plants were the lowest in the industry; workers
> doing the same kind of work were paid different wages.
> Negro workers were paid less money than white workers

for performing the same work. A woman who performed work similar to that performed by men received less wages for her work than wages paid male employees.… Workers could be called into the plant and sent home if no work was available, without receiving compensation for their efforts, and there [were] no vacation bonuses for workers in our shops.[346]

Local 212 and the UAW made a difference. Like so many other local unions in the UAW, it should not be forgotten.

• • • • • • • • • • • • •

Ken Morris served as president of Local 212 from 1948 to 1955. Ken received many awards during his career, but perhaps the award that meant more to him than any other was the 1954 Workmen's Circle Award for Social Progress from the Detroit branch of the Jewish American Fraternal Order. Only about twenty people had received the award since its Detroit inception in 1947. Ken found himself joining the likes of other elite Michigan labor pioneers and other respected people in the fight for social and economic progress, including Walter Reuther, Roy Reuther, Emil Mazey, George Edwards, Gus Scholle, and Senator Blair Moody. When the award was announced by the prestigious Jewish organization, the press release read:

Morris is being cited for his leadership in democratic trade unionism in the face of organized gangsterism, for his advocacy of the participation of union rank and file political action, and for his effective contribution to the elimination of group discrimination.[347]

Ken was extremely pleased with the award and realized his career horizons might go beyond being Local 212's president.

In 1955, the two east side coregional director positions became open. Ken announced his intention to run. In a breakfast meeting with Emil Mazey at Cupids restaurant, Ken asked Emil for his support for regional director. Emil had already committed to another candidate and said to Ken, "You're on your own." Walter Reuther, as well, remained neutral.[348]

Ken's reputation as one of the hardest working presidents of a local union paid off. His tireless support of Local 212 members and of other UAW locals in Detroit was widely known by UAW activists. He, along with longtime UAW activist George Merrelli, was elected Codirector of Region 1 at the 1955 UAW convention. Ken did not say it very often, but he took great satisfaction in the fact that from 1955 until his retirement in 1983, he held the position once held by Melvin Bishop. The difference was that Ken Morris operated as a trade unionist serving all members of his region. There was never a hint of scandal.

By the late 1930s, and especially after he married Doris, Ken visited his family in Pittsburgh, usually on Thanksgiving (a tradition still kept by the Katz/Morris families). Any disappointment Ken's father had regarding his decision to leave Pittsburgh vanished. Louis Katz was extremely proud of his son's accomplishments, especially after Ken's election to the UAW International Executive Board. Louis felt that being associated with Walter Reuther was an exceptional accomplishment.

Eventually, the two regions were broken up, and Ken headed Region 1B. He was one of the longest-serving UAW regional directors and was considered by many to be one of the best. Part of the reason for his success was his decision to get involved in the negotiations of any and every local union that needed his help. If a company, often a small supplier, could not meet worker demands, he was frank with the union members and told them their demands were unrealistic. But if a company failed to live up to its word, Ken and the power of the UAW remembered, and the next round of negotiations was much different. His direct involvement in contract negotiations was unusual for a regional director, but because of this, he was never threatened by any opposition.

Ken was also deeply involved in local Democratic politics. In the late 1940s, Soapy Williams, Neil Staebler, Martha and Hicks Griffiths, and Gus Scholle rebuilt the Michigan Democratic Party. Ken played a vital role in the east side's Fourteenth Congressional District. Much of the battle to control the Democratic Party was between the UAW and the Teamsters. At a meeting held in the Local 212 hall, seventy-five Teamsters tried to disrupt and use physical force to take over the meeting. The chairman of the Fourteenth District was labor lawyer Nick Rothe. Rothe and Ken Morris turned away the usurpers, and the meeting was able to continue. It took many years before the Teamsters returned to the state Democratic Party.

Ken was a strong supporter of Senator Blair Moody and Senator Philip Hart (the son-in-law of Walter Briggs). Years later, Ken played a pivotal role in building the Democratic Party in Oakland County and helped support the beginning efforts of Congressman (and later Governor) James Blanchard and Congressman Sander Levin.

Governor William Milliken, a Republican, appointed Ken as one of the original members of the Oakland University Board of Trustees. Governor Blanchard continued these appointments. Being on the university's board was a position that Ken, who only received a high school education, treasured for the remainder of his life.

Ken also became an expert in the area of unemployment compensation. Governor Milliken and then Governor Blanchard appointed Ken to several terms on the Michigan Employment Security Commission, which oversaw the state's unemployment insurance program. Here, Ken forged important alliances with business members to improve the delivery of unemployment insurance in Michigan. In 1977, President Jimmy Carter appointed Ken to the National Commission on Unemployment Insurance, a role that Ken enjoyed, and where, of course, he offered his special insights.

After retiring from the UAW in 1983, Ken became the chair of Coop/Optical, an optical group that had originally been set up by organized labor in 1960, long before there were optical benefits for workers. By 1983, Coop/Optical was in deep financial trouble, but under Ken's leadership, the company experienced a new period of growth. Ken essentially had a second career with Coop/Optical, spending twenty years at its helm.

By almost all accounts, Ken Morris was a well-respected labor leader and a fine human being.

**Ken's favorite photo: Introducing presidential candidate Jack
Kennedy on Labor Day 1960 at Pontiac, Michigan**

In April 2008, Ken's wife, Doris, died on the last Tuesday of the
month. Their marriage lasted nearly sixty-five years. Exactly four weeks
later, on the last Tuesday in May, Ken passed away in his sleep. He was
ninety-two years old.

The boy from Pittsburgh, who'd arrived in Detroit with nothing but
a suitcase, was proud of the fact that he had played a part in building
one of the cleanest, most socially progressive unions the world had
ever known. Like so many other working men and women from the
manufacturing sweatshops of Detroit and elsewhere, he had helped
build the United Automobile Workers.

CHAPTER NOTES

THIS BOOK IS A STORY of the UAW. I have tried to be as accurate as possible, but I know good people may debate some of the subject matters I have described. This book is not a definitive history of the UAW or its times. The following notes provided the context of many of the stories I heard from Ken Morris, Emil Mazey, Walter Reuther, and others. Quotes are generally based on transcripts, letters, or oral histories. In one instance, I created a conversation, the substantive portion of which came straight from written documents and is described in chapter notes.

Most of the material used in this book came from Ken Morris's oral histories and personal files; research conducted at the Walter P. Reuther Archives at Wayne State University; and through books purchased by Ken Morris or found in libraries. I particularly want to thank the staff from the Reuther Archives, especially William LeFevre, for all their invaluable help. I also relied heavily on microfilm of the *Detroit Free Press, the Detroit News, Detroit Times*, and other information which I found at the Library of Michigan.

Any errors in fact are accidental. I do, however, recognize that oral histories are memories that may be distorted or just plain wrong. I tried to take into account such personal weaknesses.

Key abbreviations in the notes:

KMOH—Ken Morris Oral History. There are six oral histories from Ken, some of which are drafts that were never finished. The Ken Morris

Oral Histories 1 and 6 are on file at the Reuther Archives. The others are part of the Morris family files.

KM notes—These include notes or handwritten comments Ken made for speeches or other purposes, and they are found in the Morris family files.

WSU WPR Archives—Wayne State University Walter P. Reuther Archives

Oral histories—Any oral history cited is on file at the Reuther Archives.

ENDNOTES

1. KMOH 3, pp. 27–28. Also see KMOH 6, pp. 47–50.

2. *Detroit News*, June 4, 1946.

3. KMOH 4 provides the best comments by Ken Morris on his youth, pp. 1–12 and p. 28. Much of this chapter is also composed of family stories.

4. Oliver High School yearbooks, 1933 and 1934.

5. KMOH 4, door-to-door sales at Hoyt, see pp. 20–29; also see KM Oral History 3, pp. 9–11.

6. KMOH 1, pp. 16–17.

7. KMOH 4, on soapboxers and life in Detroit, p. 30. KMOH 4 also provides the best comments by Ken Morris on his youth, pp. 1–12 and p. 28. Much of this chapter is also composed of family stories. Oliver High School yearbooks, 1933 and 1934. KM Oral History 4, door-to-door sales at Hoyt, see pp. 20–29; also see KMOH 3, pp. 9–11. KMOH 1, pp. 16–17; KM Oral History 4, on life in Detroit, p. 11.

8. KMOH 3, p. 14. KM Oral History 4, p. 30.

9. KMOH 4, pp. 31–33.

10. KMOH 3 on *Waiting for Lefty* experience pp. 11–13. Also see KM Oral History 4, pp. 25–27.

11. "Detroit Gains in Population," *Detroit News*, August 18, 1935.

12. "Briggs Slaughterhouse," see KMOH 3, p. 17.

13. For state fair job, Automobile Manufacturers Association, and Briggs, see KM Oral History 3, pp. 15–17; KMOH 4, 31–34; KM Oral History 6, pp. 5–7 and KM Oral History 2, p. 3, including KM handwritten notes.

14. KMOH 2, p. 4. Ken Morris OH 3, p. 17.

15. "No one is going to treat me like a dog," see KMOH 2, p. 5. For more information on working conditions at Briggs, see Art Vega, Joe Ferris, and Jess Ferrazza Oral Histories.

16. Superintendent taking liking to Ken, see KMOH 4, p. 35.

17. Life in the plant and on Woodward, see KMOH 2, pp. 5–9; Ken Morris OH 3, pp. 18–19; KMOH 4, pp. 36–37. The story of the finger in the glove was told to author.

18. Layoff—life during layoff and callback to Briggs, see KMOH 4, pp. 41–42.

19. On Walter Briggs background, see Boles, *A History of Local 212 UAW-CIO.* Also see Coachbuilt article on Briggs Manufacturing Company at www.Coachbuilt.com.

20. Mary Humphrey, "Briggs and Son a Winning Team," *Detroit Saturday Night,* undated (probably mid-1930s).

21. Five Dollar a Day background, see Keith Sward, *The Legend of Henry Ford* (New York: Rinehard & Company, 1948), pp. 50–62; Robert Lacey, *Ford: The Men and the Machine* (Boston: Little, Brown and Company, 1986), pp. 115–131; pp. 64–68.

22. www.Coachbuilt.com. See p. 17 of Briggs article.

23. "Briggs Build Baby's Apartment," *Saturday Night,* September 19, 1925. Also, interview with Jane Hart Briggs.

24. Interview with Jane Briggs Hart, August 2007, and May 2010 letter from Jane Briggs Hart.

25. H. G. Salsinger, "The Umpire," *Detroit News,* January 18, 1952.

26. www.Coachbuilt.com. See p. 3 of Briggs article.

27. "Spike Briggs Dies at 58," *Detroit News,* July 3, 1970. Also, Jane Hart Briggs interview.

28. Vivian M. Bauich and Patricia Zacharias, "The Day the Tigers Finally Integrated," *Detroit News,* January 22, 1996 (www.detnews.com.); Burton Folsom, Jr., "The Costs of Segregation to the Detroit Tigers," www.thefreemanonline.org, December 2003.

29. Dean Robinson coming to Briggs, see "Briggs Co.'s Robinson Dies at 59," *Detroit News,* July 21, 1958; "Briggs' Robinson Dies," *Detroit Free Press,* July 21, 1958.

30. On Fay Taylor, see Ken Morris Oral History 1, pp. 26–27. Also see Jess Ferrazza Oral History.

31. Jane Briggs Hart interview.

32. Michael D. Whitty, *Emil Mazey—Union Maverick,* (Ruther Archives Emil Mazey Personal files, Series I, Box I); "Emil Mazey Dies," *Detroit Free Press,* October 11, 1983.

33. "UAW Giant to Retire in June," *Lansing State Journal,* April 27, 1980.

34. On soapboxers, see Frank Marquart Oral History; also see Whitty.

35. Briggs 1933 strike, see: "The Story of Local 212," *Voice of Local 212,* October 1953; "The Detroit Strike," *The Nation,* February 15, 1933 (from www.Coachbuilt.com Briggs article).

36. Sidney Fine, *Frank Murphy, The Detroit Years,* University of Michigan Press, Ann Arbor, p. 413.

37. "Emil Mazey ... Father of Local 212," *Voice of Local 212,* June 24, 1976; also see Whitty.

38. KMOH 1, p. 9.

39. "Briggs Mixture," *Time* magazine, www.time.com/time/magazine/article/0.9171.757233.00.html. December 21, 1936; Letter to the editor: "Letters," *Time* magazine, December 28, 1936, www.time.com/time/magazine/article/0,9171,771873-2,00.html.

40. Whitty.

41. "Emil Mazey—Briggs Firing," personal recollections by Emil Mazey from Reuther Labor Archives, Emil Mazey series; "Emil Mazey—Father of Local 212," *Voice of Local 212,* June 24, 1976; regarding Robert Mazey firing, see Ralph Orr, "UAW Firebrand Emil Mazey Dies," *Detroit Free Press,* October 11, 1983.

42. Meldrum plant as country club and early organization, see Boles dissertation "Early Unionization Efforts, 1936–1937."

43. Richard Frankensteen Oral History, Reuther Archives.

44. Nelson Lichtenstein, *The Most Dangerous Man in Detroit: Walter Reuther and the Fate of American Labor* (New York: Basic Books, 1995), pp. 48–50. Also see Boles dissertation "Establishing a Union: 1936–1937.

45. Frankensteen OH.

46. Start of Briggs strike, see Boles dissertation "The First Strike, January–February 1937; Frankensteen OH.

47. Emil Mazey, "History of Local 212," *International Organizer,* May 15, 1937 (see Mazey collection Reuther Archives). Regarding importance of Frankensteen's Dodge Local 3, see Bole dissertation "The First Strike, January–February 1937."

48. Ken Morris joining UAW, see KMOH 1, pp. 9–10; KMOH 2, pp. 20–22; KMOH 4, p. 46; KMOH 4, p. 6.

49. Ken Morris notes 4, p. 13, and KM notes 5, p. 1.

50. The mass picket line, see Mazey, "History of Local 212"; "Emil Mazey—Father of Local 212," *Voice of Local 212,* June 24, 1976; Frankensteen OH. Regarding the ball bearings incident, see Steve Babson, *Working Detroit: The Making of a Union Town,* (New York: Adams Books, 1984), pp. 82–83.

51. Mazey, "Father of Local 212," *Voice of Local 212,* June 24, 1976.

52. For more on Harry Bennett, see Sword, *Legend of Henry Ford;* Collier and Horowitz, *The Fords: An American Epic;* Lacey, *Ford: The Men and the Machine;* and Harry Bennett's memoir: *Ford: We Never Called Him Henry.*

53. The Frankensteen experience with Gillespie and resolution of Briggs strike, see Frankensteen Oral History.

54. "Briggs Plant Re-Opens at Full Capacity as Union Accepts Offer: 350 Men Rehired," *Detroit News,* January 20, 1937.

55. Briggs support of Flint Sit-Down strikers, see Reuther, The *Brother Reuther and the Story of the UAW,* p. 159; also see Ken Morris Oral History 2, p. 49.

56. Regarding the Briggs increases in wages, see KMOH 1 and KMOH 3, pp. 24–25; also see Jess Ferrazza Oral History.

57. See Jess Ferrazza Oral History; Boles, "The First Strike, January–February 1937."

58. Leaflet on Briggs/UAW first settlement, see WSU WPR, Reuther File, Box 10.

59. Regarding Briggs contract, see Whitty; Boles "The First Strike, January-February 1937; and "Briggs-UAW Pac Is Signed," *Detroit News,* April 18, 1937.

60. For initial Local 212 structure and Knox election, see Boles, "Internal Factionalism and Union Building," and Whitty.

61. KMOH 1, pp. 13–17; KMOH 2, pp. 13–19; KMOH 3, pp. 27, 32; and KMOH 6, pp. 15–16.

62. Mazey support of Knox, see KMOH 3, p. 23, Boles, "Internal Factionalism and Union Building'; and Whitty.

63. Race and political philosophy views, see Boles, "Internal Factionalism and Union Building,"; and Whitty.

64. "Toil and Trouble," Whitty dissertation.

65. "Mazey Resigns from International Rep.," *Voice of Local 212*, July 10, 1937.

66. See telegram from Dick Leonard to Fay Taylor, November 22, 1937, WPRWSU archives, Local 212 Series, Box 4.

67. On removal of Knox, see Boles, "International Factionalism and Union Building"; Whitty, KMOH 3, p. 35, and KMOH 6, p. 22.

68. Election results, *Voice of Local 212*, December 1937.

69. On Detroit Stove Works and Santo Perrone, see Victor Reuther, *The Brothers Reuther,* pp. 271–72; US Senate, *Hearings before the Special Committee to Investigate Organized Crime in Interstate Commerce*, February 8, 1951, pp. 115–132; Jack Strohm, "Perrone, Renda Tied to Anti-Unionism," *Detroit Free Press,* January 7, 1954; article on "Santo Perrone, Labor Racketeer" (http://www.geocities.com/jiggs2000_us/perrone/html?200624), pp.1–2.

70. Jess Ferrazza Oral History.

71. Unemployment rate, see "Historical Statistics and Analysis on Unemployment, Poverty, Urbanization, Etc., in the United States," www.firesian.com/stats-2htm. Note, U.S. Bureau of Labor Statistics data only goes back to 1948.

72. Anthony Badger, *FDR: The First Hundred Days*, (New York: Hill and Wang, 2008), p. xvi.

73. On AFL organizing autoworkers, see Lichtenstein, p. 49; John Barnard, *Walter Reuther and the Rise of the Auto Workers* (Boston: Little, Brown and Company, 1983), pp. 27–33; Whitty; "National Council of United Auto Workers Meets Here on Eve of Convention," *Detroit News*, August 25, 1935; "Auto Union Convention Is on

Here," *Detroit News*, August 26, 1935; "Dillon Center of AFL Fight," *Detroit News*, August 27, 1935.

74. Irving Howe and B. J. Widick, *The U.A.W. and Walter Reuther* (New York, Random House, 1949), p. 52.

75. On Homer Martin, see Sidney Fine, *Sit-Down: The General Motors Strike of 1936–37* (Ann Arbor: The University of Michigan Press, 1969), p. 129; Barnard, p. 38; Lichtenstein, p. 112; Frank Marquart Oral History.

76. Howe and Widick, pp. 50–52; Barnard, pp. 34–35; Jean Gould and Lorena Hickok, *Walter Reuther: Labor's Rugged Individualist* (New York: Dodd, Mead & Company, 1972), pp. 92–95.

77. Lichtenstein, pp.50–51; Reuther, pp. 131–32; "Brookwood Labor College," www.wikipedia.org/wiki/Brookwood Labor College.

78. Regarding UAW staff, see Marquart Oral History and Frankensteen Oral History.

79. Homer Martin as insecure leader, see Frankensteen Oral History.

80. Martin's description of all his enemies as Communists, see Gould and Hickok, pp. 146–47; Lichtenstein, pp. 78–79, Reuther, pp. 147, 169; Howe and Widick, pp.72–73; *Voice of Local 212*, June 24, 1976; KMOH 3, p. 38.

81. For Martin firing of UAW staffers, see Mazey letter of resignation in *Voice of Local 212*, July 10, 1937; Gould and Hickok, p. 150; Reuther, pp. 185–86; and Marquart Oral History.

82. KMOH 1, pp. 17–18; Clayton W. Fountain, *Union Guy* (New York: The Viking Press, 1949), pp.60–61. For Mazey weds, see R. Whipple, Jr., "Emil Mazey Weds," the Local 212 edition of the *United Automobile Worker*, June 11, 1938.

83. Frankensteen OH; "The Story of Local 212: Revolt in the Open Shop," *Voice of Local 212*, October 1953; Lichtenstein, pp. 100–101.

84. KMOH 3, p. 44.

85. Flying squadron discussion, see KMOH 3, pp. 42–45; KMOH 6, p. 20; Ken Morris notes 5, p. 6.

86. Local 174 beginnings, see Lichtenstein, pp. 80–81; Reuther, pp. 133–142; Fine, 112–13; Barnard, pp. 40–41; Gould & Hickok, p. 109.

87. Lichtenstein, p. 98.

88. Lichtenstein, p. 99.

89. For Federal Screw battle, see Lichtenstein, pp. 99–101; "40 Injured as Mob Attacks Policemen in Plant Strike Riot," *Detroit Free Press,* March 31, 1938; "UAW Protest Up to Mayor, Fountain, p. 80.

90. KMOH 3, pp. 46–48.

91. "UAW Protest Up to Mayor," *Detroit News*, April 1, 1938; "Mayor Urges End of Strike," *Detroit News*, April 2, 1938; "Strike Truce Is Arranged," *Detroit News*, April 3, 1938.

92. American Brass battle, see "Seek Writ for 28 Held as Rioters," *Detroit News,* May

27, 1938; "Riot Victim Near Death," *Detroit Free Press*, May 27, 1938; KMOH 3, pp. 45–46; KMOH 2, pp. 20–22.

93. "Ken Morris Elected 6th time: Career Reflects Rise of UAW," *Voice of Local 212*, June 1953.

94. For more on Edwards' amazing career, see Mary M. Stolberg, *Bridging the River of Hatred: The Pioneering Efforts of Detroit Police Commissioner George Edwards* (Detroit: Wayne State University Press, 1998).

95. KMOH 3, pp. 38–40.

96. Time magazine, http://www.time.com/time/magazine/article/0,9171,989782,00.html (December 7, 1998).

97. "Reuther's Union Had a Social Conscience," *Detroit Free Press*," October 8, 1986.

98. Elisabeth Reuther Dickmeyer, *Reuther: A Daughter Strikes* (Southfield, Michigan: Spelman Publishers Division, 1989), p. 209.

99. Lichtenstein, *The Most Dangerous Man in Detroit*, pp. 160–167.

100. Irving Bluestone document, "Walter Reuther's Program for Action: Social-Economic Issues to Which WPR Gave Leadership," attached to a note from Bluestone to Ken Morris; see Ken Morris personal files.

101. Lichtenstein, pp. 383–387.

102. Irving Bluestone Oral History.

103. Reuther early days in Detroit, see Lichtenstein, pp. 6–20; Reuther, *The Brother Reuther*, pp.44–50.

104. Reuther, p. 50.

105. Reuther, p. 55.

106. For more on Reuther's high school activities, see Lichtenstein, pp. 21–24; Reuther, pp. 51–55; Merlin Bishop Oral History.

107. For Reuther's time at City College, see Lichtenstein, pp. 25–30; Reuther, pp. 57–62; Gould & Hickok, *Walter Reuther: Labor's Rugged Individualist*, pp. 40–48.

108. Reuther fired from Ford and going to Soviet Union, see Lichtenstein, pp. 32–33; Reuther, p. 6; Gould & Hickok, pp. 52–53.

109. Reuther brother's farewell, see Lichtenstein, p. 33; Reuther, p. 67.

110. Roy Reuther in Michigan and Brookwood, see Lichtenstein; Reuther, p. 125; Gould & Hickok, pp.100–101.

111. Walter Reuther's decision on education or the labor movement, see Lichtenstein, pp. 51–52; Reuther, pp. 125–127.

112. Walter Reuther and beginnings with UAW, see Lichtenstein, pp. 55–58; Reuther, pp. 127–130; Gould & Hickok, p. 108.

113. For more on the Flint Sit-Down Strike, see Lichtenstein, pp. 75–77; Reuther, pp.

143–171; Gould & Hickok, pp. 117–132; Fine, *Sit-Down: The General Motors Strike of 1936–1937*, p. 113 (this book is the definitive review of the Flint Sit-Down Strike).

114. Battle of the Overpass, see Lichtenstein, pp. 83–86; Reuther, 199–204; Gould & Hickok, pp. 135–138.

115. Attack in Reuther home, see Frank Marquart Oral History; Lichtenstein, pp. 101–103; Reuther, pp. 206–209; Gould & Hickok, pp. 139–140; Stolberg, *Bridging the River of Hatred*, pp. 59–60.

116. UAW membership data is from a May 31, 1983, memorandum from Frank Mirer (of the International UAW) to Ken Morris, from Ken Morris's personal files.

117. Lichtenstein, p. 114.

118. On Mazey and Local 212, see Witty and Boles dissertations; KMOH 1, p. 23; KMOH 6, p. 21; "Mazey Resigns from International Rep," *Voice of Local 212*, July 10, 1937.

119. Unity and Progressive Caucus discussion, see Barnard, *Walter Reuther and the Rise of the Auto Workers*, pp. 55–56; Lichtenstein, pp. 111–112; Gould and Hickok, *Walter Reuther: Labor's Rugged Individualist*, p. 151.

120. On UAW Unity Caucus members all being Communists, see Reuther, p. 184; Howe and Widick, *The UAW and Walter Reuther*, pp. 72–73; Gould and Hickok, p. 150; Witty dissertation; Ben Fischer, "Unity Group Calls Progressives to Join against Reactionaries," *Socialist Call*, August 21, 1937 (from Emil Mazey "Scrapbook box," WSU/WPU Archives).

121. On Martin's firing of UAW staffers, see Lichtenstein, p. 114; Reuther, pp. 185–186.

122. The 1937 UAW convention is described in Lichtenstein, p. 116; Howe and Widick, pp. 71–73.

123. Martin purge of UAW staffers: Reuther, p. 186; Lichtenstein, p. 114; "Purge & Pistol," *Time* magazine, October 11, 1937.

124. Additional detail on the double cross at the first Michigan CIO convention is found at Lichtenstein, pp. 124–125; Reuther, pp. 189–190; Howe & Widick, p. 75.

125. "Mr. Martin's Snuffles," *Time* magazine, September 26, 1938; Lichtenstein, pp. 125–126; Reuther, p. 190; Gould & Hickok, p. 154; Howe and Widick, p. 75.

126. Lichtenstein, p. 126; Reuther, pp. 190–192.

127. Lichtenstein, pp. 127–128; "UAW Reuther challenge at 174," *Detroit Times*, p. 22, March 2, 1938.

128. Lichtenstein, pp. 127–129; Howe & Widick, p. 77.

129. Regarding Martin and Harry Bennett deal, see Lichtenstein, p. 129; Howe & Widick, p. 76–77; Gould & Hickok, p. 155; Reuther, p. 192; Harry Bennett, as told to Paul Marcus, *Ford: We Never Called Him Henry* (New York: TOR Books, 1951, 1987), pp. 200–202; "UAW Homer Martin Dispute," *United Automobile Worker*, February 4, 1939.

130. Bennett, p. 202.

131. Minutes of Local 212 Executive Board meeting authorizing Mazey speech, January 20, 1939, Local 212 Series I, Box 24, WSU WPR Archives.

132. Text of Emil Mazey speech is at Local 212 Series, WSU WPR Archives.

133. "New Officers Elected Installation in March," *United Automobile Worker, Local 212 Edition*, February 18, 1939.

134. On Mazey-Addes meeting, see KMOH 2, handwritten insert on p. 26; Ken Morris notes 4, p. 14-c; Joe Ferris OH; Local 212 resolution directing dues to International UAW, February 5, 1939, Local 212 Series I, Box 24; Witty dissertation.

135. Regarding Local 235 and Local 212 Flying Squadron, see: KMOH 3, pp. 54–55; Clayton Fountain, *Union Guy*, (New York: The Viking Press, 1949), pp. 97–99.

136. Regarding the Moose Hall Martin convention, see *New York Times*, as quoted in "Papers Give Martinites the Ha Ha," *United Automobile Worker*, March 18, 1938.

137. The Local 212 60/40 split, see KMOH, p. 61.

138. 1939 convention's constitutional changes, see KMOH 3, pp. 62–63.

139. Chants in the street, see KMOH 3, p. 68.

140. KMOH 3, p. 65.

141. For details on the 1939 convention, see KMOH 3, pp. 66–70; KMOH 6, pp. 23–27; Lichtenstein, pp. 130–132; Howe & Widick, pp. 77–78.

142. "Wait Ruling in Briggs Row," *Detroit News*, May 31, 1939, front page.

143. "The Story of Local 212: Revolt in the Open Shop," *Voice of Local 212*, October 1953.

144. On cards regarding Local 212 member support of CIO, see Joe Ferris Oral History; "Briggs Strike Talks Reopen," *Detroit News*," May 29, 1939, which references the 12,640 cards that Mazey's people had collected.

145. Meeting with R. J. Thomas, see Joe Ferris OH.

146. Joe Ferris OH.

147. KMOH 2, pp. 26–28; KMOH 3, pp. 71–73.

148. For total number of people out of work as a result of Briggs strike, see "7 Briggs Plants Strike; 24,000 Idle," *Detroit News*, May 22, 1937, p. 1; "U.S. Sends Arbiter to Seek Settlement in Briggs Walkout," *Detroit Free Press*, May 22, 1939, p. 1; "Delay Seen on Briggs Agreement," *Detroit News*, May 25, 1939, p. 1; "U.S. Mediator Meets Officials of Briggs Firm," *Detroit Free Press*, May 25, 1939, p. 1.

149. KMOH 3, pp. 73–74; Joe Ferris OH.

150. KMOH 2, p. 30; KMOH 3, pp. 75–76.

151. Homer Martin involvement in Briggs negotiations, see "Martin Enters Briggs Parley," *Detroit Free Press*, May 26, 1939.

152. The Briggs Stadium picket battle is discussed in these articles: "Picket Line Dispersed at Ball Park," *Detroit News*, May 27, 1939, p. 1; "Rout Pickets at Ball Park," *Detroit*

News, May 28, p. 1; "18 C.I.O. Pickets Jailed As Police Repulse 2,000 in Briggs Stadium Battle," *Detroit Free Press,* May 28, 1939, p. 1.

153. KMOH 3, pp. 79–80.

154. Regarding Joe Ferris shooting, see "Official of UAW Shot in Battle," *Detroit News,* May 30, 1939, p. 1; "Dewey Seeks Strike Truce," *Detroit News,* June 1, 1939, p. 1; Joe Ferris OH.

155. Testimony of Lieutenant Meyers in court, see "Officer Charges Police Incited Stadium Riot," *Detroit Times,* June 5, 1939.

156. "The Story of Local 212: Revolt in the Open Shop," *Voice of Local 212,* October 1953.

157. NLRB vote at Local 212 between CIO and AFL, see "Local 212 History: 1939 Strike as Local 212 Members March at Plants and Stadium," *Voice of Local 212,* November 1953; Emil Mazey's speech on Local 212 History, WPR WSU Labor Archives, Local 212 series.

158. Frank Marquart Oral History.

159. For progressive attitudes by Local 212 on race relations, see August Meier and Elliott Ruwick, *Black Detroit and the Rise of the UAW* (New York: Oxford University Press, 1979), pp. 82–83; Charles J. Wartman, "UAW Local 212 Recalls Progress," the *Michigan Chronicle,* February 23, 1957.

160. Sources have indicated that African American employment at Briggs before WWII ranged from 7 to 17 percent. Based on that, I am suggested the average of the source work is somewhere over 10 percent. Sources for this data: Boles dissertation; article on Leon Bates (American Labor Leader (http://en.wikipedia.org/wiki/Leon_Bates_(American_labor_leader); JSTOR: Detroit and Negro Skill.

161. "The Story of the UAW: Revolt in the Open Shop; Union Rips Discrimination Out of the Wage Structure," *Voice of Local 212,* October 1953.

162. Charles J. Wartman, "UAW Local 212 Recalls Progress," the *Michigan Chronicle,* February 23, 1957.

163. On African American seniority, see Wartman article in *Michigan Chronicle.*

164. Regarding Mazey hiring African American staff, see Wartman article in *Michigan Chronicle.* For another example of hiring African American staff in 1941, see

165. Regarding Morris Hood Highland Park plant experience, see: Local 212 General Council Meeting, January 4, 1941, WPR WSU Archives, Local 212 Series, WPR WSU Archives.

166. First Briggs firing of Ken Morris, see KMOH 6, p. 28.

167. Motion to return Ken Morris to work, see Local 212 Membership meeting, June 8, 1940, Local 212, Series I, Box 24, WPR WSU Archives.

168. Emil Mazey, "President's Column," *United Automobile Worker* (Local 212 edition), August 15, 1940.

169. Ken Morris reinstated, see Local 212 General Council meeting, December 14, 1940, Local 212, Series 1, WPR WSU Archives.

170. Discussion on seniority and upward mobility is found in KMOH 3, p. 3, second transcript.

171. Issues regarding Mazey defeat in 1941, see Boles dissertation; Witty dissertation; KMOH 3, pp. 90–91.

172. Meier and Ruwick, p. 82–83.

173. Local 212—Compilation of history from Emil Mazey personal Files, Box 6-3, WPR WSU Archives.

174. For further information on WWII war production, see Chary, Frederick, World *War II*. March 28, 2011 (http://american-business.org/2813-world-war-ii.html); Mullin, Michael, *Preparing for War: Chrysler Military production, 1940–1942,* February 1985 (http://www.allpar.com/history/military/preparing.html).

175. Lichtenstein, pp. 177–78.

176. For discussion of WWII/UAW war interactions, see Lichtenstein, pp. 197–201. The UAW membership statistics are from a Frank Mire to Ken Morris Memorandum on UAW History, sent May 31, 1983.

177. Gould and Hickok, Walter *Reuther, Labor's Rugged Individualist,* p. 41; Merlin Bishop Oral History.

178. Reuther, *The Brothers Reuther,* pp. 214–219.

179. On Melvin Bishop's physical bullying, see Lichtenstein, note 13, p. 500.

180. UAW convention proceedings list Bishop as a delegate from west side local 157 in 1939, 1940, and 1941. At 1940 convention, Bishop spoke and said that former UAW president Homer Martin fired him.

181. For Bishop leanings, see thesis by Kenneth F. Silver, *The Dead End Kids: A History of Local 212 UAW-CIO,* University of Michigan, 1979, p. 31; Lichtenstein, footnote 13, p. 500; KMOH 1, p. 35.

182. Letter written from Emil Mazey to Jess Ferrazza, September 19, 1944, Emil Mazey Collection, WSU WPR Archives.

183. KMOH 6, p. 28.

184. On Bishop going after Mazey supporters, see Boles dissertation; Silver thesis; Briggs delegation testimony to International UAW Executive Board, December 11, 1941; also see Joe Hattley statement in UAW Executive Board, December 11, 1941.

185. Regarding Bishop effort to eliminate Mazey supporters from Local 212, see Joe Hattley statement in UAW Executive Board, December 11, 1941; also see Boles dissertation.

186. KMOH 1, pp. 35–36; KMOH 3, pp. 11–14, part II.

187. Regarding the seniority clause of the Briggs contract, see Boles dissertation.

188. For ramification of wildcat strikes and Bishop quote, see *Detroit Times,* "11,000 Idle in Auto Strike," October 1, 1941; Wells, Daniel, *Detroit Free Press,* "Auto Strike Expected to End Today," October 1, 1941.

189. KMOH 1, pp. 35–36; KMOH 6, p. 30; Ken Morris statement, part of International Executive Board minutes, December 11, 1941.

190. The workers leaving the plant and going to Local 212 is told in an unsigned handwritten statement found in Ken Morris files after Ken's death.

191. Details on the RJ Thomas meeting are found in KMOH 6, p. 31; Joe Ferris Oral History; Tom Gallery statement from UAW Executive Board, December 11, 1941.

192. KMOH, p. 31.

193. Information on this section is covered in the UAW Executive Board minutes, December 11, 1941.

194. Much of this chapter has been constructed by the military files maintained by Ken Morris. In these files are letters he received while in the service (but of course they do not reflect the letters he actually wrote). Additionally, the files contain detailed military records, including letters of commendation, promotion records, physical and health records, and other details of his four years in the military. Each of these items is not footnoted, but the author can provide details of this information, particularly letters that Ken received, by request.

195. Local 212 Series One at the WSU WPR Archives, Box 7.

196. Letter from PP McManus to Ken Morris, May 26, 1942, located in Local 212 Series I, Box 12, WSU WPR Labor Archives.

197. Briggs and wartime employment and production, see *Detroit News,* April 18, 1943, p. 8.

198. In addition to Emil Mazey's comments on Bishop's firing of Bill and Ernest Mazey while working at the Hudson plant quoted in the September 2, 1943 *Voice of Local 212,* see unsigned statement from Ken Morris files and Meier and Rudwick, *Black Detroit and the Rise of the UAW* (New York: Oxford University Press, 1979), pp. 127–29.

199. *Detroit News,* January 21, 1944.

200. Mazey letter to Ferrazza, see Mazey Series, WSU WPR Labor Archives.

201. For the meetings held between Detroit industrialists and Perrone, see Blankenhorn Collection, Box 3, WSU WPR Archives; Victor Reuther, *The Reuther Brothers,* p. 275.

202. Regarding 1946 politics of Local 212, see KMOH 1, p. 36; KMOH 3, p. 20, tape II. Also see Boles dissertation "The Post War Era: 1945–1949.

203. Regarding the women employed at Briggs, see KMOH 1, p. 37.

204. Whether this actual meeting took place is not clear, but Ken Morris indicated that such a meeting occurred, see KMOH 1 pp. 37–38.

205. Reuther quote, see Sol Dollinger and Genora Johnson Dollinger, *Not Automatic: Women and the Left in the Forging of the Auto Workers' Union,* (New York: Monthly Review Press, 2000), p. 89.

206. Local 212 did appoint a committee composed of Dollinger, Ernie Mazey, and others to investigate initial Briggs beatings—see Local 212 Membership meeting minutes

of May 20, 1945, WSU WPR Archives, Local 212 Series I, Box 24. The investigating Committee Report is in Membership minutes of October 28, 1945, WSU WPR Archives, Local 212 Series I Box 24. A summary of the report is in "Hoodlums Renew Attack on Local 212 *Members, Voice of Local 212*, October 25, 1945. Also see Dollinger, pp. 87–90.

207. It is not clear that a discussion between Ken Morris and Chester Kosmalski took place; however, the Kosmalski comments reflect almost verbatim the statement he provided to Walter Reuther on July 31, 1945. See WSU WPR Archives, Reuther Box 10.

208. For Reuther/Frankensteen letter to Detroit Police Commissioner, see: WSU WPR Archives, Reuther, Box 10.

209. See chapter 7, "Peace Becomes Cold War 1945–1950," p. 201 of history of the army at http://www.history.army.mil/books/AMH-v2/AMH%20V2/chapter7.htm.

210. Regarding Mazey role in Army demobilization, see Emil Mazey, "Mazey and the General," *Voice of Local 212*, March 15, 1945; Marcia Trbovich, "The Fighting Mazey Boys: What Happens When a Couple of Firebrands Grow Old," *Detroit Free Press*, March 31, 1974.

211. Regarding the Local 212 election, see Boles dissertation "The Post War Era: 1945–1949. For election results, see *Voice of Local 212*, March 15, 1946.

212. Ken Morris placed on Local 212 payroll, see Local 212 membership minutes, March 3, 1946, at WSU WPR Archives, Local 212 Series I, Box 24.

213. Memoranda on the Bishop/Reuther clash are found at the WSU WPR Archives, War Policy Division, Victor Reuther Box 17.

214. Memoranda from the Robert Stone incident are found at the WSU WPR Archives, Reuther, Box 7.

215. Memoranda from Bishop and Reuther are found at the WSU WPR Archives, Reuther, Box 7.

216. KMOH 6, p. 33.

217. For the Roy Reuther, Woodcock meeting with Morris, see KMOH 6, pp. 33–34.

218. Information on the nominating speeches and vote counts are from the official UAW 1946 Convention Proceedings.

219. For the best description of Emil Mazey's election as regional director, see "Emil Mazey Promoted to UAW Board; 212 Delegates Spearhead Drive to Elect Mazey," *Voice of Local 212*, April 19, 1946.

220. Description of Mazey learning of election as regional director, see Trbovich, "The Fighting Mazey Boys …," *Detroit Free Press*, March 31, 1974.

221. Regarding Emil Mazey's discharge and return to the United States, see "Mazey in Detroit on Job Ready for Work," *Voice of Local 212*, May 24, 1946.

222. Ken Morris, "Don't you Think So, MR. ROBINSON," *Voice of Local 212*, May 24, 1946.

223. Mary M. Stolberg, *Bridging the River of Hatred: The Pioneering Efforts of Detroit Police Commissioner George Edwards* (Detroit: Wayne State University Press, 1998), p. 96.

224. Tom Clampitt editorial, "Who is Behind This Terrorism?" *Voice of Local 212,* June 21, 1946.

225. Local 212 membership meeting, June 9, 1946, WSU WPR Archives, Local 212 Series I, Box 24.

226. Lack of cooperation from Detroit Police and Detective Delamaleur, see KMOH 6, p. 49.

227. "Amazing Mazey Dotes on Making Big Accusations," *Detroit Free Press*, April 8, 1951.

228. Story told by Ken Morris to his son.

229. Dollinger, *Not Automatic: Women and the Left in the Forging of the Auto Workers' Union*, p. 97.

230. Story told by Ken Morris to his son.

231. For the FE national referendum issue, see Lichtenstein, *The Most Dangerous Man in Detroit,* pp. 264–65; Reuther, *The Brother Reuther*, 261–62; Howe and Widick, *The UAW and Walter Reuther*, pp. 166–69.

232. The Morris quote is from Kenneth Silver's interview for his thesis, *The Dead End Kids: A History of Local 212 UAW-CIO,* p. 73. More information on the Local 212 referendum issue is found at Silver, *The Dead End Kids: a History of the Local 212 UAW-CIO,* pp. 72–73; Boles dissertation "The Post War Era: 1945–1949, KMOH 3, pp. 37–40; KMOH 5, p. 6; KMOH 6, pp.43–45.

233. UAW 1947 convention proceedings.

234. Frank Cormier and William J. Eaton, *Reuther* (Englewood Cliffs, NJ: Prentice-Hall, 1970), p. 261.

235. Regarding Bishop-Perrone arrest for shining, see Cormier and Eaton, p. 264; Reuther, p. 275. Hearings transcripts: "Investigation of Organized Crime in Interstate Commerce," by the Special Committee to Investigate Organized Crime in the Interstate Commerce, US Senate, February 8, 1951, pp. 130–31.

236. Bishop firing by Walter Reuther: Cormier and Eaton, p. 264.

237. Most of the story of Ken Morris's 1948 election is found at KMOH 3, pp. 54–57, tape 2; KMOH 6, pp. 55–57.

238. Gus Scholle offering position to Ken Morris, see KMOH 3, p. 57, tape 2; regarding position of CIO vice president, see KM notes 2, p. 2.

239. *Voice of Local 212,* March 18, 1948.

240. Reuther, *The Brother Reuther,* p. 277.

241. For information on the Reuther shooting and recovery, see Elisabeth Reuther Dickmeyer, *Reuther, A Daughter Strikes* (Southfield, MI: Spelman Publishers Division, 1989), pp. 3–5; Reuther, pp. 276–281; Lichtenstein, *The Most Dangerous*

Man in Detroit, pp. 271–72; Gould and Hickok, *Walter Reuther, Labor's Rugged Individualist*, pp.258–269.

242. KMOH 3, p. 34.

243. WSU WPR Archives, Blankenhorn Collection, Box 3.

244. Lichtenstein, p. 274.

245. The hoodlum-Communist connection is discussed in the following places: WSU WPR Archives, Blankenhorn memo to UAW Executive Board officers, Blankenhorn Collection, Box 3; "War on the Reuthers," *Newsweek*, January 2, 1950; Cormier and Eaton, *Reuther*, p. 261.

246. WSU WPR Archives, Ralph Winstead memorandum: "Summary Report on the Bolton Case and Investigative Developments up to December 19, 1949; WSU WPR Archives, Blankenhorn confidential memorandum to UAW officers, January 25, 1950.

247. Reuther, p. 287.

248. Almost all the information regarding the Victor Reuther shooting comes from Reuther, pp. 281–291.

249. Regarding theory that Victor Reuther's shooting was a means to take pressure off Carl Bolton, see WSU WPR Archives, Blankenhorn memorandum to UAW Officers, January 25, 1950, Blankenhorn Collection, Box 3.

250. Blankenhorn was considered an authority on industrial spying on labor unions, see Leo Huberman, *The Labor Spy Racket* (New York, Modern Age Books, 1937), p. 5; also see WSU WPR Labor Achieves, Box 5, Blankenhorn memorandum, "Origin of Senate Civil Liberties Investigation (Lafollette-Thomas Committee)," March 1952.

251. Blankenhorn, WWII, and problems with J. Edgar Hoover, see WSU WPR Archives, Blankenhorn Series, Box 3.

252. Cranefield letter to Blankenhorn, see WSU WPR Archives, Blankenhorn Collection, Box 3.

253. The "Plan R" proposal, see WSU WPR Archives, Blankenhorn Collection, Box 3.

254. Cranefield letter to Blankenhorn, see WSU WPR Archives, Blankenhorn Collection, Box 3.

255. Thomas J. Noer, *Soapy, A Biography of G. Mennen Williams* (Ann Arbor: University of Michigan Press, 2006), p. 106; also see "Secret Parley in Reuther Inquiry," the *Detroit News*, September 2, 1949.

256. For more complete information on Blankenhorn investigation of Bolton, see WSU WPR Archives, Winstead report, "Summary Report on the Bolton Case and Investigative Developments up to December 19, 1949," Blankenhorn Collection, Box 3.

257. KMOH 3, pp. 34–35; KMOH 6, pp. 49–50.

258. Reuther, *The Brothers Reuther*, p. 291.

259. "Reuther Jury Clears Bolton," *Detroit News*, February 25, 1950; Kenneth McCormick, "Bolton Acquitted," *Detroit Free Press,* February 25, 1950.

260. WSU WPR Archives, Blankenhorn memorandum to UAW Officers, "Investigation: Interim Summary of Main Clues," January 25, 1950. Blankenhorn Collection, Box 3.

261. Blankenhorn memoranda and letters to Senator Kefauver can be found at WSU WPR Archives, Blankenhorn Collection, Box 3. These include June 1950 memorandum from Blankenhorn to Kefauver; August 1950 memorandum to Kefauver listing individuals that the committee should investigate; August 11, 1950, letter from Blankenhorn to Kefauver; December 18 letter from Blankenhorn to Kefauver, and a February 5, 1951, Blankenhorn to Kefauver letter.

262. A summary of the Mafia in the United States can be found at http://www.history.com/topics/the-demise-of-the-mafia.

263. Mary M. Stolberg, *Bridging the River of Hatred,* pp. 83–92.

264. Ibid., p. 97.

265. Ibid., pp. 97–98.

266. Detroit Police Officer DeLamielleure identified as part of Murphy Grand Jury Staff: Hearings before the Special Committee to Investigate Organized Crime in Interstate Commerce, US Senate, 82nd Congress, Part 9, Michigan, February 8, 9, 19, 1951, appendix, p. 273.

267. Herbert testimony from Murphy Grand Jury records found at Hearings before the Special Committee to Investigate Organized Crime in Interstate Commerce, US Senate, 82nd Congress, Part 9, Michigan, February 8, 9, 19, 1951, appendix, pp. 318–331.

268. Lilygren grand jury testimony, Ibid., pp. 700–714.

269. Taylor grand jury testimony, Ibid., pp. 694–700.

270. "Cleary Rites Wednesday," *Detroit News*, June 3, 1946.

271. Perrone grand jury testimony, Ibid., pp. 280–318.

272. Silverstien grand jury testimony, Ibid., pp. 385–392.

273. Robinson grand jury testimony, Ibid., pp.393–403.

274. Renda grand jury testimony, Ibid., pp. 540–570.

275. Fry grand jury testimony, Ibid., pp. 570–585.

276. Bishop grand jury testimony, Ibid, pp. 642–647.

277. Spike Briggs grand jury testimony, Ibid., pp. 714–720.

278. Dewey grand jury testimony, Ibid, pp. 720–733.

279. Edwin G. Pipp, "Crime Parade on TV Stirs Public Demand for Action," *Detroit News,* February 9, 1951.

280. "Hearings before the Special Committee to Investigate Organized Crime in Interstate

Commerce, US Senate, 82nd Congress, Michigan, February 8, 9, and 19, 1951, pp.180–81.

281. Cobo and Williams's testimony, Ibid., pp. 3–6.

282. Bennett testimony, Ibid., pp. 80–103.

283. Perrone testimony, Ibid., pp. 115–132.

284. Fry testimony, Ibid., pp. 141–169.

285. Renda testimony, Ibid., pp. 161–171.

286. Freedman testimony, Ibid., pp. 172–178.

287. Lilygren testimony, Ibid., pp. 178–180.

288. Robinson testimony, Ibid., pp. 191–199.

289. Mazey testimony, Ibid., pp. 199–201; 224–228.

290. Mary M. Stolberg, *Bridging the River of Hatred*, p. 98.

291. Ken Morris Oral History 6, p. 51.

292. "Kefauver Committee Interim Report #3, *U.S. Senate Special Committee to Investigate Organized Crime in Interstate Commerce,* May 1, 1951, pp. 95–96.

293. Ibid., pp. 7–8.

294. This is from an undated, unidentified newspaper clipping, probably from spring 1951.

295. "Renda Contract Ended," *Detroit Free Press,* May 7, 1951.

296. "Briggs Victims of Beatings Lose High Court Plea," *Voice of Local 212,* December 1954.

297. Boyd Simmons, "Reuther Case Solved! Sam Perrone Vanishes," *Detroit Free Press.* January 6, 1954.

298. Ken McCormick, "Court Told of Secret Renda Quiz," *Detroit Free Press,* November 22, 1958.

299. Robert D'Arcy, "Reuther Case Detective Faces Inquiry About Bar," *Detroit News,* August 23, 1951.

300. "Briggs Co.'s Robinson Dies at 59," *Detroit News,* July 21, 1958; "Robinson, Ex-Head of Briggs, Dies," *Detroit Free Press,* July 21, 1958.

301. "Perrone Is Named in Stove Writ," *Detroit News,* November 18, 1951; "Eight Face Charges as Union Foes," *Detroit Free Press,* November 19, 1951.

302. Blankenhorn retirement, see Victor Reuther, *The Brothers Reuther,* p. 297.

303. "Hint Delay in Perrone Surrender," *Detroit News,* January 7, 1954.

304. Cormier and Eaton, *Reuther,* p. 266–267.

305. A. F. Mahan, Jr., "Famous Crimes: Reuther Reward Is Still in Waiting," *Lansing State Journal,* September 19, 1954.

306. Cormier and Eaton, pp. 267–268. For more detailed confession, see Boyd Simmons, "'Rode to Scene With Gunman,' Tipster Quoted," *Detroit News,* January 9, 1954.

307. Harry C. Sars, "Witness Flees Police! Bare His Shooting Story," *Detroit News,* January 9, 1954. For a good summary of this issue, see Reuther, *The Brothers Reuther,* pp. 297–300.

308. Robert D. Kirk, "Unionst Says UAW Knew Ritchie's Criminal Record," *Detroit News,* December 5, 1957.

309. Ken McCormick, "Renda Wins Big Point," *Detroit Free Press*, November 20, 1957.

310. Ken McCormick, "Court Told of Secret Renda Quiz," *Detroit Free Press,* November 22, 1957.

311. Ken McCormick, "Says UAW Made Own Probe," *Detroit Free Press,* November 26, 1957.

312. "Ritchie Payoff Deal Detailed," *Detroit Free Press*, November 27, 1957; "Tells of UAW Check in Reuther Shooting," *Detroit Free Press*, December 3, 1957.

313. Ken McCormick, "Mazey Tells of Payment," *Detroit Free Press,* December 5, 1957.

314. "Police Hunt Renda Case Key Witness; UAW Aide Vanishes From Home," *Detroit Free Press*, December 17, 1957; Neal Shine and James Sullivan, "Divers Fail to Find UAW Aide," *Detroit Free Press*, December 20, 1957; Robert Shogan, "The Mystery of Ralph Winstead," *Detroit Free Press*, December 22, 1957.

315. Ibid.

316. Joseph N. Hartmann, "Renda Defendant Vanishes; Damage Suit Is Held Up," *Detroit News,* December 17, 1957; Joseph N. Hartmann, "Resume Renda Suit Over UAW Protest," *Detroit News*, December 18, 1957.

317. "Winstead's Body Found," *Detroit Free Press*, December 23, 1957.

318. "'I'm Sorry,' Ritchie Told Sleuth," *Detroit Free Press*, January 9, 1958.

319. Collins George, "Tie O'Brien to Ritchie Payoff," *Detroit Free Press*, January 11, 1958.

320. "Row Puts Life into Renda Trial," *Detroit Free Press*, January 14, 1958.

321. Ibid.

322. Collins George, "Trial Told of 'Urge to Kill," *Detroit Free Press*, January 18, 1958; Collins George, "Sick Juror Hold Up Renda Trial," *Detroit Free Press*, January 21, 1958.

323. Charles C. Weber, "He's Sure Ritchie 'Knew Something,'" *Detroit Free Press*, March 11, 1958.

324. Collins George, "Renda Attorney Quizzes Reuther," *Detroit Free Press*, February 1, 1958.

325. "1954 'Haunts Us,' says Mrs. Renda," *Detroit Free Press,* February 18, 1958; "Renda Tells Life Story at Trial," *Detroit Free Press*, February 19, 1958.

326. "Court OK's Anti-Renda Testimony," *Detroit Free Press*, March 22, 1958.

327. Charles C. Weber, "Emil Mazey Angered By Verdict: 'Will Seek Remedies At Once,' He Says," *Detroit Free Press*, April 19, 1958.

328. "Renda Suit Against UAW Weighted By High Court," *Detroit News*, October 4, 1961.

329. Frank Cormier and William J. Eaton, *Reuther*, p. 269.

330. Ibid., p. 270.

331. Boyd Simmons, "Reuther Attack Tied to UAW Seizure Plot," *Detroit News*, January 8, 1954.

332. Interview Jane Briggs Hart.

333. "Spike Briggs Dies at 58," *Detroit News*, July 3, 1970. Interview Jane Briggs Hart.

334. Interview Jane Briggs Hart; WSU WPR Archives, Jess Ferrazza Oral History.

335. For more information on the Detroit Stove, see: http://apps.detnews.com/apps/history/index.php?id=198.

336. For information on Perrone assassination and activities in the 1960s, see Stolberg, *Bridging the River of Hatred*, pp. 281–285; "Statement of Police Commissioner George C. Edwards," Permanent Subcommittee on Investigation of the Committee on Government Operation, October 1963 (copy at the Edwards file, Burton Collection, Detroit Public Library; John M. Carlisle, "Perrone: 'I'll Get Bomber'"; *Detroit News*, January 20, 1964; John M Carlisle, "Perrone Bombing Shuts Underworld's Lips," *Detroit News*, January 26, 1964; "Santo Perrone; Labor Racketeer," http://www.geocities.com/jiggs2000_us/perrone.html?200624.

337. Stolberg, *Bridging the River of Hatred*, pp. 281–285; "Statement of Police Commissioner George C. Edwards," Permanent Subcommittee on Investigation of the Committee on Government Operation, October 1963 (copy at the Edwards file, Burton Collection, Detroit Public Library).

338. Lichtenstein, *The Most Dangerous Man in Detroit*, p. 333.

339. For more on the McClellan Committee and the "Vic and Wal" letter investigation, see Reuther, *The Brothers Reuther*, pp. 214–219; Lichtenstein, *The Most Dangerous Man in Detroit*, pp. 346–348; Arthur M. Schlesinger, Jr., *Robert Kennedy and His Times* (New York: Ballantine Books, 1978), pp. 190–194. The Humphrey-McClellan letter was received WSU WPR Archives.

340. John G. Fuller, *We Almost Lost Detroit* (New York: Berkley Books, 1984), pp. 49–50.

341. Edward M. Kennedy, *True Compass* (New York: Twelve, Hachette Book Group, 2009), p. 303.

342. Ralph Orr, "UAW firebrand Emil Mazey dies," *Detroit Free Press*, October 11, 1983.

343. Michael Ranville, *To Strike at a King: The Turning Point in the McCarthy Witch-Hunts* (Troy, MI: Momentum Books, Ltd., 1997), pp. 145–146.

344. Patty Proctor Park, "Solidarity: the House the UAW Build; The United Auto Workers and the United Farmworkers," Detroit Michigan, found at http://www.farmworkermovement.org/essays/essays/082%20Proctor_Patty_Park.pdf.

345. Ralph Orr, "UAW firebrand Emil Mazey dies," *Detroit Free Press*, October 11, 1983.

346. Witty dissertation.

347. For the press release and more on this award, see: WSU WPR Archives, Jewish Community Archives, Accession 1726, Box 246.

348. Ken Morris, notes 2.

BIBLIOGRAPHY

Interviews

Douglas Fraser, September 2007
Jane Hart Briggs, August 2007
Larry Mazey, February 2009

Books

Austin, Aleine. *The Labor Story, A Popular History of the Labor Movement.* New York: Coward-McCann, 1949.

Badger, Anthony F. *FDR: The First Hundred Days.* New York: Hill & Wang, 2008.

Babsom, Steve. *The Making of a Union Town.* New York: Adams Books, 1984.

Barnard, John. *Walter Reuther and the Rise of the Auto Workers.* Boston: Little, Brown and Company, 1983.

Bennett, Harry (as told to Paul Marcus). *Ford: We Never Called Him Henry.* New York: Tom Doherty Associates, 1951.

Bonosky, Phillip. *Brother Bill McKie.* New York: International Publishers, 1953.

Brophy, John. *A Miner's Life.* Madison. University Wisconsin Press, 1964.

Cohen, Adam. *Nothing to Fear.* New York: The Penguin Press, 2009.

Collier, Peter and David Horowitz. *The Fords, An American Epic*. New York: Summit Books, 1987.

Cormier, Frank and William J. Eaton. *Reuther*. Englewood Cliffs, NJ: Prentice-Hall, 1970.

Cook, Fred J. *Building the House of Labor Walter Reuther*. Chicago: *Encyclopaedia Britannica Press*, 1963.

Cooke, Alistair. *The American Home Front 1941–1942*. Grove Press, 2007.

Dollinger, Sol, and Genora Johnson Dollinger. *Not Automatic: Women and the Left in the Forging of the Auto Workers' Union*. New York: Monthly Review Press, 2000.

Edwards, George. *Pioneer-at-Law*. New York: W. W. Norton & Company, 1974.

Fountain, Clayton W. *Union Guy*. New York: The Viking Press, 1949.

Fuller, John G. *We Almost Lost Detroit*. New York: Berkley Books, 1975.Howe, Irving, and B. J. Widick. *The UAW and Walter Reuther*. New York: Random House, 1949.

Huberman, Leo. *The Labor Spy Racket*. New York: Modern Age Books, 1937.

Gould, Jean, and Lorena Hickok. *Walter Reuther Labor's Rugged Individualist*. New York: Dodd, Mead & Company, 1972.

Kennedy, Edward M. *True Compass*. New York: Twelve, Hachette Book Group, 2009.

Lacy, Robert. *Ford: The Men and the Machine*. Boston: Little, Brown and Company, 1986.

Lichtenstein, Nelson. *The Most Dangerous Man in Detroit: Walter Reuther and the Fate of American Labor*. New York: BasicBooks, a Division of HarperCollins Publishers, 1995.

Meier, August, and Elliott Rudwick. *Black Detroit and the Rise of the UAW*. New York: Oxford University Press, 1979.

Noer, Thomas J. *Soapy, A Biography of G. Mennen Williams*. Ann Arbor: University of Michigan Press, 2006.

Ranville, Michael. *To Strike at a King: The Turning Point in the McCarthy Witch-Hunts*. Troy, Michigan: Momentum Books, 1997.

Reuther Dickmeyer, Elisabeth. *Reuther: A Daughter Strikes*. Southfield, MI: Spelman Publishers Division, 1989.

Reuther, Victor. *The Brothers Reuther and the Story of the UAW*. Boston: Houghton Mifflin Company, 1976.

Reuther, Walter, ed. Henry M. Christman. *Walter P. Reuther, Selected Papers*. New York: The MacMillan Company, 1961.

Schlesinger, Jr., Arthur M. *Robert Kennedy and His Times*. New York: Random House, 1978.

Stieber, Jack. *Governing the UAW*. New York: John Wiley and Sons, 1962.

Stolberg, Mary M. *Bridging the River of Hatred: The Pioneering Efforts of Detroit Police Commissioner George Edwards*. Detroit: Wayne State University Press, 1998.

Sward, Keith. *The Legend of Henry Ford*. New York: Rinehard and Co., 1948.

Tyler, Robert L. *Walter Reuther*. William B. Eerdmans, 1973.

Wechsler, James. *Labor Baron: Portrait of John L. Lewis*. New York: William Morrow and Company, 1944.

Academic Papers

Boles, Frank Joseph. *A History of Local 212 UAW-CIO: The Briggs Manufacturing Company, Detroit, Michigan*. PhD diss., University of Michigan, 1990.

Silver, Kenneth, F. *The Dead End Kids: A History of Local 212 UAW-CIO*. Undergraduate Honors Thesis, University of Michigan, 1980.

Witty, Michael Deveran. *Emil Mazey: Radical as Liberal*. PhD diss., Syracuse University, 1969.

Congressional Reports

Hearings before the Special Committee to Investigate Organized Crime in Interstate Commerce. US Senate, Senate Resolution 202 of 81st Congress. Michigan, February 8, 9, and 19, 1951.

Third Interim Report of the Special Committee to Investigate Organized Crime in Interstate Commerce, pursuant to Senate Resolution 202, May 1, 1951.

Other Sources

Guide to the Records of the Workmen's Circle, Undated, 1903 to 1993. American Jewish Historical Society. www.ajhs.org.

Park, Patty (Proctor). *Solidarity: The House the UAW Built.* The United Auto Workers and the United Farmworkers. Detroit, MI, 1972–1975. http://www.farmworkermovement.org/essays/essays/082%20Proctor_Patty_Park.pdf.

Rosenthal, Susan. *Striking Flint*, chapter titled "Class Struggle During the War." www.historyisaweapon.com/defcon1/dollflint.html.

UAW convention minutes: 1935–1947.

Reuther Library Oral Histories

Ken Morris
Merlin Bishop
Irving Bluestone
Jack Conway
Jess Ferrazza
Joe Ferris
Richard Frankensteen
Ray Girardin
George Merrelli
Art Vega

Photo Credits

Photos on pages xiv, 4,167, and 330 are family photos, photographers unknown
Photo on page xxix courtesy of the *Detroit News* Archives
Photo on page 22 courtesy of anonymous owner
Photos on pages 47, 81, 83, 85, 95, 97, 98,126, 137, 162, 198, 226, 235, 265, 272, 275, and 309 courtesy of Walter P. Reuther Library, Wayne State University.

INDEX

Pages with "*n*" or "*nn*" in page number indicate endnote reference.
Pages with "*ph*" in page number indicate photograph reference

H

Hall, Ed, leading CIO effort against Martin, 110, 115

Hart, Jane Briggs. *see* Briggs, Jane (wife of Philip Hart)

Hart, Philip, 33, 329

Hazel Park racetrack (Detroit), 262

health-care issues, 323

Henderson, Sam, 294, 295–296, 302–303, 307

Herbert, George, 248–253, 255, 271, 273, 281, 347*n*267

Highland Park Briggs plant
activities run by Bolton in, 230
manufacturing at, 22
phasing out of, 138–139
picket lines attacked at, 126–127, 341*n*154
strike action at, 93

Hillman, Sidney, 107, 116–117, 119

Hoffa, James "Jimmy", 83,215, 247, 319

Homer Martin, end of influence of, 128

Hood, Morris, III, 131

Hood, Morris, Jr., 131, 134–135, 341*n*165

Hood, Morris, Sr., 131

Hood, Ray, 131

hoodlums (mobsters). *see also* Kefauver committee, hearing on organized crime; Perrone, Santo "Sam"
connection to Briggs, 315
gambling as Ford Motor Company connection to, 246
national investigation of organized crime, 243–244, 245
possible alliance with communists, 229, 346*n*245
possible hit on Walter Reuther, 241

Hoover, Herbert, 93

Hoover, J. Edgar, 346*n*251

Hudson, outsourcing work to Briggs, 29

Hudson Essex auto model, 28

Hudson Ordnance Plant (Detroit), 170

Humphrey, Hubert, 320

Hutchinson, Mr., 182–183

I

Iacocca, Lee, saving Chrysler, xvii

immigration workers, newspaper article on illegal, 283

Industrial Workers of World (IWW) (Wobbies)
attempt to organize Ford, 29
organizing autoworkers, 36

Ingersoll, Claud, 306

integration, of administrative office at Local 212, 134, 341*n*164

International UAW. *see also* United Automobile Workers (UAW)
becomes stronger, 145
bomb planted of headquarters of, 242–243
campaign against Emil Mazey, 139
Emil Mazey as organizer in, 45, 74
headquarters at Solidarity House, 236, 302, 304
hearings on actions taken by Melvin Bishop, 153–156
influence of, 73–74, 337*n*78
leadership battles of, 69–70
refuses to recognize removal of Knox from Local 212, 65–66
request for approval of strike against Briggs, 121–122
support of company-wide seniority system, 138–139, 342*n*170

Italian American club, Renda president of, 269–270

Iverson, Arthur, 282

J

Jacobs, Clarence, 295, 296–297, 303, 307, 309

Japan
occupation of, 170–171
surrender in WWII of, 185

Jefferson Barracks (Missouri), 157–158

Jewish American Fraternal Order, Workmen's Circle Award for Social Progress, 327

John Birch Society, 319

Jones, Kathleen, 163

M

MacArthur, Douglas, 170–171
Mack Avenue Briggs plant, 22*ph. see also* Briggs Manufacturing Company (Detroit)
  explosion at, 36
  racial tension at, 169
  seniority issues at, 138
  sit-down strikes at, 38–39
  wildcat strikes at, 149
  worker discontent at, 44, 46
Mackinac Island (Lake Huron), 31
Mafia. *see* mobsters (hoodlums)
Mahan, A. F., Jr., 295
March on Washington (1963), Walter Reuther speaking at, 89–90
Mariners' Hall (Detroit), 11
Marquart, Frank, 98
Marshall, Bill, 118, 119, 194
Martin, Charles, 248
Martin, Homer
  about, 71, 337*n*75
  causing factional problems in UAW, 111–112
  convention at Moose Hall, 116, 340*n*136
  debate with Walter Reuther, 102
  disrupting meeting at Local 235, 115
  firing of Emil Mazey, 74–75, 337*n*81
  as first elected president of UAW, xiv, 69
  followers attacking picketers in strike against Briggs, 126–127, 341*n*154
  followers harassing picketers in strike against Briggs, 124
  hires Lovestone, 73
  lack of leadership of, 74, 103–104, 337*nn*79–80
  leading Progressive Caucus, 103
  meeting with Briggs during strike, 124, 340*n*151
  presidency of, 101–102
  protesting police brutality to Detroit City Council, 83, 337*n*91
  removes Mazey as UAW International representative, 65
  secret deal with Bennett, 107–108, 339*n*129

Marxism, activists preaching from soapboxes on, 35–36, 334*n*34
Masouris, Danny, xxvi, 185
Masouris, Pete, 185
Mathews, Norman, 192, 200
Mazey, Charlotte Monser. *see* Monser, Charlotte (wife of Emil Mazey)
Mazey, Earnest "Ernie," 34, 169, 170, 187
Mazey, Emil, 137*ph*, 235*ph*
  about, 34–35, 323–326, 334*n*32
  on accomplishment of Local 212, 326–327
  as acting president of UAW after Reuther shooting, 227
  angered by verdict in suit from Renda, 309, 349*n*327
  becomes organizer for UAW Local 155, 38, 335*n*37
  as beneficiary of new UAW-CIO, 72
  campaign against, 139, 342*n*171
  compared to Ernie Mazey, 188
  coordinating investigation with Blankenhorn and Winstead, 241
  correspondence with Ken Morris during WWII, 163–164, 173–174
  death of, 326, 350–351*nn*345–346
  discharge from service in WWII, 201, 344*n*221
  dispute with Frankensteen, 51
  in "double cross" at 1938 Michigan CIO convention, 105
  drafted into service during WWII, 170–172, 343*n*199
  education of, 35, 334*n*33
  elected president of Local 212, 66, 76–77, 336*n*68
  election to UAW International Executive Board, xxiv
  finding Melvin Bishop connection to Perrone, 219, 345*n*234
  fired for union activity, 38, 39–40, 335*n*41
  getting contract at Briggs, 56–60, 336*n*59
  on grand jury investigation of assaults, 214–215, 246, 345*n*227
  helped save UAW-CIO at grassroots local union level, 110–111, 340*n*132